THE GREAT WAR

CHIPPENHAM SOLDIERS

for Harry

A frame from the memorial window to the Wilson Brothers at St. Andrew's Church, Chippenham, depicting the grief of the Great War.

THE GREAT WAR

CHIPPENHAM SOLDIERS

RICHARD BROADHEAD

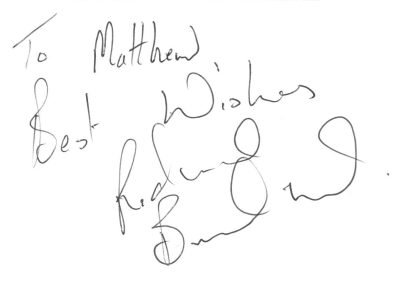

To Matthew,
Best Wishes
Richard Broadhead

The man behind the Lewis gun is Ernest Gower Baker, he was wounded twice but survived the war. After being gassed his health never recovered and he spent the last ten years of his life in hospital or in bed. He was always out of breath and passed away in 1951. A casualty of the Great War.

First published 2010

O&B Services
The Annexe
Poynder Place
Hilmarton, SN11 8SQ

British Library Cataloguing in Publication Data.
A catalogue record for this book is available from the British Library.

ISBN 978 0 9563825 28

CONTENTS

FOREWORD

In Remembrance Services across the country we always use the words "We will remember them". As the great wars of the twentieth century fade from our memories and their generations pass away, we certainly remember that we owe our liberties to those who were prepared to pay the ultimate sacrifice; but we rarely know anything now about the "them" who we say we remember.

In the Great War of 1914-18 every Wiltshire community suffered a catastrophic loss of its young sons. Richard Broadhead has researched the lives of those who fell in intimate detail, and in this book the family tragedies of Chippenham in those years begin to come alive for us. This book, which follows others that Richard has already produced for Salisbury Soldiers, Calne District Soldiers and Trowbridge Soldiers is a remarkable achievement that I warmly recommend.

J B Bush OBE, JP
HM Lord-Lieutenant for Wiltshire

INTRODUCTION

When we think about the Great War we always seem to think about the big things, we think about the big battles, we think about the huge cost in lives, history always seems to give us the big picture. Then every year, on Remembrance Day, we are told to think of all of those who have lost their lives in conflict; again another big number in the big picture. It is little wonder that the more we try to remember them, with each year passing we seem to get further away from them. 'Them' is a faceless description; perhaps if we said remember Harry or Ernest or Leonard, we could start to build a picture and remember that they all had characters, they all had stories.

Chippenham Soldiers is not simply an alphabetical list of names; you will find no index to enable the reader to find a name quickly. It portrays what happened to each of the servicemen who lost their lives in the Great War and every one of them has a story. And just as the story of each one of them is unique the collective story for Chippenham Soldiers is unique.

This is the fourth book I have written about the fallen from Wiltshire towns and when I started this research I expected each town to follow the same format with similar stories. However, the greatest impression I currently have is that every town whether it be Chippenham, Trowbridge, Calne or Salisbury is unique; just like each man featured is unique. Each major battle or minor skirmish has a different social impact on those left behind in the towns and surrounding villages; for me the Battle of the Somme impacted Salisbury heavily as many men who joined the same regiments, at the same time, fought and died in this bloody battle; Calne and District was impacted by the air accidents that took place at Yatesbury and the Great War tragedy for Trowbridge was Gallipoli. Chippenham has unfolded to show yet another view of the social impact on a town,

As with my previous books during the research I have uncovered men who are not commemorated by the Commonwealth War Graves Commission; however,,I can assure you that by the time this book is published I will have highlighted each of their individual cases to the CWGC and each will be investigated. I will continue to campaign for the recognition they deserve, no matter how long this takes.

In 2007 the Chippenham War Memorial was refurbished and a decision was made to add names of those missing; the only one added from the Great War was John William Kingsland, whose name also appears on the Devizes War Memorial as his father being a Minister at the Devizes Congregational Church. Just as each part of the stone work was scrutinized and made good, we have missed an opportunity to recognize all the men of Chippenham omitted from the list or even correct spelling mistakes. Remembrance isn't about the stone, the marble, the wood or the glass, it is about the people; similarly Remembrance isn't about the Day it is about Edwin, Frederick or John and their stories which keep their very being alive.

I would like to thank all those parishioners of local churches who have guided me to various memorials within their place of worship and have allowed me to take photographs. Also thanks to Dr Francis Willmoth of Jesus College, Cambridge and Mike Stone, Melissa Barnett and the team at Chippenham Museum and Heritage Centre.

Most of all I would like to thank my long-suffering wife, Anita, who has supported me beyond the call of duty during the writing of this book, who deserves a Long Service Medal. Thanks also to my two lovely boys, Jack-Harry and Tom, who were kind enough to give me leave from playing games with them during my first three books; and who for this fourth book have contributed to the research and taken some of the photographs of graves and headstones, both of whom I sincerely hope never have to serve their country in such a way as those listed herein.

This book is not about the battles of the First World War, or the men who directed the battles, it is a book about the great men who left Chippenham and the surrounding area, whether as a volunteer or a conscript, to fight for our future. If we forget their sacrifice we open the door for future conflicts, which will mean that their deaths were to have been in vain.

1

THE WAR OF HATE, 1914

In August 1914 the fuse was lit that would ignite a conflict that would change the world; it was to be given many names: the Great European War; The Great War for Civilisation and the First World War being but a few. There were many reasons for the commencement of hostilities, but once mobilisation of men had started, it triggered a domino effect throughout Europe and then on across the world.

Patriotism spread through countries like a plague, and, like a plague, it almost immediately claimed its victims. Men volunteered to fight for good and God against evil, in a war where keen, willing participants would be home for Christmas. The British Army was small but well trained, and had been developed to protect and control the British Empire, while relying on the powerful British Navy to protect the world trade routes.

In the August of 1914, Soldiers of the British Expeditionary Force marched across Belgium, a country that Great Britain had the treaty to protect, across fields where one hundred years earlier, the Duke of Wellington had defeated Napoleon Bonaparte. They marched to the town of Mons. The Great War had begun.

23 AUGUST 1914 – THE BATTLE OF MONS, BELGIUM
26 AUGUST 1914 – THE BATTLE OF LE CATEAU, FRANCE

Private James Idle   *1/5ᵗᵗʰBn Loyal North Lancashire Regiment*

Service No.	1878	Age:	19
Place of Birth:	Bolton, Lancashire	Home Country:	England
Date of Death:	27/08/1914	Cause of death:	Accident
Memorial:	Not known		
War cemetery:	Hullavington St Mary Churchyard		
Theatre of war:	Home		
Next of Kin:	Timothy & Helen Idle		
Address:	12 James Terrace, Blackburn Road, Bolton, Lancashire		

James was employed as a moulder and was a territorial soldier at the outbreak of the Great War. Territorials were mobilized and sent to guard important installations and infrastructure and the Loyal North Lancashires were sent to Wiltshire. On Thursday 27 August James and Private Joseph Houghton were on duty on the railway viaduct at Rodbourne Bottom. At 12.30 mid-day the Bristol to London express train was coming and James was patrolling the line

Above: Volunteers of the 8th Service Battalion Somerset Light Infantry.

Right: James Idle's grave in St. Mary Magdalene Churchyard, Hullavington.

toward the engine he passed over the bridge and it was about 10 yards further along that Private Houghton first saw the train. Private Houghton shouted to James and instead of getting off the line he turned around and the engine was almost on him. Private Houghton continued to shout but James did not seem to take any notice and he was struck by the train. After the train had passed Private Houghton saw that James had been cut to pieces. James was buried with full military honours at Hullavington St Mary Churchyard and many of the attendees were territorials, many of whom were friends of James.

Lance Corporal James Webb		*1st Bn Wiltshire Regiment*	
Service No.	6922	Age:	29
Place of Birth:	Atworth	Home Country:	England
Date of Death:	28/08/1914	Cause of death:	Killed in action
Memorial:	St. Andrew's Church Chippenham		
War cemetery:	La Ferte Sous Jouarre Memorial		
Theatre of war:	France		
Next of Kin:	Norah Webb (wife) – William Thomas & Mary Webb		
Address:	Meadow View, Frogwell, Chippenham, Wiltshire		

James, a foundry worker, married Norah Holmes in the spring of 1910 at Wilton and it is likely he was either a reservist or an ex regular soldier. He arrived with the Wiltshires in France on Friday 14 August 1914 and after their journey across France into Belgium the Wiltshire had their first engagement with casualties on 24 August 1914 at Ciply, Belgium. After meeting overwhelming odds they were forced to withdraw with the German army in pursuit. On Wednesday 26 August the Wiltshires were holding the north east edge of Caudry, France and during the morning they were heavily shelled and attacked by German infantry suffering 80 to 100 casualties. James was initially reported missing in action and later reported killed during the fighting on 24 August and admitted to hospital in Caudry on 26 August. His widow appealed for information concerning her husband and received a letter from James Britten, a native of Derry Hill, who was injured while fighting with the Wiltshires and was recovering in Charring Cross Hospital. He wrote:

"I knew that Lance Corporal that you mentioned in the letter but I am sorry to break the news to tell you that the poor chap got killed at Cambrai (Le Cateau Cambresis) on Wednesday 26th August. He was killed by a shell from the Germans about 8.30am. The one you spoke about had a locket round his neck and had two photos in it; so you see that I knew him, he used to work in the Foundry. We went into action about 3 o'clock in the morning, and the Germans very nearly surrounded us, so you can see we were in a tight corner. As I was crawling along I noticed he was hit in the head, poor chap. I should have took the locket off only I had no chance because the Germans were on top of us. We only lost about ten at Mons, that was in one trench, although we were shelled all the time by them devils."

In August 1916 the following memoriam was inserted in a local paper:

"In sweet remembrance of a true and devoted Husband and Daddie
Who fell in the battle of Mons who hath left behind a wife and darling child to mourn
Two years have passed since that sad day
When my dear husband was called away
The thought still lingers round my heart
Gods will it was that we should part
Rest in Peace"

James is remembered on the La Ferte Sous Jouarre Memorial and has no known grave. He left a widow and a young daughter, he has only recently been remembered by the Commonwealth War Grave Commision

Private Charles Ernest Yates		*1st Bn Dragoon Guards*	
Service No.	5992	Age:	30
Place of Birth:	Grittleton, Wiltshire	Home Country:	England
Date of Death:	01/09/1914	Cause of death:	Killed in action
Memorial:	Not known		
War cemetery:	Verberie French National Cemetery		
Theatre of war:	France		
Next of Kin:	Annie Yates (wife) - ELi & Elizabeth Yates		
Address:	Littlecott, Wiltshire – Preshute, Wiltshire		

It is likely Charles, a regular soldier, was in India at the commencement of hostilities, he had married his wfe Annie Dobson in Fulham in 1907. The 1st Dragoon Guards left India and arrived at Marseilles in early November 1914, Charles arrived on 11 November, however this is 2 months after records state his date of death as 1 September 1914. His medal card states that he was killed on 9 January 1915 so either the date of his death has been recorded incorrectly (01/09/1914 when it should be 09/01/1915) or he was serving with a different Dragoon Battalion. He is buried in Verberie French National Cemetery.

6 SEPTEMBER 1914 - THE BATTLE OF THE MARNE, FRANCE
9 SEPTEMBER 1914 - THE BATTLE OF FERE CHAMPENOISE, FRANCE
14 SEPTEMBER 1914 - FIRST BATTLE OF THE AISNE, FRANCE

2nd Lt Richard William Mark Lockwood   *2nd Bn Coldstream Guards*
Service No.   N/a   Age: 23
Place of Birth: Chesham Street, London   Home Country: England
Date of Death: 14/09/1914   Cause of death: Killed in action
Memorial: Lambourne Church, EssexWar cemetery: Soupir Communal Cemetery
War cemetery: Soupir Communal Cemetery
Theatre of war: France
Next of Kin: Robert and Chinty Lockwood
Address: Havering Court, Romford, Essex

Richard was the only son of Robert Lockwood, the Deputy Lieutenant of Essex, and the brother in law of Mr L Lysley of Pewsham. He was known in the area and often hunted with the Badminton Hounds. He continued the Lockwood family tradition and received a commission with the Coldstream Guards in 1913. He arrived in France on Wednesday 12 August 1914 and was killed in action on Monday 14 September 1914 during heavy fighting at La Cour de Soupir farm, near the head of the valley north-west of the village of Soupir during the Battle of the Aisne.

Corporal John Cole   *1st Bn Wiltshire Regiment*
Service No.   5540   Age: 31
Place of Birth: Lacock, Wiltshire   Home Country: England
Date of Death: 20/09/1914   Cause of death: Killed in action
Memorial: Lacock Church & Bowden Hill
War cemetery: Vailly British Cemetery
Theatre of war: France
Next of Kin: Issac & Elizabeth Cole
Address: Bowden Common, Lacock, Wiltshire

John, a regular, had originally enlisted with the Wiltshires on 27 February 1900 at a recorded age of eighteen years and one month. He arrived in France on 14 August 1914 and would have taken part in the retreat from Mons. On Sunday 20 September at 9am the Wiltshires were at Vailly on the river Aisne facing a German attack. Between 11am and 12 noon the British trenches were shelled and about 200 German Infantry men some with machine guns got through a dense wood in the line and rushed on to flank the British trenches held by the Worcester Regiment and broke through the line. After some very close fighting the Wiltshires managed to get the upper hand and stopped the Germans between 50 and 100 yards from the British trenches. After the attack was beaten off a general advance was ordered at 5.45pm. John was reported missing and in March 1915 he was reported killed in action on that day. He was one of seven of the Wiltshires to be killed during this action.

25 SEPTEMBER 1914 - THE BATTLE OF ALBERT, FRANCE

Private Robert Blanchard   *6th Wiltshire Regiment*
Service No.   3/4411   Age: 36
Place of Birth: Woolwich, London   Home Country: England
Date of Death: 27/09/1914   Cause of death: Died
Memorial: Chippenham & St. Andrew's Church Chippenham
War cemetery: Chippenham London Road Cemetery

Far left: James Edward Bindon buried In Bulford Cemetery

Left: Robert Blanchard buried in Chippenham Cemetery

Theatre of war: Home
Next of Kin: Florence Blanchard
Address: 80 London Road, Chippenham, Wiltshire

Robert, a blacksmith's striker, had married Florence Fortune at Chippenham in the spring of 1906. He had originally joined the Wiltshires on 15 November 1895 and it is likely he was a territorial soldier and volunteered to serve with the 6th Service Battalion Wiltshire Regiment. The Service element meant that he had volunteered to serve for the duration of the war. After his enlistment he was sent to Salisbury plain for training where he died of illness or disease on Sunday 27 September 1914. His body was returned to his home and he was buried in Chippenham Cemetery.

1 OCTOBER 1914 - THE BATTLE OF ARRAS, FRANCE

Sergeant James Edward Bindon   *Military Mounted Royal Military Police*
Service No.   P/82   Age: 45
Place of Birth: Bath, Somerset   Home Country: England
Date of Death: 08/10/1914   Cause of death: Died
Memorial: Not known
War cemetery: Bulford Church Cemetery
Theatre of war: Home
Next of Kin: Lillian Maria Bindon (wife) - Edward & Mary Bindon (parents)
Address: 13 Bennett Park, Blackheath, London - Bath

James was formerly a sergeant in the 1st Royal Dragoons with thirteen years service, two and a half years of these were spent in South Africa, for which he was awarded two medals and took part in the relief of Ladysmith. In the summer of 1902 he married Lilian Maria Jefferies at Chippenham and prior to the war he ran a boarding house at Blackheath. He re-enlisted in September 1914 joining the Military Mounted Police and was sent to Bulford Camp where he contracted a chill which developed into double pneumonia which he succumbed to on Tuesday 8 October 1914. He was well known in the area, his wife's parents living at Hill Corner, Langley Burrell. The funeral took place at Bulford church with full military honours and he was buried in Bulford Cemetery. James left a widow and infant daughter.

Private George Blackman   *1st Bn Wiltshire Regiment*
Service No.   9086   Age: 18
Place of Birth: Yatton Keynell, Wiltshire   Home Country: England
Date of Death: 18/10/1914   Cause of death: Killed in action
Memorial: Southwick, Wiltshire
War cemetery: Le Touret Memorial
Theatre of war: France
Next of Kin: Henry & Annie Blackman
Address: Frome Road, Southwick, Wiltshire

Prior to his enlistment in the army eighteen year old George was a gardener, he arrived in France with the Wiltshires on 14 August 1914. On Sunday 18 October 1914 the Wiltshires were attempting to advance at Ligny-le-Grand, south of Aubers, France. The German positions were too strong and they only managed to gain about 300 yards of ground. The Germans then shelled the British Trenches and George was one of three men killed. He is remembered on the Le Touret Memorial and has no known grave.

19 OCTOBER 1914 - THE FIRST BATTLE OF YPRES

Gunner Frederick Bishop   *7th Meerut Div Ammo. Col. R. F. A.*
Service No.   47981   Age: 27
Place of Birth: Yatton Keynell, Wiltshire   Home Country: England
Date of Death: 20/10/1914   Cause of death: Died
Memorial: Not Known
War cemetery: Narbone East Cemetery
Theatre of war: France
Next of Kin: William & Sarah Bishop
Address: 34 Winifred Street, Swindon, Wiltshire

Regular soldier Frederick was serving in India prior to the Great War and arrived at Marseilles France on 14 October 1914. He died of illness or disease on Tuesday 20 October 1914 and was buried at Narbone East Cemetery in the South of France. He is the only British soldier buried in this Cemetery.

Private Sidney Hurcom   *1st Bn Gloucestershire Regiment*
Service No.   7368   Age: 34
Place of Birth: Tormarton, Glos.   Home Country: England
Date of Death: 20/10/1914   Cause of death: Died of wounds
Memorial: Leigh Delamere
War cemetery: Ypres Menin Gate
Theatre of war: Belgium
Next of Kin: Leonard & Mary A Hurcom

Address: Tormarton, Gloucestershire

Regular soldier Sidney was the second son of Leonard and Mary Hurcom and it is likely he arrived in France with the 1st Battalion Gloucestershire Regiment on 13 August 1914. On Tuesday 20 October the 1st Gloucesters were ordered to advance and engage German forces near Lagemark, north east of Ypres, Belgium. Sidney was posted as missing and information was later received that he had died of wounds as the Gloucesters moved forward. He is today remembered on the Ypres Menin Gate and has no known grave.

Private Ernest Alfred Tuck		*2nd Bn Wiltshire Regiment*	
Service No.	8146	Age:	25
Place of Birth:	Castle Combe, Wiltshire	Home Country:	England
Date of Death:	24/10/1914	Cause of death:	Killed in action
Memorial:	Yatton Keynell		
War cemetery:	Ypres Menim Gate		
Theatre of war:	Belgium		
Next of Kin:	Robert & Mary Tuck		
Address:	Long Dean, Castle Combe, Wiltshire		

Ernest was the third son of Robert & Mary Tuck and had arrived in Belgium with the 2nd Battalion Wiltshire Regiment on Wednesday 7 October 1914. Just over two weeks later on Saturday 24 October 1914 the 2nd Battalion Wiltshire Regiment were holding the front line trenches at Beslare, south east of Zonnebeke, Belgium. At 5.30am as the day was breaking the Germans attacked with a superior force but the enemy were driven back with heavy casualties. The Germans then renewed the attack and after 2 hours of continuous fighting, in which the Germans had hundreds of casualties, the enemy broke through the British lines. The Wiltshires suffered very heavy casualties, a total of sixty six of their members were killed and a large number captured. A special note was inserted in the Wiltshires War Diary concerning the gallant work of Captain Comyn, the medical officer and stretcher bearers who for the previous three days and nights were continuously handling wounded or burying dead. Ernest is one of sixty six men of the 2nd Battalion Wilshire Regiment to be killed on this day. He is remembered on the Ypres Menin Gate Memorial, Belgium with over 54,000 men who have no known grave and died in Belgium during the Great War.

Private Sidney James Chivers		*2nd Bn Wiltshire Regiment*	
Service No.	8573	Age:	21
Place of Birth:	Chippenham, Wiltshire	Home Country:	England
Date of Death:	24/10/1914	Cause of death:	Killed in action
Memorial:	Chippenham & St. Andrew's Church Chippenham		
War cemetery:	Perth Cemetery China Wall		
Theatre of war:	Belgium		
Next of Kin:	George & Rosanna Chivers		
Address:	1 St Mary's Place, Chippenham, Wiltshire		

Regular soldier Sidney was serving with the 2nd Battalion Wiltshire Regiment at Gibraltar when the Great War broke out and on 7 October the Wiltshires landed at Zeebrugge in Belgium, too late to stop the German onslaught through Belgium. He was posted as missing at Belselare, Belgium in the same action as Ernest Tuck. In April 1916 George and Rosanna Chivers received an official confirmation that Sidney had been killed in action on the day he was reported missing. He is today buried in Perth China Wall Cemetery and it is likely his remains were moved here after the war. Sidney had two brothers who were to fall in the war Edwin was to die of wounds in April 1916 and Albert would be killed in action in May 1918.

Lance Corporal Walter Hancock   *2nd Bn Wiltshire Regiment*
Service No.   8655   Age: 23
Place of Birth: Chippenham, Wiltshire   Home Country: England
Date of Death: 24/10/1914   Cause of death: Killed in action
Memorial: Chippenham & St. Andrew's Church Chippenham
War cemetery: Bedford House Cemetery
Theatre of war: Belgium
Next of Kin: Jacob & Mary Hancock
Address: 7 Factory Lane, Chippenham, Wiltshire

Walter was the eldest son of Jacob & Mary Hancock and had served five years with the Wiltshires at the outbreak of hostilities and was based at Gibraltar. On 7 October the Wiltshires landed at Zeebrugge in Belgium, a little over two weeks later he was killed in action at Belselare, Belgium in the same action as Ernest Tuck. It is likely his remains were moved to Bedford House Cemetery after the end of the war.

Private Alfred Joseph Hand   *2nd Bn Wiltshire Regiment*
Service No .   8342   Age: 25
Place of Birth: Sutton Benger, Wiltshire   Home Country: England
Date of Death: 24/10/1914   Cause of death: Killed in action
Memorial: Chippenham & St. Andrew's Church Chippenham
War cemetery: Ypres Menin Gate
Theatre of war: Belgium
Next of Kin: Alfred J & Martha S. Hand
Address: 25 Park Lane, Chippenham, Wiltshire

Alfred, known as Alfie, had severed in South Africa and Gibraltar and landed with the Wiltshires at Zeebrugge in Belgium on 7 October 1914. The last news Alfie's family received was on 9 October 1914 and he was posted as missing Saturday 24 October 1914 in the same action as Ernest Tuck. Official information was later received that he had been killed in action on the same date. He is remembered on the Ypres Menin Gate. His family inserted the following memoriam in a local paper:

"Out on yonder battlefield there is a silent grave
One we loved so dearly but yet we could not save
His King and Country called him he bravely did his best
But god thought fit to take him to his eternal rest"

Private Harold George Pearce   *2nd Bn Wiltshire Regiment*
Service No.   8260   Age: 22
Place of Birth: Chippenham, Wiltshire   Home Country: England
Date of Death: 24/10/1914   Cause of death: Killed in action
Memorial: Chippenham & St. Andrew's Church Chippenham

War cemetery: Ypres Menim Gate
Theatre of war: Belgium
Next of Kin: James & Lucy Ann Pearce
Address: 31 Foghamshire, Chippenham, Wiltshire

Harold, known as Harry, was the only son of James & Lucy Ann Pearce. He had enlisted with the Wiltshire Regiment at eighteen years of age and was serving in Gibraltar at the outbreak of hostilities. He landed with the Wiltshires at Zeebrugge in Belgium on 7 October 1914 and was killed in action on Saturday 24 October 1914 at Belselare, Belgium in the same action as Ernest Tuck. He is remembered on the Ypres Menin Gate, and has no known grave. In 1916 his parents inserted the following memoriam in a local paper:

"Take his soul that died for duty in Thy tender pierced hands
Crown the faulty life with beauty offered for the Fatherland
All forgiving with the living may he in Thy kingdom stand"

Lance Corporal Arthur Hillier   *2nd Bn Wiltshire Regiment*
Service No.   8759   Age: 24
Place of Birth: Christian Malford, Wiltshire   Home Country: England
Date of Death: 24/10/1914   Cause of death: Killed in action
Memorial: Not Known
War cemetery: Ypres Menin Gate
Theatre of war: Belgium
Next of Kin: John & Selina Hillier
Address: Christian Malford, Wiltshire

Arthur was a farm labourer prior to his enlistment with the Wiltshire Regiment. He was serving in Gibraltar at the outbreak of hostilities. He landed with the Wiltshires at Zeebrugge in Belgium on 7 October 1914 and was killed in action on Saturday 24 October 1914 at Belselare, Belgium in the same action as Ernest Tuck. He is remembered on the Ypres Menin Gate, and has no known grave.

Christmas 1914: Princess Mary was the third child and only daughter of King George V and Queen Mary. The Princess set up a special fund for servicemen and nurses who were stationed overseas during the first Christmas of the war. Each received a Princess Mary Gift Box on Christmas Day. This tin contained one ounce of pipe tobacco or twenty cigarettes, a pipe, tinder lighter, or sweets for non smokers, Christmas card and photograph of the Princess. More than 355,000 were successfully delivered for Christmas 1914.

Corporal Sidney Allen Penny   *1st Bn Wiltshire Regiment*
Service No.   7531   Age: 24
Place of Birth: Wilsford, Wiltshire   Home Country: England
Date of Death: 24/10/1914   Cause of death: Killed in action
Memorial: Chippenham & St. Andrew's Church Chippenham
War cemetery: Le Touret Memorial
Theatre of war: France
Next of Kin: Charles & Julia Penny
Address: Woodtown Farm, West Parley, Dorset

Regular soldier Sidney, known as Allen, arrived in France on 14 August 1914 and took part in the retreat fom Mons and the Battle of the Aisne. On Saturday 24 October 1914 the 1st Wiltshires were at the village of Neuve Chapelle, France. During the early hours of the morning they faced a night attack from German infantry which was repulsed after two hours of fighting. The rest of the night was spent improving the trenches, which was hampered by German snipers. During the day the Wiltshires were subjected to heavy German artillery fire which resulted in some of the trenches being blown in. The Wiltshires casualties were 8 killed, 37 wounded and 23 men missing. A note in the war diary stated:

"It is feared that most of these 23 men were buried in the dug outs."

Allen was one of those killed and he is remembered on the Le Touret Memorial. He has no known grave.

Private Stephen Henry Thomas Pullen   *1st Bn Wiltshire Regiment*
Service No.   6127   Age: 30
Place of Birth: Chelsea, London   Home Country: England
Date of Death: 25/10/1914   Cause of death: Killed in action
Memorial: North Wraxall
War cemetery: Le Touret Memorial
Theatre of war: France
Next of Kin: Thomas Henry & Mary Anne Pullen
Address: Marnham Bower, North Wraxall, Wiltshire

It is likely Stephen, a gardener, had been a regular soldier and was a reservist at the commencement of hostilities. He was called to the colours and arrived in France on 22 August 1914 joining the 1st Battalion Wiltshire Regiment. He was initially reported wounded on Sunday 25 October 1914 when the Wiltshires were subjected to German shelling at Neuve Chapelle, France. Later he was officially reported killed in action on the same day. He is today remembered on the Le Touret Memorial and has no known grave.

Sergeant Maurice Dancey   *1st Bn Wiltshire Regiment*
Service No.   7583   Age: 26
Place of Birth: Great Somerford, Wiltshire   Home Country: England
Date of Death: 27/10/1914   Cause of death: Died of wounds
Memorial: Great Somerford
War cemetery: Le Touret Memorial
Theatre of war: France
Next of Kin: Mary J Dancey (wife) - George & Mary A. Dancey (parents)

Address: Abergavenny - Great Somerford, Wiltshire

Maurice originally enlisted with the Wiltshires on 19 March 1906 at the age of 18 years and one month. Prior to the war he left the army and was placed on the national reserve. Toward the end of 1913 he married Mary J. Prosser at Abergavenny where his relations lived. At the outbreak of the Great War Maurice was recalled to the army and arrived in France on 28 August 1914. On Tuesday 27 October the 1st Battalion Wiltshire Regiment were at the village of Neuve Chapelle, France and facing very stiff German opposition. Communication was becoming a problem because German snipers had nearly surrounded the Wiltshires position. An account from 2nd Lieutenant Chandler gives a good indication of the situation on that day:

"The line of trenches held by the Royal Irish Regiment on our left was vacated by that Regiment by 10a.m. And these trenches were shortly afterwards occupied by Germans. Our trenches were not pressed for some time, but, a steady fire kept up from the front. About 11a.m. our trenches were reinforced by supports under Lieutenant Ward Tetley and 2nd Lieutenant Martin. At 12.15 I reported to the Officer Commanding that we had sufficient men in the trenches and that we were holding our own (NOTE this is the last message Officer Commanding Battalion received from the trenches) About 2p.m. we became aware that the enemy had passed through the line of trenches previously held by the Royal Irish Regiment and collected in a wood near the Chateau behind our lines. About quarter hour later they deployed from there in about twenty or more lines, and proceeded to roll up the line of our trenches. From our left flank the enemy were also holding the village of Neuve Chapelle about 400 yards rear of us. After discussing the situation with the other officers present, we decided that we must give way and that further resistance in our present position was not possible. We passed down to the right along the line of our trenches, and getting out found a line in open facing the enemy's turning movement. There was some delay in getting out of the trenches as Captain Stoddart, the senior officer in the trenches, refused to move till he saw the situation for himself. When he decided that the line must go back. The losses in getting back and forming this line were heavy. We now posted our right on the left of the line still held by the Royal West Kent Regiment, and, formed a line to cover their flank and stay the enemy's advance. About 3.15p.m. having seen that neither of the previous messages sent to the Officer Commanding Battalion had got through Lieutenant Ward Tetley told me to go myself, and inform the Officer Commanding Battalion. This I did getting to him about 4.15p.m. by a circular route, the enemy being at this time between us and our HQ and reserve Coy."

Sergeant A. J. Poolman of C Company, Wiltshire Regiment gave the following account:

"I remained with Captain Stoddart, who, together with Major Buckle, West Kents, formed the line covering the West Kents flank. 2nd Lieuts Lloyd, Rose and Riley and some men of D Coy were holding a farm in the line we had taken up. Capt Stoddart was shot about dusk and died of his wounds shortly afterwards. We held on to this line till about 10p.m. when we were relieved by A Company Royal West Kents and some Indian Regiment. Shortly afterwards we were ordered to join our own Battalion HQ. From the time the enemy turned our flank we were fighting at close quarters almost up to the time we were relieved: our men using the bayonet on several occasions. An attempt was made to rescue our men from being taken prisoners by a bayonet charge, but only about 15 to 20 of this party got back without being killed or wounded."

In a casualty report which appeared on 21 December 1914 Maurice was listed as being wounded and there was hope that he would return to his home. Then a further casualty return on 17 March 1915 listed Maurice as wounded and missing. Later official news was received that Maurice had died of his wounds he received during the fighting that took place on Tuesday 27 October 1914. He has no known grave and is remembered on the Le Touret Memorial. Maurice left a widow and an unborn son who was named Maurice after the father he would never know.

Private John William Blanchard   *1st Bn Coldstream Guards*

Service No.	6834	Age:	32
Place of Birth:	Chippenham, Wiltshire	Home Country:	England
Date of Death:	29/10/1914	Cause of death:	Killed in action
Memorial:	Chippenham		
War cemetery:	Ypres Menim Gate		
Theatre of war:	Belgium		
Next of Kin:	Joseph & Elizabeth Blanchard		
Address:	Chippenham, Wiltshire		

John arrived in France on 11 September 1914 which suggests he was a reserve because the 1st Battalion Coldstream Guards had arrived in France in August 1914. He was killed in action on Thursday 29 October 1914 during heavy fighting East of Ypres, Belgium at Gheluvelt, during the First battle of Ypres. After the fighting the 1st Battalion Coldstream Guards numbered just eighty men. John is remembered on the Ypres Menin Gate and has no known grave.

Private Harry Oswald Smith   *9th Lancers*

Service No.	21	Age:	26
Place of Birth:	Hullavington, Wiltshire	Home Country:	England
Date of Death:	29/10/1914	Cause of death:	Killed in action
Memorial:	Amesbury & Police HQ Devizes		
War cemetery:	Le Touret Memorial		
Theatre of war:	France		
Next of Kin:	Frank Henry & Elizabeth Smith		
Address:	Fargo Cottages, Amesbury, Wiltshire		

It is likely Harry was a reservist, he was serving as a police officer in Wiltshire and was well known in the area. He was called up at the outbreak of hostilities and arrived in France in September 1914. Harry was killed in action on Thursday 29 October 1914 and is remembered on the Le Touret Memorial he has no known grave.

Private Thomas Self   *1st Bn Wiltshire Regiment*

Service No.	5575	Age:	33
Place of Birth:	Lacock, Wiltshire	Home Country:	England
Date of Death:	29/10/1914	Cause of death:	Killed in action
Memorial:	Warminster		
War cemetery:	Le Touret Memorial		
Theatre of war:	France		
Next of Kin:	Annie Self (wife) - Thomas & Ellen Self (parents)		
Address:	7 and 8, Victoria Road, Warminster - Lacock		

Thomas, a farm labourer. married Annie Miles Till on 19 August 1907 at Warminster and it is likely he was either a territorial or a member of reserve or special reserve. He joined the 1st Battalion Wiltshire Regiment and arrived in France on 21 September 1914. He was killed in action by German artillery fire on Thursday 29 October 1914 at Richebourg, west of Neuve Chapelle, France. He left a widow and four children, he is remembered on the Le Touret Memorial and has no known grave.

Private John Griffiths		*1st Bn Wiltshire Regiment*	
Service No.	5886	Age:	32
Place of Birth:	Malmesbury, Wiltshire	Home Country:	England
Date of Death:	30/10/1914	Cause of death:	Died of wounds
Memorial:	Chippenham & St. Andrew's Church Chippenham		
War cemetery:	Boulogne Eastern Cemetery		
Theatre of war:	France		
Next of Kin:	John & Jane Griffiths		
Address:	41 Bostock Avenue, Abingdon, Berkshire		

Regular soldier John lived at London Road, Chippenham prior to joining the army. He arrived in France on 14 August 1914 and was wounded during fighting and sent to one of the military hospitals at Boulogne, France, where he succumbed to his wounds on Friday 30 October 1914.

Private Herbert Gainey		*1st Bn Wiltshire Regiment*	
Service No.	6993	Age:	30
Place of Birth:	Kington St Michael	Home Country:	England
Date of Death:	31/10/1914	Cause of death:	Killed in action
Memorial:	Langley Burrell		
War cemetery:	Le Touret Memorial		
Theatre of war:	France		
Next of Kin:	Millicent Jane Gainey (wife) - Henry & Mary Jane Gainey (parents)		
Address:	Langley Burrell, Wiltshire - Kington St Michael, Wiltshire		

It is likely Herbert was a reservist and after leaving the Army he married Millicent J. Jefferies in the summer of 1912. At the outbreak of hostilities he was called up arriving in France on 22 August 1914. On a casualty return dated 21 December 1914 he was reported wounded; then on 11 January 1915 another casualty return stated he was wounded and missing. Later an official notification stated he had been killed in action on Saturday 31 October 1914 along with 37 other members of the Wiltshires. He is remembered on the Le Touret Memorial and has no known grave.

Lance Corporal George Bishop		*1st Bn Royal West Surrey Regiment*	
Service No.	L/8133	Age:	29
Place of Birth:	Horley, Surrey	Home Country:	England
Date of Death:	31/10/1914	Cause of death:	Killed in action
Memorial:	Not known		
War cemetery:	Ypres Menin Gate		
Theatre of war:	Belgium		
Next of Kin:	Florence Maria Bishop (wife) – George & Annie Bishop (parents)		
Address:	2 New Road, Chippenham, Wiltshire		

George originally joined the Royal West Surrey Regiment on 8 August 1904 and served for over 6 years and on leaving in 1910 was placed on the national reserve . On 10 August 1913 he married Florence Maria Heckford at Colchester and soon after this the couple moved to Chippenham. At the outbreak of hostilities George was recalled to the colours re-joining his regiment and arriving in France on 12 August 1914. On Saturday 31 October 1914 the 1st Battalion Royal West Surrey Regiment were in trenches at Gheluvelt, east of Ypres, Belgium. The Germans were preparing to attack and were dug in about 300 yards from the British lines and at 7am the RWS's trenches were subjected to a heavy German bombardment At 10am B company RWS was driven out of their trenches by machine gun fire from both flanks. At 11am the Germans had managed to get into C Company RWS trenches and also had got into the village behind D Company RWS. The Guards recaptured Gheluvelt during the afternoon but all that could be found of the RWS was about 20 men the remainder were either wounded or missing. One of those missing was George. In November 1915 Florence Bishop received a war pension of 10 shillings per week. In August 1916 he was officially presumed to have died on the day he was posted as missing. He is remembered on the Ypres Menin Gate and has no known grave.

7 NOVEMBER 1914 - BRITISH & INDIAN FORCES LAND AT MESOPOTAMIA

TO PROTECT BRITISH OIL INTERESTS

Private Herbert James Fishlock		*1st Somerset Light Infantry*	
Service No.	6762	Age:	29
Place of Birth:	Kington St Michael	Home Country:	England
Date of Death:	09/11/1914	Cause of death:	Killed in action
Memorial:	Not Known		
War cemetery:	Ploegsteert Memorial		
Theatre of war:	Belgium		
Next of Kin:	John & Ester Agnes Fishlock		
Address:	Kington St Michael, Wiltshire		

Herbert was coal miner and married Edith Lily Williams in Pontypridd South Wales in 1905. It is likely he had previously served in the army and was a reservist, being called up returning to the 1st Battalion Somerset Light Infantry arriving in France on 21 August 1914. On 6 November 1914 the Somersets went into the front line in trenches north west of Saint Yvon near Plugstreet Wood (Ploegsteert, Belgium). While in these trenches the Somersets were subjected to German shell fire and it is likely Herbert was killed at this time. He was one of nine members of the Battalion to be killed on Monday 9 November. He is remembered on the Ploegsteert Memorial and has no known grave.

Driver Oscar Bush		*54th Bde Royal Field Artillery*	
Service No.	42248	Age:	27
Place of Birth:	Biddestone	Home Country:	England
Date of Death:	12/11/1914	Cause of death:	Died of wounds
Memorial:	Biddestone & Corsham		
War cemetery:	Poperinghe Old Military Cemetery		
Theatre of war:	Belgium		
Next of Kin:	Annie Bush (wife) - Jos & Emma Bush (parents)		
Address:	Biddestone, Wiltshire		

Oscar originally joined The Royal Artillery on 13 March 1906 and after six years with the colours he left the army marrying Annie Strong at Windsor Registry Office on 5 March 1912. Oscar and Annie settled in Biddestone and Oscar found employment working in the gardens of Lord Islington's Estate at Hartham Park. Oscar was a reservist and at the commencement of the Great War was called back to the Royal Artillery being sent to the Continent where he arrived on 16 August 1914. He was wounded with a gun shot wound to the chest on 11 November 1914 and taken to No. 4 Clearing Hospital at Poperinghe, Belgium, where he succumbed to his wounds on Thursday 12 November 1914. Oscar was buried in Poperinghe Old Military Cemetery and the funeral was conducted by Chaplain Rev. E.A.S. Gell who was a former Corsham Vicar. Oscar left a Widow and two small children.

Private William Arthur Brewer   *1st Wiltshire Regiment*

Service No.	10398	Age:	21
Place of Birth:	Chippenham, Wiltshire	Home Country:	England
Date of Death:	13/11/1914	Cause of death:	Killed in action
Memorial:	Chippenham		
War cemetery:	Ypres Menim Gate		
Theatre of war:	Belgium		
Next of Kin:	George & Sarah Brewer		
Address:	81 Wood Lane, Chippenham		

William, known as Billy, had served as a territorial soldier for three years at the start of the Great War and had played as a forward for Swindon Town Football Club in the 1913/1914 season. He volunteered for service with the regulars and was posted to the 1st Battalion arriving on the continent on 27 October 1914. He was killed in action on Friday 13 November 1914 when the Wiltshires were shelled and then attacked by German infantry at Hooge east of Ypres in Belgium. The German attack was repulsed and Billy was one of three members of the Wiltshire Regiment to be killed. He is remembered on the Ypres Menin Gate and has no known grave.

Private William Ernest Jones   *1st Wiltshire Regiment*

Service No.	7253	Age:	30
Place of Birth:	Walcot, Somerset	Home Country:	England
Date of Death:	05/12/1914	Cause of death:	Died of wounds
Memorial:	Chippenham & St. Andrew's Church Chippenham		
War cemetery:	Wimereux Communal Cemetery		
Theatre of war:	France		
Next of Kin:	William Edward & Helen Jones		
Address:	Lowden Hill, Chippenham, Wiltshire		

Regular soldier William originally enlisted with the Wiltshires on 7 March 1905 at the age of eighteen years and two months. He arrived in France on 14 August 1914 and was wounded in subsequent fighting succumbing to his wound at a military hospital at Wimereux, France on Saturday 5 December 1914. Official sources tell uthough were informed he had died on the 6 December 1914. The following memoriam was inserted in a local paper in November 1916:s he died on 5 December 1914, his family

We often sit and think of him
His face we oft recall
There's nothing left to Answer
But his photo on the wall

Private John Newman   *2nd Bn Wiltshire Regiment*
Service No.   8208   Age: 22
Place of Birth: Bremhill, Wiltshire   Home Country: England
Date of Death: 07/12/1914   Cause of death: Died of wounds
Memorial: Not known
War cemetery: Merville Communal Cemetery
Theatre of war: France
Next of Kin: Frederick James & Dora Annie Newman
Address: 30 Christian Malford, Wiltshire

It is likely John was a regular soldier. He arrived at Zeebrugge, Belgium with the 2nd Battalion Wiltshire Regiment on Sunday 7 October 1914. Early in 1915 news was received that he had died of wounds at a casualty clearing station at Merville, France, on Monday 7 December 1914, he had been on the continent just two months.

Private William Hadrill   *2nd Wiltshire Regiment*
Service No.   3/9363   Age: 23
Place of Birth: Box, Wiltshire   Home Country: England
Date of Death: 09/12/1914   Cause of death: Died of wounds
Memorial: Great Somerford
War cemetery: Great Somerford (SS.Peter and Paul) Churchyard
Theatre of war: Home
Next of Kin: Herbert & Mercy Hadrill
Address: 17 Jeffery Street, Kentish Town, London

William, a farm labourer, had been brought up by his grandparents in Great Somerford, and was the only son of Herbert & Mercy Hadrill. His father had died when William was young and his mother worked as a cook in London. He was a territorial soldier and at the outbreak of hostilities he volunteered to serve with the regulars arriving on the Continent on 20 October 1914. He had just reached the front when he was severely wounded in fierce fighting at Ypres. He had been struck by a piece of shrapnel in his back and had a bullet wound to the head. He was evacuated to England and sent to a Hospital in Oxford and then on to Milton House, Steventon, near Abingdon which had been converted to a convalescent hospital. William wrote the following letter to his Aunt while in the hospital:

"I am shifted from Oxford to this place. This is a nice place. I have a piece of shrapnel which cut my head, it is nearly better now. My chum next to me in the trench had his eye cut right out, and two or three more chums got killed on the spot. I had a bullet through my cap but it so happened it never touched my head – lucky! I was the luckiest of them all. I was talking to a chap from Malmesbury out there one day, and half an hour later after he was shot right through the head. It is not war, it is murder. I have seen some sights – some arms and legs off.. This happened in the battle of Ypres which is on now. One night I lost my chums in a wood. I didn't know what to do wandering about all night up to my knees in mud and water, then stop in it

all day. But never mind; I'm come back to England again, thank God."

William succumbed to his wounds on Wednesday 9 December. His body was brought back to Great Somerford where he was buried with full military honours.

LtFelix Charles Hurbert Hanbury-Tracey   *2nd Bn Scots Guards*

Service No.	N/A	Age:	30
Place of Birth:	Buckingham Gate, London	Home Country:	England
Date of Death:	10/12/1914	Cause of death:	Killed in action
Memorial:	All Saints Church, Eastbourne		
War cemetery:	Ploegsteert Memorial		
Theatre of war:	Belgium		
Next of Kin:	Madeline Hanbury-Tracy (wife) – Charles 4th Baron Sudeley (parent)		
Address:	46, Montague Square, London		

Felix was educated at Harrow and the Royal Military College Sandhurst and received a commission with the Scots Guards on 8 May 1901. He retired form the army in 1907 and on 11 June 1908 he married Madeline Llewellyn at Lacock, Wiltshire. He arrived in France on 7 November and on the night of 18-19 December he took part in an attack on German positions at Fromelles with the 2nd Battalion Scots Guards. He was slightly wounded during the start of the attack but carried on and led his men. He was then seriously wounded on the parapet of the German Trench. Some of his men attempted to carry him to safety but he ordered them to leave him where he was and not risk their lives. The Germans counterattacked recapturing the trench and Felix died in German hands a few hours later. He was subsequently buried by his captors. A few days later during the 1914 Christmas truce information was received from the Germans that Felix had been buried in Fromelles German cemetery. He is today remembered on the Ploegsteert Memorial. A memorial service was held at Trowbridge and Madeline, his wife, laid a wreath of myrtle, which had been grown at Lackham from a spray taken from her bridal bouquet.

Left: Felix Charles Hurbert Hanbury-Tracey.

Below: The Cloth Hall, Ypres in flames 22 November 1914.

18 DECEMBER 1914 - BATTLE OF GIVENCHY, BELGIUM

Private Clifford Alfred James Wiltshire

Service No.   1640
Place of Birth: Chippenham
Date of Death: 22/12/1914
Memorial: Not known
War cemetery: Le Touret Memorial
Theatre of war: France
Next of Kin: Alfred & Florence Wiltshire
Address: 52 Church Road, Redfield, Bristol

1st Bn Gloucestershire Regiment

Age: 17
Home Country: England
Cause of death: Killed in action

Seventeen year old Clifford was under age when he arrived in France on 11 November 1914. To serve abroad at this time soldiers were supposed to be 19 or over. He was killed in action, most likely by German shell fire near Le Bassee, France, on Tuesday 22 December 1914, along with 7 other members of the 1st Battalion Gloucestershire Regiment. He is remembered on the Le Touret Memorial and has no known grave.

25 DECEMBER 1914 - UNOFFICIAL CHRISTMAS TRUCE

Private Frederick Philip Cole

Service No.   6449
Place of Birth: Lacock, Wiltshire
Date of Death: 26/12/1914
Memorial: Not known
War cemetery: Ypres Menin Gate
Theatre of war: Belgium
Next of Kin: Frederick William & Lydia Cole
Address: 41 Hillside View, Peasedown, Somerset

1st Wiltshire Regiment

Age: 29
Home Country: England
Cause of death: Killed in action

Frederick was an apprentice painter with Gowen and Stevens of Trowbridge, and enlisted in the Wiltshires on 12 October 1903 at the age of 18 yeas and 7 months. At the outbreak of war he was working in Weston-Super-Mare and was engaged to be married. However, being on reserve he was called up and returned to the Wiltshires, arriving in France on Friday 14 October 1914. He took part in all the actions the Wiltshire Regiment were involved in. Frederick was killed in action on Boxing day 1914. At Kemmel in Belgium there was no Christmas truce and the 1st Battalion Wiltshire Regiments war diary states;

"In trenches. Germans did a good deal of shelling, but most of their shells did not burst. A good deal of sniping in trenches. Cold and frost. 2 killed, 1 wounded."

In December 1915 the following memoriam was inserted in a local paper:

In loving memory of Frederick Philip Cole killed in action while serving with the 1st Wiltshire Regiment on Boxing Day 1914

For him the Warfare's over
The sounds of battle cease
Angels have bourne his soul away
To realms of endless peace"

Private Herbert Kington		*2nd Bn Wiltshire Regiment*	
Service No.	12929	Age:	20
Place of Birth:	Castle Combe, Wiltshire	Home Country:	England
Date of Death:	31/12/1914	Cause of death:	Killed in action
Memorial:	Grittleton		
War cemetery:	Ploegsteert Memorial		
Theatre of war:	Belgium		
Next of Kin:	George & Harriet Kington		
Address:	Foscote, Grittleton, Wiltshire		

Herbert, a groom, volunteered for service with the Wiltshire Regiment most likely as part of Lord Kitcheners call for more men, and arrived in France on 11 December 1914. He had been in France a little over a month when he was killed in action on New Years Eve 1914. The Wiltshires war diary gives an indication of conditions in the trenches at this time:

"Casualties from 18 December being 6 killed, 12 wounded, 20 admitted to hospital with sickness. Considering the trying conditions the percentage of sickness was not so great as might have been expected, and most of the men admitted to hospital were Kitcheners Army. The time serving men and reservists in majority of cases standing the hardship with great fortitude and even cheerfulness."

Herbert is remembered on the Ploegsteert Memorial and has no known grave.

Sergeant Hancock (below) took his camera to the front and took a number of photographs of trench life (left).

2
1915 - The War That Should Have Been Over By Christmas

Private John Waddie Wishart
Service No.   8394
Place of Birth: Manchester, Lancashire
Date of Death: 07/01/1915
Memorial: Chippenham & St. Andrew' Church Chippenham
War cemetery: Le Touret Memorial
Theatre of war: France
Next of Kin: Emily Louise Wishart (wife) – Helen Wishart (parent)
Address: 5 Timber Street, Chippenham, Wiltshire – St Paul's, Bristol

1st Bn South Wales Borderers
Age: 30
Home Country: England
Cause of death: Killed in action

John, a chauffeur, married his wife Emily in Cheltenham in 1910 and soon after moved to Chippenham. It is likely he had served with the South Wales Borderers and was a reservist being called back to the colours at the start of the Great War. He arrived in France on 13 August 1914 and was posted as missing on Thursday 7 January 1915 near Neuve Chapelle, France. Later he was assumed to have died on that day. He is remembered on the Le Touret Memorial and has no known grave.

Private Frederick Evans
Service No.   8913
Place of Birth: Calne, Wiltshire
Date of Death: 16/01/1915
Memorial: Derry Hill - Lacock & Lacock Church
War cemetery: Wytschaete Military Cemetery
Theatre of war: Belgium
Next of Kin: Harry & Annie Evans
Address: Cantax Hill, Lacock, Wiltshire

1st Bn Wiltshire Regiment
Age: 19
Home Country: England
Cause of death: Killed in action

Nineteen year old regular soldier Frederick, known as Fred who had been a farm labourer, arrived in France on 14 August 1914. He was killed in action on Saturday 16 January 1915 while in the trenches facing the Germans at Kemmel, Belgium. The war diary of the Wiltshires for the day states;

"Trenches. A quiet day, a farm just in rear of Battn. HQ took fire, and the enemy put some shrapnel over, presumably at the smoke. Relieved about 7p.m. by 5th Fusiliers. 2 men killed.1 man wounded."

Frederick was one of the two men killed, he is buried in Wytschaete Military Cemetery, Belgium with 329 casualties of the Great War.

Sergeant Major George Ralph Thomas		*Royal Scots Greys*	
Service No.	3112	Age:	52
Place of Birth:	Bow, London	Home Country:	England
Date of Death:	20/01/1915	Cause of death:	Died
Memorial:	Chippenham		
War cemetery:	Chippenham London Road Cemetery		
Theatre of war:	Home		
Next of Kin:	Mabel Thomas (wife)		
Address:	London Road, Chippenham, Wiltshire		

George, known as Ralph, had joined the Scots Greys and taken part in the South African war and after recovering and being invalided home he was attached to the Wiltshire Yeomanry. In 1908 he was promoted to Regimental Sergeant Major. At the outbreak of hostilities he was transferred to Cheltenham where he was involved with training the Wiltshire Yeomanry for war service. On the evening of Wednesday 20 January Ralph went to the bedroom in the hotel where he was billeted. Shortly afterward one of Ralph's comrades found him seated on the bed, and he was described as very unwell. Ralph asked his friend to go for a doctor but when his friend arrived at the doctor's house he was not there. He then met another doctor in the street but he declined to go to Ralphs aid. The friend then returned to the hotel and found that Ralph was in a state of collapse and went again to find a doctor. This time the friend was successful but when they returned to the hotel they found Ralph had died from heart failure. Ralph's body was returned to Chippenham and he was given a funeral with full military honours. His coffin was covered with a Union Jack, on which laid his sword belt and cap, and taken from the Armoury (Yeald Hall) to the Cemetery, the route was lined with people. Three volleys were fired over the grave and the last post was sounded. Ralph left a Widow and four children.

Cptn Eustace Arundel De St Barbe Sladen Watkins		*2nd Bn Devonshire Regiment*	
Service No.	N/a	Age:	26
Place of Birth:	Castle Combe, Wiltshire	Home Country:	England
Date of Death:	31/01/1915	Cause of death:	Died of wounds
Memorial:	Castle Combe		
War cemetery:	Merville Communal Cemetery		
Theatre of war:	France		
Next of Kin:	Robert Arundel & Mary Etheldesh Watkins		
Address:	The Shrub, Castle Combe, Wiltshire		

Regular soldier Eustace arrived in France on 7 November 1915. He had been with the 3rd Battalion Devonshire Regiment and transferred to the 2nd Battalion where he served with C Company. On 30 January the Devons were in trenches near Neuve Chapelle, France, where

Above: Men of the 1st Battalion Wiltshire Regiment in the trenches.

The grave of Sergeant Major George Ralph Thomas in Chippenham Cemetery.

no man's land was 50 to 100 yards away. A portion of the British trenches was under water and to the rear a breastwork (raised bank) was being built where the British trenches were unoccupied. Eustace had been warned not to stand out in the open but at about 10pm he went to the end of the breastwork to see how the men were getting on. While he was bending down he was hit in the right shoulder by a bullet. The bullet passed downwards through his back injuring his internal organs and breaking two ribs. He was in a serious condition and was sent by motor ambulance direct to a clearing hospital where he peacefully died about 15 hours later. It was found he had also been wounded by a bullet in the leg and it was thought that he had been hit by chance because it had been quite dark when he was hit. Robert and Mary also received the following details of his burial:

"He was buried in a quiet corner of the cemetery which was reserved for officers and near to the graves of the men of his company whom he loved and who loved him."

Sergeant Richard Harold Marsden   *38th Coy Royal Garrison Artillery*

Service No.	23084	Age:	34
Place of Birth:	Winterbourne Gunner	Home Country:	England
Date of Death:	11/02/1915	Cause of death:	Died
Memorial:	Not Known		
War cemetery:	Plymouth Weston Mill Cemetery		
Theatre of war:	Home		
Next of Kin:	Alice Marion Powell (foster sister)		
Address:	Near the Chapel, Christian Malford, Wiltshire		

Regular soldier Richard was the foster brother of Alice Powell. No 38 Company, Royal Garrison Artillery were part of the UK coastal defence batteries and were based in the Plymouth area. It is likely Richard died of illness or disease.

Sergeant Frank Phillips   *Plymouth Bn RN Div RMLI*

Service No.	PLY/8707	Age:	36
Place of Birth:	Swindon	Home Country:	England
Date of Death:	24/02/1915	Cause of death:	Died of wounds
Memorial:	Chippenham & St. Andrew's Church		
War cemetery:	Berlin South Western Cemetery		
Theatre of war:	Germany		
Next of Kin:	Beatrice Alice Philips (wife) - Elijah & Rebecca Phillips (parents)		
Address:	33 Sheldon Road, Chippenham - Rowden Hill, Chippenham		

Frank, a Blacksmiths labourer, enlisted with the Royal Marine Light Infantry on 16 July 1897. In 1900 he served in China during the Boxer rebellion and won the China Medal with clasp. Returning to England he married Beatrice Alice Kingston at Chippenham in 1906. He was promoted to the rank of sergeant in 1909 and in 1912 he received a long service and good conduct medal. The Royal Marine Light Infantry were landed at Ostend on 27 August 1914 and remained there until 31 August and were then employed in the defence of Dunkirk and Antwerp from 19 September to 12 October. Frank was taken prisoner during the defence of Antwerp in 1914 and sent to a prisoner of war camp in Germany where he died of his wounds on Wednesday 24 February 1915.

Private Christopher Herbert Dawson   *Princess Patricia's Canadian Light Inf.*

Service No.	218	Age:	28
Place of Birth:	Jhansi, Inda	Home Country:	Canada
Date of Death:	28/02/1915	Cause of death:	Killed in action
Memorial:	Christian Malford		
War cemetery:	Voormezeele Enclosure No 3		
Theatre of war:	Belgium		
Next of Kin:	Marion Dawson		
Address:	Hartfield, Eastbourne, Sussex		

Christopher, an electrician, was born in Jhansi, India and arrived in Canada via the United States in September 1909. He had previously served with the Ceylon Rifle Corps and volunteered for service on 24 August 1914 joining Princess Patricia's Canadian Light Infantry. After completing their training in England the Princess Patricia's arrived in France on 22 December 1914 and were sent to the front in Belgium. On Saturday 28 February Christopher and the Princes Patricia's were in trenches at St Eloi, Belgium. At 4.30 No 4 Company with snipers and bomb throwers attacked and captured a German Sap (trench extending into no man's land). The German Sap was opposite the position of Shelley Farm. The raid was successful as the sap was demolished and the parapet knocked in and No. 4 Company withdrew at daybreak. The Princes Patricia's War diary states:

"The attack was carried out with considerable dash notwithstanding the fact that the men had been for six weeks employed in trenches under not very favourable conditions."

After 3 days in the trenches the Princes Patricia's had the following casualties: 17 killed, 47 wounded and 3 missing. Christopher was the nephew of Alfred Clark of Christian Malford and Alfred was to lose his own son Guy in April 1915.

Private Sidney Iver Morse   *1st Bn Wiltshire Regiment*

Service No.   10257   Age: 17
Place of Birth: Chippenham   Home Country: England
Date of Death: 02/03/1915   Cause of death: Killed in action
Memorial: Chippenham
War cemetery: Kemmel Chateau Military Cenetery
Theatre of war: Belgium
Next of Kin: Arthur & Diana Morse
Address: 25 Causeway, Chippenham, Wiltshire

Seventeen year old under age soldier, Sidney, volunteered for service with the Wiltshire Regiment and arrived on the continent on 26 January 1915. On Tuesday 2 March 1915 the Wiltshires were in trenches at Kemmel, Belgium, and had been shelled by the Germans The Medical Officer Lieutenant P.M.J. Power and one man were killed and buried in the cemetery near Kemmel Chateau. The one man killed was Sidney and his father, Arthur Morse received the following letter from Major Ernest Barnard of the 3rd Wiltshires dated 9 March 1915:

"I very much regret to inform you that a post card arrived here today from Lance Corporal S. Leggett, 1st Battalion Wiltshire Regiment, announcing that your son, Sidney, had been killed in action on 2nd March. Lance Corporal Leggett asks that you should be informed as soon as possible. Personally I offer you my very great sympathy for your boy was well known to me and he was everything that was straight and manly. Lance Corporal Leggett's own words were as follows: "Poor Kid, he was liked by everyone," and I can certainly endorse that for a cheerier lad has never yet put on a uniform. I will write at once for further information, and if you like I will send further details later on."

Sidney's sister, Amy Gough, received the following letter from Captain E Harvey of C Company 1st Wiltshires dated 9 March:

"I regret to inform you that your brother Private Morse was killed instantaneously by a German bullet last Tuesday afternoon while in the trenches. He was buried the same evening with other men of the Regiment. His grave was marked with a little wooden cross bearing his name and the date of his death. Private Morse was a good soldier and always Cheerful. He is a great loss to his comrades."

10 MARCH 1915 - BATTLE OF NEUVE CHAPELLE

Private Montague Rowland Bridgeman   *1st Bn Wiltshire Regiment*

Service No.   8003   Age: 27
Place of Birth: Dauntsey, Wiltshire   Home Country: England
Date of Death: 12/03/1915   Cause of death: Killed in action
Memorial: Calne & Christian Malford
War cemetery: Ypres Menin Gate
Theatre of war: Belgium
Next of Kin: Gertrude Bridgeman (wife) - Frederick & Myrah Bridgeman (parents)
Address: 11 Dodford Cottages, Christian Malford, Wiltshire

Regular soldier Montague married Gertrude Louise Merrett toward the end of 1910 and arrived on the continent on Wednesday 7 October 1914 with the 2nd Battalion Wiltshire Regiment. It is likely he was wounded and after his recovery was transferred to the 1st Battalion Wiltshire Regiment. On Friday 12 March 1915 the Wiltshires were in the trenches near Kemmel in Belgium opposite a German position called the Spranbroek Molen, waiting to assault the Germans. The Wiltshires had arrived at 5.30 and the morning was dull and misty. The Artillery bombardment which was to precede the assault on Spranbroek Molen had to be delayed because of the weather. The mist began to clear and the war diary states;

"At 2.30pm the Artillery bombardment began and continued with a slight pause till 4.10p.m. It consisted of field guns firing shrapnel to cut the hostile wire, and large quantities of heavy HE (High Explosives) *to beat down the German parapets and blow in his trenches, in this it appeared to be fairly successful, but, it was afterwards observed that the enemy's front line trenches were almost intact."*

At 4.10pm the Wiltshires attacked and as soon as they passed the British wire the Germans opened fire with what was described as very heavy using both rifles and machine guns. Some small parties of men managed to get to the German wire which was a distance of 200 yards away but the majority of the Wiltshires were unable to get more than 50 yards from the British trenches, unable to move because of the heavy fire. At 5pm the British began to fall back to their trenches and suffered many casualties from the German fire and most of the Wiltshires withdrew at 7pm under the cover of darkness. The war diary goes on to tell us:

"It was observed that the enemy were holding this position very strongly and did not seem unduly shaken by our Artillery fire".

The Wiltshires casualties for the day were 33 killed, 48 wounded and 12 missing. Montague was first reported as missing, then reported wounded and then reported killed in action on that day. He is remembered on Ypres Menin gate and has no known grave. Montague left a widow and baby daughter. His brother, Walter, was to die of wounds just six days later while serving with the 2nd Battalion Wiltshire Regiment at Neuve Chapelle

Private Arthur Stinchcombe		*1st Bn Wiltshire Regiment*	
Service No.	3/535	Age:	28
Place of Birth:	Bristol, Gloucestershire	Home Country:	England
Date of Death:	12/03/1915	Cause of death:	Killed in action
Memorial:	Chippenham		
War cemetery:	Ypres Menin Gate		
Theatre of war:	Belgium		
Next of Kin:	James F & Ellen E Stinchcombe		
Address:	Albert Street, Bristol, Gloucestershire		

It is likely Arthur, who had served in the navy, was a territorial soldier and volunteered for service with the Wiltshires Regular Battalions. His brother Edwin lived at 73 Park lane Chippenham. Arthur arrived in France on 11 November 1914. He was killed in action in the same action as Montague Bridgeman at Kemmel, Belgium, on Friday 12 March 1915. He is remembered on the Ypres Menin Gate and has no known grave.

Private William James Wilkins		*1st Bn Wiltshire Regiment*	
Service No.	3/363	Age:	43
Place of Birth:	Chippenham, Wiltshire	Home Country:	England

Date of Death:	12/03/1915	Cause of death:	Killed in action
Memorial:	Chippenham		
War cemetery:	Ypres Menin Gate		
Theatre of war:	Belgium		
Next of Kin:	George Henry Wilkins (brother) - Sydney & Mary Anne Wilkins (parents)		
Address:	1 Beard's Cottage Allington, Chippenham, Wiltshire		

William, a builder's labourer, was the second son of Sydney and Mary Anne Wilkins. He originally joined the Wiltshires on 7 September 1893 and arrived in France on 11 November 1914. He was killed in action in the same action as Montague Bridgeman at Kemmel, Belgium, on Friday 12 March 1915. He is remembered on the Ypres Menin Gate and has no known grave.

Private Arthur Joseph Ricketts   *1st Bn Wiltshire Regiment*

Service No.	10030	Age:	22
Place of Birth:	London	Home Country:	England
Date of Death:	12/03/1915	Cause of death:	Killed in action
Memorial:	Bradford on Avon		
War cemetery:	Ypres Menin Gate – Devizes Odd Fellows – Lacock & Westwood		
Theatre of war:	Belgium		
Next of Kin:	Albert Edward and Charlotte Ricketts		
Address:	Avoncliffe Bungalow, Upper Westwood, Wiltshire		

Arthur was the youngest son of Albert and Charlotte Ricketts and was a promising sportsman especially at cycle handicaps. He won the shield at Trowbridge Wednesday Evening Sports in the summer of 1914 as well as many other prizes for various sports in the county. He was also a member of the Society of Odd fellows and volunteered for service in August 1914 being sent to Weymouth for training. Arthur was later sent to France arriving on 28 November 1914 and went through the weary wet winter campaign. He was killed in action in the same action as Montague Bridgeman at Kemmel, Belgium, on Friday 12 March 1915. He is remembered on the Ypres Menin Gate and has no known grave. His brother John Albert Ricketts was to die in Mesopotamia in December 1917.

Private Frederick Escott   *2nd Bn Wiltshire Regiment*

Service No.	10243	Age:	21
Place of Birth:	Chippenham	Home Country:	England
Date of Death:	12/03/1915	Cause of death:	Killed in action
Memorial:	Chippenham		
War cemetery:	Le Touret Memorial		
Theatre of war:	France		
Next of Kin:	William & Annie Escott		
Address:	102 Wood Lane, Chippenham, Wiltshire		

Frederick, a machinist, was the youngest son of William & Annie Escott and volunteered for service arriving in France on 11 December 1914. On Friday 12 March the 2nd Battalion Wiltshire Regiment was at the heart of the battle of Neuve Chapelle in the forward trenches. Just as the rations arrived at 5.30am the Germans attacked with bombs (hand grenades) and confusion overtook the British trenches. Eventually the Germans were stopped and the Wiltshires counter attacked to try to retake the trenches that had been lost. Initially the attack made good progress but coming under heavy machine gun fire the British were driven back; these attacks prevented some of the Wiltshires getting water and their rations. Other Regiments attacked the Germans during the day but all ended in failure and by the end of the day the British front line was held by a jumbled mass of Wiltshires, Gordons, Warwicks and Scots Guards. About 50 members of the 2nd Battalion Wiltshire Regiment were killed and one of these was Frederick. He is remembered on the Le Touret Memorial and has no known grave. In March 1918 his parents inserted the following memoriam in a local paper:

"We think we see his smiling face as he bade us his last goodbye
And left home for ever in a foreign land to die
But the bitterest blow has yet to come when the warriors return
And we miss among the cheering crowd the face of our dear son"

Lance Corporal Thomas Henry Wallace Powell 2nd Bn Wiltshire Regiment

Service No.	8730	Age:	21
Place of Birth:	Yatton Keynell	Home Country:	England
Date of Death:	12/03/1915	Cause of death:	Killed in action
Memorial:	Chippenahm & St. Andrew's Church Chippenham		
War cemetery:	Le Touret Memorial		
Theatre of war:	France		
Next of Kin:	Henry Daniel & Eliza J Powell		
Address:	Sheldon Road, Chippenham, Wiltshire		

Thomas, a farm labourer, was the only son of Henry Daniel and Eliza Powell. It is likely he volunteered for service with the Wiltshires. He was killed on Friday 12 March 1915 at Neuve Chapelle, France, in the same action as Frederick Escott. He is remembered on the Le Touret Memorial and has no known grave.

Private Walter Victor Bridgeman   *2nd Bn Wiltshire Regiment*

Service No.	8114	Age:	31
Place of Birth:	Dauntsey, Wiltshire	Home Country:	England
Date of Death:	18/03/1915	Cause of death:	Died of wounds
Memorial:	Christian Malford		
War cemetery:	St Sever Cemetery Rouen		
Theatre of war:	France		
Next of Kin:	Frederick Edward & Myrah Urania Bridgeman		
Address:	11 Dodford Cottage, Christian Malford, Wiltshire		

Regular soldier Walter had been a farm labourer before joining the army and arrived on the continent on 7 October 1914. He was wounded in action at Neuve Chapelle most likely in the same action as Frederick Escott. He was then evacuated to No. 3 military hospital at Rouen, France where he succumbed to his wounds on Monday 8 March 1915. His brother Montague Rowland Bridgeman had been killed in action on 12 March 1915 while serving with the 1st Battalion Wiltshire Regiment in Belgium.

Private Arthur Harry John Swanborough   *1st Bn Gloucestershire Regiment*

Service No.	9775	Age:	21
Place of Birth:	Chippenham	Home Country:	England

Left above: Chippenham's Neeld Hall became a Red Cross Hospital. Patients and staff inside the main hall.

Right above: The grave of Arthur Swanborough in Chippenham Cemetery.

Date of Death: 10/04/1915   Cause of death: Died
Memorial: Chippenham & St. Andrew's Church Chippenham
War cemetery: Chippenham London Road Cemetery
Theatre of war: Home
Next of Kin: Arthur Henry & Ellen Swanborough
Address: Englands Wood Lane, Chippenham

Arthur, a milk factory worker, was the eldest son of Arthur and Ellen Swanborough and enlisted with the Gloucesters at Bristol on 6 January 1913. At the outbreak of hostilities he was sent to France arriving on 13 August 1914 and was evacuated to England on 2 November 1914 and sent to a London Hospital. He was discharged from the army on 2 April 1915 and it is likely at this time he was transferred to Chippenham Cottage Hospital where he died of pulmonary tuberculosis on Saturday 10 April 1915. Pulmonary tuberculosis is a contagious bacterial infection and has a incubation period of about 4 to 8 weeks and it is likely he contracted this disease while on active service while living in the unsanitary conditions the soldiers were living in during the war.

Driver Ernest Egbert Slade   *237th H T Coy Army Service Corps*
Service No.   T4/059845   Age: 19
Place of Birth: Yatton Keynell   Home Country: England
Date of Death: 15/04/1915   Cause of death: Died
Memorial: Corsham & Chippenham Secondary School Memorial
War cemetery: Corsham St Bartholemew Burial Ground Ladbrook Lane
Theatre of war: Home
Next of Kin: Andrew George & Fanny Slade
Address: Monks Lane, Corsham, Wiltshire

Ernest, known as Egbert, volunteered for service in February 1915 and while in training he developed spinal meningitis, which he died from on Thursday 16 April 1915. Andrew and Fanny Slade received the following letter From Major T.C.R. Moore, Egbert's commanding Officer:

"I much regret to have to inform you of the death of your son Egbert, which took place at 10.15 last night in the isolation hospital, Aldershot. Your son came under my command on the 5th March and was admitted to hospital on the 8th March suffering from cerebro spinal meningitis. I desire to express my deep sympathy with you in your sad bereavement. I would like to add that your son will be sadly missed in his train by both officers and men; he was a good comrade and gave every promise of being a good soldier."

Egbert's body was conveyed to Chippenham by train and then transported by a hearse to Corsham where he was buried with full Military honours.

17 APRIL 1915 - THE CAPTURE OF HILL 60, BELGIUM

Lance Coporal Joseph Stanley Victor Fox   *1st Bn Wiltshire Regiment*

Service No.	8992
Place of Birth:	Chippenham
Date of Death:	20/04/1915
Memorial:	Chippenham
War cemetery:	Dickebusch New Military Cemetery
Theatre of war:	Belgium
Next of Kin:	Charles & Harriet Fox
Address:	45 The Causeway, Chippenham, Wiltshire

Age:	20
Home Country:	England
Cause of death:	Executed

Joseph was employed by his father who had a bill posting business. At the age of 16 he had enlisted with 3rd Bn Gloucestershire Regiment at Horfield, Bristol under the name Stanley Victor Fox and giving the place of birth as Corsham and his age as 17. It is likely he was under age and had joined without the consent of his parents. He then joined the Somersets but was bought out most likely by his parents. He then enlisted with the Wiltshires on 12 February 1913 and went with the 1st Battalion Wiltshire Regiment to France arriving on 14 August 1914. On about 17 August 1914 Joseph was attached to the Divisional Cyclist Corps. On 9 February 1915 Joseph was arrested for being a deserter and taken to General Headquarters at St. Omer France where he was questioned by the Intelligence Corps on 11 February 1915 and the following statement was taken:

Intelligence Corps
G.H.Q.
St.Omer
11.2.1915

Statement of Joseph Stanley Victor Fox.

I am a lance corporal of the 1st Wilts Regiment No. 8992. I enlisted on the 12th February 1913 at Devizes Barracks and remained with my regiment. On 13th August 1914 I left with my regiment for France, (from Gellalabad Barracks Tidworth), and arrived at Rouen on the 14th

On 16th went about 16 hours by train to a place of which I do not know the name, then marched about 7 miles rested for the night, then continued the march to a spot in Belgium (name of place not known) 3 days march from Mons, then was attached to the Divisional Cyclist Corps under Capt. Foster of the Northumberland Fusiliers. I finished with my regiment then. There were 98 Cyclists in the Corps. We all went to a village for the night of Mons and the following day the battle of Mons commenced. We retired from this village the same day as the battle started. We went on our cycles with the D.H.Q. (3rdDiv.) and kept with the H.Q. during the retirement. We were employed in reconnoitring during the day with the 15th Hussars. We went to Meaux and I kept with the divisional Cyclists till I got to Vieille Chappelle. When I there (about 15th). I was directed by Capt. Foster to take 3 men and go to a village La Fosse to ascertain whether the bridge there was guarded by the French or the Germans.

We went about 1 1/4 kilometres, and was then fired up by the Germans. We threw our bicycles on the bank of a canal and jumped into the canal, which had a high bank. We swam across and got away all four safely. We found the H.Q. of the Royal Scots in a field about 1 Kilometre from the canal. We saw a church burning and went to look at it. We had taken off our uniform and left it to dry in a brewery. We were supplied with civilian clothing to wear whilst our uniform was drying. When we came back three of us found our clothing had been burnt. My trousers were so much burnt that I could not wear them so I kept the civilian and I wore them till December when I exchanged them for the trousers I am now wearing.

Capt. Foster ordered us to go back and get our Bicycles. We went back I found my bicycle so damaged by rifle shot that I could not use it.

The other 3 men took their bicycles and I went with them to the 3rd Div. H.Q. 2 kilometres from Vieille Chapelle there I was directed to remain for the night. The next morning the lieutenant took the three men away and directed me to follow on foot to La Couture.

I ought to have told you that when I went (was going) from Meaux to a place called Vailly about September 15th I stayed with my Corps about 19 days, we went to Braisne and joined the 15th Hussars, rode about 40 Kilometres on cycle, took train to Conchil-le-Tempe. I was then handed over with 3 men to a R.E. (Royal Engineers) Captain. I don't know his name. I and the 3 men were placed on guard at Conchil-le-Tempe. I had to see the passes of civilians were in good order. I did this during the night. This was during the 1st week of October. In the morning I made enquires and found the Cyclists had gone, I asked where they had gone and was told they had gone in the direction of Montreuil. I went to Montreuil with the men 6 in number who had formed the guard. I there met Mr Stevenson of Montreuil. He took us to dinner at the Hotel de France. Afterwards we were informed that our Division was at Vailly and We went to Abbeville and there found the Divisional H.Q. I reported to a Captain of the Gordon Highlanders on the Staff. He sent me to a place about 8 Kilometres away and there we all 7 joined the Divisional Cyclists (I reported to Captain Foster) and went same day with them to Vailly Vieille Chapelle. It was there that I got the order to go to La Fosse and ascertain whether the French or Germans were holding the bridge as I have stated.

I now come back to where I was ordered to go on foot to La Couture, I got as far as Vaielle Chapelle and met about 30 of the Div. Cyclists. I spoke to the Sergt. Major. He told me that as I had no bicycle it would be better for me to find my regiment (the 1st Wilts) and join them. I made my my way to Richebourg Saint Vaast. I there saw Lieutenant Broome who was on the 7th Brigade Staff. He is a lieutenant of my regiment. He told me that the Wilts Regiment was further on the other side of the village. Half way through the village I met the Wilts transport.

They gave me food and I stayed the night at the house of a Mon Victor Chapnis. The Transport left during the night. The next day I followed in the direction they had gone. I came up with the Artillery and then the following day with the 5th Division R.A.M.C. and stated with them for 7 days at a place ten kilometres from Bethune. I tried to find the 3rd Division. This was about the later end of October. I made my way to a village I do not remember the name and reported myself to a Lieutenant of the Artillery (an intelligence Officer). I went then to Levantie and from there to La Gorgue. I did not report myself to any one there. I stayed there for about 6 or 7 weeks. I stayed part of the time with a bridging Company of the R.E. and part of the time in a café kept by a Madame Bondley. I after stopped with the 2nd Battalion of the Wilts Reg. Private Hatheral of C or D Company, Private Hunt of B Coy and Private Rolls of C or D Coy and the Captain of the Battalion spoke to me. I realised that I had stayed away too long from my Regiment and I was afraid to go back. I made up my mind to go to Montreuil and see Mr Stevenson. I had found a bicycle at Richebourg and I made my way to Montreuil on it. I arrived about the 4th of December. I stayed with Mr Stevenson I told him I was on my way to join my Battalion at Abbeville. I slept at Mr Stevenson's house for 4 or 5 days and then he told me he wanted the room for a Lady who was coming from England. He then paid for my bed at the Hotel de France. I had meals with Mr & Mrs Stevenson. After 6 days I told Mr Stevenson that I had permission from Capt. Foster to remain from Wednesday till Saturday. I said I had met Capt. Foster at Montreuil, this was untrue.

Whilst I was at Mr Stevenson's I met Miss E. Ridgeway , she is the lady who came to stay with Mr Stevenson I became very friendly with her. When I left the Stevenson's after 9 or 10 days stay. I went to Conchil le Temp and stayed there with a Madame Lebland who has a farm there. I stayed two nights in a café kept by a Madame Derrin, went back to Montreuil slept with French Guards stayed with them 20 days up to the 8th January.

In the mean time I was corresponding with Miss Ridgeway and she was visiting me at Montreuil. She is attached to the Red Cross (French) Hospital at Headin. I have been to the hospital and seen her there. She told me that she has a brother a priest at St Thomas's Vicarage Clapton Common, London. She went to London on the 25th January and wrote to me from that address.

After I left the French Guard on 8th January I went to Remortier a village 12 kilometres from Montreuil stayed 2 days then to a café kept by Mon Morenval at La Secheress near Fauguemberges there four days. I then went to Hesdin, put my bicycle up in a house near the French Guards, visited Miss Ridgeway. She paid for my food and lodgings at the Hotel de France, I day, and Hotel de Commerce I day, I then remained for 5 or 6 days at a café kept by a man named Fernand Richard. I was meeting Miss Ridgeway daily. Miss Ridgeway went to England on the 25th as I had said. I left my lodging and stayed 2 days with the French Gendarmes at the Railway station at Hesdin, then returned to the café at La Secheresse and was there until I was arrested 9th ins.

I have never known a Captain Ridgeway, neither have I known or seen a Captain of the A.S. Corps at Montreuil.

I do not know Colonel Barnfield, but I know his chauffeur I have met him at the Hotel De France.

The above statement is willingly made by me and is correct

Signed Victor Fox" (In Pencil)

On the 6 April 1915 Joseph was tried by a General Court Martial on the charge of :

"When on active service, deserting His Majesty's Service"

He was found guilty and on 8 April the following statement was made by the Captain in charge of the 3rd Division Mounted Troops:

1)   Lance Corporal Fox was considered to be reliable and liked both in the field and in billets. No question was ever raised as to his conduct in front of the enemy. At Vailly Bridge, where a post was established by me in September when the 3rd Division first arrived in that neighborhood, the corporal volunteered to remain on the post an extra 24 hours. At the time Vailly Bridge was under shrapnel fire continually. This man had been out here since the beginning of the war.
2)   The state of discipline in the Cyclist Company is good.
3)   In my opinion the crime was not deliberately committed, when the prisoner first went about, as the prisoner did volunteer for particular service at the time.

The Commander of the 3rd Division wrote the following on 8th April 1915:

I endorse the remark (2) of the Officer Commanding Divisional Mounted Troops. This information was not originally included with the proceedings because both the court and I myself considered that the extreme penalty should not be inflicted, and, therefore recommended the accused to mercy.

However, on 10 April 1915 Lieutenant General Fergusson wrote:

I cannot see the slightest reason for leniency in this case, which in my opinion is one for deliberate and prolonged desertion, without a shadow of excuse. From the man's own statement he is evidently perfectly capable of finding his way about, and had constant opportunities of reporting himself as an absentee of which he deliberately did not avail himself. It appears to me a particularly flagrant case and I recommend that the extreme penalty be inflicted."

His views were personally endorsed by General Smith-Dorian commander of the 2nd Army on 10 April 1915:

I agree with the Commander of the 2nd Corps and recommend that the extreme penalty be inflicted.

Twenty year old Joseph was executed by firing squad on Tuesday 20 April 1915 at Dickebusch, south of Ypres, Belgium and buried in Dickebushe Cemetery.

On 22 April Joseph's father Charles received unofficial information that his son had been killed at the front and to avenge his sons death he enlisted in the army. At this time Charles and Harriet had another son who was serving with the army who was a prisoner of war in Germany.

It is not known if or when Joseph's parents were informed on their son's true cause of death but on 16 July 1919 Charles Fox applied for his son's 1914 Star only to be told that his son

A British firing squad

was not eligible for service medals on account that he had been shot for desertion. For many years the details of Joseph's execution and for those of over 300 other men were kept secret and it is only in relatively recent times that this information has been in the public domain.

In 2006 Des Browne, Minister of Defence, announced that 306 men executed during the Great War were to be posthumously pardoned. Joseph was one of those pardoned and his pardon states

"The pardon stands as recognition that he was one of the many victims of the First World War and that execution was not the fate he deserved."

Joseph's statement is written in ink but he signed it in pencil. This would indicate that he was questioned and the answers written by the person or persons who questioned him. At the end of the statement he answers:

"I have never known a Captain Ridgeway"

Did Captain Ridgeway have any influence on the outcome of the court martial?

25 APRIL 1915 - GALLIPOLI LANDINGS, TURKEY

28 APRIL 1915 - FIRST BATTLE OF KRITHIA, GALLIPOLI, TURKEY

Rifleman Guy Clark

Service No.	2771
Place of Birth:	Badulla, Ceylon
Date of Death:	29/04/1915
Memorial:	Christian Malford
War cemetery:	Ypres Menin Gate
Theatre of war:	Belgium
Next of Kin:	Alfred & Jessie Clark
Address:	The Homestead, Christian Malford, Wiltshire

9th Bn London Regiment

Age:	20
Home Country:	England
Cause of death:	Killed in action

Guy was the son of Alfred and Jessie Clark, and Alfred was the church warden at Christian Malford. Guy volunteered for service with the London Regiment and after completing his training he arrived on the continent on 20 January 1915 being posted to the 9th London Regiment known as Queen Victoria's Rifles. He was one of five members of the 9th Londons to be killed in action on Thursday 29 April 1915 during the German attack on Ypres, Belgium, most likely from German shell fire. He is remembered on the Ypres Menin Gate and has no known. His cousin Christopher Dawson was killed in February 1915.

Above left: Hill 60 today, looking up from the inside of the crater to the lip of the crater.

Above right: The Memorial to the Queen Victoria's Rifles at Hill 60 east of Ypres, Belgium. It was the scene of desperate fighting during April 1915 when the QVR's suffered heavy casualties. The original memorial was destroyed by the Germans in 1940.

3
BELGIUM & FRANCE

6 MAY 1915 - SECOND BATTLE OF KRITHIA, GALLIPOLI, TURKEY

9 MAY 1915 - THE BATTLE OF AUBERS RIDGE, FRANCE

Gunner John Smith   *118th Bde Royal Field Artillery*

Service No.	86704	Age: 40
Place of Birth:	Stanton St Quintin	Home Country: England
Date of Death:	09/05/1915	Cause of death: Killed in action
Memorial:	Kington Langley	
War cemetery:	Le Touret Memorial	
Theatre of war:	France	
Next of Kin:	James & Fanny Smith	
Address:	Silver Street, Kington Langley, Wiltshire	

John was a masons labourer, his father had died when he was young and he lived with his step father and mother, Fanny Dowsell. He volunteered for service and arrived in France on 13 March 1915. He was killed in action during the British bombardment that accompanied the attack on Aubers Ridge, France. The attack was a failure mainly due to a shell shortage which had, prior to the attack, limited the 18 pounder ammunition to just two shells per gun per day and led to the resignation of Lord Kitchener as minister for munitions. John was most likely killed by German counter battery fire on his gun position. He is remembered on the Le Touret Memorial and has no known grave.

Private Frederick Pepler   *H.M.S. Goliath R.M.L.I.*

Service No.	PLY/12005	Age: 30
Place of Birth:	Bradford on Avon	Home Country: England
Date of Death:	13/05/1915	Cause of death: Died
Memorial:	Not known	
War cemetery:	Plymouth Naval Memorial	
Theatre of war:	At Sea	
Next of Kin:	Annie Pepler (wife) – Mary Hancock (mother)	
Address:	Chapel Hill, Gastard – 7 Factory Lane, Chippenham	

H.M.S. Goliath

Frederick a carter enlisted with the Royal Marine Light Infantry on 31 December 1901 and in 1909 he married Annie Townsend at Chippenham. In October 1910 he bought himself out of the marines and was placed on reserve, Frederick and his wife moved to South Wales where he was employed as a coal miner. Being part of the reserve each year Frederick had to attend annual training and in 1913 he was transferred to the immediate reserve. This meant that he served each year two weeks on board a ship which was engaged on war manoeuvres. On 29 July 1914 Frederick joined H.M.S. Goliath for his annual service and in the following week war was declared, Frederick did not return home but remained on active service with this ship. The Goliath was first used to cover the Royal Marine landings at Ostend in late August 1914 and was then sent to the East Indies in September 1914. In November 1914 the Goliath took part in the action against the German ship Konigsberg at the Rufiji River in East Africa. With the operations at the Dardanelles and the landing at Gallipoli the Goliath was used for fire support for the Landings at Cape Helles and she was damaged by Turkish Gun fire on 28th April and on 2nd May 1915 . During the night of 13 May 1915 the Goliath was torpedoed by the Turkish motor torpedo boat Muavenet and sank soon after with a loss of 570 men. Frederick was one of the men lost on the Goliath and is remembered on the Plymouth Naval Memorial.

15 MAY 1915 - THE BATTLE OF FESTUBERT, BELGIUM

Private Edward Scott
Service No.   10519
Place of Birth: Lea, Wiltshire
Date of Death: 16/05/1915
Memorial: Not Known
War cemetery: Loos Memorial
Theatre of war: France
Next of Kin: Charles & Harriet Scott
Address: Little Somerford, Wiltshire

1st Bn Royal Welsh Fusiliers
Age: 22
Home Country: England
Cause of death: Killed in action

Edward enlisted with the Royal Welsh Fusiliers on 25 November 1910 at the age of 18 years and five months. His father had died when he was young and his mother married Oliver Higgs, after his mothers death Edward went to live with his brother in South Wales. In 1912 Edward was posted to India and then in March 1914 he and the R.W.F. were sent to Malta where they were at the outbreak of the war. After returning to Britain the R.W.F. were sent to the continent where they arrived on 4 October 1914. At 3.15am on 16 May 1915 Edward and the R.W.F. were at Festubert, France and were in the first wave of the attack. As they advanced they were subjected to heavy machine gun fire causing a large number of casualties and the advance was halted for an extra 15 minutes shelling. By 6.00am they R.W.F. had advanced to the German position of the Orchard but by 7.30pm they were forced to withdraw to La Quinque Rue by lack of support and heavy German shelling. Edward was posted as missing in action and on 25 September 1915 it was assumed he had died on Sunday 16 May 1915. Nearly 200 members of the R.F.W. were killed; Edward is remembered on the Loos Memorial.

Private Isaac Charles Watts   *2nd Bn Wiltshire Regiment*

Service No.	7210	Age:	34
Place of Birth:	Kington St Michael	Home Country:	England
Date of Death:	17/05/1915	Cause of death:	Killed in action
Memorial:	St Augustines Swindon		
War cemetery:	Le Touret Memorial		
Theatre of war:	France		
Next of Kin:	Charles & Elizabeth Watts		
Address:	Haydon Wick, Swindon		

Regular soldier Isaac known as Charles, initially arrived in France with the 1st Battalion Wiltshire Regiment on 28 August 1914 and it is likely he was wounded during fighting in the early part of the war and then transferred to the 2nd Battalion Wiltshire Regiment. He was killed on Monday 17 May near Festubert, France when the Wiltshires were ordered forward to occupy trenches. As they went forward they faced a barrage of German shells and machine gun fire and were eventually forced to retire. Charles is remembered on the Le Touret Memorial and has no known grave.

Private Herbert Knighton   *2nd Wiltshire Regiment*

Service No.	8253	Age:	21
Place of Birth:	Langley Burrell, Wiltshire	Home Country:	England
Date of Death:	17/05/1915	Cause of death:	Died of wounds
Memorial:	Christian Malford		
War cemetery:	Bethune Town Cemetery		
Theatre of war:	France		
Next of Kin:	Sam Dudley & Emily E. Knighton (parents) – George Knighton (brother)		
Address:	Not known		

Herbert had lived in Christian Malford when he was a boy with his three brothers. It is likely Herbert was under age when he joined the army and had served with the 1st Battalion Wiltshire Regiment in Natal, South Africa. At some stage prior to the Great War he was transferred to the 2nd Battalion Wiltshire Regiment and arrived with them in France on 7 October 1914. He was wounded in fighting in early May 1915 and evacuated to 33rd Casualty Clearing Station at Bethune, France, where he succumbed to his wounds on Monday 17 May 1915. His Brother Percy was to die while serving with the 5th Wiltshires in August 1915.

Private William James Taylor *2nd Bn Wiltshire Regiment*

Service No.	3/376	Age:	36
Place of Birth:	Tower Hill, London	Home Country:	England
Date of Death:	18/05/1915	Cause of death:	Died of wounds
Memorial:	Chippenham & St. Andrew's Church Chippenham		
War cemetery:	Merville Communal Cemetery		
Theatre of war:	France		
Next of Kin:	Harriet Taylor (mother)		
Address:	Union Court, Chippenham, Wiltshire		

William, a painter, was also a member of the 2nd Wiltshire Volunteers prior to the Great War. He volunteered for service with the regular army joining the 2nd Battalion Wiltshire Regiment arriving in France on 3 November 1914. On Tuesday 18 May the Wiltshires were in trenches at Rue De L'Epinette near Festubert, France and were subjected to heavy German shelling which was composed of high explosive and shrapnel shells which fell every eight or nine seconds. William was wounded in the face and was then evacuated to a casualty clearing station where he died of his wounds shortly afterwards.

Private James Richard Few *14th Bn Quebec Regiment*

Service No.	25581	Age:	32
Place of Birth:	Great Cheverell, Wiltshire	Home Country:	Canada
Date of Death:	24/05/1915	Cause of death:	Died of wounds
Memorial:	Not Known		
War cemetery:	Longuenesse St.Omer Souvenir Cemetery		
Theatre of war:	France		
Next of Kin:	Jesse & Mary Few		
Address:	Royal Hythe Farm, Staines, Middlesex		

James was well known in Great Somerford where his parents had farmed. In 1911 he emigrated to Canada and married but his wife died two years later. On 21 September 1914 James volunteered for service with the Canadian Army. The 14th Battalion went into action between 18 and 20 May and the Canadians captured German trenches at Festubert, France. It was at this time that James was wounded and evacuated to one of the military hospitals near St. Omer. He succumbed to his wounds on Monday 24 May 1915.

Captain Arthur Noel Edwards *9th Lancers*

Service No.	N/A	Age:	31
Place of Birth:	Kensington, London	Home Country:	England
Date of Death:	25/05/1915	Cause of death:	Died of wounds
Memorial:	Chippenham & St. Andrew's Church Chippenham		
War cemetery:	Bailleul Communal Cemetery Extension Nord		
Theatre of war:	France		
Next of Kin:	Evelyn M Edwards (wife) - Arthur J & Hilda M. Edwards (parents)		
Address:	Hawking Down, Hindon, Wiltshire - Beech Hill Park, Waltham Abbey		

Arthur, known as Noel, received a commission with the 9th Lancers in 1903 and was promoted to Lieutenant in 1905. He was a keen polo player and had been a member of two English teams that had visited America. Late in 1911 he married Evelyn M. Hargreaves at London and was made Adjutant of the Wiltshire Yeomanry, a post which he held for three years, being promoted to Captain in 1912. While in the post of Adjutant he lived at Rowden Hill Chippenham in a house that had been occupied by the late Delme Awdry. He was also vice president of the Chippenham sports club. At the outbreak of the Great War he rejoined the 9th Lancers arriving in France on 28 March 1915. He was gassed on 24 May 1915 and evacuated to hospital where he died from the effects of gas poisoning the following day.

4 JUNE 1915 - THIRD BATTLE OF KRITHIA, GALLIPOLI, TURKEY

Private Archibald Herbert Wheeler   *1st Bn Wiltshire Regiment*

Service No.	18230	Age:	28
Place of Birth:	Christian Malford, Wiltshire	Home Country:	England
Date of Death:	12/06/1915	Cause of death:	Died of wounds
Memorial:	Christian Malford		
War cemetery:	Bedford House Cemetery		
Theatre of war:	Belgium		
Next of Kin:	Jacob & Eliza Wheeler		
Address:	59 The Green, Christian Malford		

Farm labourer Archibald volunteered for service with the Wiltshire Regiment and arrived on the Continent on 4 May 1915. He was wounded little over a month later during the afternoon of Saturday 12 June near Zilebeke Village, east of Ypres, Belgium. An accident occurred with a lyddite grenade and Archibald succumbed to his wounds soon after. The accident also claimed the life of 2nd Lieutenant Stansfield-Smith and wounded 23 other men.

Private Albert John Payne   *14th Reserve Cavalry Regiment*

Service No.	29352	Age:	20
Place of Birth:	Hullavington, Wiltshire	Home Country:	England
Date of Death:	14/06/1915	Cause of death:	Died
Memorial:	Not known		
War cemetery:	Bordon Military Cemetery		
Theatre of war:	Home		
Next of Kin:	John & Elizabeth Payne		
Address:	Cranmore Cottages, Shipton Moyne, Tetbury, Gloucestershire		

Albert, a shepherd, was the eldest son of John and Elizabeth Payne and volunteered for service with the cavalry. He died while in training at Longmoor near Liss, Hampshire on Monday 14 June 1915 most likely from illness or disease.

Private Albert Fry   *2nd Bn Wiltshire Regiment*

Service No.	5524	Age:	31
Place of Birth:	Castle Combe, Wiltshire	Home Country:	England
Date of Death:	15/06/1915	Cause of death:	Killed in action
Memorial:	Calne & Leigh Delamere		
War cemetery:	Le Touret Memorial		
Theatre of war:	France		
Next of Kin:	Sarah Fry (wife) - Isaac & Rhoda Fry (Parents)		

Address: Sevington, Wiltshire - Yatton Keynell, Wiltshire

Albert a farm labourer, married Sarah Bird in 1905 and at the outbreak of war they had three children. He had arrived in France on Monday 21 September 1914 and was wounded twice. On Tuesday 15 June he was in the trenches at Givenchy, France, with the 2nd Battalion Wiltshire Regiment. As they left the trenches they were subjected to heavy machine gun fire from the front and the sides. The British reached a point 50 yards from the German trenches and in the leading Companies all but 1 officer were hit. At 9pm the Wiltshires were occupying an old German trench and orders were received to make a further assault on the German lines at 9.15pm. The old German trench was not safe and was being fired upon by German machine guns from the side and because of this situation the attack was cancelled. The war diary states;

"During the action of 15th and 16th, the Germans used incendiary bullets, and also sniped the wounded in front of their trenches."

In July Sarah received the news that Albert was missing and later it became known he had been killed along with 70 men of the 2nd Battalion Wiltshire Regiment. He has no known grave.

Private Frank Stapleford   *2nd Bn Wiltshire Regiment*
Service No.   13757   Age: 26
Place of Birth: Calne, Wiltshire   Home Country: England
Date of Death: 15/06/1915   Cause of death: Killed in action
Memorial: Calne & Derry Hill & Chippenham
War cemetery: Le Touret Memorial
Theatre of war: France
Next of Kin: George & Elizabeth Stapleford
Address: Studley, Wiltshire

Frank was a brick layers labourer who lodged at Lowden Chippenham. He volunteered for service and arrived in France on Wednesday 24 March 1915. He fell in the same action as Albert Fry at Givenchy, France. News of his death reached home in early July 1915. Frank is remembered on the Le Touret Memorial, France, with over 13,000 men who fell in the area before 25 September 1915 and who have no known grave.

Private Harvey William Cole   *2nd Bn Wiltshire Regiment*
Service No.   13609   Age: 18
Place of Birth: Biddestone, Wiltshire   Home Country: England
Date of Death: 15/06/1915   Cause of death: Killed in action
Memorial: Biddestone
War cemetery: Le Touret Memorial
Theatre of war: France
Next of Kin: William & Sarah Anne Cole
Address: Giddea Hall, Biddestone, Wiltshire

Harvey, known as William, was a paper mill labourer. He was an under age soldier because at this stage in the war a soldier was supposed to be nineteen and a half years of age to serve abroad. He was the third son of William & Sarah Annie Cole and volunteered for service arriving in France on 6 March 1915. He was initially posted as wounded on Tuesday 15 June 1915 in the same action as Albert Fry at Givenchy, France. On 21 July 1915 new information was received that William was wounded and missing. Later it was assumed that William had died on the day he had first become wounded. He is remembered on the Le Touret Memorial, France, he has no known grave. At the time of William's death his father and two of his brothers were also serving their country.

Private William Herbert Spencer		*2nd Bn Wiltshire Regiment*	
Service No.	18443	Age:	19
Place of Birth:	Pewsham, Wiltshire	Home Country:	England
Date of Death:	15/06/1915	Cause of death:	Killed in action
Memorial:	Not known		
War cemetery:	Le Touret Memorial		
Theatre of war:	France		
Next of Kin:	Herbert and Edith Spencer		
Address:	Church Brook Cottage, Broughton Gifford, Wiltshire		

Nineteen year old William, a carter, was the eldest son of Herbert & Edith Spencer and volunteered for service joining the Wiltshire Regiment. He arrived in France on 1 June 1915 and just two weeks later on Tuesday 15 June he was posted as missing in the same action as Albert Fry at Givenchy, France. Later it was assumed he had died on the day he was posted as missing. He is remembered on the Le Touret Memorial, France and has no known grave.

Private William Pearce		*2nd Bn Wiltshire Regiment*	
Service No.	3/630	Age:	37
Place of Birth:	Whitley, Wiltshire	Home Country:	England
Date of Death:	15/06/1915	Cause of death:	Killed in action
Memorial:	Not known		
War cemetery:	Le Touret Memorial		
Theatre of war:	France		
Next of Kin:	Elizabeth Pearce (wife) - Robert & Sarah Pearce (parents)		
Address:	13 Victoria Road Warminster - Thingley, Corsham		

William married Elizabeth Ruddle in 1904 at Chippenham and they moved to Warminster where he was employed as a farm labourer. William volunteered for service and arrived in France on 25 May 1915. He was killed in action on Tuesday 15 June 1915 in the same action as Albert Fry at Givenchy, France. He is remembered on the Le Touret Memorial, France and has no known grave. He left a widow and a young son.

Private Herbert Ernest Crew		*1st Bn Wiltshire Regiment*	
Service No.	10628	Age:	19
Place of Birth:	Chippenham, Wiltshire	Home Country:	England
Date of Death:	16/06/1915	Cause of death:	Killed in action
Memorial:	Lacock Church & Lacock Village		
War cemetery:	Ypres Menin Gate		
Theatre of war:	Belgium		
Next of Kin:	Mrs Vines (mother) – Samuel & Sarah Crew (grandparents)		
Address:	Showell Cottage, Lacock – Wick Lane, Lacock		

Nineteen year old Herbert was employed in a bake house and had been brought up by his grandparents. He volunteered for service with the 2nd Battalion Wiltshire Regiment and when he arrived on the continent on 12 May 1915 he was attached to the 1st Battalion Wiltshire Regiment. At 4.20 am on Wednesday 16 June 1915 the 1st Wiltshires were in Belgium on the Menin road near Hooge East of Ypres. The Wiltshires were assaulting German trenches at Hooge Village. Initially the Wiltshires were successful and had got within 50 yards of Hooge but by 9am the Germans started advancing down a communication trench under cover of a heavy barrage. During the next hour and a half a bombing (hand grenade) action took place between the Germans and the Wiltshires but by 10.30am the Wiltshires began to run out of grenades and the Germans began to regain their lost ground. During this time the Wiltshires suffered heavy casualties. By 11 am the Wiltshires were forced to retire over open ground and again lost a considerable amount of men. The Wiltshires were then subject to a German bombardment for the remainder of the day. Toward the end of June 1915 Herbert's Family were informed that he was missing and late in July 1915 he was reported to have been killed in action. He is remembered on the Ypres Menin Gate and has no known grave.

30 JUNE 1915 - ALLIED CASUALTIES AT GALLIPOLI REACH 42,434

Captain Philip Simons Picot   *14th Bn Sherwood Foresters*

Service No.	N/A	Age:	26
Place of Birth:	Kensington, London	Home Country:	England
Date of Death:	11/07/1915	Cause of death:	Killed in action
Memorial:	Singapore Cenotaph		
War cemetery:	Twelve Tree Copse Cemetery		
Theatre of war:	Gallipoli		
Next of Kin:	Lt. Col Francis Slater & Ada Melville Picot		
Address:	The Hawthorns, Langley Road, Langley Burrell		

Philip was the only son of Francis Slater and Ada Melville Picot and was educated at Malvern College then on to Sandhurst and on completion served three years with the West Yorkshire Regiment. He then spent the next three years at Camborne School of Mines and on 20 December 1912 he married Marjorie Putnam the daughter of Thomas Putman, chairman of the Darlington Forge Company. Philip was well known in Wiltshire and was a fine athlete and a winner of many skiing trophies in Switzerland. He was also an examiner with the British Ski Association. After finishing his studies he went to Penang in the Far East where he was on active service at the outbreak of the Great War. He then returned to England and joined the 14th Battalion Sherwood Foresters as a lieutenant and was then promoted to the rank of captain. He volunteered for active service and was attached to the 4th Battalion Royal Scots and was sent to the Dardenelles arriving on the Gallipoli peninsular in June 1915. He was killed in action on Sunday 11 July 1915 most likely by Turkish shell fire as the Royal Scots prepared to assault the Turkish position near Krithia, Gallipoli. Philip left nearly £6,000 in his will and is remembered on a special memorial in Twelve Tree Copse Cemetery, Gallipoli.

Private William Isaac Henry Thomas Hobbs   *F coy. 3rd Bn Wiltshire Regiment*

Service No.	19144	Age:	36
Place of Birth:	Kington St Michael	Home Country:	England
Date of Death:	12/07/1915	Cause of death:	Died
Memorial:	Not Known		
War cemetery:	Weymouth Cemetery		
Theatre of war:	Home		

Next of Kin: Violet May Hobbs (wife) - George & Annie Hobbs (parents)
Address: Church Street, Beaminster, Dorset - Nether Street, Bromham

William, a Prudential Insurance Agent, was the eldest son of George and Annie Hobbs and married Violet May Kemp in the spring of 1907 at Great Yarmouth. He volunteered for service with the Wiltshire regiment and while in training he developed an illness or disease and was admitted to Weymouth Isolation Hospital where he died on Monday 12 July 1915. He left a widow and young son.

Private Edmund John Clark   *1/5th Bn Lincolnshire Regiment*
Service No.   2743   Age: 18
Place of Birth: Chippenham, Wiltshire   Home Country: England
Date of Death: 19/07/1915   Cause of death: Killed in action
Memorial: Not known
War cemetery: Railway Dugouts Burial Ground
Theatre of war: Belgium
Next of Kin: Edwin & Rosa Frances Clark
Address: Bradford on Avon

Under age soldier Edmund was born in Chippenham Union Workhouse at the beginning of 1897. It is likely his father had died and his mother returned from London to her home town. His mother remarried in 1900 probably to escape the work house. Edmund, a farm labourer, volunteered for service joining the Lincolnshire Regiment and arrived on the continent on 25 June 1915. Less than one month later Edmund was killed near Zillebeke, Belgium, on Monday 19 July 1915. He was the only soldier of the 1/5th battalion to be killed on that day.

Pioneer Albert George Bishop   *87th Field Coy Royal Engineers*
Service No.   48470   Age: 21
Place of Birth: North Wraxall, Wiltshire   Home Country: England
Date of Death: 20/07/1915   Cause of death: Died of wounds
Memorial: Chippenham - St. Andrews Church Chippenham & North Wraxall
War cemetery: Bailleul Communal Cemetery Extension Nord
Theatre of war: France
Next of Kin: George & Jane Bishop
Address: North Wraxall, Wiltshire

Twenty one year old Albert, a farm labour, volunteered for service with the Royal Engineers and arrived in France on 2 June 1915. The division he was attached were sent to an area of the line between Armentieres, France and Ploegstreet Wood, Belgium, for further training. This area was considered a quiet part of the front line. Albert was wounded while on duty in this area and evacuated to one of the casualty clearing stations based at Bailleul, France where he succumbed to his wounds on Tuesday 20 July 1915.

4
GALLIPOLI

Private Frederick Gideon Beasley   *5th Bn Wiltshire Regiment*

Service No.   9866   Age: 26
Place of Birth: Chippenham   Home Country: England
Date of Death: 23/07/1915   Cause of death: Died of wounds
Memorial: Chippenham & St. Andrews Church
War cemetery: Helles Memorial
Theatre of war: Gallipoli
Next of Kin: Gideon & Elizabeth Beasley
Address: 56 Wood Lane, Chippenham

Frederick, a moulder, volunteered to serve and was sent to the 5th Service Battalion Wiltshire Regiment, a regiment that was formed for the duration of the war. He arrived on the Gallipoli peninsular in Mid July 1915 and was wounded most likely by Turkish shell fire while the Wiltshires were serving in trenches around Cape Helles. He succumbed to his wounds and was either buried at sea or on the peninsular and his grave was later lost. He is remembered on the Helles Memorial with 21,000 men who lost their lives during the Gallipoli campaign and have no known grave.

25 JULY 1915 - NASRIYA IN MESOPOTAMIA IS CAPTURED BY BRITISH FORCES

Private Clement Harold Taylor   *15th Bn Civil Service Rifles London Reg.*

Service No.   1785   Age: 22
Place of Birth: Chippenham   Home Country: England
Date of Death: 25/07/1915   Cause of death: Died of wounds
Memorial: St. Pauls Church & Chippenham Secondary School
War cemetery: Nouex Les Mines Communal Cemetery
Theatre of war: France
Next of Kin: Francis & Florence Annie Taylor
Address: 18 St. Paul's Street, Chippenham

Clement, a student teacher, volunteered for service joining the Civil Service Rifles, part of the

London Regiment, and arrived in France on 17 March 1915. He died of wounds on Sunday 25 July 1915, his elder brother Bernard, inserted the following memorial in a local paper:

In loving memory of my dear brother
Who gave his life for King and Empire
Greater love hath no man than that he lay down his life for his friends
He died for you and me

30 JULY 1915 - GERMANS ATTACK WITH FLAME THROWERS AT HOOGE, BELGIUM

Private Frederick Eli George Ashe   *2nd Bn Wiltshire Regiment*

Service No.	10976	Age:	21
Place of Birth:	Chippenham	Home Country:	England
Date of Death	01/08/1915	Cause of death:	Killed in action
Memorial:	Chippenham & St Andrew's Church Memorial		
War cemetery:	Le Touret Memorial		
Theatre of war:	France		
Next of Kin:	Eli & Elizabeth Ashe		
Address:	6 Bailey Close, Chippenham		

Twenty one year old Frederick, a stoker, volunteered for service with the Wiltshire Regiment arriving in France on 11 December 1914. He was killed in action on Sunday 1 August 1915 when the Wiltshire were in trenches at Richebourg St Vaast, France. The battalion war diary for the day states, *"position quiet"*. Frederick is remembered on the Le Touret Memorial and has no known grave.

Two views of trench life at the Gallipoli Peninsular, Turkey.

Sapper Stephen Bull   *GHQ Signal Coy Royal Engineers*
Service No.   72405   Age: 24
Place of Birth: Chippenham, Wiltshire   Home Country: England
Date of Death: 02/08/1915   Cause of death: Killed in action
Memorial: Chippenham & St Andrew's Church Memorial
War cemetery: Lancashire Landing Cemetery
Theatre of war: Gallipoli
Next of Kin: George & Eliza Bull
Address: 26 Causeway, Chippenham

Stephen, a butcher's assistant, was originally a member of the Royal Wiltshire Yeomanry but was transferred to the Royal Engineers. He arrived on the Gallipoli peninsular in May 1915 and was a member of the Signal Company for the General headquarters at Helles, Gallipoli. It would have been a very dangerous job because the small area the British occupied was subjected to heavy Turkish shell fire and sniper fire. Stephen was killed on Monday 2 August 1915 and was buried in Lancashire Landing Cemetery, named after the men of the 1st Battalion Lancashire Fusiliers who landed near by and died in the first two days of the Gallipoli campaign.

6 AUGUST - BATTLE OF SARI BAIR AND LANDINGS AT SUVLA BAY AND ACHI BABA, GALLIPOLI, TURKEY

Corporal Charlie Clifford   *4th Bn Worcestershire Regiment*
Service No.   9036   Age: 42
Place of Birth: Chippenham, Wiltshire   Home Country: England
Date of Death: 06/08/1915   Cause of death: Killed in action
Memorial: Not known
War cemetery: Helles Memorial
Theatre of war: Gallipoli
Next of Kin: Philip & Sophia Clifford (parents) - Julia Elizabeth Jackson (niece)
Address: Chippenham, Wiltshire – Sheffield

Charlie, a labourer, had served in the Wiltshire Regiment prior to the war and at the outbreak of hostilities at the age of nearly 42 he enlisted with the Worcestershire Regiment on 22 August 1914. He was promoted to corporal on 1 May 1915 before arriving on the Gallipoli peninsular on 21 May. He was shot in the left arm on 4 June 1915 during the Third Battle of Krithia and after his recovery he was returned to the trenches on 7 July. On 6 August a plan was made to attack Turkish positions at Krithia Orchard in support of the landings at Suvla Bay. The 4th Battalion Worcestors had been reinforced and numbered over 800 men and were sent to the front line trenches on the morning of 6 August, attack was to take place during the cool of the evening. The Worcesters spent the day in the trenches under the mid day sun and were plagued by flies and had little water. At 2.20 the British heavy artillery began to shell Turkish positions and the Turkish replied by shelling the British trenches with high explosive and shrapnel shells. At 3.15 pm the British machine guns opened fire followed by British field guns which continued for half an hour. At 3.50pm the Worcesters advanced in four waves towards a rise in no man's land and as they reached the rise they were in full view of the Turkish trenches. Each wave was met by withering machine gun fire from both sides, the Worcestors quickened their pace but as they got nearer the Turkish trenches the fire became more intense. Small groups of the

Worcesters entered the Turkish trenches and those who were left in no mans land were raked by Turkish machine gun fire. All those who entered the Turkish trenches (apart from a group of about twelve men who made their way back to British lines under the cover of darkness), were overwhelmed by the Turkish defenders. About sixty Worcestors were taken prisoner and casualties for the day were 16 Officers and 752 men. Charlie was posted as missing and following a board of enquiry in February 1916 concluded he had been killed in action on Friday 6 August 1915. He is remembered on the Helles Memorial and has no known grave.

Private Ernest Walter Scott   *4th Bn Worcestorshire Regiment*
Service No.   21945   Age: 24
Place of Birth: Lea, Wiltshire   Home Country: England
Date of Death: 06/08/1915   Cause of death: Killed in action
Memorial: Not known
War cemetery: Helles Memorial
Theatre of war: Gallipoli
Next of Kin: Charles & Harriet Scott
Address: Little Somerford, Wiltshire

Ernest, a coal miner hewer, had moved to Pontypridd South Wales, where he lived with his brother. He volunteered for service with the Worcestershire Regiment and was sent to Gallipoli where he arrived on 15 July 1915 as part of a reinforcement draft. It is likely he was posted as missing on Friday 6 August 1915 in the same action as Charlie Clifford. He was later assumed to have died on the same day, he is remembered on the Helles Memorial and has no known grave.

Private Frank Goulding   *7th Bn Gloucestershire Regiment*
Service No.   2549   Age: 26
Place of Birth: Pinkney, Wiltshire   Home Country: England
Date of Death: 08/08/1915   Cause of death: Killed in action
Memorial: St. Andrew's Church Memorial
War cemetery: Helles Memorial
Theatre of war: Gallipoli
Next of Kin: William & Dorothy Goulding
Address: Pipsmore Cottage, Chippenham

Farm labourer Frank was the third son of William and Dorothy Goulding and volunteered for service with the 7th Service Battalion Gloucester Regiment and arrived at Cape Helles on the Gallipoli Peninsular in July 1915 and the Gloucesters were transferred to Anzac Cove on the 3 August1915. He was killed during fighting at Russell's Top and Sari Bair on Sunday 8 August 1915. He is remembered on the Helles Memorial and has no known grave. His brother Frederick Orlando Goulding was to be killed in Mesopotamia in April 1916.

Private Albert George Newman   *7th Bn Gloucestershire Regiment*
Service No.   2474   Age: 42
Place of Birth: Chippenham   Home Country: England
Date of Death: 08/08/1915   Cause of death: Killed in action
Memorial: Chippenham & St Andrews Church Memorial
War cemetery: Helles Memorial
Theatre of war: Gallipoli

Russell's Top Gallipoli.

Next of Kin: Ann Newton Newman (wife) - Thomas & Elizabeth Newman (parents)
Address: 9 St. Mary Street, Chippenham

Albert, known as George, was a masons labouer. He originally enlisted with the Wiltshires on 7 September 1893 and married Ann Newton Bowen in the summer of 1908 in Chippenham. He volunteered for service joining the 7th Service Battalion, Gloucestershire Regiment and arrived at Helles on the Gallipoli Peninsular at the start of July 1915, George and the 7th Gloucesters were then sent to the island of Murdos, Greece at the end of July. On 3 August the 13th Western Division , of which the 7th Gloucesters were a part, landed at Anzac to support attacks during the landings at Suvla Bay on Sari Bair and Russell's Top. George was one of 186 men to either die from wounds or be killed in action on Sunday 8 August 1915 he is remembered on the Helles Memorial and has no known grave.

In January 1916 a report in the local paper lead with the headline *"5th Wilts Almost Annihilated"*.

It referred to Sir Ian Hamiltons' (who had been the commander of the Gallipoli Peninsula Operations), dispatches describing the events of 6 to 10 August 1915 when a great attack had taken place from the ANZAC area. The aims were to break out of ANZAC and cut off the bulk of the Turkish forces on the peninsula from Constantinople and to gain a commanding position for the artillery to cut off the Turkish army with sea traffic. The 5th Wiltshire Regiment were part of the left covering column and were to march northwards along the beach and seize a hill called Damakjelik Bair some 1400 yards north of Table Top. This would enable 9th corps to be aided as it landed south of Nibrunei Point, while protecting the flank of the other assaulting columns.During the main attack hill Chunuk Bair had been taken and on the night of Monday 9th and Tuesday 10th August 1915 the 5th Battalion Wiltshire Regiment and the 6th Loyal North Lancashire Regiment were chosen to hold this position. The Loyal North Lancashire's arrived first and their commanding officer, even though it was dark, recognised how dangerously the trenches were sited. He at once ordered that observation posts were dug on the actual crest of the hill. The Wiltshire's were delayed by the rough terrain of the intricate country and did not reach the position until 4am The war diary disagrees with this time stating that the Wiltshire's arrived at 3am and lays the blame on a New Zealand officer who was their guide. When the Wiltshire's did arrive they were told to lie down in what was believed, erroneously, to be a covered and safe position.

At daybreak on Tuesday 10 August the Turks delivered a grand attack from the line at Chunuk Bair Hill against the Wiltshires and the Loyal North Lancashires, which were already weakened in numbers by previous fighting. First the British were shelled and then at 5.30am they were assaulted by a huge column, consisting of a division plus a regiment and three battalions. The Loyal North Lancashire Regiment were overwhelmed in their shallow trenches by the sheer weight of the Turkish attack while the Wilts Regiment were caught out in the open and were almost annihilated. The War diary for the Wiltshire states the Turks attacked 15 minutes after machine guns opened fire at 4.30am It also gives an indication of how desperate the British were to escape from the fighting and during the desperate fighting Lieutenant Colonel J. Carden commanding the 5th Wiltshire's was killed.

Another account is given from Captain (then Lieutenant) Bush who was honoured for his conspicuous service during the Gallipoli campaign. According to the dispatches, the Wiltshire's and another regiment had a whole division of Turks and two other Battalions against them on 10 August 1915. Fire was opened on them at dawn with terrible results. Those who could, retired down a narrow gully, only to come under fire from more machine guns, and here, the two remaining senior officers being killed, Lieutenant Bush found himself left in command. He immediately, with the help of two sergeants, rallied the men and lined them against the side of the gully just out of reach of the machine guns. He, himself, went up and across the gully, finding a fairly practicable though terribly steep way up, got the men across by twos and threes, and led them to a place of safety under the top of the cliffs. Leaving them with the two remaining subalterns with orders not to move till after dark if he did not return, and then to make their way to the beach, he went across the open, under machine gun and rifle fire about 300 yards, finally reaching a New Zealand trench. From there he was passed down to Headquarters, and was able to pass word along the line to look out for the men as they came in after dark. A party was sent out to clear the bottom of the gully - about 150 to 200 men came in that night. Lieutenant Bush was invalided home about 10 days afterwards, with dysentery.

Some of the men of the 5th Wiltshire's lay hidden and survived the attack returning to their unit as late as 26 August 1914. However, almost 150 members of the 5th Wiltshire's were killed on Tuesday 10 August 1915 the majority have no known grave and are remembered on Helles Memorial.

Lance Coporal Oscar James Kidd		*5th Bn Wiltshire Regiment*	
Service No.	11604	Age:	29
Place of Birth:	Chippenham, Wiltshire	Home Country:	England
Date of Death:	10/08/1915	Cause of death:	Killed in action
Memorial:	Chippenham - St Andrews Church Memorial & Liberal Club Memorial		
War cemetery:	Helles Memorial		
Theatre of war:	Gallipoli		
Next of Kin:	Eli & Charlotte Kidd		
Address:	21 Blind Lane, Chippenham, Wiltshire		

Oscar, a labourer, volunteered with the 5th Service Battalion Wiltshire Regiment and arrived at Helles on the Gallipoli peninsular at the start of July 1915. Oscar and the 5th Wiltshires were then sent to the island of Murdos, Greece at the end of July. On 3 August the 13th Western Division, of which the 5th Wiltshires were a part, were landed at Anzac Cove to give support

*The medals and memorial scroll of Oscar Kidd killed at Chunuk Bair,
Gallipoli on 10 August 1915.*

to the landings at Suvla Bay. Oscar was killed in action on 10 August when the Wiltshires were
nearly annihilated at Chunuk Bair. He is remembered on the Helles Memorial and has no known
grave.

Private Albert Russ		*5th Bn Wiltshire Regiment*	
Service No.	9700	Age:	22
Place of Birth:	Sutton Benger	Home Country:	England
Date of Death:	10/08/1915	Cause of death:	Killed in action
Memorial:	Sutton Benger		
War cemetery:	Helles Memorial		
Theatre of war:	Gallipoli		
Next of Kin:	Henry W & Annie Mary Russ		
Address:	High Street, Sutton Benger, Wiltshire		

Albert, a mason's labourer, volunteered for service with the 5th Service Battalion Wiltshire
Regiment. He was posted as wounded and missing in the same action at Chunuk Bair, Gallipoli
as Oscar Kidd. He is remembered on the Helles Memorial and has no known grave.

Private Frederick John Walker		*5th Bn Wiltshire Regiment*	
Service No.	18363	Age:	20
Place of Birth:	Chippenham	Home Country:	England
Date of Death:	10/08/1915	Cause of death:	Killed in action
Memorial:	Chippenham & St Andrews Church Memorial		
War cemetery:	Helles Memorial		
Theatre of war:	Gallipoli		
Next of Kin:	Thomas & Mary Jane Walker		
Address:	51 Parliment Street, Chippenham, Wiltshire		

Twenty year old Frederick, known as Fred and a grocer's porter, volunteered for service with the 5th Service Battalion Wiltshire Regiment. He was posted as wounded and missing in the same action at Chunuk Bair, Gallipoli as Oscar Kidd. He is remembered on the Helles Memorial and has no known grave.

Private Montague Douglas Snell		*5th Bn Wiltshire Regiment*	
Service No.	10800	Age:	19
Place of Birth:	Yatton Keynell	Home Country:	England
Date of Death:	10/08/1915	Cause of death:	Killed in action
Memorial:	Yatton Keynell		
War cemetery:	No 2 Outpost Cemetery		
Theatre of war:	Gallipoli		
Next of Kin:	Emanuel & Georgina Snell		
Address:	Tidley Winks, Yatton Keynell, Wiltshire		

Nineteen year old Monatgue, a farm labourer, was the eldest son of Emanuel & Georgina Snell. He volunteered for service with the 5th Service Battalion Wiltshire Regiment. He was killed in the same action at Chunuk Bair, Gallipoli as Oscar Kidd. He is remembered on the Helles Memorial and has no known grave. Montague's mother died and his father married Mary Greenman and her son, Edward James Greenman, died of wounds at Gallipoi on 16 September 1915.

Private Joseph Harry Dew		*5th Bn Wiltshire Regiment*	
Service No.	9300	Age:	21
Place of Birth:	Surbiton, Surrey	Home Country:	England
Date of Death:	10/08/1915	Cause of death:	Killed in action
Memorial:	Kington St Michael		
War cemetery:	Helles Memorial		
Theatre of war:	Gallipoli		
Next of Kin:	Henry Duncan & Ellen Dew		
Address:	Laburnum Cottage, Giddea Hall, Wiltshire		

Twenty one year old Joseph, a fish seller, was the eldest son of Henry Duncan and Ellen Dew and volunteered for service with the 5th Service Battalion Wiltshire Regiment He was posted as missing in the same action at Chunuk Bair, Gallipoli as Oscar Kidd and it was later assumed he had died on that date. He is remembered on the Helles Memorial and has no known grave.

Private Percy Harold Augustus Knighton		*5th Bn Wiltshire Regiment*	
Service No.	18025	Age:	17
Place of Birth:	Chippenham	Home Country:	England
Date of Death:	10/08/1915	Cause of death:	Killed in action
Memorial:	Not known		
War cemetery:	Helles Memorial		
Theatre of war:	Gallipoli		
Next of Kin:	Sam Dudley & Emily Elizabeth Knighton		
Address:	Not known		

Under age soldier Percy volunteered for service with the 5th Service Battalion Wiltshire

Regiment. He was killed in the same action at Chunuk Bair, Gallipoli as Oscar Kidd. He is remembered on the Helles Memorial and has no known grave. His brother Herbert died of wounds in France in May 1915.

Private James Sly		*6th Bn Leinster Regiment*	
Service No.	1305	Age:	22
Place of Birth:	Brinkworth	Home Country:	England
Date of Death:	10/08/1915	Cause of death:	Killed in action
Memorial:	Little Somerford		
War cemetery:	Embarkation Pier Cemetery		
Theatre of war:	Gallipoli		
Next of Kin:	William & Elizabeth Sly		
Address:	Winkworth Cottages, Lea, Wiltshire		

James, a farm labourer, volunteered for service initially joining the Wiltshire Regiment but because the Wiltshires had so many volunteers, and Irish regiments so few, he was transferred to the 6th Service Battalion Leinster Regiment. On 6 August 1915 the Leinsters landed at Anzac Cove and James was one of twenty members of the 6th Leinsters to be killed in action on Tuesday 10 August 1915 during actions against Turkish forces. His brother William Sly was to be killed at the Somme in July 1916.

Private Allen Richard Wicks		*6th Bn Royal Munster Fusiliers*	
Service No.	2988	Age:	29
Place of Birth:	Hullavington	Home Country:	England
Date of Death:	13/08/1915	Cause of death:	Killed in action
Memorial:	Hullavington		
War cemetery:	Helles Memorial		
Theatre of war:	Gallipoli		
Next of Kin:	Richard & Rose Hannah Wicks		
Address:	The Green, Hullavington, Wiltshire		

Allen a labourer for the Great Western Railway was the eldest son of Richard and Rose Wicks. He volunteered for service initially joining the Wiltshire Regiment but because the Wiltshires had so many volunteers, and Irish regiments so few, he was transferred to the 6th Service Battalion Royal Munster Fusiliers. The Munsters landed at Anzac Cove, Allen was one of five members of the 6th Munsters to be killed in action on Friday 13 August 1915 during actions against Turkish forces. He is remembered on the Helles Memorial and has no known grave.

Private Harry Arthur William Penton		*6th Bn Shropshire Light Infantry*	
Service No.	13153	Age:	19
Place of Birth:	Bowden Hill, Wiltshire	Home Country:	England
Date of Death:	14/08/1915	Cause of death:	Died of wounds
Memorial:	Not Known		
War cemetery:	Trois Arbres Cemetery Steenwerck		
Theatre of war:	France		
Next of Kin:	William James & Lena Penton		
Address:	Kingston Hill, Norbiton, Kingston-on-Thames, Surrey		

Nineteen year old Harry volunteered for service with the 6th Battalion Shropshire Light Infantry and arrived in France on 24 July 1915. On 11 August the Shropshires were sent to the trenches near Armentieres, France occupied by the West Yorkshire Regiment for instructional purposes. During his first tour in what were described as safe trenches, Harry was wounded and it is likely he died soon after. He had been in France just three weeks.

Gunner Roland Baish		*122nd Heavy Bty Royal Garrison Artillery*	
Service No.	26606	Age:	26
Place of Birth:	Chippenham	Home Country:	England
Date of Death:	19/08/1915	Cause of death:	Died of wounds
Memorial:	Not known		
War cemetery:	Lijssenthoek Military Cemetery		
Theatre of war:	Belgium		
Next of Kin:	Herbert & Ellen Baish		
Address:	Chippenham		

Regular soldier Roland was the eldest son of Herbert & Ellen Baish and arrived in France on 9 September 1914. He was wounded, most likely from German shell fire, and evacuated to a casualty clearing station at Lijssenthoek west of Ypres, Belgium, where he succumbed to his wounds on Thursday 19 August 1915. Roland's brothers Harold, who served with the Wiltshire Regiment, and Sidney who served with the Royal Marines, both survived the war.

21 AUGUST 1915 - ANZAC ATTACK AT ANAFARTA, SUVLA BAY AND THE START OF THE BATTLE OF SCIMITAR HILL, GALLIPOLI

Private Harold Mortimer		*5th Bn Dorsetshire Regiment*	
Service No.	10504	Age:	21
Place of Birth:	Grittleton, Wiltshire	Home Country:	England
Date of Death:	21/08/1915	Cause of death:	Killed in action
Memorial:	Devizes		
War cemetery:	Helles Memorial		
Theatre of war:	Gallipoli		
Next of Kin:	Joseph & Emily Mortimer		
Address:	Longcroft Road, Devizes		

Twenty one year old Harold volunteered for service on 27 August 1915 joining the 5th Service Battalion Dorsetshire Regiment. He arrived with the Dorsets at Suvla Bay, Gallipoli on 6 August 1916 and on 21 August the Dorsets were in trenches south of Dead Man's House. The British had a shortage of shells and the bombardment of the Turkish positions only lasted thirty minutes and inflicted little damage. At 3pm the Dorsets advanced over 500 yards of no man's land under Turkish shrapnel fire and took the Turkish first line trench, many of the defenders being killed with the bayonet. The Dorsets then found an even stronger held position 40 yards further on and set off to capture the position but at this time the British units on the left had veered off leaving un attacked Turkish position from which the Dorsets were coming under fire. Many of those who attacked this trench failed to return and it is likely Harold was one of these men. He was posted as missing and later presumed to have been killed in action with over 120 members of the 5th Dorsets on Saturday 21 August 1915. He is remembered on the Helles Memorial and has no known grave

---

31 AUGUST 1915 - THE ALLIES LOSSES AT GALLIPOLI DURING AUGUST NUMBER 40,000 SOLDIERS, FROM DEATH DUE TO FIGHTING OR THROUGH DYSENTERY AND OTHER DISEASES

Private Edgar Wallace Couzens | *1st Bn Wiltshire Regiment*

Service No.	10418	Age:	20
Place of Birth:	Langley Burrell	Home Country:	England
Date of Death:	02/09/1915	Cause of death:	Killed in action
Memorial:	Langley Burrell & St. Paul's Church Memorial		
War cemetery:	Ypres Menin Gate		
Theatre of war:	France		
Next of Kin:	Frederick & Mary Couzens		
Address:	Greenway Hill, Chippenham		

Twenty year old Edgar, known a Wallace and a machinist, volunteered for service with the 1st Battalion Wiltshire Regiment arriving in France on 4 January 1915. On Thursday 2 September 1915 the Wiltshires were in the front line at Hooge, east of Ypres, Belgium. It was raining heavily and at 3.55am the British bombarded the German front line. The Germans believing the bombardment was a prelude to an attack retaliated by bombarding the British trenches. The enemy fire was very intense and much of the British trench system was blown in by heavy shells. The Wiltshires were also occupying a trench in a crater to the front of the British front line and this area was targeted by the German artillery and trench mortars, the British dugouts in the crater were destroyed. The Wiltshire casualties were 14 killed, 38 wounded and 21 missing believed killed. Many of those who were killed were in the dugouts in the crater. One of those killed was Edgar, he is remembered on the Ypres Menin Gate and has no known grave. In September 1918 the following memoriam was inserted by his family in a local paper:

In ever loving memory of our dear son and brother
Sleep on dear one and take thy rest
They miss you most who loved you best
When days are dark and friends are few
Oh dear one how we long for you
Ever remembered by his loving father mother brother and sisters.

Private Sutcliffe Couzens | *1st Bn Wiltshire Regiment*

Service No.	7095	Age:	32
Place of Birth:	Seagry, Wiltshire	Home Country:	England
Date of Death:	03/09/1915	Cause of death:	Killed in action
Memorial:	Sutton Benger		
War cemetery:	Ypres Menin Gate		
Theatre of war:	Belgium		
Next of Kin:	John & Elizabeth Couzens		
Address:	Sutton Benger, Wiltshire		

Regular soldier Sutcliffe enlisted with the Wiltshires under the name of Cousins. He arrived in France on 14 August 1914 and would have been involved in all the engagements involving the Wiltshires. He was hit by German shell fire when the Wiltshires were subjected to German bombardment at Hooge, east of Ypres, Belgium, in the same action as Edgar Wallace Couzens. He is remembered on the Ypres Menin Gate and has no known grave. The Wiltshires were sent the following message from General Haldane:

"Convey to Wiltshire Regt my appreciation of stout hearted manner they stood bombardment yesterday. Regret heavy casualties."

Private Jesse Heath		*1st Bn Wiltshire Regiment*	
Service No.	14125	Age:	21
Place of Birth:	Sutton Benger, Wiltshire	Home Country:	England
Date of Death:	03/09/1915	Cause of death:	Died
Memorial:	Sutton Benger		
War cemetery:	Longuenesse St.Omer Souvenir Cemetery		
Theatre of war:	France		
Next of Kin:	Lewin and Emma Heath		
Address:	Old Post Office, Sutton Benger, Wiltshire		

Jessie was the second son of Lewin and Emma Heath. He volunteered for service with the 1st Battalion Wiltshire Regiment and arrived in France on 7 April 1915. He was taken ill and evacuated to a stationary hospital at St. Omer where he died from appendicitis on Friday 3 September 1915.

Lance Corporal Edward James Greenman		*7th Bn Royal Dublin Fusiliers*	
Service No.	15034	Age:	22
Place of Birth:	Yatton Keynell	Home Country:	England
Date of Death:	16/09/1915	Cause of death:	Died of wounds
Memorial:	Yatton Keynell		
War cemetery:	Helles Memorial		
Theatre of war:	Gallipoli		
Next of Kin:	George & Mary Anne Greenman		
Address:	Yatton Keynell, Wiltshire		

Edward, known as James and a farm labourer, was the only son of George and Mary Anne Greenman and volunteered for service joining the Wiltshire Regiment but because the Wiltshires had so many volunteers and Irish regiments so few he was transferred to the 7th Service Battalion Royal Dublin Fusiliers. He arrived in Gallipoli in July 1915 and was wounded in fighting likely to have been around the Turkish position at Chocolate Hill. James died of his wounds on Thursday 16 September 1915. He has no known grave and is remembered on the Helles Memorial. James's father died and his mother remarried Emanuel Snell whose son Montague Douglas Snell was killed in action at Gallipoli on 10 August 1915.

5
LOOS

Sergeant Mervyn Percy Powell　　　　　　　*8th Royal Berkshire Regiment*
Service No.　　　7752　　　　　　　　　　Age:　　　　　27
Place of Birth:　　Farringdon, Berkshire　　　Home Country:　England
Date of Death:　　25/09/1915　　　　　　　Cause of death:　Killed in action
Memorial:　　　　Chippenham & St Paul's Church Memorial
War cemetery:　　Loos Memorial
Theatre of war:　France
Next of Kin:　　　Emily Louisa Powell (wife) - William & Louisa Powell (parents)
Address:　　　　49 Oak Cottage, Marshfield Road, Chippenham

Regular soldier Mervyn, known as Percy, married Emily Louisa Smart in the summer of 1912. He arrived in France with the 2nd Battalion Royal Berkshire Regiment on 6 November 1914. It is likely Percy was wounded and on his recovery transferred to the 8th Battalion Royal Berkshire Regiment. On Saturday 25 September 1915 the Royal Berkshires were south west of Loos South of the Hulloch Road, preparing to attack. At 5.50am the preliminary British bombardment took place to which the Germans retaliated but caused little damage. The Gas Company in the front line trenches began to open the gas cylinders and several casualties from gas poisoning were caused by leaks from the cylinders. At 6.28 the gas ceased, smoke bombs were thrown screening the British advance and at 6.30 am the British artillery fire lifted from the German front line trenches. The Royal Berkshires then advanced in quick time, they were met by heavy artillery and machine gun fire and as they reached the German wire it was found to be almost intact. Most of the Royal Berkshires casualties occurred while the British tried to cut through the German wire and were caused by shrapnel and machine gun fire. It was also found that the wind had changed and the British gas was now blowing back into the ranks of the Royal Berkshires. However they managed to penetrate the obstacle and found the German front line trenches almost deserted. The Royal Berkshires then advanced capturing the German second and third line positions with little opposition. After the third line they then went on to capture an enemy field gun and a forth German line was then captured. The Forth line was in such a bad state that it gave little protection and the Royal Berkshires withdrew to the German third line. Over one hundred and seventy members of the 8th Battalion Royal Berkshire Regiment were killed, one of those was Percy. He is remembered on Loos Memorial and has no known grave.

Private Tom Canter   *8th Bn Royal Berkshire Regiment*
Service No.   14509   Age: 30
Place of Birth: Minety, Wiltshire   Home Country: England
Date of Death: 25/09/1915   Cause of death: Killed in action
Memorial: Swindon
War cemetery: Loos Memorial
Theatre of war: France
Next of Kin: Ella Alice Canter (wife) - Thomas and Dinah Canter (parents)
Address: 11 Unity Street, Chippenham - Silver St., Minety, Wiltshire

Tom worked as a boiler makers labourer in Swindon and toward the end of 1914 he married Ella Alice Gardner. He volunteered for service joining the 8th Battalion Royal Berkshire Regiment arriving in France on 7 August 1915. A little over a month later he was killed in action on Saturday 25 September in the same action as Mervyn Percy Powell. Tom has no known grave and is remembered on the Loos Memorial.

Lance Coporal Alfred George Hunt   *2nd Bn Wiltshire Regiment*
Service No.   8969   Age: 17
Place of Birth: Chippenham   Home Country: England
Date of Death: 25/09/1915   Cause of death: Killed in action
Memorial: Chippenham & St. Andrews Church Memorial
War cemetery: Loos Memorial
Theatre of war: France
Next of Kin: Charles & Jane Hunt
Address: London Road, Chippenham

Under age regular soldier Alfred, know as George, was the youngest son of Charles & Jane Hunt. He had enlisted prior to the commencement of hostilities with the 1st Battalion Wiltshire Regiment and arrived in France on 14 August 1914. He was wounded at the battle of Aisne in September 1914 and after his recovery he returned to the front joining 2nd Battalion Wiltshire Regiment. At 12.30am on Saturday 25 September 1915 the 2nd Battalion Wiltshire Regiment Verquin, South East of Loos, France, and marched via Labourse ans Sailly Labourse and arrived at a reserve line of trenches south east of Noyelles-les-Vermelles At 3am the British bombardment became intense and at 6am the British launched their attack which would become the Battle of Loos. The Wiltshires moved through the communication trench through Vermelles to occupy the front line trenches. The 20th Brigade which had taken part in the initial attack was now occupying the front and support line defences and the Wiltshires then advanced keeping north of the Hulluch Road. As the Wiltshires advanced they were subjected to heavy rifle and machine gun fire from the front. When the Wiltshires arrived at the former German trenches they found that they were weakly held by some British troops and contained 4 German field guns and ammunition. George was one of thirty men killed during the advance. He is remembered on the Loos Memorial and has no known grave. A letter to George's father from one of the Wiltshires officers stated:

"It may be some comfort to you that he died in the victorious advance with his face to the enemy"

Private William John Hoye   *9th Bn Welsh Regiment*
Service No.   24826   Age: 22
Place of Birth: Littlebury Green, Essex   Home Country: England

Date of Death: 25/09/1915   Cause of death: Killed in action
Memorial: Not known
War cemetery: Pont Du Hem Military Cemetery La Gorgue
Theatre of war: France
Next of Kin: Alice Maude Hoye (wife) - William & Susan Hoye (parents)
Address: Rhoose, Cardiff - Debden Essex

William, a farm labourer, volunteered for service with the Welsh Regiment giving his residence as Chippenham, Wiltshire. It may have been he was working on a farm near Chippenham. Just before William went to France on 14 August 1915 he married Alice Maude Dimmond at Cardiff. He was killed in action during fighting at Loos, France on Saturday 25 September 1915.

2nd Lieutenant Ernest Philip Morris Panes   *9th Bn Kings Royal Rifle Corps*
Service No.   N/A   Age: 22
Place of Birth: Blagdon, Somerset   Home Country: England
Date of Death: 25/09/1915   Cause of death: Killed in action
Memorial: Not known
War cemetery: Ypres Menin Gate
Theatre of war: Belgium
Next of Kin: Rev. John Benjamin & Louisa C Panes
Address: The Rectory, Torver, Coniston, Lancashire

Ernest was the youngest son of Rev. John Benjamin Panes who served at St. Paul's Church, Chippenham, during the absence of the Rector. He was educated at Dean Close Memorial School, Cheltenham and Brasenose College, Oxford. At the commencement of hostilities he obtained a commission with the 9th Service Battalion Kings Royal Rifle Corps and was attached to the 2nd Battalion Royal Irish Rifles. Ernest had, on a visit to Chippenham, read a lesson at St.Paul's Church. He was killed in action on Saturday 25 September 1915 during an attack on Bellewarde Farm near Hooge, Belgium, an attack which was supported by the 1st Wiltshires. He is remembered on the Ypres Menin Gate Memorial and has no known grave.

Private Roland Rose   *1st Bn Wiltshire Regiment*
Service No.   6186   Age: 29
Place of Birth: Urchfont, Wiltshire   Home Country: England
Date of Death: 25/09/1915   Cause of death: Killed in action
Memorial: Chippenham & St. Andrew's Chippenham
War cemetery: Ypres Menin Gate
Theatre of war: Belgium
Next of Kin: Joseph & Anne Rose
Address: 6 Nelsons Place, Chippenham

Roland was a coal carter and it is likely that he was a territorial soldier or a member of the special reserve. He joined the 1st Battalion Wiltshire Regiment arriving in France on 31 August 1914. He was wounded during fighting at the front and after recovering was granted a short leave in England. On 6 September 1915 Roland wrote the following letter to his parents stating that he had been recommended for the Distinguished Conduct Medal:

"You will be pleased to know that I have been recommended for the DCM. I hope I shall be

fortunate enough to get it. I don't think there is one DCM in our town at present and it will be a great honour to be the first Chippenham man to get it. I think myself lucky I am alive as we have just had a terrible bombardment losing about 130 of our chaps. It is said by some of the men that it was the worst bombardment all through the war. The Germans shelled our trenches for 3 days without stopping. I was recommended for digging a poor chap out who got buried by one of the German shells."

The terrible bombardment that Roland had written about was at Hooge, Belgium and had started on 3 September 1915 (see Edgar Wallace Couzens).

At 2am on Saturday 25 September 1915 the 1st Battalion Wiltshire Regiment were back in the trenches at Hooge, Belgium and were supporting a British attack on Bellewaard Farm. At 3.50am a British bombardment commenced, the Germans then replied fierce shell fire targeting the British front line and communication trenches. Rear areas along the Menin Road and communication trenches were also targeted, all the telephone wires were cut and the German shelling continued throughout the day. At 7.30am the Wiltshires were ordered to move up to the firing line to take the place of the attacking units. No information was received concerning the results of the attack and the situation was considered to be very uncertain but British troops on the left were seen to retire from the German Trenches that had apparently been captured. The Germans continued to bombard the British trenches throughout the night and into the morning of 26 September and the trenches were in a very bad condition with many dead lying about. At the end of the day the Wiltshires were by this time under strength and could only muster about 400 men, the majority of whom were very exhausted. For the past week the Wiltshires had few chances of getting any sleep. The casualties for the day were 16 killed and 54 wounded, one of those killed was Roland. His parents received the following letter from Captain Arthur Hales:

"Dear Mrs Rose. I much regret to have to inform you that Private Rose was killed by a shell when supporting an attack on the 25 September. He had been my servant for a few weeks and I had time to admire his courage and many good qualities. I feel that I have lost a good servant and a good friend. He was splendidly cool under the bombardment. It may be of some consolation to you to know that he did not suffer any pain being rendered unconscious at once. I had the pleasure at the beginning of the month of recommending Private Rose for bravery. A man was buried by the explosion of a shell and he volunteered to go out under heavy bombardment and dig him out. His sergeant who had asked for volunteers, and who has already been mentioned for this received the DCM, so you can be sure it was a gallant act. Be sure that every one act of bravery is seldom recognised officially; if it were so, few of them could remain long undiscovered."

Roland did not receive the Distinguished Conduct Medal, he is remembered on the Ypres Menin Gate and has no known grave.

Private Edward Hinchliffe Carvey		*2nd Bn Wiltshire Regiment*	
Service No.	10391	Age:	25
Place of Birth:	Swindon, Wiltshire	Home Country:	England
Date of Death:	26/09/1915	Cause of death:	Killed in action
Memorial:	Chippenham & St. Andrews Church Memorial		
War cemetery:	Loos Memorial		
Theatre of war:	France		
Next of Kin:	Maud E Carvey (wife) – Cecillia Carvey (mother)		

Address: 11 Palmer Street, Chippenham

Edward, a fitter and a Wiltshire territorial, was brought up by his grandparents William and Anne Carvey of 5 Park Lane, Chippenham. He was a keen footballer playing for Rovers football team and in the spring of 1912 he married Maud E. Ellison. He volunteered for service joining the 2nd Battalion Wiltshire Regiment and arrived in France on 17 February 1915. He was wounded in May 1915 and after his recovery was given some home leave before returning to the front. On the night of Sunday 26 September the Wiltshires were in trenches north of the road between Vermelles and Hulluch, France. An urgent request for support was made from the British front line trenches and as they went forward they were met by heavy German machine gun and rifle fire causing heavy casualties. One of those killed was Edward. He was buried at Vermelles but his grave was lost in subsequent fighting. He is today remembered on the Loos Memorial and has no known grave. He left a widow and two small children and in September 1916 the following memoriam was inserted in a local paper:

He has gone for aye but not forgotten
To our hearts he still appeals
He who gave his life so freely
Out on yonder battlefields
Never forgotten and ever lovingly remembered
By his wife and children and other relations.

Act.Captain Geoffrey Mervyn Underhill Wilson   B Coy 2nd Bn Wiltshire Regiment

Service No.	N/A	Age:	21
Place of Birth:	Chippenham, Wiltshire	Home Country:	England
Date of Death:	26/09/1915	Cause of death:	Killed in action
Memorial:	Chippenham & St Andrews Church Memorial		
War cemetery:	Loos Memorial		
Theatre of war:	France		
Next of Kin:	Mervyn Seppins & Helena Jane Wilson OBE		
Address:	19 St Marys Street, Chippenham		

Twenty one year old Geoffrey was educated at King's School Bruton Somerset and Marlborough College. He volunteered for service obtaining a commission as a Lieutenant with the 2nd

A panel of the memorial window in St. Andrew's Church, Chippenham denoting the Wiltshire Regiment in which Geoffrey Wilson served.

Battalion Wiltshire Regiment arriving in France on 9 February 1915. In July he was promoted in the field to Captain. He was killed in action in trenches north of the road between Vermelles and Hulluch, France, (See Alfred Hunt and Edward Carvey). The Commonwealth War Grave Commission gives the date of death as 26 September 1915 while the Wiltshires War Diary states he was killed on 25 September 1915. This may indicate he was killed during the evening or night but does give a good indication of the confusion that took place and the strain the officers and men were under when they were in action. The answer though may be held by his medal card, which originally stated he was killed on 26 September but was then changed to 25 September. Geoffrey's parents were to lose three sons during the war; Evelyn was killed at Loos three days after his brother and Herbert was to die from wounds in Iraq in January 1917. On 29 September 1918 a stained glass window in St. Andrews Church, Chippenham was dedicated to the memory of the three brothers. The date of 29 September was very significant, it was the date when Geoffrey was born, Herbert was baptized and Evelyn was killed. The window was intended to contrast the desolation and sorrow of that which was felt toward the end of the war, with a higher hope for the future world, which was the remedy. Geoffrey is remembered on the Loos Memorial and has no known grave.

Private Richard Edward John Wilkins	*2nd Bn Wiltshire Regiment*	
Service No.	18259	Age:	21
Place of Birth:	Chippenham, Wiltshire	Home Country:	England
Date of Death:	26/09/1915	Cause of death:	Killed in action
Memorial:	St Pauls Church Memorial, Chippenham & Allington		
War cemetery:	Loos Memorial		
Theatre of war:	France		
Next of Kin:	George Henry & Eliza Jane Wilkins		
Address:	The Pitts, Allington, Chippenham		

Twenty one year old Richard, known as Jack and a blacksmith, was the eldest son of George & Eliza Wilkins. He volunteered for service with the 2nd Battalion Wiltshire Regiment arriving in France on 27 April 1915. In mid October 1915 his parents received the following letters from the front, the first from a comrade Willie Curtis:

"I am writing these few lines to break the news to you about poor Jack, and I am sorry to inform you that he was killed in action on September 25th He was buried in the trench and also a lance corporal. Poor Jack is gone but not forgotten. I was cut up when I new it. I am sending your photo back, as that was all we found on him of any use to you. I can tell you it was an awful sight to see after we attacked. I am sorry I could not let you know before, but I had not much time for letter writing. I must conclude now, hoping you will cheer up as much as you can. I will write again within a day or two. I remain your loving friend"

The second letter from was 2nd lieutenant G. Bryer-Ash of the 2nd Battalion Wiltshire Regiment:

"I very much regret to inform you that No. 18529 Private R.E. Wilkins was killed in action on September 25th, during the great advance and whilst fighting gallantly for his country. Please accept my deepest sympathy."

Jack was killed in action in trenches north of the road between Vermelles and Hulluch, France, (See Alfred Hunt and Edward Carvey). The Commonwealth War Grave Commission gives the date of death as 26 September 1915 while the Wiltshires War Diary states he was killed on 25

September 1915. This may indicate he was killed during the evening or night but does give a good indication of the confusion that took place and the strain the officers and men were under when they were in action. Jack's grave was lost and he is today remembered on the Loos Memorial but has no known grave.

Private Arthur Henry Selby   *2nd Bn Wiltshire Regiment*

Service No.	10651	
Place of Birth:	Kington St Michael	
Date of Death:	26/09/1915	
Memorial:	BSE BE LJB BB Shop Memorial Swindon Railway Museum	
War cemetery:	Loos Memorial	
Theatre of war:	France	
Next of Kin:	Thomas & Emma Selby (parents) – Frederick J. Selby (brother)	
Address:	39 George Street, Swindon - 112 Princes Street, Swindon	

Age: 35
Home Country: England
Cause of death: Killed in action

Arthur was employed as an engineers labourer with the Great Western Railway Works in Swindon. He volunteered for service with the 2nd battalion Wiltshire Regiment arriving in France on 11 December 1914. He was killed in action in trenches north of the road between Vermelles and Hulluch, France, (See Alfred Hunt and Edward Carvey). He is remembered on the Loos Memorial and has no known grave.

27 SEPTEMBER 1915 - BRITISH GUARDS DIVISION CAPTURE HILL 70 AT LOOS, FRANCE

Captain Evelyn Seppings Wilson   *2nd Bn East Yorkshire Regiment*

Service No.	N/A
Place of Birth:	Chippenham, Wiltshire
Date of Death:	29/09/1915
Memorial:	Chippenham
War cemetery:	Loos Memorial
Theatre of war:	France
Next of Kin:	Mervyn Seppings & Helena Jane Wilson OBE
Address:	19 St Marys Street, Chippenham

Age: 22
Home Country: England
Cause of death: Killed in action

Regular soldier Evelyn was educated at St. Peter's School, Weston Supper Mare and Marlborough College before attending the Military College at Sandhurst. He was a keen cricketer and footballer and whilst at Marlborough College he played for the school eleven. On his graduation he received a commission with the East Yorkshire Regiment and proceeded to India in 1913 where he was stationed at the outbreak of hostilities. In December 1914 he returned with his regiment to England and was taken ill for a time and then placed in charge of a camp in Yorkshire. He was promoted to Captain and in June 1915 and went to France to join his regiment. He was killed on Wednesday 29 September 1915 during fighting at Loos, France. Evelyn's parents were to lose three sons during the war Geoffrey was killed at Loos three days before his brother and Herbert was to die from wounds in Iraq. On 29 September 1918 a stained glass window in St. Andrews Church, Chippenham was dedicated to the memory of the three brothers. The date of the 29 September was very significant, it was the date when Geoffrey was born, Herbert was baptized and Evelyn was killed. The window was intended toontrast the desolation and sorrow of that was felt toward the end of the war, with a higher hope for the future world, which was the remedy. Evelyn is remembered on the Loos Memorial.

Left: Ernest Albert Young

Above: A panel of the memorial window in St. Andrew's Church, Chippenham denoting the East Yorkshire Regiment in which Evelyn Wilson served.

Private Ernest Albert Young

Service No.	15298		

10th Bn Gloucestershire Regiment

Service No.   15298
Place of Birth: Castle Combe, Wiltshire
Date of Death: 01/10/1915
Memorial: Castle Combe
War cemetery: Etaples Military Cemetery
Theatre of war: France
Next of Kin: Annie Maria Young (wife) - Albert & Elizabeth Young (parents)
Address: Park Street, Stow-on-the-Wold, Gloucestershire - Castle Combe

Age: 37
Home Country: England
Cause of death: Died of wounds

Ernest, a gardener, married Annie Maria Haynes in 1902 in Castle Combe. He volunteered for service enlisting first with the Grenadier Guards but was transferred to the 10th Service Battalion Gloucestershire Regiment. He arrived in France on 9 August 1915. He was severely wounded and died of his wounds shortly after his admittance to a military hospital at Etaples, France on Friday 1 October 1915. He left a widow and three young children.

5 OCTOBER 1915 - A BRITISH AND FRENCH FORCE LANDS AT SALONIKA , GREECE TO SUPPORT SERBIA

Private John Randolph Lea   *7th Bn Gloucestershire Regiment*

Service No.   22309   Age: 20
Place of Birth: Sutton Benger, Wiltshire Home Country: England
Date of Death: 06/10/1915   Cause of death: Died
Memorial: Sutton Benger - Church & Chippen Secodary School
War cemetery: Alexandria Chatby Military and War Memorial Cemetery
Theatre of war: Gallipoli
Next of Kin: John & Lucy Lea

The private memorial to John Randolph Lea in All Saints Church Sutton Benger.

Address: Poplar Farm, Sutton Benger, Wiltshire

Farmers son John was the only son of John and Lucy Lea and volunteered for service with the Hussars and after being told cavalry were not required he volunteered to join the Gloucestershire Regiment, being sent to the 7th Service Battalion. He arrived with a reinforcement draft to Gallipoli on 16 August 1915 and while serving he was taken ill and evacuated to a base hospital at Alexandria, Egypt. He died at the base hospital of pneumonia on Wednesday 6 October 1915. John's parents erected a private Memorial to their son in All Saints Church, Sutton Benger.

Private John Taylor   *2nd Bn Wiltshire Regiment*
Service No.   10437   Age: 22
Place of Birth: Chippenham   Home Country: England
Date of Death: 09/10/1915   Cause of death: Died of wounds
Memorial: Hardenhuish Church Memorial & Seagry Memorial
War cemetery: Chocques Military Cemetery
Theatre of war: France
Next of Kin: Alfred & Mrs Taylor
Address: Woodlands, Chippenham

John, a farm labourer, volunteered for service with the 2nd Battalion Wiltshire Regiment and arrived in France on 17 February 1917. He was wounded in fighting most likely in trenches north of the road between Vermelles and Hulluch, France, and evacuated to No 1 Casualty Clearing Station, Chocques, France where he died on Saturday 9 October 1915.

TUESDAY 12 OCTOBER 1915 - ENGLISH NURSE EDITH CAVELL WAS SHOT BY THE GERMANS FOR HELPING BRITISH PRISONERS OF WAR ESCAPE FROM BELGIUM TO NEUTRAL HOLLAND

Chaplain 4th Class William Preston Ainley   *Royal Army Chaplains Department*
Service No.   N/A   Age: 27
Place of Birth: Cork, Ireland   Home Country: England
Date of Death: 12/10/1915   Cause of death: Died
Memorial: St. Paul's Church Chippenham

Left:Rev. William Preston Ainley.

Above: Wounded soldiers at Charring Cross station.

War cemetery:	Uffington Lincolnshire
Theatre of war:	Home
Next of Kin:	Frederick W Ainley & Annie Preston
Address:	St Andrews Vicarage, Islington, London

William was the second son of Rev. Frederick and Annie Ainley and was educated at Cork Grammar School and Merchant Taylors School, London. He was admitted to Jesus College, Cambridge in 1906 and read theology and attained a B.A. in 1909. He was a keen sportsman and a cox in the college rowing team. From 1909 to 1914 he was curate at St. Paul's Church Chippeham, he had intended to carry out missionary work in China but at the outbreak of hostilities he obtained a commission as a Chaplain 4th Class with the Royal Army Chaplains Department and served as a chaplain at Aldershot and Whitley. He was about to proceed to France when he contracted cerebo spinal meningitis and died at Uffington on Tuesday 12 October 1915. He left over £268 in his will. At the time of this book being publish William is not remembered by the Commonwealth War Graves Commission.

Private George William Fields		*26th Bn Austrailian Infantry AIF*	
Service No.	1895	Age:	29
Place of Birth:	Chippenham, Wiltshire	Home Country:	Australia
Date of Death:	21/10/1915	Cause of death:	Killed in action
Memorial:	Chippenham & St. Andrew Church Memorial		
War cemetery:	7th Field Ambulance Cemetery		
Theatre of war:	Gallipoli		
Next of Kin:	Evelyn B. Fields (wife) – George & Agnes Fields (parents)		
Address:	Deagon, Sandgate, Queensland - 92 Lowden Road, Chippenham		

George, a labourer, emigrated to Australia prior to the Great War where he married and had a young family. He volunteered for service with the Australian Army on 12 June 1915 and after completing his training he left Brisbane on the troopship Kyarra on 16 August 1915. He arrived on the Gallipoli peninsular as part of a 3rd reinforcement draft on 12 October 1915. He was killed in action just nine days later on Thursday 21 October 1915. He was buried the same day at 7th Field Ambulance Cemetery at Gallipoli and left a widow and 3 young children. In late

October 1915 George's family in England inserted the following memoriam in a local paper:

We think of him in silence no eye can see us weep.
But ever to our aching hearts his name we keep
Not now but in a better land some day we'll understand
We never thought his time so short in this world to remain
When from our home he went away he thought to come again
Ever remembered by Mother, Father, Brother and Sisters.

Private Edwin Kent		*2nd Bn Wiltshire Regiment*	
Service No.	18255	Age:	33
Place of Birth:	Binfield, Berkshire	Home Country:	England
Date of Death:	22/10/1915	Cause of death:	Died of wounds
Memorial:	Nettleton & Burton		
War cemetery:	Nettleton St Mary Churchyard		
Theatre of war:	Home		
Next of Kin:	Elizabeth Eliza Kent (wife) - William & Anne Kent (parents)		
Address:	The Gibb, Burton, Wiltshire – Yatton Keynell, Wiltshire		

Edwin was employed by Mr Higgs, a coal merchant at Burton, and married Elizabeth Eliza West at the beginning of 1903. He volunteered for service with the 2nd Battalion Wiltshire Regiment. He was shot in the spine while serving at the front and was evacuated to England and sent to Norwich Hospital where he succumbed to his wounds on Friday 22 October 1915. He was buried with full military honours at Nettleton St. Mary Churchyard and left a widow and a little girl. In October 1916 his wife inserted the following memoriam in a local paper:

O'may we meet our dear one again
Far up in that home above
Where war and strife will be no more
But all will be peace and love
Ever remembered by his wife and child.

Sergeant Charles William Scriven		*2nd Bn Wiltshire Regiment*	
Service No.	19155	Age:	28
Place of Birth:	Minety, Wiltshire	Home Country:	England
Date of Death:	28/10/1915	Cause of death:	Died of wounds
Memorial:	Hullavington		
War cemetery:	Chocques Military Cemetery		
Theatre of war:	France		
Next of Kin:	Sarah Ann Scriven (wife) – Edwin & Ann Mary Scriven (parents)		
Address:	Ivy Court, Hullavington, Wiltshire – Woodbine Cottage, Hullavington		

Charles originally joined the Wiltshire Militia on 14 November 1904 at the age of 17 years and 11 months. The following year he became a regular soldier enlisting with the 2nd Battalion Wiltshire Regiment on 4 January 1905. Toward the end of 1907 he married Sarah Tull in South Wales and in 1911 was transferred to the reserve. At the commencement of hostilities he was called to the colours on 5 August 1914 but was discharged on 28 November 1914 being physically unfit for further service. Charles then re-enlisted with the 2nd Battalion Wiltshire Regiment and arrived in France on 21 April 1915. He was wounded in fighting most likely in trenches north of the road between Vermelles and Hulluch, France, and evacuated to No 1 Casualty Clearing Station, Chocques, France where he died on Thursday 28 October 1915.

Private Gilbert John Mahoney   *1st Bn Wiltshire Regiment*
Service No.   3/558   Age: 19
Place of Birth: Allington, Wiltshire   Home Country: England
Date of Death: 30/10/1915   Cause of death: Killed in action
Memorial: Chippenham - St Paul's Church Memorial - Allington
War cemetery: Ploegsteert Wood Military Cemetery
Theatre of war: Belgium
Next of Kin: Angelina Keel
Address: 9 Nelsons Place London Road, Chippenham, Wiltshire

Nineteen year old Gilbert, known as John, was the only son of Gilbert John Mahoney & Angelina Mahoney and after the death of his father his mother remarried Isaac Keel. John volunteered for service with 1st Battalion Wiltshire Regiment and arrived in France on 26 January 1915. He was killed while working in the trenches near Ploegsteert Wood, called Plog Street by British troops, on Saturday 30 October 1915.

Corporal William Arthur Sealy   *8th Bn Royal Fusiliers*
Service No.   1213   Age: 26
Place of Birth: Great Somerford, Wiltshire Home Country: England
Date of Death: 09/11/1915   Cause of death: Killed in action
Memorial: Not known
War cemetery: Loos Memorial
Theatre of war: France
Next of Kin: Thomas & Louisa Sealy
Address: 23 Blundells Road, Tilehurst, Berkshire

William, a shop assistant, volunteered for service with the 8th Battalion Royal Fusiliers and arrived in France on 1 June 1916. He was killed in action on Tuesday 9 November 1915 north of the town of Loos, France. He is remembered on the Loos Memorial and has no known grave.

22 NOVEMBER 1915 - THE BATTLE OF CTESIPHON, MESOPOTAMIA

Private George Edwin Duck   *1/4th TF Somerset Light Infantry*
Service No.   2757   Age: 21
Place of Birth: St.Thomas, Bristol   Home Country: England
Date of Death: 22/11/1915   Cause of death: Killed in action
Memorial: Chippenham & St. Paul's Church Memorial
War cemetery: Basra Memorial
Theatre of war: Mesopotamia
Next of Kin: Edwin Nathan & Susan Duck
Address: 20 Park Lane, Chippenham

Nineteen year old George was the only son of Edwin and Susan Duck. He had worked at the bookstall firstly at Chippenham railway station and then in 1911 he transferred to the same role at Frome railway station, being well known in both towns. At the outbreak of the Great War he volunteered for service with the 1/4th Territorial Battalion Somerset Light Infantry and was sent to India for garrison duties in order that regular British units could be sent back to Europe. He arrived in India, landing at Bombay, on 9 November 1914 and when a call for volunteers to serve in Mesopotamia came George stepped forward. He arrived in Mesopotamia, modern day Iraq on 14 August 1915 and was attached to the 2nd Battalion Dorsetshire Regiment. On Monday 22 November 1915 the Dorsets were preparing to attack Turkish positions at Ctessphon, in modern day Iraq. At the start of the attack they were in support, advancing behind the attacking formation over a vast plain which gave them an unprecedented view of the battle. At 11am as the British advance forces captured the Turkish strong point, known as VP, the two companies of the Dorsets C and D, continued to advance a further distance, under fire from Turkish snipers they captured the Turkish 2nd line trenches at about 12:30pm, pushing on and capturing the Turkish reserve trenches which were full of dead and wounded Turks. From these trenches the Dorsets could see the Turkish artillery and a further advance was made but as the Dorsets reached the Turkish guns that had been abandoned they were shelled by other Turkish artillery units using shrapnel. The Dorsets then pushed forward to upset the ranging of the Turkish gunners and were met by intense fire from further Turkish lines. The other two companies of the Dorsets which had been held in reserve now attacked Water Redoubt, another Turkish strong point. Meanwhile C and D companies of the Dorsets were now facing an attack from Turkish reserve forces and so heavy was the Dorsets rifle fire on attacking troops, that the grease was beginning to bubble through the woodwork on the British rifles and the sights became to hot to touch. Dorsets were now running short of ammunition and were compelled to retreat to the position of VP leaving the Turkish guns that they had captured. The Dorsets casualties were 9 officers and 200 men and in January 1916 the news reached George's parents that he had been killed, he is remembered on the Basra Memorial and has no known grave.

Private Arthur Tanner   *2/4th TF Bn Wiltshire Regiment*
Service No.   3175   Age: 29
Place of Birth: Kington St Michael   Home Country: England
Date of Death: 22/11/1915   Cause of death: Killed in action
Memorial: Kington St Michael & Trowbridge St. James Church Memorial
War cemetery: Basra Memorial
Theatre of war: Mesopotamia
Next of Kin: Alfred James & Jane Tanner
Address: Kington St Michael, Wiltshire

Arthur, a farm labourer, volunteered for service with the 2/4th Battalion Wiltshire Regiment and was initially sent to India for garrison duty. When a call came for men to fight in Mesopotamia Arthur again volunteered and arrived in modern day Iraq on 25 August 1915. He was killed in action on Monday 22 November 1915 at the Battle of Ctesiphon, Iraq, in action against Turkish forces, (see George Duck). He is remembered on the Basra Memorial and has no known grave.

Lance Corporal James William Milford   *5th Bn Wiltshire Regiment*
Service No.   18043   Age: 30
Place of Birth: Walcot, Somerset   Home Country: England
Date of Death: 28/11/1915   Cause of death: Died
Memorial: Chippenham & St. Andrew's Church memorial

War cemetery: Green Hill Cemetery
Theatre of war: Gallipoli
Next of Kin: Rose Milford (wife) - Charles William & Margaret Milford (parents)
Address: 52 St. Mary Street, Chippenham - 11 James's Buildings, Bath, Somerset

James, a labourer, married his wife Rose in 1906 and at the outbreak of hostilities he volunteered for service with the 5th Battalion Wiltshire Regiment. He arrived on the Gallipoli peninsular in July 1915 and it is likely that he was weakened by the fighting and depravations he had to face at Gallipoli. On Friday 26 November as winter arrived in Gallipoli, the men of the 5th Battalion Wiltshire Regiment were at Suvla Bay. They were dressed in their thin warm climate uniforms and had little protection from what was to come. During the night there was a tremendous thunder storm. Water rushed into the trenches destroying parapets and washing away the soldier's kit, blankets and other equipment. After the rain stopped the night was bitterly cold and the Wiltshires attempted to repair the trenches. At dawn the trenches were full of deep water, the cook house was flooded and with no fires conditions were described as deplorable. The following day the rain continued and orders were received to evacuate any unfit men. Unfortunately the roads were flooded and the unfit men had to remain. As night fell the rain turned to snow and the Turks fired artillery shells at the British positions. On Sunday 28 November there was a heavy blizzard and the Wiltshires were in the fire trenches huddling around braziers and biscuit tins trying to keep the fires burning. One man died of exposure and some were described as comatose. The war diary states:

"The majority kept up their spirits admirably and continued rifle and machine gun fire during night."

The following day, Monday 29 November, the Wiltshires were still in the fire trenches, the war diary states;

"Two of the sick awaiting removal on stretchers which did not arrive from ambulance died and then 3 others were found dead from exhaustion in the trenches. Frost began to dry trenches and conditions improved, fires being started and cookhouses in good working order. Extra issues of rum during these days of bitter cold were much appreciated. Unfit men still awaiting embarkation."

It is likely that James died of exposure and he was buried by his comrades. After the armistice his grave was moved to Green Hill Cemetery which is situated between Suvla Bay and Anzac Cove.

Private Albert Walter Cullimore		*2/4th TF Wiltshire Regiment*	
Service No.	2658	Age:	25
Place of Birth:	Biddestone, Wiltshire	Home Country:	England
Date of Death:	28/11/1915	Cause of death:	Died of wounds
Memorial:	Biddestone & Trowbridge St James's Church Memorial		
War cemetery:	Kut War Cemetery		
Theatre of war:	Mesopotamia		
Next of Kin:	Albert & Ellen Cullimore		
Address:	Pickwick, Corsham, Wiltshire		

Albert, known as Walter and a labourer, volunteered for service with the 2/4th Battalion Wiltshire Regiment and was sent to India for Garrison duties. After a call for more men for

Mesopotamia campaign he again volunteered arriving on 25 May 1915. He was wounded in fighting most likely at Ctesiphon between 20 and 23 November 1915 (see George Duck). He was evacuated to a field hospital at Kut where he died of his wounds on Sunday 28 November 1915.

5 DECEMBER 1915 - BRITISH FORCE AT KUT ARE SURROUNDED BY TURKISH TROOPS

Private John Edward Griffin

Service No.	15294	

7th Bn Royal Dublin Fusiliers

Service No.   15294
Place of Birth: Giddeahall, Wiltshire
Date of Death: 07/12/1915
Memorial: Chippenham – Liddington – St. Andrew's Church & Liberal Club Mem.
War cemetery: Doiran Memorial
Theatre of war: Balkans
Next of Kin: John Sherman & Eliza Griffin
Address: 22 Parliament Street, Chippenham

Age: 36
Home Country: England
Cause of death: Killed in action

John, a stone sawyer, was the eldest son of John and Eliza Sherman and originally enlisted with the Wiltshires on 23 March 1897 at the age of 17 years and 9 months. At the outbreak of the Great War he volunteered for service, originally joining the Wiltshire Regiment but because the Wiltshires had so many volunteers and Irish regiments so few he was transferred to the 7th Service Battalion Royal Dublin Fusiliers. He arrived at Gallipoli in early August 1915 and after taking part in actions in August and September the Royal Dublin Fusiliers were withdrawn from the peninsular on 30 September 1915. They were then sent to Salonika, Greece, the Serbian army was in retreat and was threatened by the Bulgarians. The British and French commenced a campaign against the Bulgarians to aid the Serbians allowing the retreating army to fall back through Macedonia to Greece. The Serbs however were forced to retreat through Albainia and embark by sea for Greece. In December British advanced to Kosturino, in modern day Macedonia, north of Doiran, Greece. They were holding the only road to pass through the Mountains to the Vardar Valley, which was held by the French. If the Bulgarians had broken through the French armys' line of retreat would have been cut off. John was killed in action during fighting against the Bugarian army on Tuesday 7 December 1915, before British retreated to prepared positions at Doiran. John is remembered on the Doiran Memorial, in Greece with over 2,000 men who died while fighting in Salonika and have no known grave. John's brother Francis Griffin was to die of dysentery in Egypt in September 1918.

8 DECEMBER 1915 - EVACUATION OF GALLIPOLI BEGINS

4 JANUARY 1916 - THE BATTLE OF SHEIK SA'AD, MESOPOTAMIA - AN ATTEMPT TO RELIEVE THE BRITISH GARRISON IN KUT

9 JANUARY 1916 - GALLIPOLI EVACUATION COMPLETED

Private Arthur James Blackford · *19th Bn Royal Fusilers*

Service No.	94	Age:	21
Place of Birth:	Dorchester, Dorset	Home Country:	England
Date of Death:	17/01/1916	Cause of death:	Killed in action
Memorial:	Peasenhall, Suffolk		
War cemetery:	Cambrin Churchyard Extension		
Theatre of war:	France		
Next of Kin:	Arthur Albert James Smyth & Adela Fanny Blackford		
Address:	4 Avondale Road, Gorleston, Great Yarmouth, Norfolk		

Arthur Blackford senior had an ironmongers shop at 23 High Street, Chippenham and though he moved to Peasenhall Suffolk, he still carried on the business. Arthur junior was educated at Weston-Super- Mare and Merchant Ventures School, Bristol. He volunteered for service with the 19th Battalion Royal Fusilers, known as the 2nd Public Schools Battalion which was made up of men who had attended public schools or universities. He arrived in France on 14 November 1915 and was killed a little over two month later near Cambrin, east of Bethune, France on Monday 17 January 1916. He was buried in Cambrin Churchyard Extension and the service was performed by the Brigade Chaplain.

24 JANUARY 1916 - THE MILITARY SERVICE ACT IS PASSED IN PARLIAMENT CONSCRIPTION WILL COMMENCE IN MAY 1916

Rifleman Reginald Percy Bennett · *3/8th London Regiment*

Service No.	3711	Age:	23
Place of Birth:	Chippenham, Wiltshire	Home Country:	England
Date of Death:	29/01/1916	Cause of death:	Died
Memorial:	Chippenham & Poole Dorset		
War cemetery:	Longfleet St Mary Churcuyard		
Theatre of war:	Home		
Next of Kin:	Bessie Selina Bennett (wife) - Thomas & Ellen Bennett (parents)		
Address:	12 Hill Street, Poole, Dorset - Lowden Hill, Chippenham		

Reginald, a labourer, moved to Poole, Dorset prior to the Great War and in the spring 1915 he married Bessie Selina Chaffey at Poole, Dorset. It is likely he joined the army under the Derby Scheme which meant a man could enlist in the army but would not join until the army needed him. He died at Poole, most likely of illness or disease, on Saturday 21 January 1916.

Stoker 2nd Class Joseph John Hulance · *HMS New Zealand Royal Navy*

Service No.	K/28036(Dev)	Age:	18
Place of Birth:	Hullavington, Wiltshire	Home Country:	England
Date of Death:	01/02/1916	Cause of death:	Died
Memorial:	Hullavington		
War cemetery:	Hullavington St Mary Churchyard		
Theatre of war:	Home		
Next of Kin:	Lewin Trimmer & Martha Hulance		
Address:	The Street, Hullavington, Wiltshire		

Above H.M.S. New Zealand.

Right: The grave of Joe Hulance in St. Mary Magdalene Churchyard, Hullavington.

Eighteen year old Joseph, known as Joe, was the fifth son of Martha Hulance serving his country; three of his brothers were in the Navy and one was serving with the 1st Battalion Wiltshire Regiment. He died after a short illness at the Royal Naval Hospital, South Queensferry, Scotland, on Tuesday 1 February 1916. His body was returned to his home in Hullavington and was buried in St May's Churchyard.

Rifleman Alfred Edward Bray		*8th Bn Rifle Brigade*	
Service No.	B/1493	Age:	20
Place of Birth:	Fishponds, Bristol	Home Country:	England
Date of Death:	11/02/1916	Cause of death:	Died of wounds
Memorial:	Not known		
War cemetery:	Boulogne Eastern Cemetery		
Theatre of war:	France		
Next of Kin:	Henry William & Rose Ann Bray		
Address:	Southsea Cottages, Kington Langley, Wiltshire		

Twenty year old Alfred, a grocers assistant, volunteered for service joining the 8th Service Battalion the Rifle Brigade on 31 August 1914. After completing his training he arrived in France on 20 May 1915 and took part in actions in Belgium Hooge, in July 1915 and Bellewaarde, in September 1915. He was wounded with a gun shot wound to his back on 3 February 1916 and evacuated to 44th Field Ambulance and then on to No 10 Casualty Clearing Station were he succumbed to his wounds on Friday 11 February 1916. His personal effects returned to his family consisted of two discs, one 10 Franc coin, one Prayer book and a Macintosh cape.

Driver Arthur Francis Baggs		*20th Bde Ammo. Col Royal Field Artillery*	
Service No.	18184	Age:	32
Place of Birth:	Chippenham	Home Country:	England
Date of Death:	13/02/1916	Cause of death:	Died
Memorial:	Not Known		

War cemetery: Netley Military Cemetery
Theatre of war: Home
Next of Kin: Thomas & Elizabeth Baggs
Address: 6 Prince of Wales Road, Weymouth, Dorset

Arthur, a labourer, was the eldest son of Thomas and Elizabeth Baggs and volunteered for service with the Royal Field Artillery. He arrived in France on 18 January 1915. While serving on the continent he was taken ill and evacuated to Netley Military Hospital, England where he died of illness or disease on Sunday 13 February 1916.

Private Walter George Greenman   *16th Bn Welsh Regiment*
Service No.   23511   Age: 20
Place of Birth: Box, Wiltshire   Home Country: England
Date of Death: 16/03/1916   Cause of death: Died of wounds
Memorial: Biddestone
War cemetery: St Venant Communal Cemetery
Theatre of war: France
Next of Kin: Henry & Lily Greenman
Address: Box, Wiltshire

Walter, a farm labourer, was the second son of Henry and Lily Greenman. In the spring of 1901 Henry Greenman died and six years later Lily Greenman married Charles Toghill and for a time Walter was known as Walter Toghill. When he volunteered for service Walter enlisted under his true surname Greenman and joined the Welsh Regiment. He arrived in France on 4 December 1915 and the 16th Welsh spent the first few months of 1916 training in trench warfare. Part of this training involved gaining experience in the front line and this was done in the area of Givenchy, France. It is likely that Walter was wounded while in these trenches and evacuated to a casualty clearing station at St. Venant, North West of Bethune, France, where he succumbed to his wounds on Thursday 16 March 1915.

Private Joseph Alfred Wood   *6th Bn Wiltshire Regiment*
Service No.   18943   Age: 19
Place of Birth: Bath, Somerset   Home Country: England
Date of Death: 18/03/1916   Cause of death: Killed in action
Memorial: Chippenham & St. Andrews Church Memorial
War cemetery: St Vaast Post Military Cemetery Richebourg Lavoue
Theatre of war: France
Next of Kin: Joseph & Johanna Wood
Address: 49 Blind Lane, Chippenham

Nineteen year old Joseph volunteered for service joining the 6th Service Battalion Willtshire Regiment and arrived in France early in 1916. He was killed, most likely by German shell fire, while improving the British trenches at the position of Port Arthur Redoubt which was near the Estaires to Le Bassee Road, France, on Saturday 18 March 1916.

5 APRIL 1916 - FIRST BATTLE OF KUT

5

MESOPOTAMIA

Private William James Lemm		*5th Bn Wiltshire Regiment*	
Service No.	3/541	Age:	19
Place of Birth:	Maryport, Cumberland	Home Country:	England
Date of Death:	06/04/1916	Cause of death:	Died of wounds
Memorial:	Chippenham & Hardenhuish Church Memorial		
War cemetery:	Amara War Cemetery		
Theatre of war:	Mesopotamia		
Next of Kin:	James & Violet S Lemm		
Address:	50 St Mary Street, Chippenham		

Nineteen year old William, known as James, was the only son of James senior and Violet Lemm. He volunteered for service with the 5th Battalion Wiltshire Regiment and arrived at Gallipoli on 22 November 1915. In January 1916 Gallipoli was evacuated and the Wiltshires were first sent to Egypt and then on to Mesopotamia arriving at Basra on 29 February 1914. The Wiltshire then proceeded north in an attempt to relieve the British Garrison at Kut Al Amara in Modern day Iraq. James was wounded while fighting Turkish forces most likely near Falahiyeh. It is also likely he was evacuated to one of the hospitals at Amara where he died of his wounds on Thursday 6 April 1916.

Sergeant Edwin George Chivers		*5th Bn Wiltshire Regiment*	
Service No.	10056	Age:	25
Place of Birth:	Chippenham	Home Country:	England
Date of Death:	09/04/1916	Cause of death:	Died of wounds
Memorial:	Chippenham – St. Andrews Church & Causeway Methodist Church		
War cemetery:	Amara War Cemetery		
Theatre of war:	Mesopotamia		
Next of Kin:	George & Rosanna Chivers		
Address:	1 St Mary's Place, Chippenham		

Edwin, a factory worker was the eldest son of George & Rosanna Chivers and volunteered for service with the 5th Battalion Wiltshire Regiment arriving at Gallipoli in June 1915. In January 1916 Gallipoli was evacuated and the Wiltshires were first sent to Egypt and then on to Mesopotamia arriving at Basra on 29 February 1914. On 6 April 1914 the 5th Wiltshire were at Sannaiyat, North east of Kut-al-Amara in modern day Iraq. At 4.20am the Wiltshires

British troops on the march in Mesopotamia.

advanced toward the Turkish positions and were subjected to enemy sniper and machine gun fire. They also had the darkness and terrain to contend with and on their left was a marsh. The Wiltshires lost their bearings and in the confusion many of the men were seperated from their companies. The main body of the Wiltshires dug in 650 yards from the Turkish positions andgradually the seperated men came in from the front. During the next day many wounded crawled in to the Wiltshires position and two privates, James Nelson and William Price, both won the Distinguished Conduct Medal for collecting wounded members of the Battalion and evacuating them from the battle front. The Wiltshires casualties were 25 killed including their commanding officer, 165 wounded and 40 missing. One of those posted as missing at Sannaiyat on Sunday 9 April 1916 was Edwin and his parents waited anxiously for news. Over eighteen months later in November 1917 George and Rosanna Chivers received the news they hoped would never come that their son Edwin had died of wounds on the same day that he was posted missing. Edwin's brother Sidney had been killed in action in 1914 and his brother Albert would be killed in 1918.

Private Ernest Townsend   *5th Bn Wiltshire Regiment*

Service No.   3/536   Age: 20
Place of Birth: Chippenham   Home Country: England
Date of Death: 09/04/1916   Cause of death: Killed in action
Memorial: Chippenham & St Andrews Church Memorial
War cemetery: Basra Memorial
Theatre of war: Mesopotamia
Next of Kin: Eden & Charlotte Townsend
Address: 55 Wood Lane, Chippenham

Twenty year old Ernest volunteered for service with the 5th Battalion Wiltshire Regiment and arrived at Gallipoli on 22 November 1915. In January 1916 Gallipoli was evacuated and the Wiltshires were first sent to Egypt and then on to Mesopotamia arriving at Basra on 29 February 1914. He was reported missing at Sannaiyat on Sunday 9 April 1916 in the same action as Edwin Chivers. In November 1917 Eden and Charlotte Townsend received the news that their son had been killed in action on the day he was reported missing. Ernest is remembered on the Basra Memorial and has no known grave.

Private Frank Monk   *5th Bn Wiltshire Regiment*
Service No.   18209   Age: 25
Place of Birth: Grittleton, Wiltshire Home Country: England
Date of Death: 09/04/1916   Cause of death: Killed in action
Memorial: Grittleton
War cemetery: Basra Memorial
Theatre of war: Mesopotamia
Next of Kin: Thomas & Arraminta Monk
Address: Alderton Road, Grittleton, Wiltshire

Frank, a farm labourer, was a member of the local lodge of the Wiltshire Working Men's Conservative Benefit Society. He volunteered for service with the either the 1st or 2nd Battalion Wiltshire Regiment and arrived in France on 27 April 1915. It is likely he became ill or was wounded and was evacuated to England and on his recovery sent to the 5th Battalion Wiltshire Regiment. Frank was reported missing at Sannaiyat on Sunday 9th April 1916 in the same action as Edwin Chivers. Thomas and Arraminta Monk contacted the Red Cross society to find out if there son was a prisoner of war but no news was heard. In January 1917 the official news was received that Frank was killed in action on the same day as he was reported missing. He is remembered on the Basra Memorial and has no known grave. Franks brother John was to be killed in action in September 1916 while fighting at the Somme, France.

Private William Sutton   *5th Bn Wiltshire Regiment*
Service No.   18425   Age: 17
Place of Birth: Corsham   Home Country: England
Date of Death: 09/04/1916   Cause of death: Killed in action
Memorial: Hardenhuish Church Memorial
War cemetery: Basra Memorial
Theatre of war: Mesopotamia
Next of Kin: John & Elizabeth Sutton
Address: Allington, Wiltshire

Seventeen year old under age soldier William volunteered for service with the 5th Battalion Wiltshire Regiment at the age of 16 years and arrived at Gallipoli on 17 November 1915. In January 1916 Gallipoli was evacuated and the Wiltshires were first sent to Egypt and then on to Mesopotamia arriving at Basra on the 29 February 1914. He was killed in action at Sannaiyat on Sunday 9th April 1916 in the same action as Edwin Chivers. He is remembered on the Basra Memorial and has no known grave.

Private Alfred Tom Drew   *5th Bn Wiltshire Regiment*
Service No.   18408   Age: 27
Place of Birth: Wick, Wiltshire   Home Country: England
Date of Death: 09/04/1916   Cause of death: Killed in action
Memorial: West Kington
War cemetery: Basra Memorial
Theatre of war: Mesopotamia
Next of Kin: Thomas & Edith Annie Drew
Address: West Kington Wick, Wiltshire

Alfred, a farm labourer, volunteered for service with the 5th Battalion Wiltshire Regiment and arrived at Gallipoli on 2 October 1915. In January 1916 Gallipoli was evacuated and the Wiltshires were first sent to Egypt and then on to Mesopotamia arriving at Basra on 29 February 1914. He was posted as missing at Sannaiyat on Sunday 9th April 1916 in the same action as Edwin Chivers. Some time later Alfred was officially reported to have been killed in action on the day he was reported missing. He is remembered on the Basra Memorial and has no known grave.

Private Frederick James Drewett   *8th Bn Royal Welsh Fusiliers*
Service No.   24098   Age: 19
Place of Birth: Kington Langley   Home Country: England
Date of Death: 09/04/1916   Cause of death: Killed in action
Memorial: Kington Langley
War cemetery: Basra Memorial
Theatre of war: Mesopotamia
Next of Kin: Stephen & Ellen Maria Drewett
Address: Silver Street, Kington Langley, Wiltshire

Nineteen year old Frederick, a farm labourer, originally volunteered to join the Wiltshire Regiment but was transferred to the 8th Service Battalion Royal Welsh Fusiliers which were part of the 13th Western Division of which the 5th Battalion Wiltshires were a part. He arrived at Gallipoli in July 1915. In January 1916 Gallipoli was evacuated and the 13th Division were first sent to Egypt and then on to Mesopotamia arriving at Basra on 29 February 1914. He was killed in action most likely at Sannaiyat, north east of Kut-al Amara, in modern day Iraq, on Sunday 9 April 1916. He is remembered on the Basra memorial and has no known grave. His brother Leonard Drewett was to die of wounds in March 1918.

2nd Lt Hugh Guy Daniel Clutterbuck   *7th Bn Gurkha Rifles*
Service No   N/a   Age: 22
Place of Birth: Boyton, Wiltshire   Home Country: England
Date of Death: 17/04/1916   Cause of death: Killed in action
Memorial: Corsham
War cemetery: Basra Memorial
Theatre of war: Mesopotamia
Next of Kin: Col Hugh F. Clutterbuck & late Mrs Clutterbuck
Address: Dicketts, Corsham, Wiltshire

Hugh was the only son of Col. Hugh and Margaret Clutterbuck and was educated at Harris Hill, Newbury before attending Wellington College where he joined the Officer Training Corps. He was a prefect of his house and won the long distance cup for running and in 1910 he left Wellington after passing the entrance examination for the Royal Military Academy Sandhurst. Hugh did not go to Sandhurst but accompanied his family to Ceylon in 1911 joining the Ceylon Planters' Rifles. At the outbreak of the Great War the Ceylon Planters' were mobilized and sent to Cairo. Hugh was given a commission on 20 January 1915 with the Indian Army and attached to the Infantry. At the beginning of April 1915 he arrived in Mesopotamia, modern day Iraq and took part in all actions until 1 August 1915 when he was evacuated to India. He returned to Mesopotamia on 7 December 1915 and was with the force that set out for the relief of Kut Al Amara. Around 24 February 1916 Hugh was severely wounded while crossing the Tigris at the Shurman Loop but after his recovery rejoined his unit in April 1916. He was involved in fighting against Turkish forces on 16 and 17 April and on the morning of the

*Private memorial to Hugh Clutterbuck
at St. Nicholas Church, Hardenhuish*

18 April he was missing. On 21 April 1916 Hugh's Colonel wrote:

"In the attack on the Bait Isa *trenches on the 17 April he did splendidly, and was still alive and well up to the evening of the 17 April when the Turks counter attacked; since then nothing definite can be heard of him."*

In October 1916 Hugh's Colonel gained information that Hugh was killed on the night of 17 April 1916. He is remembered on the Basra Memorial and has no known grave.

Gunner Ladas Harcourt Hancock		*60th Howitzer Bty Royal Field Artillery*	
Service No.	71111	Age:	21
Place of Birth:	Chippenham	Home Country:	England
Date of Death:	18/04/1916	Cause of death:	Died of wounds
Memorial:	Chippenham & St Andrews Church Memorial		
War cemetery:	Basra Memorial		
Theatre of war:	Mesopotamia		
Next of Kin:	Alfred Joseph & Alice Hancock		
Address:	Chestnut Cottage, 79 Wood Lane, Chippenham		

Ladas, an auxiliary postman, was the youngest son of Alfred and Alice Hancock. He enlisted with the Royal Artillery on 18 November 1912, most likely due to lack of work, at the age of eighteen years and one month. In October 1913 his commanding officer described his character stating:

"He is stupid, he does what he is told to the best of his ability."

At the outbreak of hostilities Ladas went to France with the 2nd Division arriving on the continent on 16 August 1914 and took part in every action from Mons to Loos. On one occasion he was the only man left at the gun he was working, all his comrades being killed. He was eventually granted leave and brought home a piece of fuse which had killed his captain, who had been standing close by him at the time. Ladas spent sixteen months in France and after a short leave he was drafted to Mesopotamia landing at Basra in modern day Iraq in January 1916 with the 13th Western Division of which the 5th Battalion Wiltshires were a part. He was wounded while fighting Turkish forces most likely near Sannaiyat, north east of Kut-al Amara, in Modern day Iraq, and succumbed to his wounds on Tuesday 18 April 1916. Ladas had been a member of the Wesleyan Sunday School in Chippenham and was one of five boys in a class who had been taught by Miss May Beaven and at this time only one was left alive. A memorial service was held at the Wesleyan Chapel, Chippenham and the Rev. Watson referred to:

"The terrible toll in human life which this war was exacting."

Ladas is remembered on the Basra Memorial and has no known grave

Private James Egbert Wilkins   *5th Bn Wiltshire Regiment*

Service No.	10073	Age:	30
Place of Birth:	Clack (Bradenstoke)	Home Country:	England
Date of Death:	18/04/1916	Cause of death:	Killed in action
Memorial:	Christian Malford		
War cemetery:	Basra Memorial		
Theatre of war:	Mesopotamia		
Next of Kin:	Benjamin & Sarah Jane Wilkins		
Address:	Avon Lane, Kellaways, Wiltshire		

After the death of his father in 1912 James, a farm labourer, supported his mother. At the outbreak of war he volunteered for service with the 5th Battalion Wiltshire Regiment and arrived at Gallipoli in July 1915. In January 1916 Gallipoli was evacuated and the Wiltshires were first sent to Egypt and then on to Mesopotamia arriving at Basra on 29 February 1916. On 16 April 1916 the Wiltshires took part in the Capture of the Bait Isa line, part of the Es Sinn defenses supporting the Sanniyat position on the opposite bank of the Tigris River. On the night of the 16-17 April 1916 the Turkish forces committed their reserves launching a counter attack to retake Bait Isa The counter attack took place as the Wiltshires were preparing to attack further Turkish defensive positions. The British and Indian divisions involved maintained control of Bait Isa but their plan for further advances was stalled. James was one of eleven members of the Wiltshires to be killed in action on Tuesday 18 April 1916. He is remembered on the Basra Memorial and has no known grave.

Lance Coporal William Augustus Marks   *7th Bn Gloucestershire Regiment*

Service No.	8420	Age:	27
Place of Birth:	Corsham, Wiltshire	Home Country:	England
Date of Death:	21/04/1916	Cause of death:	Killed in action
Memorial:	Corsham – North Wraxall		
War cemetery:	Basra Memorial		
Theatre of war:	Mesopotamia		
Next of Kin:	Alfred & Bertha E Marks		
Address:	Haskings Road, Corsham, Wiltshire		

Regular soldier William was serving in Tientsin, China with the 2nd Battalion Gloucestershire Regiment at the outbreak of hostilities and returned to England arriving in Southampton on 8 November 1914. The 2nd Gloucesters arrived in France on 19 December 1914 and at some time William was evacuated to England after either being wounded or suffering from illness or disease. On his recovery he was transferred to the 7th Battalion Gloucestershire Regiment and sent to serve in Mesopotamia, modern day Iraq. He was killed in action during fighting against Turkish forces near Sanniyat on Friday 21 April when the British were attempting to relieve the British Garrison at Kut Al Amara, Iraq. He is remembered on the Basra Memorial and has no known grave.

Lance Coporal Reginald Daly   *1st Bn Seaforth Highlanders*
Service No.   S/9502   Age: 25
Place of Birth: Marlborourgh   Home Country: England
Date of Death: 22/04/1916   Cause of death: Killed in action
Memorial: Newport
War cemetery: Basra Memorial
Theatre of war: Mesopotamia
Next of Kin: John & Mary A Daly
Address: 1 Morden Road, Newport, Gwent

Reginald, a regular soldier, was the youngest son of John & Mary Daly, John was a police superintendent and the family lived at the Police Station at 25 New Road, Chippenham. It is likely Reginald volunteered for service joining the 1st Battalion Seaforth Highlanders and was sent to Mesopotamia in modern day Iraq arriving in January 1916. The Seaforth Highlanders became part of the 7th Indian Division and on the morning of 21 April 1916 they attacked Turkish positions at Istabulat Station, in modern day Iraq. It is likely Reginald was killed in action during this attack. He is remembered on the Basra Memorial and has no known grave.

Private Frederick Orlando Goulding   *1st Bn Ox &Bucks Light Infantry*
Service No.   21701   Age: 22
Place of Birth: Sherston, Wiltshire   Home Country: England
Date of Death: 28/04/1916   Cause of death: Killed in action
Memorial: St. Andrew's Church Memorial
War cemetery: Basra Memorial
Theatre of war: Mesopotamia
Next of Kin: William & Dorothy Goulding
Address: Pipsmore Cottage, Chippenham

Farm labourer Frederick was the fifth son of William and Dorothy Goulding. He volunteered for service with the 1/4th Wiltshire Regiment and was sent to India to replace regular units who were needed for the war. While in India he volunteered to serve in Mesopotamia and was attached to the 1st Battalion OX & Bucks Light Infantry. He was killed in action while fighting the day before the British Garrison at Kut el Amara in modern day Iraq, was surrendered to Turkish forces . He is remembered on the Basra Memorial and has no known grave. His brother Frank Goulding was killed at Gallipoli in August 1915.

Private Henry Godfrey Vincent Chapman   *1/4th Bn Somerset Light Infantry*
Service No.   2601   Age: 20
Place of Birth: Corsham   Home Country: England
Date of Death: 05/05/1916   Cause of death: Died of wounds
Memorial: Corsham & Secondary School Memorial Chippenham
War cemetery: Amara War Cemetery
Theatre of war: Mesopotamia
Next of Kin: Frederick Jeffery & Maggie Chapman

Address: The Cleeve, Corsham, Wiltshire

Henry, known as Harry and an estate clerk, was the eldest son of Frederick and Maggie Chapman and enlisted with the army joining the 1/4th Battalion Somerset Light Infantry. The 1/4th Somersets arrived at Bombay on 9 October 1914 and landed at Basra in modern day Iraq on 23 February 1916. It is likely he was wounded in action in April 1917 and succumbed to his wounds at a military hospital at Amara Iraq on Friday 5 May 1916.

31 MAY 1916 - THE BATTLE OF JUTLAND

Able Seaman Frank Beaven   *HMS Queen Mary Royal Navy*
Service No   J/6136   Age: 23
Place of Birth: Chippenham   Home Country: England
Date of Death: 31/05/1916   Cause of death: Killed in action
Memorial: Chippenham & St Andrews Church Memorial
War cemetery: Portsmouth Naval Memorial
Theatre of war: At Sea
Next of Kin: William & Rebecca Beaven
Address: 46 Victoria Buildings, London Road, Chippenham

Frank joined the Royal Navy prior to the Great War. On Wednesday 31 May 1916 he was serving on the HMS Queen Mary which at the time was one of the fastest and most accurate firing British battleships. The Queen Mary was involved in the largest last major sea battle of the Great War off the Danish coast at Jutland. At around 5.25am the Queen Mary was in action and under fire from the German Ships, Seydlitz and Derfflinger. A little after a tremendous explosion with red flame occurred breaking the Queen Mary in two and throwing the roofs of her turrets 100 feet in the air. All but the stern section with the propellers still turning disappeared and a further explosion then took place sinking the stern section. There were only eight survivors and Frank was one of the 1,266 crew to be lost. He is remembered on the Portsmouth Naval Memorial.

Stoker 1st Class George Stevens   *HMS Black Prince Royal Navy*
Service No.   SS/101473   Age: 29
Place of Birth: Lacock   Home Country: England
Date of Death: 31/05/1916   Cause of death: Killed in action
Memorial: Lacock Church & Lacock
War cemetery: Portsmouth Naval Memorial
Theatre of war: At sea
Next of Kin: Eva Stevens (wife) - Joseph & Susannah Stevens (parents)
Address: Bradford on Avon – Lacock

George, a gardener, married Eva Morris at the beginning of 1915 most likely prior to joining the navy. He was posted as missing when H.M.S. Black Prince was sunk during the battle of Jutland on Wednesday 31 May 1916. Later it was assumed he had been killed and he was one of 857 lives lost when the Black Prince sank. He is remembered on the Portsmouth Naval Memorial.

Arthur Tom Humphries

5 JUNE 1916 - LORD KITCHENER IS DROWNED AFTER HMS HAMPSHIRE SINKS AFTER HITTING A MINE

Private Arthur Tom Humphries   *5th Bn Wiltshire Regiment*

Service No.	18379	Age:	18
Place of Birth:	Kington Langley	Home Country:	England
Date of Death:	17/06/1916	Cause of death:	Died
Memorial:	Kington St Michael		
War cemetery:	Basra War Cemetery		
Theatre of war:	Mesopotamia		
Next of Kin:	Arthur & Margaret Humphries		
Address:	Sebastopol Place, Kington St Michael, Wiltshire		

Eighteen year old under age soldier Arthur was the youngest son of Arthur and Margaret Humphries. It is likely he volunteered for service arriving at Basra in Mesopotamia in modern day Iraq in the early months of 1916. He died most likely of illness or disease on Saturday 17 June 1916.

Lance Coporal Reginald Tucker   *26th Bn Royal Fusiliers*

Service No.	20257	Age:	25
Place of Birth:	Chippenham	Home Country:	England

Date of Death: 18/06/1916   Cause of death: Killed in action
Memorial: Chippenham - St Andrews Church Memorial & Liberal Club Memorial.
War cemetery: Hyde Park Corner Royal Berks Cemetery
Theatre of war: Belgium
Next of Kin: Jonah & Elizabeth Tucker
Address   Kenilworth 98 Sheldon Road, Chippenham

Reginald, a miller's clerk, volunteered for service with the 26th Service Battalion Royal Fusiliers who were composed mainly of bank clerks and accountants. The 26th Royal Fusiliers arrived in France on 4 May 1916 and were sent for further training in what was considered to be a quiet part of the front at Ploegsteert Belgium. Reginald was the only member of the Royal Fusiliers to be killed on Sunday 18 June which may indicate he was killed by a sniper. Reginald's brother Percy was to be killed at the Somme in September 1916. In June 1917 Reginald's family inserted the following memoriam in a local paper:

Only a step removed
And that step into the bliss
Our own our dearly loved
Whom here on earth we miss
Only a step removed
We soon again shall meet
Our own our dearly loved
Around the Saviours feet

Private Edwin Frank Scammell   *1/4th TF Bn Wiltshire Regiment*
Service No.   200991   Age: 23
Place of Birth: Lanhill, Wiltshire   Home Country: England
Date of Death: 21/06/1916   Cause of death: Died
Memorial: Chippenham - St. Andrew's - St. Paul's - Causeway Methodist -Liberal Club Memorials
War cemetery: Baghdad North Gate War Cemetery
Theatre of war: Mesopotamia
Next of Kin: James & Emily Scammell
Address: Lanhill, Yatton Kennel, Wiltshire

Edwin was a farm labourer and a territorial soldier. On 14 October 1914 the 1/4th Battalion Wiltshire Regiment were sent to India on garrison duties to allow regular British army units be released for war service. They arrived in Bombay, India on 9 November 1914. In May 1915 a call was made for volunteers to fight with the Dorset Regiment in Mesopotamia, modern day Iraq Edwin stepped forward and arrived at Basra on 25 May 1915. It is likely Edwin was captured by Turkish forces during fighting at Kut-al-Amara. The prisoners of war were marched northwards to Baghdad and in general were treated very badly by their Turkish captors who took much of their clothing and gave their prisoners little food or water. It is likely Edwin became ill during this march and died of illness or disease.

> *24 JUNE 1916 - A WEEK LONG BRITISH ARTILLERY BOMBARDMENT COMMENCED*

7
THE SOMME

Rifleman Reginald William Davies		*5th Bn London Regiment*	
Service No.	301369	Age:	29
Place of Birth:	Bath, Somerset	Home Country:	England
Date of Death:	01/07/1916	Cause of death:	Killed in action
Memorial:	Chippenham & St. Paul's Church Memorial		
War cemetery:	Gommecourt British Cemetery No2 Hebuterne		
Theatre of war:	France		
Next of Kin:	Stephen & Eleanor Davies		
Address:	7 St. Paul Street, Chippenham		

Shop assistant Reginald was the eldest son of Stephen and Eleanor Davies and prior to the Great War he lived at Kingston on Thames, Surrey. Reginald volunteered for service joining the 5th London Regiment and arriving in France on 17 October 1915. On the first day of the Battle of the Somme the 5th Londons were in trenches south west of Gommecourt , France. At 7.20am smoke was released to cover the attacking troops and the 5th Londons advanced. When they reached the German wire they found much of it had been cut and the first and second line of German trenches were captured with little loss of life. The third line was then attacked and was only taken after hard fighting but by 2pm the third line had been lost to German counter attacks and by 9.30pm the majority of the 5th Londons were back at their start point from the morning suffering heavy casualties while falling back through no mans land. Reginald was one of 268 members of the 5th Londons to die on Saturday 1 July 1916.

Rifleman Gilbert Arthur Robbins		*5th Bn London Regiment*	
Service No.	300223	Age:	25
Place of Birth:	Chippenham	Home Country:	England
Date of Death:	01/07/1916	Cause of death:	Killed in action
Memorial:	Not known		

War cemetery	Thiepval Memorial
Theatre of war:	France
Next of Kin:	Samuel Arthur & Melinda Jane Robbins
Address:	The Grove, Slough, Berkshire

Gilbert, an assurance clerk, was living in London prior to the war and at the outbreak of hostilities he volunteered for service with the 5th London Regiment arriving in France on 4 November 1914. On the first day of the Battle of the Somme the 5th Londons were in trenches south west of Gommecourt France. At 7.20am smoke was released to cover the attacking troops and the 5th Londons advanced, see Reginald Davies. Gilbert was posted as missing in action and it was later presumed that he had been killed in action on the day he was reported missing. He is remembered on the Thiepval Memorial which today bears the names of over 72,000 men declared missing at the Somme.

Corporal Anthony George Greenway		*10th Bn Yorkshire Light Infantry*	
Service No.	16472	Age:	34
Place of Birth:	Great Somerford	Home Country:	England
Date of Death:	01/07/1916	Cause of death:	Killed in action
Memorial:	Great Somerford		
War cemetery:	Gordon Dump Cemetery Ovillers La Boisselle		
Theatre of war:	France		
Next of Kin:	Annie Greenway (wife) - Thomas & Hester Greenway (parents)		
Address:	Glen View Fritchley Ambergate, Derby, Deryshire - Great Somerford		

Anthony, known as George and a coal miner, was the eldest son of Thomas and Hester Greenway. In 1901 he married his wife Annie and the couple moved to the coalfields of the north of England. George volunteered for service with the 10th Service Battalion Yorkshire Light Infantry and arrived in France on 11 September 1915. The 10th Yorkshire light infantry then took part in the Battle of Loos after which it was withdrawn from the line and sent for further training at Armentieres before continuing service in the front line. On the first day the of the Battle of the Somme on Saturday 1 July 1916 the 10th Yorkshire Light Infantry were attacking German positions north of Fricourt, France. After an initial break through of two companies to the position of Red Cottage the following companies of the 10th Yorkshire Light Infantry were met with German machine gun fire and almost wiped out before they reached the enemy front line. The men at Red Cottage were over whelmed on the morning of 2 July by German attacks. George was one of 156 men of the 10th Yorkshire Light Infantry to be killed or die from wounds on the first day at the Battle of the Somme. He left a widow and a young son.

Private Reginald Stanley James		*12th Bn Middlesex Regiment*	
Service No.	G/6218	Age:	22
Place of Birth:	Castle Combe, Wiltshire	Home Country:	England
Date of Death:	01/07/1916	Cause of death:	Died of wounds
Memorial:	Castle Combe		
War cemetery:	Dive Copse British Cemetery Sailly Le Sec		
Theatre of war:	France		
Next of Kin:	Frederick John & ELizabeth James		
Address:	Castle Combe, Wiltshire		

Reginald, a gardener, volunteered for service with the 10th reserve Hussars with Harold Melsom also from Castle Combe. Reginanld's original service number being 14335 and Harold's was 14334. They both transferred to the 12th Service Battalion Middlesex Regiment, arriving in France on 25 July 1915. On Saturday 1 July 1916 on the first day of the Battle of the Somme the 12th Middlesex were at Carnoy, in reserve most likely used for carrying duties and it is probable Reginald was wounded by German shell fire. He was evacuated to one of the field ambulances at Sailly Le Sec, where he succumbed to his wounds. Harold Melsom was to be killed four days later

Private Edgar George Vines   *2nd Bn Wiltshire Regiment*

Service No.	8644	Age:	23
Place of Birth:	Chippenham	Home Country:	England
Date of Death:	01/07/1916	Cause of death:	Killed in action
Memorial:	Swindon		
War cemetery:	Peronne Road Cemetery Maricourt		
Theatre of war:	France		
Next of Kin:	Charles William & Mary Elizabeth Vines		
Address:	3 Grove Cottgaes Drove Road, Swindon, Wiltshire		

During the Great War Edgar, his brother William and their father Charles all served in the Army. William a regular with the Dorset Regiment, Charles with the Wiltshire territorials in India and Edgar a regular with the 2nd Battalion Wiltshire Regiment arriving on the continent on 7 November 1914. Edgar's mother Mary moved to Chippenham during the war living at Baydons Lane. On Saturday 1 July 1916 the Wiltshires were in reserve near Cambridge Copse northwest of Maricourt. Three companies were on carrying duties to supply the attacking troops and the other D Company was sent to the British front line trenches. When the position of Moutauban had been taken by the attacking British troops the Wiltshires spent the day and night carrying water, rations and material to the forward troops under German shell fire. It is likely Edgar was killed while carrying these supplies forward. His brother William was a prisoner of war of the Turks and died of illness or disease while in captivity in Mesopotamia modern day Iraq on New Years Eve 1916.

Private Francis Edward Porter   *2nd Bn Wiltshire Regiment*

Service No.	8574	Age:	24
Place of Birth:	Great Somerford, Wiltshire	Home Country:	England
Date of Death:	02/07/1916	Cause of death:	Killed in action
Memorial:	Great Somerford		
War cemetery:	Thiepval Memorial		
Theatre of war:	France		
Next of Kin:	Maurice & Elen Porter		
Address:	Park Lane, Great Somerford, Wiltshire		

Regular soldier Francis, known as Edward, was well known in Great Somerford and had for some years been the organ blower, but because of his high spirits and love of fun it was often to the detriment of the choir boys behaviour. He joined the 2nd Battalion Wiltshire Regiment and at the outbreak of war was serving in India. The Wiltshires returned to England and were then landed at Zeebrugge on 7 October 1914 where Edward was wounded in the leg by a piece of shell and evacuated to England. Recovery from his leg wound was to take many months and during his convalescents he was placed with a reserve battalion. At the start of 1916, by his own request, Edward returned to the front. During the early hours of Sunday 2 July 1916 the Wiltshires were still on carrying duties when at about 3.30am orders were received to reinforce British troops at the north end of Moutauban. All through the day the Wiltshires were subjected to heavy German shell fire. The Germans had attacked from Bernafay Wood and during British artillery attempted unsuccessfully to set fire to the wood with an experimental Thermite Barrage. Edward was killed in action and is today remembered on the Thiepval Memorial. He has no known grave.

Lance Corporal Fred Purbrick   *2nd Bn Wiltshire Regiment*
Service No.   18878   Age: 31
Place of Birth: Patchway, Glocestershire   Home Country: England
Date of Death: 02/07/1916   Cause of death: Killed in action
Memorial: Castle Combe
War cemetery: Thiepval Memorial
Theatre of war: France
Next of Kin: Mabel Beatrice Purbrick (wife)
Address: Salutation Lodge, Burton, Wiltshire

For eleven years Fred, a carter, had been in the employee of Mr Cryer of the Gibb and in 1904 he married Mable Beatrice M. King. In February 1915 he volunteered for service with the 3rd Battalion Wiltshire Regiment and was then transferred to the 2nd Battalion Wiltshire Regiment. In January 1916 he was promoted to Lance Corporal and in May 1916 he arrived in France. In mid July 1916 Mabel Purbrick received the following letter from Sergeant Clyde of the Wiltshires, dated 5 July 1916:

"With deep regret I have to let you know that Lance Corporal Purbrick was killed in action on the 3rd of this month and is greatly missed by all his comrades. But it gives me the honour of letting you know that your husband was one of the brave men from Wiltshire, for he died upholding the honour of his King and Country. Lance Corporal Purbrick was greatly admired by all officers and men of the 2nd Battalion Wiltshire Regiment, and I myself found him very reliable and one hard to replace. From all his comrades especially the Lewis Gun Section, I through them express their great sympathy in your loss. May God guard you in the future, I do not belong to Wiltshire, but it is a pleasure to have such men under one as Lance Corporal Purbrick, he was killed serving the gun to the very end, and he was only one of the many upholding the honour of the Wiltshire men. That very evening I got a party of men to dig the grave, and buried him and placed the cross over his grave. Not being in holy orders I could not read the burial service, so I called all men present to attention and saluted poor lance Corporal Purbrick for the last time, for he was a soldier and a man. I myself have gathered his personal belongings and shall forward to you at an early date, including his regimental badge."

Fred was killed during his first action at the front, it is most likely he was killed on 2 July at the north end of Moutauban in the same action as Francis Edward Porter, as the Wiltshire were relieved on the evening of 2 July. Fred's grave was lost in later fighting and today he is remembered on the Thiepval Memorial. He left a widow and four children.

Lance Corporal Arthur Frederick Clark   *6th Bn Wiltshire Regiment*
Service No.   9109   Age: 21
Place of Birth: Norton St Philip, Somerset   Home Country: England
Date of Death: 02/07/1916   Cause of death: Killed in action

Memorial: Langley Burrell
War cemetery: Gordon Dump Cemetery Ovillers La Boisselle
Theatre of war: France
Next of Kin: Roland & Edith Clark
Address: Hill Corner, Langley Burrell, Wiltshire

Twenty one year old Arthur volunteered for service with the 6th Battalion Wiltshire Regiment and arrived in France on 19 July 1915, taking part in the Battle of Loos in September 1915. At 4pm on Sunday 6 July 1916 the 6th Wiltshires attacked German trenches to the South of La Boisselle at the Somme. Arthur was one of 60 members of the 6th Wiltshires killed or died of wounds on that day.

Private George Neate   *D Coy 1st Bn Wiltshire Regiment*
Service No.   18360   Age: 22
Place of Birth: Slauhterford, Wiltshire   Home Country: England
Date of Death: 05/07/1916   Cause of death: Killed in action
Memorial: North Wraxall
War cemetery: Thiepval Memorial
Theatre of war: France
Next of Kin: George & Alice Maude Mary Neate
Address: Ford, Wiltshire

George was a cutter boy employed in the paper mill at Slaughterford and the eldest son of George & Alice Neate. He volunteered for service with the 1st Battalion Wiltshire Regiment and arrived in France on 22 June 1915. At 4pm on Wednesday 5 July the Wiltshire moved forward into an old German trench at the Liepzig Salient which was south west of Thiepval, with a view to attacking the strongly defended Hindenburg which formed part of the German 2nd line. C and D Companies were selected for the attack. The attack was to take place at 7pm and 30 seconds before there was an intense British Artillery bombardment supported by Stokes Mortars. The Wiltshires left the trenches in the first wave advancing under heavy machine gun and rifle fire. It is likely George was killed while serving with D Company in this attack. After a tough fight the Wiltshires gained the position but shortly afterward the Germans intensely bombarded their old front line which was occupied by the Wiltshires. The 1st Wiltshires casualties for the day were 20 killed, 22 missing, 158 wounded and 2 missing believed killed. One of those missing was George and in March 1917 his parents received an official notification that he had been killed in action on Wednesday 5 July 1916. He is remembered on the Thiepval Memorial and has no known grave.

Private Harold Melsom   *12th Bn Middlesex Regiment*
Service No.   G/6207   Age: 26
Place of Birth: Castle Combe   Home Country: England
Date of Death: 05/07/1916   Cause of death: Killed in action
Memorial: Castle Combe
War cemetery: Dantzig Alley British Cemetery Mametz
Theatre of war: France
Next of Kin: George & Elizabeth Melsom
Address: Castle Combe, Wiltshire

Harold, known as Harry and an invoice clerk, was the youngest son of George & Elizabeth

Harold Melsom killed at the Somme.

Melsom. He volunteered for service with the 10th Reserve Hussars with Reginald James also from Castle Combe. .Harold's original service number being 14334 and Reginald's was 14335. They both transferred to the 12th Service Battalion Middlesex Regiment, arriving in France on 25 July 1915. On 4 July 1916 the 12th Middlesex were near Caterpillar Wood north of Montauban at the Somme and the 18th Division of which they were a part occupied Marlborough Wood further north during the night meeting no opposition. Harold was one of nine members the 12th Middlesex to die from wounds or be killed in action on Wednesday 5 July 1916. Reginald James had died of wounds 4 days before.

Private Frederick James Tanner		*1st Bn Wiltshire Regiment*	
Service No.	22899	Age:	24
Place of Birth:	Chippenham, Wiltshire	Home Country:	England
Date of Death:	06/07/1916	Cause of death:	Killed in action
Memorial:	Brinkworth		
War cemetery:	Thiepval Memorial		
Theatre of war:	France		
Next of Kin:	Fred Charles & Ruth C Tanner		
Address:	Callow Hill, Brinkworth, Wiltshire		

Frederick, known as Fred and a hairdresser was the eldest son of Frederick and Ruth Tanner who had lived at 73 Wood Lane, Chippenham. It is likely that Fred joined the army under the Derby Scheme which allowed a man to enlist but he would only be called up when he was needed. He arrived in France in the spring of 1916 and on 6 July 1916 was at the Leipzig Salient, south west of Thiepval at the Somme. The Wiltshiures were holding the trench they had captured the previous day and were subjected to German attacks from bombing (hand grenades), trench mortars and rifle grenades and enemy shelling throughout the day. It is likely Fred was one of twenty three members of the 1st Wiltshires killed on this day. He is remembered on the Thiepval Memorial and has no known grave.

Private Edgar Thomas Pearce   *9th Bn West Riding Regiment*

Service No.	11166		Age:	23
Place of Birth:	Chippenham		Home Country:	England
Date of Death:	07/07/1916		Cause of death:	Killed in action

Memorial: Chippenham & St. Andrew's Church Memorial
War cemetery: Gordon Dump Cemetery Ovillers La Boisselle
Theatre of war: France
Next of Kin: Thomas & Agnes Pearce
Address: The Causeway, Chippenham

Edgar, a baker, was the second son of Thomas and Agnes Pearce and volunteered originally with the 8th Service Battalion West Riding Regiment. He arrived on the Gallipoli Peninsular in July 1915 and was either wounded or taken sick with illness or disease and evacuated to England. On his recovery he was transferred to the 9th Service Battalion West Riding Regiment and was sent to serve with them in France. On 7 July 1916 the 9th West Riding Regiment were preparing to attack the German position of the Quadrangle south West of Mametz Wood at the Somme. There was confusion about the start time of the attack and during the delay the British barrage which preceded the attack lifted and as the 9th West Riding Regiment advanced in broad daylight they were cut down by a hail of German machine gun fire from Mametez Wood. Edgar was posted as missing and later it was assumed he had died on Friday 7 July 1916, he was one of 68 men to be killed during the attack.

Private Frederick John Pollard   *1st Bn Wiltshire Regiment*

Service No.	13954		Age:	23
Place of Birth:	Sutton Benger		Home Country:	England
Date of Death:	07/07/1916		Cause of death:	Killed in action

Memorial: Sutton Benger
War cemetery: A I F Burial Ground Flers
Theatre of war: France
Next of Kin: Ernest Walter & Mary Anne Pollard
Address: Sutton Lane, Sutton Benger, Wiltshire

Frederick, known as John and a farm labourer, was well known in Sutton Benger and regularly attended the Church, he had been a member of the choir. He volunteered for service joining the 1st Battalion Wiltshire Regiment and arrived in France on 1 April 1915. He was wounded in action in July 1915 and after his recovery he returned to the front. On 7 July 1916 the 1st Wiltshires were at the Leipzig Salient at the Somme. At 1:15am the Germans mounted a counter attack on the Wiltshires position and the war diary states:

"With great coolness beat off this attack and inflicted heavy casualties on the enemy."

Aided by artillery the attack was beaten off but for the next two hours bombing (hand grenades) exchanges between the Wiltshires and the Germans took place but the Wiltshires gained the upper hand. At 9.30 am the Wilthires then attacked the German lines and after a 30 second intense British artillery and stokes mortar bombardment they successfully captured the German position. At 1pm the Wiltshires attacked another German trench and were then subjected to a five hour German bombardment. The Wiltshires war diary described the casualties as *"enormous"*. One of those killed was John who was buried near where he fell and later moved to the A.I.F. Burial Ground at Flers, France.

Men of the Wiltshire Regiment on their way to the front at the Somme.

Private Albert Edward Millard   *2nd Bn Wiltshire Regiment*

Service No.	18257	Age:	25
Place of Birth:	Stanton St Quentin	Home Country:	England
Date of Death:	08/07/1916	Cause of death:	Killed in action
Memorial:	Chippenham & St. Andrews Church Memorial		
War cemetery:	Thiepval Memorial		
Theatre of war:	France		
Next of Kin:	Charles Emily Millard		
Address:	Lower Stanton, Stanton St Quentin, Wiltshire		

Albert was employed working with horses on a farm and volunteered for service with the 2nd Battalion Wiltshire Regiment arriving in France on 8 June 1915. On 8 July 1916 the 2nd Wiltshires were preparing to attack German positions at Maltz Horn Farm, east of Montauban at the Somme. Two companies, A and D, were moved to the Bricqueterie in reserve and B and C companies were sent to Bernfray Wood where they were to follow the 2nd Yorkshire Regiment on to Trones Wood and attack Maltz Horn trench with 2 companies of a French Regiment who were attacking on the left. When B and C companies reached the south east edge of Bernfray Wood they found the 2nd Yorkshires had been forced back by the enemy. A company in reserve were then ordered to advance across the open and capture German trenches south of Maltz Horn Farm, which they succeeded in doing. At the same time the British artillery bombarded Trones Wood for a second time and at 1pm C and D companies advanced capturing the southern half of Trones Wood which was by now a mass of undergrowth, shell holes and fallen trees. They then established a trench line and during the evening were attacked from the north by small parties of Germans which were beaten off. At midnight the Germans made a strong attack from the north but this was repulsed and the only German success was capturing a Lewis gun and throwing two hand grenades into the Wiltshires line. Albert was one of 51 members of the 2nd Wiltshires to be killed or die of wounds on Saturday 8 July 1916. He is remembered on the Thiepval Memorial and has no known grave.

Sergeant William Sly   *2nd Bn Wiltshire Regiment*
Service No.   8053   Age: 28
Place of Birth: Wootton Bassett, Wiltshire Home Country: England
Date of Death: 08/07/1916   Cause of death: Killed in action
Memorial: Little Somerford
War cemetery: Thiepval Memorial
Theatre of war: France
Next of Kin   William & Elizabeth Sly
Address: Winkwork Cottages, Lea, Wiltshire

Regular soldier William was the eldest son of William and Elizabeth Sly and arrived on the continent on 7 October 1914. He was killed in action on Saturday 8 July 1916 in the same action as Albert Millward. He is remembered on the Thiepval Memorial and has no known grave. His brother was killed at Gallipoli while serving with the Leinster Regiment in August 1915.

Private Thomas Strange   *2nd Bn Wiltshire Regiment*
Service No.   22421   Age: 32
Place of Birth: Little Somerford   Home Country: England
Date of Death: 08/07/1916   Cause of death: Died of wounds
Memorial: Litte Somerford
War cemetery: Thiepval Memorial
Theatre of war: France
Next of Kin: John & Emily Strange
Address: Somerford Hill, Little Somerford, Wiltshire

Thomas had been employed as a gardener for fourteen years in the service of Lord Estcourt at Estcourt House, Shipton Moyne. He was the youngest son of John and Emily Strange and it is likely he joined the army under the Derby Scheme where a man could enlist and the army would call him up when he was needed. Thomas arrived in France in the spring of 1916 and was mortally wounded and succumbed shortly after on Saturday 8 July 1916 in the same action as Albert Millward. He is remembered on the Thiepval Memorial and has no known grave.

Private Arthur Lewis   *2nd Bn Wiltshire Regiment*
Service No.   18233   Age: 25
Place of Birth: Sutton Benger, Wiltshire   Home Country: England
Date of Death: 08/07/1916   Cause of death: Killed in action
Memorial: Sutton Benger
War cemetery: Thiepval Memorial
Theatre of war: France
Next of Kin: Alfred & Annie Lewis
Address: Sutton Benger, Wiltshire

Arthur, a gardeners labourer, was the eldest son of Alfred and Annie Lewis. He volunteered for service with the 2nd battalion Wiltshire Regiment and arrived in France on 4 May 1915. He was killed in action on Saturday 8 July 1916 in the same action as Albert Millward. He is remembered on the Thiepval Memorial and has no known grave.

Private Herbert Jesse Wiltshire   *2nd Bn Wiltshire Regiment*

Service No.	7972	Age:	28
Place of Birth:	Bulkington, Wiltshire	Home Country:	England
Date of Death:	08/07/1916	Cause of death:	Killed in action
Memorial:	Chippenham		
War cemetery:	Bernafay Wood British Cemetery Montauban		
Theatre of war:	France		
Next of Kin:	Jane Drewett		
Address:	Lowden, Chippenham, Wiltshire		

Regular soldier Herbert originally joined the Wiltshire militia on 16 December 1904 at the age of seventeen years and five months. He was the son of John and Jane Wiltshire and after the death of her husband Jane Drewett married James Drewett in 1907. Herbert arrived on the continent on 7 October 1914. Herbert was killed in action on Saturday 8 July 1916 in the same action as Albert Millward.

Private Frederick Mark Wilkins   *2nd Bn Wiltshire Regiment*

Service No.	13979	Age:	18
Place of Birth:	Startley, Wiltshire	Home Country:	England
Date of Death:	09/07/1916	Cause of death:	Killed in action
Memorial:	Great Somerford		
War cemetery:	Bernafay Wood British Cemetery Montauban		
Theatre of war:	France		
Next of Kin:	Frank & Emily Wilkins		
Address:	Great Somerford, Wiltshire		

Under age soldier Frederick volunteered for service with the 2nd Battalion Wiltshire Regiment arriving in France on 1 April 1915. He was killed in action on Saturday 8 July 1916 in the same action as Albert Millward. Frederick is remembered on the Thiepval Memorial and has no known grave.

Refreshment caravans for the walking wounded at the Somme.

Private Arthur Thomas   *6th Bn Wiltshire Regiment*

Service No.	18365	Age:	21
Place of Birth:	Stanton St Quentin	Home Country:	England
Date of Death:	08/07/1916	Cause of death:	Killed in action
Memorial:	Not known		
War cemetery:	Thiepval Memorial		
Theatre of war:	France		
Next of Kin:	Charles & Margaret Thomas		
Address:	Lower Stanton, Stanton St Quentin, Wiltshire		

Farm labourer Arthur volunteered for service with the 6th Battalion Wiltshire Regiment and arrived in France on 30 June 1916. On Saturday 8 July 1916 the 6th Wiltshire were south west of Contalmaison at the Somme and were subject to constant heavy German artillery fire. It is likely Arthur was killed by the German bombardment, he is remembered on the Thiepval Memorial and has no known grave.

Gunner Thomas Percy Snell   *B Bty 51st Bde Royal Field Artillery*

Service No.	61758	Age:	38
Place of Birth:	Corsham	Home Country:	England
Date of Death:	08/07/1916	Cause of death:	Died of wounds
Memorial:	Yatton Keynell		
War cemetery:	Dantzig Alley British Cemetery Mametz		
Theatre of war:	France		
Next of Kin:	William & Agnes Snell		
Address:	Yatton Keynell, Wiltshire		

Thomas, a carter on a farm, volunteered for service joining the Royal Field Artillery and arrived in France on 12 May 1915. It is likely Thomas was killed by German counter battery fire on Saturday 8 July 1916 near Montauban at the Somme, while supporting troops of the 9th Division. In 1917 his family inserted the following memoriam in a local paper:

May the winds of heaven blow softly
O'er that still and silent grave
Where the one we loved so dearly
Gave his life our homes to save

Private Henry Crook   *2nd Bn Wiltshire Regiment*

Service No.	10387	Age:	35
Place of Birth:	Hullavington, Wiltshire	Home Country:	England
Date of Death:	13/07/1916	Cause of death:	Died of wounds
Memorial:	Swindon		
War cemetery:	Abbeville Communal Cemetery		
Theatre of war:	France		
Next of Kin:	Laban and Elizabeth Crook		
Address:	Stonehouse Quarries, Swindon, Wiltshire		

Henry was a cowman on a farm and volunteered for service with the 2nd Battalion Wiltshire Regiment. He arrived in France on 11 December 1914 and it is likely he was wounded during fighting at the Somme earlier in July 1916. He was evacuated to one of the hospitals based at

Abbeville where he succumbed to his wounds on Thursday 13 July 1916.

Private Harry Lucas		*1st Bn Wiltshire Regiment*	
Service No.	10064	Age:	22
Place of Birth:	Chippenham	Home Country:	England
Date of Death:	14/07/1916	Cause of death:	Died of wounds
Memorial:	Chippenham & St. Paul's Church Memorial		
War cemetery:	Millencourt Communal Cemetery Extension		
Theatre of war:	France		
Next of Kin:	Eli & Mary Lucas		
Address:	74 Park Lane, Chippenham		

Harry was a postman and described as bright and cheery, he was a keen footballer and a member of the Rovers team. He was also a regular member of the Men's Own Brotherhood at the Primitive Church. Harry volunteered for service initially joining the 5th Battalion Wiltshire Regiment and arrived on the Gallipoli peninsular in July 1915. He was evacuated to England later in 1915 most likely suffering from illness or disease and after his recovery he was drafted to the 1st Battalion Wiltshire Regiment in France. On 14 July 1916 the 1st Wiltshires were in the old German dugouts 1km west of La Boisselle, France at the position called Usna hill. They were subjected to shelling by German artillery and it is probable Harry was killed during this shelling. In mid August 1916 Harry's parents received the following letter from Sergeant William George Thomas of the platoon to which Harry belonged:

"I feel it is my duty to write and answer the letter which you enclosed in the last parcel which you sent to your son, Harry. In accordance with our usual custom, the contents of the parcel were distributed amongst his old comrades. Although I know that it is impossible for me to comfort you in your great sorrow, I am now trying my best to forward to you the great

Left: Harry Lucas.

Below: A German dugout at La Boisselle at the end of the war.

sympathies of his comrades and myself. When your dear son was killed it seemed to throw a cloud over the whole company to which he belonged. He was always well liked by officers, NCO's and men, and often was the means of cheering many of us up, by his own cheery and pleasant nature. As his platoon sergeant, I was extremely sorry to lose him, as he was one of my best boys, always willing and ready to undertake any duty with a cheery spirit. He was also an extremely plucky and brave boy and is greatly missed by all who knew him. His death was caused through the bursting of a shell and I am thankful to be able to tell you that he suffered no pain, as his death was instantaneous. We buried him in the small cemetery about 3 miles behind the lines and erected a small wooden cross over his grave."

Official records state that Harry died of wounds, but Sergeant Thomas informs us that Harry died instantly. He may have done this to ease the grief of Harry's parents. The cemetery where Harry is buried was used by a dressing station and Harry could have been taken to this dressing station and died of wounds. In July 1919 Harry's parents inserted the following memoriam in a local paper:

Rest well dear son for at the great awakening
When Christ shall call his soldiers to His side
His promise stands there shall be no forsaking
Of those who fought for Him and nobly died
From his loving Mother, Father, Sisters and Brothers

Private Richard Elmes   *D Coy 16th Bn Kings Royal Rifle Corps*
Service No.   R/16894   Age: 21
Place of Birth: Lacock   Home Country: England
Date of Death: 15/07/1916   Cause of death: Died of wounds
Memorial: Lacock Church – Lacock Village St. Andrews Memorial, Chippenham
War cemetery: Thiepval Memorial
Theatre of war: France
Next of Kin: Emily Elmes (wife) - Job & Lucy Elmes (parents)
Address: 2 Parliament Street, Chippenham – Vine Cottage, Wick Lane, Lacock

Twenty one year old labourer Richard volunteered for service with the King's Royal Rifle Corps on 18 November 1915. While on leave he married Emily Strange at St. Mary's Church on Boxing Day 1915 and shortly after the wedding he returned to his unit. He arrived in France on 22 June 1916 and was posted to the 16th Service Battalion King's Royal Rifle Corps part of the 100th Brigade of 33rd Division. On 14 July 1916 the 100th Brigade took up positions between High Wood and Bazentin-le-Petit at the Somme. At 9am on Saturday 15 July 1916 after a 30 minute bombardment they attacked the German position of the Switch Trench south of Martipunch. However the attack was unsuccessful, a German machine gun situated at the western side of the High wood hampered the attack. The 16th King's Royal Rifle Corps was sent in to reinforce the attack and it was during this advance that Richard was posted as missing. By 4pm the 100th Brigade was back at position it had started from in the morning. On 6 September Richard's wife Emily wrote the following letter to the Rifles Record Office:

"I shall be glad if will kindly let me know if any further information has been found concerning the above who was reported missing on July 15th 1916. A report (not official) reached us the other day that he was wounded and taken to the 101st dressing station. Will you kindly provide any news. Thanking you in anticipation for an early reply."

Richard's mother then wrote the following to the army:

"Could you give me any news of my Darling boy as I have not heard from him for a long time and I am nearly worried to death. I shouldn't be so worried if you could give me some tidings of where he is. I hope please god I shall hear some thing of the dear one."

In April 1917 Richard's sister wrote the following letter to the Rifles Record Office:

"I have been advised to write to you concerning my missing brother. My mother is in such a dangerous state of health at present. It has been for some time and the Doctor states that it is the suspense of his fate that is doing her mental harm. He says it may prove fatal if in her condition, if something final is not known of her son. Begging you to do your best for us and thanking you greatly in the anticipation of your kindness"

In June 1917 news was received that Richard was regarded for official purposes as having died on or since Saturday 15 July 1916. He is remembered on the Thiepval Memorial and has no known grave. Richard's mother Lucy passed away at the beginning of 1921 and never discovered the true fate of her son.

Private Robert Barclay		*20th Bn Liverpool Regiment*	
Service No.	22921	Age:	32
Place of Birth:	Liverpool, Lancashire	Home Country:	England
Date of Death:	21/07/1916	Cause of death:	Died of wounds
Memorial:	Not known		
War cemetery:	Bronfay Farm Military Cemetery Bray Sur Somme		
Theatre of war:	France		
Next of Kin:	John & Janet Barclay (parents) – Agnes Barclay (sister)		
Address:	Liverpool, Lancashire - School House, Nettleton		

Robert, a tailor's salesman, was the youngest brother of Agnes Barclay School Mistress of Nettleton and he volunteered for service with the 20th Service Battalion Liverpool Regiment on 10 November 1914. Robert's mother Janet had been living with her daughter in Nettleton

Left: The grave of Janet Barclay at St. Mary's Nettleton & Burton Churchyard and below the inscription remembering her son.

and died in 1911. He arrived in France on 7 November 1915 and on 23 February 1916 he was sent on a trench mortar course and on his return he joined the Liverpools trench mortar battery. In March 1916 he was transferred to the 3rd Army as a signaler and servant to a Lieutenant Laurie. After two bouts of influenza in March and April 1916, and on both occasions he had spells at 96th Field & 97th Field Ambulance, he rejoined his unit on 26 April 1916. He was wounded during fighting at the Somme and evacuated to 142 Field Ambulance where he succumbed to his wounds at on Friday 21 July 1916. His personal property was sent to his sister at Nettleton and consisted of 1 disc, letters and photos and a cigarette case containing four cigarettes. Robert's sister Agnes had the following memoriam inscribed on her mother's headstone:

Robert Barclay, son of Janet and John Barclay, Kings Liverpool Regt. Killed on active service, 21st July 1916, in France.

2nd Lieutenant William Bryan Wood   *B Coy 8th Bn Gloucestershire Regiment*

Service No.	N/a	Age:	21
Place of Birth:	Tytherton, Wiltshire	Home Country:	England
Date of Death:	23/07/1916	Cause of death:	Killed in action
Memorial:	Chippenham - Wotton Under Edge - Private Memorial Tytherton Lucas		
War cemetery:	Thiepval Memorial		
Theatre of war:	France		
Next of Kin:	William Gent & Kate Annie Wood		
Address:	The Hawthorns, 18 Langley Road, Chippenham		

William known as Bryan, was the eldest son of William and Kate Wood and volunteered for service joining the 12th Service Battalion Gloucestershire Regiment. He was given a commission on 25 June 1916 and transferred to 8th Service Battalion Gloucestershire Regiment. At 12.30am on Sunday 23 July 1916 the Gloucesters attacked German positions at International trench north of Bazentin-le-Petit at the Somme. They were halted by German machine gun fire and the attack failed. William is remembered on the Thiepval Memorial and has no known grave.

The Memorial to William Bryan Wood at St. Nicholas' Thytherton Lucas.

Private Albert Kearton   *2nd Bn Wiltshire Regiment*

Service No.	10001	Age:	20
Place of Birth:	Allington, Wiltshire	Home Country:	England
Date of Death:	23/07/1916	Cause of death:	Killed in action
Memorial:	Allington		
War cemetery:	Dantzig Alley British Cemetery Mametz		
Theatre of war:	France		
Next of Kin:	Thomas & Mary Kearton		
Address:	Allington, Chippenham, Wiltshire		

Albert was the youngest son of Thomas and Mary Kearton. He originally volunteered for service with the 5th Battalion Wiltshire Regiment and arrived on the Gallipoli peninsular in July 1915. He was evacuated to England later in 1915 most likely suffering from illness or disease and after his recovery was drafted to the 2nd Battalion Wiltshire Regiment in France. On Sunday 23 July 1916 the Wiltshires were between Bernafray Wood and Trones Wood at the Somme. At 4.30 am the 19th Battalion Manchester Regiment attacked Guillemont and A Company of the 2nd Wiltshires were detailed to support the Manchesters. The attack failed and A Company got no further than the eastern side of Trones Wood. It is likely Albert was killed in Trones Wood in support of this attack, along with five other members of the Wiltshire Regiment.

Private Walter George Brain   *6th Bn Wiltshire Regiment*

Service No.	10000	Age:	22
Place of Birth:	Biddestone	Home Country:	England
Date of Death:	26/07/1916	Cause of death:	Killed in action
Memorial:	Biddestone		
War cemetery:	Flatrion Copse Cemetery Mametz		
Theatre of war:	France		
Next of Kin:	Alfred David Brain & Ellen Eliza Brain		
Address:	Biddestone, Wiltshire		

Twenty two year Walter worked in the saw mills near Biddestone and was the youngest son of Alfred and Ellen Brain. He originally volunteered for service with the 5th Battalion Wiltshire Regiment and arrived on the Gallipoli peninsular in July 1915. He was evacuated to England later in 1915, most likely suffering from illness or disease, and after his recovery he was drafted to the 2nd Battalion Wiltshire Regiment in France. On Wednesday 26 July 1915 the 6th Wiltshires were in the front line near Bazentin-le -Petit, at the Somme. It is likely Walter was killed by a sniper possibly when B Company were wiring in front of the British trenches. His brother Albert was to be killed in April 1917.

Private Harry Vincent Calkin   *17th Bn Welsh Regiment*

Service No.	25521	Age:	23
Place of Birth:	Chippenham	Home Country:	England
Date of Death:	28/07/1916	Cause of death:	Died of wounds
Memorial:	Not known		
War cemetery:	Bethune Town Cemetery		
Theatre of war:	France		
Next of Kin:	John Henry & Amy Elizabeth Calkin		
Address:	Wickham Road, Stockcross, Newbury, Berkshire.		

Harry, a house decorator, was the eldest son of John & Amy Calkin. He volunteered for service with the 17th Service Battalion Welsh Regiment which was a Bantam Regiment which means that the minimum height requirement was reduced to 5 feet. He arrived in France in June 1916. It is likely he was wounded in action in the Lens area while the 17th Welsh were in training in what were known as quiet trenches. He was evacuated to a hospital at Bethune, France, where he died of his wounds on Friday 28 July 1916.

Lance Corporal Gerald Herbert Wooster   *1st Bn East Surrey Regiment*

Service No.   11763   Age: 29
Place of Birth: Chippenham   Home Country: England
Date of Death: 29/07/1916   Cause of death: Killed in action
Memorial: Clyffe Pypard, Wiltshire
War cemetery: Thiepval Memorial
Theatre of war: France
Next of Kin: Walter Henry & Blanche Wooster
Address: Southampton, Hampshire

Gerald was a bank clerk and it is likely he joined the East Surrey Regiment under the Derby Scheme where a man could enlist and would not be called up until the army needed him. He arrived in France in 1916 and on Saturday 29 July 1916 the East Surreys were in trenches between Longueval and Delville Wood known as Devil Wood. They had been subjected throughout the night of the 28/29 July to heavy shelling by German Artillery. Which continued into the morning of 29 July and communication was described as almost impossible. The East Surreys war diary states:

"Many wounded of several days duration are occupying shell holes in and around the village, it is impossible to get them away or even to provide them with the water, which they cry for as one passes. Water is a great difficulty. Many attempts were made to get water up through the barrage but much more was actually required than received."

At 3.30pm the East Surreys were ordered to attack. As they went forward they were met by heavy German machine gun fire and were pinned down unable to move forward or back. After dusk the survivors made their way back to their original positions. Gerald was one of over forty members of the East Surreys to be killed. He is remembered on the Thiepval Memorial and has no known grave.

Private Arthur George Hiscox   *2/4th TF Bn Wiltshire Regiment*

Service No.   1636   Age: 23
Place of Birth: Trowbridge   Home Country: England
Date of Death: 30/07/1916   Cause of death: Died
Memorial: St Andrews Chippenham – Melksham & Trowbridge St. James Church
War cemetery: Basra Memorial
Theatre of war: Mesopotamia
Next of Kin: James & Alice Hiscox
Address: Avondale Road, Melksham, Wiltshire

Twenty three year old Arthur, a labourer, had volunteered to go to India with the Wiltshires to relieve regular regiments. He arrived in Bombay in January 1915 and when a call was made for volunteers to go to Mesopotamia he stepped forward and arrived in what is modern day

Iraq on 28 August 1915. He was attached to the Oxford and Buckinghamshire Light Infantry and was captured by the Turkish forces at the surrender of Kut on 29April 1916. He was one of over 10,000 British and Commonwealth troops marched through the desert, into captivity at Mosul in modern day Iraq. In December 1916 news reached Melksham that Arthur had died of dysentery at Mosel while a prisoner of the Turks and a letter was received via the Red Cross Society in Geneva stating:

"We fear that any word of ours must inevitably prove very inadequate at this time, but we trust that it may be of some slight consolation to you in your sorrow to know from the signature at the end of this document, it is evident that Private Arthur Hiscox received as much medical care and attention as possible under the circumstances from one of his own countrymen, and also that his last moments were passed in the presence of familiar comrades who had shared, we may suppose, at least some weeks of his captivity with him at Mosul. Will you allow us to express our sincere sympathy with you in your sad loss, and our deep regret that your suspense and anxiety should be ended in so sad a manner."

Arthur is remembered on the Basra memorial and has no known grave. In August 1918 his parents inserted the following memoriam in a local paper:

Out in that foreign land
Lies one we all love well
We could not hold his dying hand
We could not say farewell
"Until the Day Breaks"
From his loving Mother, Dad, Sisters and Brothers

Private Henry John Wicks		*14th Bn Royal Warwickshire Regiment*	
Service No.	16694	Age:	27
Place of Birth:	Chippenham	Home Country:	England
Date of Death:	30/07/1916	Cause of death:	Died of wounds
Memorial:	Chippenham		
War cemetery:	Thiepval Memorial		
Theatre of war:	France		
Next of Kin:	Henry John & Mary Anne Wicks		
Address:	36 St Marys Street, Chippenham		

Henry was a teacher with the Royal Institution for Deaf and Dumb Children at Church Road, Edgbaston. It is likely he joined the Royal Warwickshire Regiment under the Derby Scheme where a man could enlist and would not be called up until the army needed him. He arrived in France in 1916 and on Sunday 30 July 1916 he was killed in action when the Warwicks attacked German positions at Delville Wood at the Somme. The Warwicks were pinned down by German machine gun fire and went to ground in shell holes. Henry is remembered on the Thiepval Memorial and has no known grave.

Stoker 1st Class Henry George Morse		*HMS Lasoo Royal Navy*	
Service No.	SS 113560	Age:	22
Place of Birth:	Tonyrefail, Glamorgan	Home Country:	England
Date of Death:	13/08/1916	Cause of death:	Died
Memorial:	Chippenham & St. Andrews Church Memorial		

War cemetery: Plymouth Naval Memorial
Theatre of war: At Sea
Next of Kin: William E & Lucy Morse
Address: 10 Timber Street, Chippenham, Wiltshire

Twenty two year old farm hand Henry joined the Royal Navy. His father, William had died and his mother married William Hemmings. Originally the Laforey class destroyer was to be named HMS Magic, she was renamed HMS Lasoo. The Ship struck a mine off the Maas lightship on Sunday 13 August 1916 and sank. Henry was one of those lost and is remembered on the Plymouth Naval Memorial. In August 1917 Henry's mother inserted the following memoriam in a local paper:

I often sit and think of him
When I am all alone
For memory is the only friend
That grief can call its own
Like ivy on withered oak
All other thing decay
My love for him will still keep green
And never fade away
Ever remembered by his loving Mother

Trooper Herbert Arthur Tanner   *D Squadron Royal Wiltshire Yeomanry*
Service No.   1560   Age: 21
Place of Birth: Chippenham   Home Country: England
Date of Death: 14/08/1916   Cause of death: Accident
Memorial: Chippenham & St Andrews Church Memorial
War cemetery: St Sever Cemetery Rouen
Theatre of war: France
Next of Kin: Frederick Charles & Ruth Tanner
Address: Hazlebury, 73 Englands, Chippenham

Twenty one year old Herbert, known as Bert, was the second son of Frederick and Ruth Tanner and was educated at Westmead School. He had been a member of the Boy Scouts and the Church Lads Brigade, and also had a talent for sketching and painting. He was a keen angler, being a member of the Chippenham Angling Club and had served an apprenticeship as a dentist with Mr T Hamblyn of Chippenham. In February 1915 he volunteered for service with the Royal Wiltshire Yeomanry and after serving in Chippenham he was sent to Tidworth at Easter 1915. At the start of June 1916 the Royal Wiltshire Yeomanry were sent to France and Herbert served at Rouen and later at the front and had written home stating he had some:

"Interesting and exciting time under shrapnel."

Unfortunately Bert was accidentally kicked by a horse and serious complications set in and he was sent to a hospital at Rouen. It was hoped that Bert would make a swift recovery but after a week in hospital his condition worsened and he died soon after. He was buried at Rouen with full military honours. In August 1918 the following memoriam was inserted in a local paper:

Death took thee from us in a foreign land
We were not near to clasp a dying hand

But though parting's left us heart sore and desolate
For thee the hand of death did but unlock the golden gate
And thou hast passed within it's hallowed portal
Whilst we in hopeful sorrow wait blest reunion in the life immortal
Ever lovingly remembered by his Mother, Father, Brothers and Sisters

Corporal Robert Wilton Tuck   *63rd Bty Royal Field Artillery*
Service No.   54425   Age: 31
Place of Birth: Chippenham, Wiltshire   Home Country: England
Date of Death: 15/08/1916   Cause of death: Died of wounds
Memorial: Not known
War cemetery: Baghdad North Gate War Cemetery
Theatre of war: Mesopotamia
Next of Kin: Not Known
Address: Not Known

Regular soldier Robert was serving in India prior to the Great War and arrived in Mesopotamia in modern day Iraq on the 17 November 1914. He was wounded during fighting with Turkish forces at Kut Al Amara and taken into captivity when the British surrendered on 29 April 1916. He succumbed to his wounds while a prisoner of war most likely at Baghdad on Tuesday 15 August 1916. His medals were never applied for and in the 1920's The Records Office made a request for the disposal of his medals which were probably scrapped. While researching Robert I could find no birth record for a Robert Wilton Cook and it is a possibility that he enlisted in the army under an assumed name.

Private Henry Charles Bowsher   *1st Bn Wiltshire Regiment*
Service No.   23742   Age: 26
Place of Birth: Chippenham   Home Country: England
Date of Death: 23/08/1916   Cause of death: Died of wounds
Memorial: Kington Langley
War cemetery: Puchevillers British Cemetery
Theatre of war: France
Next of Kin: Henry & Mary Ann Bowsher
Address: Day's Lane, Kington Langley, Wiltshire

Henry, known as Charles and a farm labourer, was the only surviving son of Henry and Mary Bowsher and it is likely he joined the army under the Derby scheme arriving in France in 1916. He was wounded in fighting at the Somme and evacuated to one of the casualty clearing stations based at Puchevillers north east of Amiens, France, where he succumbed to his wounds on Wednesday 23 August 1916.

Sergeant George John Collins MM   *6th Bn Somerset Light Infantry*
Service No.   10192   Age: 23
Place of Birth: Chippenham   Home Country: England
Date of Death: 27/08/1916   Cause of death: Killed in action
Memorial: Not known
War cemetery: Thiepval Memorial
Theatre of war: France
Next of Kin: George & Mary Collins

Men of the 1st Battalion Wiltshire Regiment displaying captured trophies after their attack on Thiepval on the 25/26 August 1916.

Address: 67 Coronation Avenue, Twerton, Somerset

George, a moulder in an iron factory, was the eldest son of George and Mary Collin. He volunteered for service with the 6th Service Battalion Somerset Light Infantry and arrived in France on 21 May 1915. On Sunday 27 August 1916 the Somersets were in reserve trenches 300 yard in front Berfray Wood at the Somme. One company was sent forward to reinforce the 10th Durham Light Infantry who had driven the Germans out and occupied Edge trench on the right side of Delville Wood. It also allowed a barricade to be placed across the communication trench Ale Alley and left Delville Wood completely in British hands. While assisting the Durhams four members of the Somerset were killed and one of these was George. He is remembered on the Thiepval Memorial and has no known grave.

Sergeant Frank Porter   *1st Bn Wiltshire Regiment*

Service No.   4911   Age: 36
Place of Birth: Neston, Wiltshire   Home Country: England
Date of Death: 28/08/1916   Cause of death: Died of wounds
Memorial: Not known
War cemetery: Puchevillers British Cemetery
Theatre of war: France
Next of Kin: William & Jane Porter
Address: High Street, Hilperton, Wiltshire

Regular soldier Frank arrived in France with the British Expeditionary Force on 14 August 1914. He was wounded in fighting at the Somme most likely in an attack on Thiepval on 25/26 August 1916. Frank was evacuated to one of the casualty clearing stations based at Puchevillers north east of Amiens, France, where he succumbed to his wounds on Monday 28 August 1916. In August 1917 Frank's family inserted the following memoriam in a local paper:

We never knew the pain you bore

We did not see you die
We only know you passed away
And we could not say goodbye
Although the sea divide us
And your grave we cannot see
Let this little token tell
That we still think of thee
Never forgotten by his Mother, Sisters and Brother

Major Ronald Henry Greig DSO		*54th Coy Royal Engineers*	
Service No.	N/a	Age:	40
Place of Birth:	Haselmere, Surrey	Home Country:	England
Date of Death:	28/08/1916	Cause of death:	Killed in action
Memorial:	Private Memorial St. Nicholas Hardenhuish		
War cemetery:	Fricourt British Cemetery		
Theatre of war:	France		
Next of Kin:	Mary Hope Greig (wife)– Lt. Col. Banks & Florence Greig (parents)		
Address:	54 Palace Gardens Terrace, Kensington, London		

Ronald was the Eldest son of Banks and Florence Greig and passed out of The Royal Military Academy Woolwich in 1896 joining the Royal Engineers. He was promoted to Lieutenant in March 1899 and fought in the South African War where he was severely wounded. He took part in the advance at Kimberly, including the actions at Belmont, Enslin and Modder River. Afterwards he served on many operations in various colonies. He was mentioned in dispatches being made a Companion of the Distinguished Service Order and awarded the Queen's Medal with four clasps and the King's Medal with 2 clasps. On 5 October 1909 he married Mary Hope Laetitia Clutterbuck, daughter of Edmund Henry Clutterbuck of Hardenhuish, whose son David was to die as a consequence of the war. He arrived in France with the Royal Engineers on the 20 April 1915 and on Monday 28 August 1916 he was with 54th Company Royal Engineers near Trones Wood at the Somme. During the early hours of the morning he was killed while superintending advanced trench work. He was buried Fricourt British Cemetery and left a widow and three children.

Memorial to Ronald Greig in St. Nicholas Church, Hardenhuish

Private Albert George Daniels   *1st/1st Royal East Kent Yeomanry*

Service No.	1754
Place of Birth:	Hardenhuish, Wiltshire
Date of Death:	30/08/1916
Memorial:	Derry Hill
War cemetery:	Alexandria Hadra War Memorial Cemetery
Theatre of war:	Egypt
Next of Kin:	Tom and Louisa Daniels
Address:	Derry Hill, Wiltshire.

Age:	20
Home Country:	England
Cause of death:	Died

Albert, a gardener, arrived in Egypt in October 1915 and it is likely he served at Gallipoli with the East Kent Yeomanry in a dismounted role. After the evacuation of Gallipoli in January 1916 he returned to Egypt. He died most likely of illness or disease on Wednesday 30 August 1916. He is buried in Alexandria Hadra War Memorial Cemetery, with 1700 other soldiers who died during the Great War.

Corporal Edward James Barrington MM   *12th Bn Royal Fusiliers*

Service No.	5396
Place of Birth:	Sutton Benger
Date of Death:	02/09/1916
Memorial:	Sutton Benger
War cemetery:	Thiepval Memorial
Theatre of war:	France
Next of Kin:	John & Rosa Barrington
Address:	Sutton Benger, Wiltshire

Age:	24
Home Country:	England
Cause of death:	Killed in action

Edward, known as James, volunteered for service with the 12th Service Battalion Royal Fusiliers arriving in France on 1 September 1915. On 2 February 1916 while serving east of Ypres, Belgium, James won the Military Medal for his coolness under fire the citation states:

"The Divisional Commander wishes to bring to the notice of all ranks the exceptionally good work performed by No. 5396, Lance-Corporal E. J. Barrington, 12th Royal. Fusiliers when in charge of a Machine Gun Post, on February 2nd. When his part of the line was shelled and damaged he took charge not only of his own post, but an adjoining post which suffered heavily. He showed gallantry and presence of mind under most trying circumstances and rose to the occasion in a very commendable manner."

After winning the Military Medal James was granted four days home leave, however on his return to the front he was severely wounded and had to have an operation and spent Easter 1916 in hospital. After his recovery he returned to the front and on Saturday 2 September 1916 the 12th Royal Fusiliers were near Delville Wood at the Somme. James was killed in action during a German counter attack and at the end of September 1916 his parent's received the following letter from James's company commander:

"I write to assure you of my deep sympathy with you in the loss of your Son, No 5396, Corporal Barrington, who was killed in action whilst performing his duty with consummate bravery under the following circumstances. On the 2nd inst. we were holding a recently captured trench which was subject to almost incessant shell fire. The enemy launched an unexpected counter attack, in which we were hard pressed from both front and rear. Your Son placed his 'Lewis' machine gun on the parapet and gave us valuable help in driving back the enemy until he was

killed instantaneously by a bullet wound in the head. I cannot tell you what a loss he is to us. As you know his bravery was recognised before by the well-merited decoration he received. It is only a few days since he performed a similar valuable service to his Company, when he remained in a forward trench with his 'Lewis' machine gun after the rest of his team had been either killed or wounded. The fact that he suffered no pain will be some consolation to you. The trench he gave his life for is still ours and likely to be so. My brother Officers desire to be associated with his comrades and myself in assuring you of our sense of loss both his country and you have sustained."

James is remembered on the Thiepval memorial and has no known grave.

Private George Hulbert		*1st Bn Wiltshire Regiment*	
Service No.	18358	Age:	19
Place of Birth:	Chippenham, Wiltshire	Home Country:	England
Date of Death:	03/09/1916	Cause of death:	Killed in action
Memorial:	Chippenham & St Andrews Church Memorial		
War cemetery:	Thiepval Memorial		
Theatre of war:	France		
Next of Kin:	Frederick & Lucy Anne Hulbert		
Address:	29 Wood Lane, Chippenham		

Nineteen year old George would have been underage when he enlisted with the 1st Battalion Wiltshire Regiment and he arrived in France on 5 December 1915. In May 1916 Geroge was wounded suffering from shell shock, we will never know if he recovered or not but it must have been terrible for this young man to return to the trenches. On Sunday 3 September 1916 the 1st Wiltshires were at the Leipzig Salient South of Thiepval and were preparing to attack the Hindenburg trench of the German front line. At 5.10 the British artillery bombarded the German line and the Wiltshires moved into no man's land and formed up fifty yards from their objective. As soon as they left the safety of their trenches they were subjected to German *Whizbang* and machine gun fire. On the right D Company got into the German trench but were wiped out as the British artillery barrage which did not lift in time. By the time the Wiltshires reached their objective their numbers had been depleted and the Wiltshires were forced to withdraw, the attack having failed. George was one of seventeen members of the 1st Wiltshires killed. He is remembered on the Thiepval Memorial and has no known grave.

Private Alfred John Smith		*1st Bn Wiltshire Regiment*	
Service No.	18229	Age:	28
Place of Birth:	Knowle St Giles, Somerset	Home Country:	England
Date of Death:	03/09/1916	Cause of death:	Killed in action
Memorial:	Sutton Benger		
War cemetery:	Thiepval Memorial		
Theatre of war:	France		
Next of Kin:	Evelyn May Smith (wife) - John & Clara Smith (parents)		
Address:	1 Burnt Cottage, Beanacre, Wiltshire - The Turnpike, Christian Malford		

Cowman Alfred married Evelyn May Broom in 1912 and at the outbreak of hostilities he volunteered for service with the 1st Battalion Wiltshire Regiment arriving in France on 4 May 1915. He was wounded by a bullet wound to the chest at the battle of Loos, France and after his recovery he returned to the front and was attached to the Lewis gun section. He was killed in action Sunday 3 September 1916 when the 1st Wiltshires attacked Hindenburg Trench, the same action as George Hulbert. Evelyn Smith had received no details from the War Office concerning her husband's death, so Reverend Westlake of Sutton Benger wrote to Captain Horncastle, Alfred's company commander, who stated that he had heard:

"Private Smith was killed on September 3rd during an attack. He was in the Lewis gun section and while moving from one shell hole to another in front of the trench was hit in the side and died almost immediately. Please convey to his family my deepest sympathy."

At the time of his death Alfred had been in France 17 months and left a widow and two tiny children. He is remembered on the Thiepval Memorial and has no known grave.

Captain Eric Robert Donner		*11th Bn Rifle Brigade*	
Service No.	N/A	Age:	21
Place of Birth:	Camberwell, London	Home Country:	England
Date of Death:	03/09/1916	Cause of death:	Killed in action
Memorial:	Kington Langley		
War cemetery:	Thiepval Memorial		
Theatre of war:	France		
Next of Kin:	Harry Philip & Lilly Donner		
Address:	The Ridge, Kington Langley, Wiltshire		

Twenty one year old Eric, known as Robin, was the twin son of Harry & Lily Donner, he was educated at Warren Hill School and Harrow where he became Head of Mr Kemps House. He was a keen footballer and represented Harrow for two years at association football and at the outbreak of the Great War he enlisted with the East Kent Regiment, known as the Buffs. On 22 October 1914 he was given a commission with the Rifle Brigade and was promoted to full Lieutenant in February 1915 and arrived in France on 21 July. In September 1915 he was given his Captaincy, and was subsequently mentioned in Dispatches. He was killed leading his men on Sunday 3 September 1916 when the 11th Rifle Brigade attacked German positions at Guilemont at the Somme. His commanding officer stated:

"He was in the third line of German trenches, gallantly leading his Company, when he was shot through the spine and dropped dead. When he was in the front line I knew our companies were then all right; I felt absolute security. For a boy just over twenty-one he was phenomenal."

Another officer stated:

"You knew Donner well, so I need not tell you in what universal respect he was held by both Officers and men. His Company was not all that one might desire in many ways, when he took command of it nine months ago. After two or three months, when he had had time to impress his personality on it, it became the best in the Battalion, and more than equal to many companies under the command of regular soldiers of many years' experience."

Colonel Harrington, commanding 11th Rifle Brigade, wrote to Robin's mother stating:

"I had been in command of the nth Battalion until August 25th, when I was wounded, so I was not with the Battalion when they did so brilliantly on the 3rd September. I had many opportunities of appreciating your son's excellent qualities, both as an Officer and a comrade. He was a splendid Company leader and his loss to the Battalion will be very great. He met his

death, as all our best do, as a leader of men in a successful enterprise; but he was of a type that the British Army and the nation, for that matter cannot afford to lose."

Robin left in his will £11532 19s 6d, he is remembered on the Thiepval Memorial and has no known grave.

Private Reginald Frank Bailey		*2/4th TF Gloucestershire Regiment*	
Service No.	201924	Age:	22
Place of Birth:	Hooke, Dorset	Home Country:	England
Date of Death:	04/09/1916	Cause of death:	Died
Memorial:	Not known		
War cemetery:	Loos Memorial		
Theatre of war:	France		
Next of Kin:	Henry & Lucy Alice Bailey		
Address:	Ivy Villa, Bradford Road, Trowbidge,		

Reginald known as Frank was the third son of Henry and Lucy Bailey and worked on his fathers Farm. He enlisted with the army joining the 2/4th Battalion Gloucestershire Regiment. He took part in the ill fated attack at Fromelles, France in July and it is possible he could have been taken prisoner. He died of illness or disease on Monday 4 September 1916. Frank is remembered on the Loos Memorial and has no known grave. His name also appears on his sisters grave marker in St. Mary the Virgin, Grittleton, Churchyard.

15 SEPTEMBER 1916 - FIRST USE OF THE BRITISH SECRET WEAPON THE "TANK" - GREAT ADVANCES WERE MADE AND A TANK DROVE DOWN THE MAIN STREET OF FLERS

Left: Frank Bailey remembered on his sister's grave marker at St. Mary the Virgin, Grittleton, Churchyard.

Below: A British Tank on the way to the front.

Private George Goodwin Cook   *32193 D Coy MGC Heavy Branch*
Service No.   206158   Age: 28
Place of Birth: Westminster, Middlesex Home Country: England
Date of Death: 15/09/1916   Cause of death: Killed in action
Memorial: Lacock Church – Lacock & Bowden Hill
War cemetery: Thiepval Memorial
Theatre of war: France
Next of Kin: George & Sarah Ann Cook
Address: Bowden Cottage, Lacock, Wiltshire

George was the only son of George & Sarah Ann Cook and originally joined the Machine Gun Corps later volunteering to join the Machine Gun Corp Heavy Branch which was the former name of the Tank Corps. The first use of tanks was at Flers at the Somme, France on Friday 15 September 1916 George was one of nine members of the Tank Corps killed in action most likely when his tank was hit by German shell fire. The British captured over 4,000 Germans during the attack which would eventually change the way battles were fought. George is remembered on the Thiepval Memorial and has no known grave.

Lance Corporal John Monk   *8th Bn Bedfordshire Regiment*
Service No.   20121   Age: 26
Place of Birth: Littleton Drew, Wiltshire Home Country: England
Date of Death: 15/09/1916   Cause of death: Killed in action
Memorial: Grittleton
War cemetery: Thiepval Memorial
Theatre of war: France
Next of Kin: Thomas & Arraminta Monk
Address: Alderton Road, Grittleton, Wiltshire

John, a farm labourer, was a member of the local lodge of the Wiltshire Working Men's Conservative Benefit Society. He volunteered for service with the 8th Battalion Bedfordshire Regiment and arrived in France on 30 August 1915. September 1916 was the first time the British used Tanks and on 15 September 1916 the 8th Bedfords were preparing to attack the German strong point called the Quadrilateral, north east of Guillemont at the Somme. At 6.20am the 8th Bedfords moved forward but were stopped by machine gun fire John was posted as missing in action. Thomas and Arraminta Monk contacted the Red Cross society to find out if their son was a prisoner of war but no news was heard. In January 1917 the official news was received that john was killed in action on the same day as he was reported missing. He is remembered on the Thiepval Memorial and has no known grave. John's brother Frank was killed in action in April 1916 while fighting in Mesopotamia in modern day Iraq.

Lance Corporal Frank Mason   *8th Bn Rifle Brigade*
Service No.   S/14400   Age: 32
Place of Birth: Winchester, Hampshire   Home Country: England
Date of Death: 15/09/1916   Cause of death: Killed in action
Memorial: Not known
War cemetery: Thiepval Memorial
Theatre of war: France
Next of Kin: Edward and Ellen Elizabeth Mason
Address: High St, Lacock, Wiltshire

Frank was the youngest son of Edward and Ellen Elizabeth Mason a housekeeper for Frances Awdry of Lacock. He was posted as wounded and missing while serving with the 8th Battalion Rifle Brigade while attacking German positions at Pint Trench and Tea Support Trench South of Flers at the Somme. The attack commenced at 6.20am on Friday 15 September 1916. The 8th Rifle Brigade were initially held up by a German machine gun then ran into the British barrage. In December 1916 Ellen Mason was officially informed her son had been killed in action on the day he was posted missing. He is remembered on the Thiepval Memorial and has no known grave.

Guardsman Josiah Whitmore   *2nd Bn Grenadier Guards*

Service No.	12178	Age:	35
Place of Birth:	Stoke on Trent, Staffs	Home Country:	England
Date of Death:	15/09/1916	Cause of death:	Killed in action
Memorial:	Castle Combe Church Memorial		
War cemetery:	Guards Cemetery Lesboeufs		
Theatre of war:	France		
Next of Kin:	Ellen Mary Whitmore (wife) - Mary A Whitmore (parent)		
Address:	Castle Combe - Stoke on Trent, Staffordshire		

General labourer Josiah had served in the navy prior to his marriage to Ellen May Daniells in the summer of 1909. He volunteered for service joining the Grenadier Guards and arrived in France on 20 October 1915. At 7.20am on Friday 15 September 1916 the 2nd Grenadier Guards were attacking from Ginchy at the Somme during the Battle of Flers – Courcelette. They were fired on from German forces at Serpentine Trench but managed to enter the German positions and after bombing along the trench they captured the enemy position. Josiah was killed during the attack and later buried in the Guards Cemetery, Lesboeufs, leaving a widow and two children. It is interesting to note he does not appear on Castle Combe Village War Memorial.

Private Victor Clare Tarling   *6th Bn Somerset Light Infantry*

Service No.	11266	Age:	21
Place of Birth:	Lacock, Wiltshire	Home Country:	England
Date of Death:	16/09/1916	Cause of death:	Killed in action
Memorial:	Nettleton		
War cemetery:	Guards Cemetery Lesboeufs		
Theatre of war:	France		
Next of Kin:	Richard & Helen Tarling		
Address:	Nettleton, Wiltshire.		

Twenty one year old Victor, a farm labourer, volunteered for service with the 6th Service Battalion Somerset Light Infantry and arrived in France on 24 July 1915. On 16 September 1916 the 6th Somersets were north of Ginchy at the Somme and were preparing to attack Grid Trench. There was no time for reconnaissance and and they had not been informed about a partially dug trench called XX. At 9.25 the Somersets advanced following the barrage and captured what they thought was Grid Trench but was in fact XX. A new attack was then planned to attack Grid Trench and at 6.55pm the attack went forward behind a weak barrage that the Somersets war diary described as *"very feeble"*. The Somersets were met by German machine gun fire which caused heavy casualties and the attack failed. Victor was assumed to have died during the attack and later his remains were discovered and buried in Guards Cemetery Lesboeufs, which on Saturday 16 September 1916 was still occupied by the Germans.

Sergeant Percy Tucker   *2nd Bn London Regiment*
Service No.   2866   Age: 31
Place of Birth: Chippenham, Wiltshire   Home Country: England
Date of Death: 17/09/1916   Cause of death: Killed in action
Memorial: Chippenham - St Andrews Church Memorial & Liberal Club Memorial
War cemetery: Combles Communal Cemetery Extension
Theatre of war: France
Next of Kin: Jonah & Elizabeth Tucker
Address: Kenilworth, 98 Sheldon Road, Chippenham

Percy was an elementary school teacher at Wimbledon and volunteered for service with the 2nd Battalion London Regiment and arrived in Egypt on 30 August 1915 before landing on Gallipoli. After the evacuation of Gallipoli the 2nd Londons returned to Europe. On 17 September 1916 the 2nd Londons were engaged in at the Battle of Flers – Courcellette. Percy was one of 24 members of the 2nd Londons to be killed in action or die of wounds on Sunday 1 September 1916. Percy's brother Reginald had been killed at Ploegsteert, Belgium, in June 1916.

Private Frederick Henry Keyte   *3rd Coldstream Guards*
Service No.   16789   Age: 32
Place of Birth: Wolverhampton, Staffordshire Home Country: England
Date of Death: 23/09/1916   Cause of death: Killed in action
Memorial: Private Memorial St Mary-le-Strand London
War cemetery: Thiepval Memorial
Theatre of war: France
Next of Kin: Florence Jane Keyte
Address: Melba, Chippenham, Wiltshire

Fredrick had a long career as a manager in the hotels and restaurants industry and was described as a restaurateur and auditor to the trade, which could indicate he was a food & resturant critic. He joined the army most likely under the Derby Scheme and just before he was sent to France he married by special licence Florence Jane Deham at St.Mary-le-Strand church in Westminster. Florence's uncle had been rector of St.Mary-le-Strand and this is likely to be the reason they married at the church. Frederick's fate is best told by an inscription on a plaque almost hidden in the corner of St.Mary-le-Strand church:

"Frederick Harry Keyte. Survivor of the 3rd Coldstream attack outside Ginchy, France on 15th September 1916 in which some 361 of the battalion became casualties from machine guns located in the Sunken Road, but only to lose his life on the 23rd as the Coldstream awaited the next attack."

On 15 September 1916 the 3rd Coldstram Guards attacked north east of Ginchy at the Somme during the Battle of Flers-Courcelette. It is likely that Frederick was killed near Guillemont, the rear area of the Guards Division. He is remembered on the Thiepval Memorial and has no known grave.

Guardsman Willis Spear Robbins   *4th Bn Grenadier Guards*
Service No.   23564   Age: 19
Place of Birth: Chippenham   Home Country: England

Date of Death:	25/09/1916	Cause of death:	Killed in action
Memorial:	Not known		
War cemetery:	Thiepval Memorial		
Theatre of war:	France		
Next of Kin:	Louis & Hannah Sybella Robbins		
Address:	Marlborough, Wiltshire		

Nineteen year old Willis was the grandson of Frederic Robbins who was the proprietor of the Old Southbroom Brewery. He was educated at Marlborough Grammar School after which he went to Canada, but returned to England to join the army. He enlisted with the 4th Battalion Grenadier Guards and arrived in France in 1916. While in the trenches Willis wrote to his mother stating how he had carried with assistance a wounded man out of the trenches and taking him a mile and a half under heavy shell fire. On Monday 25 September 1916 the 4th Grenadiers were involved in the attack on Les Boeufs at the Somme. They were forced to hold the left flank of the attack when the 21 Division failed to capture Grid trench. Willis's company officer stated:

"He died in an action as glorious to our arms as any recorded in the annuals of the regiment, or as our General told us, any in our whole history."

The Company Quarter Master Sergeant also wrote to Willis's mother:

"Your boy received a Christian burial, and all was done for him that was possible."

However one of Willis's comrades summed up his character:

"He was afraid of nothing."

Willis grave was lost in subsequent fighting and he is today remembered on the Thiepval Memorial.

Private George William Tanner			*1st Bn West Yorkshire Regiment*	
Service No.	13227		Age:	29
Place of Birth:	Great Somerford		Home Country:	England
Date of Death:	25/09/1916		Cause of death:	Killed in action
Memorial:	Great Somerford			
War cemetery:	Thiepval Memorial			
Theatre of war:	France			
Next of Kin:	Albert & Alice Tanner			
Address:	Great Somerford, Wiltshire			

George was the only son of Albert and Alice Tanner and volunteered for service most likely with the 9th Service Battalion West Yorkshire Regiment and was sent to Gallipoli arriving at Suvla bay in August 1915. It is likely George was either wounded or suffering from illness or disease and evacuated to England. On his recovery he was transferred to the 1st Battalion West Yorkshire Regiment and was sent to France. On Monday 25 September 1916 the 1st West Yorks took part in the capture of Les Boeufs, at the Somme and were responsible for clearing the southern part of the village of enemy forces. It is likely George was killed while performing this duty, he is remembered on the Thiepval Memorial and has no known grave.

Above: Vimy Memorial

Right : Frank Mortimer Webb

Private Frank Moritmer Webb

		5th Saskatchewan Regiment	
Service No.	147770	Age:	22
Place of Birth:	Chippenham, Wiltshire	Home Country:	Canada
Date of Death:	26/09/1916	Cause of death:	Killed in action
Memorial:	Not known		
War cemetery:	Vimy Memorial		
Theatre of war:	France		
Next of Kin:	Arthur John & Selina Webb		
Address:	302 Bruce Street, Woodstock, Ontario		

Frank, a tinsmith, emigrated to Canada with his family before the Great War. He was the eldest son of Arthur and Selina Webb who had lived at 27 Park Field, Chippenham. He was a member of the militia and had served with the 34th Fort Garry Horse and on 9 July 1915 he volunteered to serve with the Canadian Army. He arrived in France on 13 March 1916 and on Tuesday 26 September 1916 the 5th Battalion were attacking Zollern trench east of Coucelette at the Somme. The trench was captured and then the attack was pressed on to Hessian Trench and it is likely Frank was killed during this attack. He is today remembered on the Vimy Memorial which bears the names of over 11,000 Canadian servicemen who died in France during the Great War and have no known grave.

Gunner Francis John Pullen

		24th Siege Bty Royal Garrison Artillery	
Service No.	27771	Age:	28
Place of Birth:	Box	Home Country:	England
Date of Death:	30/09/1916	Cause of death:	Killed in action
Memorial:	Not known		
War cemetery:	Bernafay Wood British Cemetery Montauban		
Theatre of war:	France		
Next of Kin:	Thomas & Emily Pullen		
Address:	Box, Wiltshire		

Left: Reginald Hancock.

Above: Brtish heavy howitzers in action.

Regular soldier Francis, known as John lived in Grittleton prior to enlisting with the Royal Garrison Artillery. He had served in Singapore before the Great War and arrived in France on 21 August 1915. He was killed most likely by German artillery fire on Saturday 30 September near Guillemont at the Somme.

Private Reginald Hancock		*1st Bn Wiltshire Regiment*	
Service No.	29794	Age:	19
Place of Birth:	Chippenham	Home Country:	England
Date of Death:	04/10/1916	Cause of death:	Died of wounds
Memorial:	Corsham		
War cemetery:	Puchevillers British Cemetery		
Theatre of war:	France		
Next of Kin:	Henry John & Eliza Hancock		
Address:	Hope Villa, Bradford Road, Corsham		

Nineteen year old Reginald was the eldest son of Henry and Eliza Hancock and originally enlisted with the Somerset Light infantry. He was then transferred to the 1st battalion Wiltshire Regiment and arrived in France in 1916. He was wounded during fighting at the Somme and taken to a casualty clearing station at Puchevillers, France, where he succumbed to his wounds on Wednesday 4 October 1916. At the time of his death Reginald's father and two brothers were also serving in the army.

Private Ivan Cecil Francis Joy		*Royal Canadian Regiment*	
Service No.	455279	Age:	23
Place of Birth:	Thetford, Norfolk	Home Country:	England
Date of Death:	08/10/1916	Cause of death:	Killed in action
Memorial:	Chippenham		
War cemetery:	Regina Trench Cemetery Grandcourt		

Theatre of war: France
Next of Kin: Cecil S Joy
Address: Buckstone Upton Hellons, Crediton, Devon

Ivan was educated Felsted School, Essex, was the eldest son of Cecil Joy and the grandson of
Cannon John Rich of St Andrews, Chippenham. Prior to the Great war Ivan went to Canada
where he was a farmer. He enlisted with the Royal Canadian Regiment on 6 August 1915 and
sailed for England on the Olympic on 1 April 1916. He was then sent to France and on Sunday
8 October 1916 was posted as missing, believed killed in action, during an attack on Regina
trench south of Le Sars at the Somme. His remains were later found and he is today buried in
Regina Trench Cemetery Grandcourt.

Private Frederick Edward Avery   *2nd Bn   Wiltshire Regiment*
Service No.   8796   Age: 23
Place of Birth: Chirton, Wiltshire   Home Country: England
Date of Death: 16/10/1916   Cause of death: Killed in action
Memorial: Chippenham – Chirton & St Andrews Chippenham
War cemetery: Thiepval Memorial
Theatre of war: France
Next of Kin: Richard & Lily Avery (parents) - Mary J Hayward (Grandparent)
Address: 24 The Causeway, Chippenham - Next to the Post Office, Chirton

Regular soldier Frederick, known as Edward, was the second son of Richard and Lily Avery
and had been a baker's assistant prior to his enlistment. He arrived on the continent on 7 October
1914. Edward was killed in action on Monday 16 September 1916 when the 2nd Battalion
Wiltshire Regiment was in reserve resting at Flers Trench near Flers at the Somme and were
subject to heavy German shelling. He is remembered on the Thiepval Memorial and has no
known grave.

Private William Ernest Rose   *2nd Bn Wiltshire Regiment*
Service No   10978   Age: 22
Place of Birth: Calne, Wiltshire   Home Country: England
Date of Death: 17/10/1916   Cause of death: Killed in action
Memorial: Chippenham
War cemetery: Thiepval Memorial
Theatre of war: France
Next of Kin: Joseph & Anne Rose
Address: 6 London Road, Chippenham

Twenty two year old William, who was a labourer, arrived in France on 11 December 1914
with the 2nd Battalion Wiltshire Regiment. He was wounded in September 1915 and after his
recovery he returned to the front. On Tuesday 17 October 1916 he was taking part in 'the big
push', the battle of the Somme now being in its fourth month. The Wiltshires were in the
trenches at Flers, France. Flers had been made famous in England when a journalist made a
report of the new wonder weapon the Tank - he had seen this marvel rolling through the centre
of the French town. In October the weather was described as awful and all the Wiltshires were
soaked. The German shelling was very active and it is likely William was killed during this
bombardment. He may have been one of the rations party that was shelled on that day and is
recorded in the war diary. William has no known grave and is remembered on the Thiepval
Memorial.

Left: Francis Tom Tanner

Above:The effect of a 9.2 inch British shell on a German concrete bunker

Private Francis Tom Tanner   *2nd BnWiltshire Regiment*

Service No.	7695	Age:	27
Place of Birth:	Chippenham, Wiltshire	Home Country:	South Africa
Date of Death:	18/10/1916	Cause of death:	Killed in action

Memorial: Chippenham & St Andrews Church Memorial
War cemetery: Warlencourt British Cemetery
Theatre of war: France
Next of Kin: Elizabeth Lally Tanner (wife) - John & Elizabeth Tanner
Address: 94 Berg Street, Pietermaritzburg, Natal – 10 Ladds Lane, Chippenham

Francis, known as Frank, while serving with the 1st Battalion Wiltshire Regiment in South Africa, met his wife and settled at Pietermaritzburg, Natal. He was the eldest son of John and Elizabeth Tanner and at the outbreak of hostilities being a reserve he was called to the colours and arrived in France on 20 October 1914, joining the 2nd Battalion Wiltshire Regiment. Frank took part in all the major engagement the 2nd Wiltshire took part in during the first two years of the war and was one of five sons serving in the army. At 3.40am on Wednesday 18 October after a heavy British bombardment the 2nd Wiltshires made a frontal attack on German held Bite and Bayonet Trenches, north of Flers at the Somme. The Wiltshires were held up by uncut wire but some got into the trench and bombed (hand grenades) along it only to be machine gunned out of it by the enemy. The Wiltshires were reinforced by the Cameron Highlanders the trench was captured and a block (barrier) was put up. Frank was posted as wounded and missing and in September 1917 an official notification was received informing his wife and parents that he had been killed in action on the day he was reported missing. His remains were located and he was buried in Warlencourt British Cemetery. In October 1918 the following memoriam was inserted in a local paper by his parents:

In loving memory of our dear son Lance Corporal Frank Tanner who was killed at the battle of the Somme.

Somewhere in France our loved one is sleeping
While angels Bright are watching near
Still at home our hearts our aching
For we have lost a son most dear
All his sufferings are now ended
His wounded body is at rest
His soul from every ill defended
Reposes on his Saviour's Breast
Deeply Mourned By his Father, Mother, Sisters and Brothers

Private Henry John Godfrey Herrington   *2nd Bn Wiltshire Regiment*
Service No.   22374   Age: 22
Place of Birth: Biddestone, Wiltshire   Home Country: England
Date of Death: 18/10/1916   Cause of death: Killed in action
Memorial: Bradford on Avon
War cemetery: Thiepval Memorial
Theatre of war: France
Next of Kin: John & Harriet Herrington
Address: 4 Regents Place, Trowbridge Road, Bradford on Avon

Henry, known as Godfrey and a gardener, enlisted with the 2nd Battalion Wiltshire Regiment arriving in France during 1916. He was posted as missing in action on Wednesday 18 October 1916 when the 2nd Wiltshires made a frontal attack on German held Bite and Bayonet Trenches, north of Flers at the Somme in the same action as Francis Tanner. It was later assumed that Godfrey had died on the day he was listed as missing. He is remembered on the Thiepval Memorial and has no known grave.

Private Arthur Bridgeman   *2nd Bn Wiltshire Regiment*
Service No.   22600   Age: 18
Place of Birth: Dauntsey, Wiltshire   Home Country: England
Date of Death: 18/10/1916   Cause of death: Killed in action
Memorial: Christian Malford & Carriage & Waggon Paint Shop Memorial, Swindon
War cemetery: Warlencourt British Cemetery
Theatre of war: France
Next of Kin: John & Elizabeth Jane Bridgeman
Address: Wood Farm Cottages, Wroughton, Wiltshire

Arthur worked for the Great Western Railway in the carriage and wagon department. He volunteered for service with the 2nd Battalion Wiltshire Regiment arriving in France during 1916. He was posted as missing in action on Wednesday 18 October 1916 when the 2nd Wiltshires made a frontal attack on German held Bite and Bayonet Trenches, north of Flers at the Somme in the same action as Francis Tanner. His remains were later recovered and he is today buried in Warlencourt British Cemetery.

Lance Corporal Arthur Martin Ricketts   *2nd Bn Wiltshire Regiment*
Service No.   18364   Age: 36
Place of Birth: Chippenham   Home Country: England
Date of Death: 18/10/1916   Cause of death: Killed in action

Memorial: North Wraxall
War cemetery: Warlencourt British Cemetery
Theatre of war: France
Next of Kin: Ethell Rickets (wife) - William & Sarah Ricketts (parents)
Address: Giddea Hall, Wiltshire - 28 Blind Lane, Chippenham

Arthur, a blacksmith's striker, married Ethel Skues in the summer of 1907. It is likely he joined the army under the Derby Scheme and was called up and sent to France during 1916. He was posted as missing in action on Wednesday 18 October 1916 when the 2nd Wiltshires made a frontal attack on German held Bite and Bayonet Trenches, north of Flers at the Somme in the same action as Francis Tanner. His remains were later recovered and he is today buried in Warlencourt British Cemetery.

Private Walter Stiles   *2nd Bn Wiltshire Regiment*
Service No.   18251   Age: 20
Place of Birth: Christian Malford   Home Country: England
Date of Death: 18/10/1916   Cause of death: Killed in action
Memorial: Not known
War cemetery: Thiepval Memorial
Theatre of war: France
Next of Kin: Henry & Martha Stiles
Address: Alderton, Wiltshire

Farm labourer Walter volunteered for service with the 2nd Battalion Wiltshire Regiment and arrived in France on 8 June 1915. He was posted as missing in action on Wednesday 18 October 1916 when the 2nd Wiltshires made a frontal attack on German held Bite and Bayonet Trenches, north of Flers at the Somme in the same action as Francis Tanner. It was later assumed that Walter had died on the day he was listed as missing. He is remembered on the Thiepval Memorial and has no known grave.

Private Wilfred Hunt   *5th Bn Wiltshire Regiment*
Service No.   10376   Age: 21
Place of Birth: Bowden Hill, Wiltshire   Home Country: England
Date of Death: 19/10/1916   Cause of death: Died
Memorial: Lacock – Lacock Church & Bowden Hill Memorial
War cemetery: Basra Memorial
Theatre of war: Mesopotamia
Next of Kin: Elizabeth Ann Hunt
Address: Bowden Hill, Lacock, Wiltshire

Twenty one year old Wilfred, a farm labourer, was the second son of Elizabeth Hunt and volunteered for service with the Wilshire Regiment. He was sent to France arriving on 11 December 1914 and was posted to either the 1st or 2nd Battalion. It is likely he was evacuated to England suffering from either wounds or illness during the first winter of the war. On his recovery he was sent to serve with the 5th Battalion Wiltshire Regiment in Mesopotamia, modern day Iraq. In April 1916 Wilfred was reported missing in action and as no news was heard of him and he was presumed to have been killed in action. For seventeen months Elizabeth Hunt mourned her dead son and had been receiving a pension when in September 1917 she received a letter from Wilfred with a Baghdad postmark stating that he had been taken prisoner by the Turks and was being treated well. The letter was dated 16 April 1916. Her hopes were dashed for a second time when Wilfred did not return from the war and had died while a prisoner of war on Thursday 19 October 1916. Official records state he was killed in action on the same date. He is remembered on the Basra Memorial and has no known grave.

Private Ernest William Hacker		*7th Bn Royal West Surrey Regiment*	
Service No.	G/21764	Age:	25
Place of Birth:	Hilmarton, Wiltshire	Home Country:	England
Date of Death:	26/10/1916	Cause of death:	Killed in action
Memorial:	Nettleton		
War cemetery:	Thiepval Memorial		
Theatre of war:	France		
Next of Kin:	Eli Henry & Elizabeth E Hacker		
Address:	The Keeper's Lodge, Nettleton, Wiltshire		

Ernest, known as William and a carter on a farm, enlisted with the 7th Battalion Royal West Surrey Regiment and arrived in France during 1916. On Thursday 26 October 1916 Ernest was in Fabick Trench, east of Mouquet Farm on the Somme; the weather was showery. The previous day the 7th West Surreys had been under intense German bombardment and the war diary states Thursday was a *"quiet day"*. Their Casualties for the four day tour in the trenches was killed 15, wounded 98 and missing 1. Ernest was probably killed by German shell fire. He is remembered on the Thiepval memorial and has no known grave. His brother Percival John Hacker was to be killed in Belgium in November 1917.

Private William Albert Baker		*2/4th TF Bn Wiltshire Regiment*	
Service No.	200973	Age:	25
Place of Birth:	Langley Burrell	Home Country:	England
Date of Death:	30/10/1916	Cause of death:	Died
Memorial:	Chippenham - St Andrews & Trowbridge St. James Church Memorial		
War cemetery:	Baghdad North Gate War Cemetery		
Theatre of war:	Mesopotamia		
Next of Kin:	Albert & Louisa A Baker		
Address:	20 River Street, Chippenham, Wiltshire		

William, a farm labourer, was the eldest son of Albert and Louisa Baker and a Wiltshire territorial. He was sent to India at the outbreak of hostilities and served at Poona. He volunteered for service in Mesopotamia arriving in 1916 and attached to the Oxford & Buckinghamshire Light Infantry. He was captured at the surrender of Kut Al Amara to Turkish forces on 29 April in the same year and marched into captivity. He died most likely of disease on Monday 30 October 1916 while a prisoner of war. His parents were informed he had died at Adana in Turkey, official records state he is buried at Baghdad North Gate War Cemetery in Iraq. In November 1918 William's parents inserted the following memoriam in a local paper:

Only a mother can know the sorrow
Only a mother can know the pain
Of a the loss of a son she loved so dearly
She never on earth will see again.
Sleep on dear Will, in an unknown grave.
Never forgotten by his sorrowing Mother, Father, Sisters and Brothers.

Private Percy Saunders Pearce   *3rd Bn London Regiment*
Service No   6064   Age: 29
Place of Birth: Chippenham   Home Country: England
Date of Death: 31/10/1916   Cause of death: Killed in action
Memorial: Chippenham & St Andrews Church Memorial.
War cemetery: Vielle-Chappelle New Military Cemetery Lacouture
Theatre of war: France
Next of Kin: Sarah Farmilo (mother)
Address: 10 The Butts, Chippenham

Prior to his enlistment in the army Percy was a barman at the Hat & Feathers public house in Clerkenwell Street, London. It is likely he was called up in May 1916 and subsequently sent to France and was killed in action soon after his arrival while undergoing training in so called quiet parts of the line.

Private George Frederick Bright   *6th Bn Wiltshire Regiment*
Service No.   19505   Age: 21
Place of Birth: Bath, Somerset   Home Country: England
Date of Death: 03/11/1916   Cause of death: Killed in action
Memorial: Chippenham & St. Andrews Church Memorial
War cemetery: Thiepval Memorial
Theatre of war: France
Next of Kin: Thomas & Kate Bright
Address: 20 Emery Lane, Chippenham

George was employed as a signal worker by Saxby & Farmer Ltd which later became Westinghouse. He originally volunteered for service with the Wiltshire Regiment on 30 August 1914 but was discharged just seventeen days later because "*he had poor physiche and was not likely to become an efficient soldier.*" It would appear he was then called up in 1916 joining the 6th Battalion Wiltshire Regiment and sent to France. On Friday 3 November 1916 the 6th Wiltshires were in trenches south of Grancourt which were described as being in a very bad state and they were continuously shelled by German artillery. One of those killed was George. He is remembered on the Thiepval Memorial and has no known grave.

CQMS Leopold John Jordan   *6th Bn Wiltshire Regiment*
Service No.   11836   Age: 32
Place of Birth: Axebridge, Somerset   Home Country: England
Date of Death: 04/11/1916   Cause of death: Killed in action
Memorial: Chippenham & Chippenham Secondary School Memorial
War cemetery: Thiepval Memorial
Theatre of war: France
Next of Kin: Frederick W & Elizabeth Anne Jordan
Address: 2 Park Lane, Chippenham

Prior to the Great War Leopold, known as Leo, had been a member of the 2nd Wiltshire Volunteer Battalion and he was one of the first to enroll in the National Reseves when they were formed. He had a love of music being a member of the Amateur Operatic Society and the the Parish Church Choir, pocessing what was described as a powerful and cultivated bass voice. Leo was also a member of the Constitutional Club, the Swimming Club and was also assistant overseer for the Parish of Christian Malford a post which he suceeded on the death of his father, Frederick, who had been headmaster of Christian Malford School. At the outbreak of hostilities Leo resigned from Smith and Marshall estate agents where he was employed as a land surveyor and volunteered for service with the 6th Battalion Wiltshire Regiment. He was promoted to the rank of Sergeant then later to Quarter Master Sergeant and was sent to France arriving on 19 July 1915. In September 1916 while out of the line Leo wrote:

"The place where we are now seems very quiet after the Somme district, where we were in the thick of it. It looks as if the rainy season has started: yesterday afternoon the water was up to the tops of the tent walls and our belongings were floating about. Today is bad too; I am wet through in my dugout , but still merry and bright."

On 4 November 1916 the 6th Wiltshires were in trenches south of Grancourt which were described as being in a very bad state and they were continuously shelled by German artillery. In mid November Leo's mother received the following letter from Captain Pullen:

"It is with great regret I write you to communicate the death of Quartermaster Jordan. He, as no doubt you have heard died last week. He was killed by a shell whilst taking rations up to my company in the trenches. I am sure that no man could have done his duty better than he. I have not been in this company long, but during the three months I have been here I have got to know him as a man to be absolutely trusted, and one who always did his best for his company, which has the reputation of being the best looked after as for food, comfort and clothing went in the regiment, and that was due to his hard work. You will understand from this that not only I, but every man in the company, feel with you in your loss. His grave I will have properly marked, and later on, if you apply to the war office, you will be able to obtain the particulars. I will send you a photograph, but am not allowed to tell you where. With every sympathy with you in your sorrow."

Sergeant Major F.W. Pike wrote the following:

"I am set one of the most difficult tasks I have ever experienced in my life, and that is to tell you that your dear son, Leo, whilst taking up rations to his company, who are in the firing line, was killed. Personally, it is the hardest blow I have had during this fearful war, as I was fortunate enough to be one of his personal friends, and a better friend than he was I am sure it would be impossible to find. The company absolutely worshiped him, and so did everybody in the whole Battalion. Corporal Pollard, his clerk, joins with me in sending you his deepest sympathy"

Leo was killed by a shell on Saturday 4 November 1916 and his grave was lost in subsequent fighting. He is today remembered on the Thiepval Memorial.

Private Walter John Martin		*6th Bn Wiltshire Regiment*	
Service No.	22876	Age:	24
Place of Birth:	Kington Langley	Home Country:	England
Date of Death:	04/11/1916	Cause of death:	Killed in action
Memorial:	Chippenham & St. Andrews Church Memorial		
War cemetery:	Regina Trench Cemetery Grandcourt		
Theatre of war:	France		
Next of Kin:	Frances Isabella P. Martin (wife) - Arthur H. & Eliza Martin (parents)		
Address:	Lowden, Chippenham - 36 Thomas Street, Swindon		

Walter was employed as a rubber worker and lived with his aunt at Bradford on Avon. At the end of 1915 he married Frances Isabella P. Gulliver just before enlisting with the 6 Battalion Wiltshire Regiment. On Saturday 4 November 1916 the 6th Wiltshires were in trenches south of Grancourt which were described as being in a very bad state and they were continuously shelled by German artillery. It is possible Walter was killed while bringing rations with Leopold Jordan, he is today buried in Regina Trench Cemetery Grandcourt. In October 1917 Walter's wife inserted the following memoriam in a local paper:

He did his duty and died a hero for King and country and now lies at rest in a British soldier's grave.

Private Frederick James Young		*6th Bn Wiltshire Regiment*	
Service No.	10024	Age:	21
Place of Birth:	Nettleton, Wiltshire	Home Country:	England
Date of Death:	04/11/1916	Cause of death:	Died of wounds
Memorial:	Nettleton		
War cemetery:	Puchevillers British Cemetery		
Theatre of war:	France		
Next of Kin:	Charles & Kate Young		
Address:	The Green, Nettleton, Wiltshire		

Frederick, known as Fred and a farm labourer, was the only son of Charles and Kate Young. He volunteered for service with the 6th Battalion Wiltshire Regiment and arrived in France on 19 July 1915. Fred was wounded on Saturday 4 November 1916 when the 6th Wiltshires were in trenches south of Grancourt which were described as being in a very bad state and they were continuously shelled by German artillery. The following letter from Chaplain George S. Ducan of No. 44 Casualty Clearing Station was received by Fred's parents in mid November 1916:

"I am sorry to be the bearer of sad news to you. Your son, Private F.J. Young, 10024, of the Wilts Regiment, was brought into this hospital in the early hours of this morning, about 1.30am suffering from very severe gun shot wounds in the legs and arms. He was quite unconscious and at 2.15am he passed to his rest. This I know will be a very sore blow to you, but every mother who sent a son to the war knew that, like Abraham of old, she was laying her dearest upon the altar. However much you might have prayed that if it were God's will he might be spared to return, I hope you have also learned trustfully to leave him where you placed him, in the hands of God who loves with more than a mother's love. God has thought best to accept your sacrifice and your boy, and that means that He has taken your boy to be more near to Himself and He called him, I hope to higher service. I buried his broken body this forenoon in the little military cemetery adjoining the C.C.S. I am not allowed to tell you the name of the place. A small wooden cross will be erected in a few days to mark the spot, with his name, regiment and the date of death inscribed on it. The cemetery will be looked after, May our heavenly Father who spared not His own son, give you and yours abundantly of His strength, comfort and peace."

The following memoriam was inserted by Fred's parents in a local paper:

We think of how he bravely went
For freedom's cause to fight
Laid down his life so willingly
For God, King, and the Right

Left: Major Allen Llewellyn Palmer

Above: Major Allen Llewellyn Palmer's Sword in Trowbridge St. James Church

Major Allen Llewellyn Palmer   *1st Royal Wiltshire Yeomanry*

Service No.	N/A	Age:	34
Place of Birth:	Trowbridge, Wiltshire	Home Country:	England
Date of Death:	15/11/1916	Cause of death:	Died
Memorial:	Trowbridge & Lacock Church & Lacock		
War cemetery:	St Pierre Cemetery Amiens		
Theatre of war:	France		
Next of Kin:	Brig. Gen. George & Madeleine Palmer		
Address:	Berryfield, Bradford on Avon, Wiltshire		

Allen was educated at Harrow and Sandhurst and he obtained a commission in the 14th Hussars in May 1901. He served in the South African war receiving the Queens Medal and two clasps. He resigned his captaincy in 1907 and was commissioned into the Royal Wiltshire Yeomanry in 1908. From 1910 to 1911 he was the A.D.C. to the Governor of Bombay and was master of the Hounds at Ootacamund, India. After his return to England he became Joint Master of the Cattistock Hunt and had strong interests in agriculture and was an active member of many agricultural societies in Wiltshire. In December 1915 he left for France with his Regiment. On 29 October 1916 Allen underwent an operation after being taken seriously ill with appendicitis at No. 1 New Zealand Stationary Hospital at Amiens, France. News reached Allen's parents that he was seriously ill and his father left Trowbridge early on the morning of Wednesday 15 November but before he could reach his son he had died of peritonitis. On the day of Allen's funeral a memorial service was held simultaneously in Trowbridge. In April 1917 Allen's parents donated a pair of Flags and their sons' sword to the Parish Church in Trowbridge. In 1923 his parents donated eight bells to Christchurch, Bradford on Avon in memory of Felix Hanbury-Tracy, their son in law who was killed in action in December 1914 and their two sons, Michael George who died in 1911 and Allen who died in November 1916. Allen Llewellyn Palmer was described as a real English Gentleman.

18 NOVEMBER 1916 - THE END OF THE BATTLE OF THE SOMME

Private James Blake   *AO 411 RFR Royal Marine Light Infantry*

Service No.	PO/2015	Age:	49
Place of Birth:	Bishops Cannings	Home Country:	England
Date of Death:	30/11/1916	Cause of death:	Died
Memorial:	Lacock & Lacock Church		
War cemetery:	Haslar Royal Naval Cemetery		
Theatre of war:	Home		
Next of Kin:	Alice Blake (wife) - James and Ann Blake (parents)		
Address:	Raybridge Lacock, Wiltshire – Devizes		

James had originally enlisted with the marines on 7 January 1884 leaving in 1905 and being placed on reserve. He married Margaret Alice Self at the beginning of 1909 and he was working as a general labourer at the outbreak of hostilities. Being a member of the special reserve he was called up and returned to the colours. He was sent to serve at sea on H.M.S. Calgarian and armed merchant cruiser and returned to Forton Barracks in October 1916. On 25 November 1916 Alice Bake was informed that her husband had been admitted to Haslar Military Hospital suffering from pneumonia and on Thursday 30 November 1916 after returning from her mother's funeral she received the news that her husband had died. He was buried at Haslar Royal Naval Cemetery and left a widow and two children.

Private Simeon Rowe   *26th Bn Royal Fusiliers*

Service No.	23286	Age:	23
Place of Birth:	Fowey, Cornwall	Home Country:	England
Date of Death:	14/12/1916	Cause of death:	Killed in action
Memorial:	Chippenham		
War cemetery:	Ridge Wood Military Cemetery		
Theatre of war:	Belgium		
Next of Kin:	Simeon & Ada C Rowe		
Address:	Fowey, Cornwall		

Simeon was the youngest son of Alderman Simeon and Ada Rowe and had come to Chippenham in 1910 to take employment with Capital and Counties Bank. He was a member of the parish choir and was invited to become honoury secretary of Chippenham Swimming Club. His services to the club were much appreciated and in January 1916 the committee presented him with a watch when he left to join the army. After completing his training he was sent to France with the 26th Battalion Royal Fusiliers, known as the Bankers battalion, arriving in May 1916. He took park in the capture of Flers at the Somme in September 1916 and had received a slight shrapnell wound in his leg. On Thursday 14 December 1916 the 26th Royal Fusiliers were in the front line near St.Eloi, south of Ypres in Belgium. Simeon was one of three men killed repelling a German night attack on the British trenches. The Chaplain of the Division wrote the following to Simeon's parents:

"He was killed bravely resisting a heavy night attack of the enemy. He fought bravely and with great demeanor, he was always loyal to duty and ready to help a comrade; he was endeared to all who knew him and we shall all miss him. He was laid to rest in a small cemetery with the rites and prayers of the Church of England and his sorrowing comrades attending."

Just before Simeon was killed he had been invited to take up a commission and had been expected to be given home furlough in the New Year. In December 1916 Simeon's parents inserted the following memoriam in a local paper:

But what put glory or grace into what they did is that they did it of pure love for their country

Private William Francis Vines   *2nd Bn Dorsetshire Regiment*

Service No.   9112

Age: 26

Place of Birth: Chippenham, Wiltshire

Home Country: England

Date of Death: 31/12/1916

Cause of death: Died

Memorial: Swindon

War cemetery: Basra Memorial

Theatre of war: Mesopotamia

Next of Kin: Charles William & Mary Elizabeth Vines

Address: 3 Grove Cottgaes, Drove Road, Swindon, Wiltshire

During the Great War William, his brother Edgar and their father Charles all served in the Army. William a regular with the 2nd Battalion Dorset Regiment, Charles with the Wiltshire territorials in India and Edgar a regular with the 2nd Battalion Wiltshire Regiment William's mother Mary moved to Chippenham during the war living at Baydons Lane. The 2nd Dorsets arrived at Basra on 6 November 1914 part of a force sent to protect Britain's oil interests. William was presumed to have been taken prisoner at the surrender of Kut al Amra on 29 April 1916. It is thought he died of illness or disease on New Years Eve 1916. He is remembered on the Basra Memorial and has no known grave. Edgar Vines was killed in July 1916 on the first day of the Battle of The Somme.

8
1917

Private George Victor Jim Elmes

Service No.	6921	
Place of Birth:	Derry Hill, Wiltshire	
Date of Death:	03/01/1917	
Memorial:	Chippenham	
War cemetery:	Trowbridge Cemetery	
Theatre of war:	Home	
Next of Kin:	Nelson Jim & Hannah Elmes	
Address:	6 Park Lane, Chippenham, Wiltshire	

F Bn Tank Corps

Age:	19
Home Country:	England
Cause of death:	Died

George was a member of the newly formed Tank Corps originally named the Machine Gun Corps Heavy. He was a new recruit and in training at Bovington, Dorset (which later became home of the Tank Corps). He was taken ill on New Years Day 1917 while travelling to his home from Bovington to visit his mother. At Trowbridge he was found to be so seriously ill that he was admitted to the Red Cross Hospital, Trowbridge where he died two days later of illness. He was buried with full military honours at Trowbridge Cemetery.

Left: George Victor Jim Elmes grave in Trowbridge Cemetery

Below: A panel of the memorial window in St. Andrew's Church, Chippenham remembering Captain Herbert Raymond Wilson

Private Roland Alpheus Pullin   *12th Bn Gloucestershire Regiment*
Service No.   22647   Age: 19
Place of Birth: Castle Combe   Home Country: England
Date of Death: 09/01/1917   Cause of death: Died of wounds
Memorial: Castle Combe
War cemetery: Castle Combe St Andrew Church Yard
Theatre of war: Home
Next of Kin: Albert & Stevena Pullin
Address: Park Lane, Castle Combe, Wiltshire

Under age soldier Roland volunteered for service with the 12th Service Battalion Gloucestershire Regiment and arrived in France on Christmas Eve 1915. He was wounded on 4 September 1916 at the Somme, most likely by German artillery fire when the 12th Gloucesters were out of the line. He was evacuated to England being sent to King George's Lambeth, Hospital, London where he succumbed to his wounds on Tuesday 9 January 1917. His body was returned to Castle Combe where he was buried on Wedneasday 24 January 1917. Many of the people of the village who attended were disappointed that military honours were not accorded, the Dead March was not played nor any other mark of honour shown to a soldier who had died for his country.

Captain Herbert Raymond Wilson   *105th Mahratta Light Infantry*
Service No.   N/A   Age: 28
Place of Birth: Chippenham, Wiltshire   Home Country: India
Date of Death: 09/01/1917   Cause of death: Died of wounds
Memorial: Chippenham & St. Andrews Church Memorial
War cemetery: Amara War Cemetery
Theatre of war: Mesopotamia
Next of Kin: Mervyn Seppings & Helena Jane Wilson
Address: 19 St Mary Street, Chippenham

Herbert was the eldest son of Mervyn and Helena Wilson and was educated at St. Peter's School, Weston-Super-Mare and Repton where he was awarded with an open Army Class Scholarship and went on to Sandhurst in 1906. He was a keen sportsman being an enthusiastic angler, a skilled marksman and a member of the Beaufort Hunt which he regularly took part in. He was a member of Chippenham Swimming Club but it was football which he excelled at and had played on many occasions for Chippenham Town. In 1907 he passed out of Sandhurst with an Indian Army Cadetship and for a year was attached to the York and Lancaster Regiment at Quetta. He was gazetted to the 114th Mahrattas in 1909 serving in Tibet then on to Northern Assam with the Chinese Frontier Commission where, for one year, he was Political Agent to the Chief Commissioner Sir Archdale Earle. At the outbreak of hostilities he was recalled to his regiment being sent to Mesopotamia and involved in fighting with Turkish forces. While in the Persian Gulf Herbert contracted typhoid and was invalided back to his home in England for six months. In March 1916 he returned to India and was sent back to Mesopotamia in October 1916. He was wounded while serving with the 105th Mahrattas at Sannayat in modern day Iraq on Tuesday 9 January 1917 and succumbed to his wounds shortly after. Herberts's parents were to loose three sons during the war; Geoffrey and Evelyn were both killed at Loos, in 1915. On 29 September 1918 a stained glass window in St. Andrews Church, Chippenham was dedicated to the memory of the three brothers. The date of 29 September was very significant, it was the date when Geoffrey was born, Herbert was baptized and Evelyn was killed. The window was intended to contrast the desolation and sorrow of that which was felt toward the end of the war, with a higher hope for the future world, which was the remedy.

Private George Bodman   *5th Bn Wiltshire Regiment*

Service No.	9883	Age:	19
Place of Birth:	Chippenham	Home Country:	England
Date of Death:	12/01/1917	Cause of death:	Died of wounds
Memorial:	Chippenham & St. Andrew's Church Memorial		
War cemetery:	Amara War Cemetery		
Theatre of war:	Mesopotamia		
Next of Kin:	John & Annie Bodman		
Address:	1 Avondale Villa, London Road, Chippenham		

Nineteen year old George was a gardener at a nursery and was under age when he volunteered to serve with the 5th Service Battalion Wiltshire Regiment arriving in Gallipoli on 30 June 1915. After the evacuation of the Peninsular, the 5th Wiltshires were sent to Iraq in an attempt to relieve the besieged City of Kut Al Amara. George was wounded, most likely at Sannayat in modern day Iraq, and died of his wound on Friday 12 January 1917.

Private Harold Augustus Lewis   *5th Bn Wiltshire Regiment*

Service No.	11192	Age:	30
Place of Birth:	Allington, Wiltshire	Home Country:	England
Date of Death:	02/02/1917	Cause of death:	Died of wounds
Memorial:	St Augustines Church, Swindon		
War cemetery:	Amara War Cemetery		
Theatre of war:	Mesopotamia		
Next of Kin:	Frederick & Mary T Lewis		
Address:	23 Beatrice Street, Swindon, Wiltshire		

Harold, a monumental mason, volunteered for service with the 5th Battalion Service Regiment arriving in Gallipoli on 30 June 1915. After the evacuation of the Peninsular the 5th Wiltshires were sent to Iraq in an attempt to relieve the besieged City of Kut Al Amara. Harold was wounded, most likely at Sannayat in modern day Iraq, succumbing to his wounds on Friday 2 February 1917.

Private Edgar William Godwin   *10th Bn Liverpool Regiment*

Service No.	61113	Age:	26
Place of Birth:	Seagry, Wiltshire	Home Country:	England
Date of Death:	03/02/1917	Cause of death:	Died
Memorial:	Christian Malford Church Memorial		
War cemetery:	Seagry St. Mary Churchyard		
Theatre of war:	Home		
Next of Kin:	Beatrice Godwin (wife) - John & Mary Godwin (parents)		
Address:	Christian Malford - Church Farm, Seagry, Wiltshire		

Edgar, a farm worker and youngest son of John and Mary Godwin, emigrated to Canada prior to the war but returned to England where he worked on a farm near Tetbury, before moving to Christian Malford. During the summer of 1916 he married Beatrice A. Gready at Bradford on Avon and soon after was called up initially joining the Wiltshire Regiment before being

Right: Edgar Godwin's grave in Seagry St Mary Churchyard.

Far Right: Raymond Stubbert died at the Red Cross Hospital at the Neeld Hall Chippenham, buried in Chippeham cemetery.

transferred to the 10th Battalion Liverpool Regiment. Whilst in training Edgar developed acute bronchitis and asthma and was sent to Connaught Hospital, Aldershot where he died on Saturday 3 February 1917. His body was brought back to Seagry and he was buried in Seagry St Mary Churchyard. He left a widow and baby daughter.

Captain Glenville Richard Cattarns MC	*6th Bn South Lancashire Regiment*	
Service No.	N/a	Age:	32
Place of Birth:	Lewisham, London	Home Country:	England
Date of Death:	12/02/1917	Cause of death:	Killed in action
Memorial:	Great Somerford		
War cemetery:	Basra Memorial		
Theatre of war:	Mesopotamia		
Next of Kin:	Richard & Emily Cattarns		
Address:	Lee, Kent.		

Solicitor Glenville was the youngest son of Richard and Emily Cattarns who had resided in Great Somerford. He was assisting his father, also a solicitor, in London prior to the war and volunteered for service with the 5th Lancashire Regiment receiving a commission. He was then transferred to the 6th Service Battalion South Lancashire Regiment and arrived at Gallipoli in July 1915 where he was wounded on 15 August during fighting at Sari Bair, Anzac. He was evacuated to Egypt where he spent some months in hospital and on his recovery he rejoined his regiment in Mesopotamia. He was mentioned in dispatches on 19 October 1916 and awarded the Military Cross on 22 December 1916. He was killed during operations against Turkish forces near Kut Al Amara on Monday 12 February 1917. Glenville is remembered on the Basra Memorial and has no known grave.

Private Raymond Stubbert	*MT Coy Army Service Corps*	
Service No.	M2/268200	Age:	29
Place of Birth:	Nova Scotia	Home Country:	Canada

Date of Death:	14/02/1917	Cause of death:	Died
Memorial:	Not Known		
War cemetery:	Chippenham London Road Cemetery		
Theatre of war:	Home		
Next of Kin:	William P. & Caroline Stubbert		
Address:	Cape Breton, Nova Scotia		

William, a machinist, left Canada and arrived at Liverpool on 31 August 1915 on the Corsican. He volunteered for service with the Army Service Corps and was taken ill and sent to the Red Cross Hospital at the Neald Hall, Chippenham. He died of double pneumonia on Valentines Day 1917 and was buried in Chippenham Cemetery.

Sapper Bertie Basil Blackman		*145 Army Troops Coy Royal Engineers*	
Service No.	89922	Age:	37
Place of Birth:	Bishops Waltham	Home Country:	England
Date of Death:	20/02/1917	Cause of death:	Died
Memorial:	Chippenham		
War cemetery:	Mont Huon Military Cemetery Le Treport		
Theatre of war:	France		
Next of Kin:	Elizabeth Jane Blackman (wife) - Walter & Martha Blackman (parents)		
Address:	Park Lane, Chippenham - West Cottage, Bishops Waltham, Hampshire		

Bertie was a stone mason who worked for an undertaker and in the spring of 1898 he married Elizabeth Jane Bulpett at Windsor. Prior to the Great War he lived in Park Lane, Chippenham and volunteered for service with the Royal Engineers arriving in France on 28 September 1915. He was taken ill and sent to a hospital in Le Treport, France, where he died of pneumonia on Tuesday 20 February 1917. He left a widow and seven children.

25 FEBRUARY 1917 - KUT EL AMARA IS RE-OCCUPIED BY THE BRITISH

Shoeing Smith Herbert William Carter		*No. 1 Convalescent Horse Depot RAVC*	
Service No.	SE/25303	Age:	23
Place of Birth:	Steeple Langford	Home Country:	England
Date of Death:	02/03/1917	Cause of death:	Died
Memorial:	Steeple Langford & Police HQ Devizes		
War cemetery:	St Sever Cemetery Extension Rouen		
Theatre of war:	France		
Next of Kin:	Edward & Maria Carter		
Address:	Hanging Langford, Steeple Langford, Wiltshire		

Herbert was the youngest son of Edward and Maria Carter and had been a police constable at Chippenham prior to the outbreak of hostilities. Before joining the police Herbert had assisted his father who was a blacksmith. He enlisted with the army and was sent to the Royal Army Veterinary Corps on 22 January 1917 and arrived in France on 1 February 1917 being attached to the 29th Infantry Base Depot. Soon after Herbert was taken ill which proved to be serious and his parents travelled to France to be with him. He died on Friday 2 March 1917 at a Military Hospital in Rouen, France. Herbert is buried in St. Sever Cemetery Extension Rouen.

Corporal Frederick Walter Whale   *2nd Bn Royal Berkshire Regiment*

Service No.	23561	Age:	21
Place of Birth:	Calne	Home Country:	England
Date of Death:	04/03/1917	Cause of death:	Killed in action
Memorial:	Chippenham & St. Paul's Church Memorial		
War cemetery:	Thiepval Memorial		
Theatre of war:	France		
Next of Kin:	Arthur & Katherine Whale		
Address:	40 Tegula Road, Chippenham		

Frederick, known as Fred, worked for a butcher prior to the war and initially enlisted in the Somerset Light Infantry before being transferred to the 2nd Royal Berkshire Regiment arriving in France during 1916. As dawn broke on 4 March 1917 the 2nd Royal Berks were in trenches at Bouchavesnes-Bergen south of the Moislains Road at the Somme. They attacked the German first line Pallas which was easily overrun and then Fritz Trench was taken after a fifteen minute fight. The position offered commanding views over the enemy held Moislains Valley and German forces immediately counter attacked the newly won British positions but were repulsed. The Germans then continually shelled their former trenches. Fred was one of 42 members of the 2nd Royal Berks to be killed or die of wounds on Sunday 4 March 1917. He is remembered on the Thiepval Memorial and has no known grave.

11 MARCH 1917 - BAGHDAD IS CAPTURED BY THE BRITISH

Private Harry John Wheeler   *3rd Bn Wiltshire Regiment*

Service No.	32281	Age:	19
Place of Birth:	Chippenham, Wiltshire	Home Country:	England
Date of Death:	12/03/1917	Cause of death:	Died
Memorial:	Chippenham & St.Andrews Church Memorial		
War cemetery:	Weymouth Cemetery		
Theatre of war:	Home		
Next of Kin:	Alfred & Elizabeth Wheeler		
Address:	4 Parliament Street, Chippenham		

Harry was the eldest son of Alfred and Elizabeth Wheeler and it is likely he was called up joining the Wiltshire Regiment. He was sent to Weymouth where the Wiltshires had a training depot. He died of illness or disease on Monday 12 March 1917.

15 MARCH 1917 - RUSSIAN TSAR NICHOLAS II ABDICATES FOLLOWING THE START OF THE RUSSIAN REVOLUTION

18 MARCH 1917 - GERMANS RETIRE TO THE HINDENBURG LINE

Lance Corporal Francis John Eddolls   *SS Joshua Nicholson R.M.L.I*

Service No.	PLY/5543	Age:	43
Place of Birth:	Chippeham, Wiltshire	Home Country:	England
Date of Death:	18/03/1917	Cause of death:	Died
Memorial:	Not known		

War cemetery: Plymouth Naval Memorial
Theatre of war: At Sea
Next of Kin: Ida Maud Eddolls (wife) - John & Matilda Eddolls (parents)
Address: 45 Cromwell Street, Burnley, Lancashire – Chippeham

Francis was the eldest son of John and Matilda Eddolls and enlisted with the Royal Marine Light Infantry on 19 January 1891. In the spring of 1907 Francis married Ida Maud Champion at Plymouth where they lived until 1913 when they moved to Burnley, Lancashire. On Sunday 18 March 1917 Francis was serving on the armed merchant ship SS Joshua Nicholson when the ship was torpedoed off Wolf Rock, Lands End by the German Submarine U70 and was one of 26 men killed. He is remembered on the Plymouth Naval Memorial and left a widow and four children.

25 MARCH 1917 - BATTLE OF JEBEL HAMRIN, MESOPOTAMIA

26 MARCH 1917 - THE FIRST BATTLE OF GAZA, PALESTINE

Private Thomas Baker   *2nd Bn Wiltshire Regiment*
Service No.   8258   Age: 26
Place of Birth: Langley Burrell, Wiltshire   Home Country: England
Date of Death: 26/03/1917   Cause of death: Died
Memorial: Bremhill - St Andrews Church Chippenham - Foxham - East Tytherton
War cemetery: Cologne Southern Cemetery
Theatre of war: Germany
Next of Kin: Thomas & Hannah Baker
Address: Stanley, Wiltshire

Thomas was the sixth son of Thomas and Hannah Baker. He was a regular soldier and landed at Zeebrugge, Belgium on 7 October 1914. On Saturday 24 October the 2nd Battalion Wiltshire Regiment were in trenches at Beselare, Belgium. At 5.30am, just before daybreak, the Germans attacked with a very superior force but were driven back with heavy losses. The Germans then attacked again and fighting carried on continuously for 2 hours. The Germans had hundreds of casualties killed and wounded, but eventually they broke through. With the exception of about 30 NCOs and men mostly from trenches on the right, the remainder of the Battalion were either killed or captured. One of those taken prisoner was Thomas. He was transported to Germany and confined in Dulmen prison camp in Westphalia. He became sick most likely due to malnutrition and forced labour. During the war prisoners of war in Germany were forced to work and the British naval blockade prevented not only war materials but food being transported to Germany. By 1917 food products were in short supply for the whole German population and the rations given to prisoners of war were very poor. William died on Monday 26 March 1917 after two years and five months in captivity. He was buried in the Dulmen Prisoner of War Cemetery with ninety six other inmates. At the end of the Great War all the burials at Dulmes were exhumed and relocated to Cologne Southern Cemetery, which today contains the remains of over 2500 casualties of the Great War. His family inserted the following memoriam in a local paper:

A light from our household has gone
A voice we loved is still
A place is vacant in our home
Which never can be filled

Private Arthur John Payne   *5th Bn Wiltshire Regiment*
Service No.   19409   Age: 19
Place of Birth: Walcot, Somerset   Home Country: England
Date of Death: 29/03/1917   Cause of death: Killed in action
Memorial: Chippenham & St. Andrew's Church Memorial
War cemetery: Basra Memorial
Theatre of war: Mesopotamia
Next of Kin: Alfred Henry & Harriet Mary Payne
Address: 27 Park Lane, Chippenham

Under age soldier Arthur volunteered for service with the 5th Battalion Wiltshire Regiment and arrived at Gallipoli at the end of 1915. After the evacuation of the Peninsular the Wiltshires were first sent to Egypt and then on to Mesopotamia, modern day Iraq. On 29 March 1917 the Wiltshires were at Palm Tree Post near the Nahrwan Canal and came under heavy Turkish shell and machine gun fire. They were finally held up about 1300 yards from the Turkish position. The Wiltshires casualties were described as very heavy with 28 killed and 139 wounded. Arthur was one of those killed and he is remembered on the Basra Memorial and has no known grave.

Private Ernest William Maslen   *5th Bn Wiltshire Regiment*
Service No.   26200   Age: 21
Place of Birth: Melksham, Wiltshire   Home Country: England
Date of Death: 01/04/1917   Cause of death: Died of wounds
Memorial: Melksham
War cemetery: Basra Memorial
Theatre of war: Mesopotamia
Next of Kin: Rose Maslen (wife) - Charles & Elizabeth Maslen (parents)
Address: 43 Factory Lane, Chippenham - Coburg Square, Spa Road, Melksham

Ernest was the youngest son of Charles and Elizabeth Maslen and had been a manager at Eastmans Ltd. He was a married man and was called up for service in June 1916 joining the Wiltshire regiment and being sent to Mesopotamia, now modern day Iraq. He was wounded during fighting at the Nahrawan Canal near Baghdad and succumbed to his wounds moat likely at 41st Field Hospital. Ernest was within a day of his 22nd birthday and left a widow and baby son who was only weeks old when he left England. He is remembered on the Basra Memorial and has no known grave.

Private Everett Ferriday   *16th Reserve Gloucestershire Regiment*
Service No.   TR7/10126   Age: 18
Place of Birth: Camborne, Cornwall   Home Country: England
Date of Death: 03/04/1917   Cause of death: Died
Memorial: Frome & Chippenham Secondary School Memorial
War cemetery: Frome Vallis Road Cemetery
Theatre of war: Home
Next of Kin: Rev Jonah Grieves & Elizabeth Ferriday
Address: 5 Portland Road, Frome, Somerset

Eighteen year old Everett was the eldest son of the Rev Jonah who had served as Primitive Methodist Minister at Frome for six years and Elizabeth Ferriday. Everett was educated at Chippenham Secondary School then was employed at a motor and cycle works in Bristol. On reaching eighteen years of age he joined the army and was sent to the 94th Territorial Reserve

Battalion of the Gloucestershire Regiment. He was stationed at Chisedon Camp, near Swindon and caught a chill almost immediately which developed into bronchial pneumonia, from which he died on Tuesday 3 April 1917. His body was sent to Frome where he was buried with full military honours. On the Chippenham Secondary School Memorial it is stated that Eric Ferriday died in the war. Eric was Everett's younger brother and also attended the school but is not recorded as being a casualty of the war.

Private Henry John Whale		*6th Bn Wiltshire Regiment*	
Service No.	10079	Age:	23
Place of Birth:	Box, Wiltshire	Home Country:	England
Date of Death:	04/04/1917	Cause of death:	Killed in action
Memorial:	Not known		
War cemetery:	Elzenwalle Brasserie Cemetery		
Theatre of war:	Belgium		
Next of Kin:	John Thomas & Fanny Whale		
Address:	Stanton St Quentin, Wiltshire.		

Henry, known as Harry and a carter on a farm, volunteered for service on 31 August 1914 joining the 5th Battalion Wiltshire Regiment and was sent to Gallipoli arriving on the Peninsular in July 1915. While serving at Gallipoli Harry became ill with dysentery and fever and was invalided home. On his recovery he was transferred to the 6th Battalion Wiltshire Regiment arriving on the continent in December 1915. On Wednesday 4 April 1917 the 6th Wiltshires were in trenches at Diependaalhoek sector just south of St Elooi, Belgium. They were caught in the middle of an artillery dual between British and German gunners throughout the day and night. Harry was one of those killed most likely by the trench mortar fire. In early May 1917 his parent's received the following letter from 2nd Lieutenant Percy Hart:

"I am writing to you with very real sympathy with regard to the death of your son. As his platoon officer I was near him at the time, when he and two of his friends were instantaneously killed. He was one of the best men in all respects that one could wish, and we all mourn his loss. He was buried in a little cemetery just behind our line and if you should wish it at any time I will send you a description of the exact spot. If there is anything I can do for you, please let me know. Trusting you will bear up bravely in your affliction."

In April 1918 Harry's parents inserted the following memoriam in a local paper:

I think I see his smiling face
As he bade his last goodbye
And left his home for ever more
In a foreign land to die
Oh for the touch of a vanished hand
And a sound of a voice that is stilled
Never forgotten by his Father, Mother, Brother and Sisters

6 APRIL 1917 - THE UNITED STATES DECLARES WAR ON GERMANY

9
ARRAS

Private Sylvester Thomas Cook

Service No.	32978
Place of Birth:	Chippeham
Date of Death:	09/04/1917
Memorial:	Chippenham & St. Andrew's Church Memorial.
War cemetery:	Neuville-Vitasse Road Cemetery
Theatre of war:	France
Next of Kin:	Agnes Cook (wife) – Roland and Rhoda Cook
Address:	18 Blind Lane, Chippenham

2nd Bn Wiltshire Regiment

Age:	24
Home Country:	England
Cause of death:	Killed in action

Sylvester, known as Thomas, was the eldest son of Roland and Rhoda Cook and married Agnes E. C. Rogers at the beginning of 1914 in Chippenham. He initially joined the Royal Wiltshire Yeomary before transferring to the 2nd Battalion Wiltshire Regiment. On Monday 9 April 1917 the 2nd Battalion Wiltshire Regiment were preparing to make attacks on the German Hindenburg line. Their first objective was a Mill on the Henin - Neuville Vitasse Road, south west of Arras, France. At 1.30am D Company of the 2nd Wiltshires went forward, but they met considerable resistance from the German defenders, which it was later found numbered about 120 men and two machine guns. The Wiltshires suffered 37 casualties and were forced

Sylvester Thomas Cook on his wedding day in 1914.

to retire. The main British attack had started at 5.30am. Thomas and the 2nd Battalion Wiltshire Regiment attacked at 11.38am and were met by heavy shelling from the Germans, causing many casualties before the objective could be seen. When the Wiltshires arrived at the German wire it was found to be uncut and British troops took cover in shell holes in front of the German line, but were eventually forced to retire. All that was left of the 2nd Battalion was about 90 men. Total casualties for the second attack were 342. Thomas left a widow and two small children and in April 1919 Thomas's family inserted the following memoriam in a local paper:

In memory of my dear husband
Lost to sight, but to memory dear
From our happy home and circle
God has taken one we loved
Borne away from pain and sorrow
To a nobler rest above
From his Wife and Children Betty and Ronnie; also his Mother, Father, Sisters and Brothers

Private Frederick Willis   *2nd Bn Wiltshire Regiment*
Service No.   18160   Age: 30
Place of Birth: Bremhill   Home Country: England
Date of Death: 09/04/1917   Cause of death: Killed in action
Memorial: Chippenham & St. Andrew's Church Memorial
War cemetery: Arras Memorial
Theatre of war: France
Next of Kin: Beatrice Willis (wife) - George & Ellen Willis (parents)
Address: 30 London Road, Chippenham - Bremhill, Wiltshire

Frederick, a flour miller, had married his wife in Chippenham in the summer of 1908. He volunteered for the army leaving behind a young family and arrived in France on 8 December 1915. He was killed in the same action as Sylvester Thomas Cook near Arras on Easter Monday 1917. He is remembered on the Arras Memorial and has no known grave.

Private Joseph Hawkins   *2nd Bn Wiltshire Regiment*
Service No.   21319   Age: 22
Place of Birth: Kington Langley   Home Country: England
Date of Death: 09/04/1917   Cause of death: Killed in action
Memorial: Not known
War cemetery: Bucquoy Road Cemetery Ficheux
Theatre of war: France
Next of Kin: Albert & Harriet Hawkins
Address: Southsea Cottage, Day's Lane, Kington Langley, Wiltshire

Joseph a farm labourer was the eldest son of Albert and Harriet Hawkins. It is likely he was conscripted into the army joining the 2nd Battalion Wiltshire Regiment. He was killed in the same action as Sylvester Thomas Cook near Arras on Easter Monday 1917.

Private William Bert Mills   *1st Bn London Regiment*
Service No.   203501   Age: 19
Place of Birth: Kilburn, London   Home Country: England
Date of Death: 09/04/1917   Cause of death: Killed in action

Memorial: Chippenham - St. Paul's & Hardenhuish Church Memorials
War cemetery: Arras Memorial
Theatre of war: France
Next of Kin: William Thomas & Florence Gertrude Mills
Address: 3 Canterbury Street, Chippenham

William was the eldest son of William and Florence Mills joinied the 1st Battalion London Regiment and proceeded to France. He was killed in action on Easter Monday 1917 near Neuville Vitasse south west of Arras, France. He is remembered on the Memorial that bears the same name and has no known grave.

Private Percy James Perkins MM   *28th Bn Saskatchewan Regiment*
Service No.   73822   Age: 35
Place of Birth: Chippenham   Home Country: Canada
Date of Death: 09/04/1917   Cause of death: Killed in action
Memorial: Chippenham & St. Andrew's Church Memorial
War cemetery: Ecoivres Military Cemetery Mont St Eloi
Theatre of war: France
Next of Kin: James & Mary Anne Perkins
Address: The Vaults, Chippenham

Percy was the youngest of James and Mary Perkins. He was educated at the National School and served an apprenticeship as a draper, working in Reading and Folkestone. In 1912 Percy emigrated to Canada where he hoped to become a farmer but on his arrival at Regina, Saskatchewan he started a new career as first a waiter and then a restaurant manager. At the outbreak of hostilities he was about to be offered a partnership in the business where he worked but he made the decision to join the army enlisting on 24 October 1914. His employers assured him that his position would be held until his return and he was presented with a gold ring and a safety razor in a silver case. Percy's work colleagues marked their respect, by presenting him with a gold watch prior to his departure. On his arrival in England he was sent for further training and was given the opportunity of visiting his parents. In January 1916 he went to France with his regiment and on 15 September 1916 he won the Military Medal while taking part in the Battle of Courcelette at the Somme. While in France Percy met his brother Fred who he had not seen for some years and who was a Gunner serving with the Royal Marine Artillery. It was in a letter from Fred that James and Mary Perkins first heard that Percy had been seriously wounded. Later official information was received that Percy had been killed on Easter Monday 1917 during fighting on Vimy Ridge.

Sergeant Alfred Henry Herbert Brain   *C Bty 71st Bde Royal Field Artillery*
Service No.   18179   Age: 27
Place of Birth: Biddestone, Wiltshire   Home Country: England
Date of Death: 09/04/1917   Cause of death: Killed in action
Memorial: Biddestone
War cemetery: Beaurains Road Cemetery Beaurains
Theatre of war: France
Next of Kin: Alfred David & Ellen Eliza Brain
Address: Biddestone, Wiltshire

Alfred, known as Harry a carter at the saw mills at Biddestone, volunteered for service joining The Royal Field Artillery and arrived in France on 9 July 1915. He was killed near Beaurains, on the outskirts of Arras, most likely by German counter battery fire while supporting the British attacks on Easter Monday 1917. His brother Walter George Brain had been Killed in July 1916 at the Somme.

Private Stanley William James Pearce   *2nd Bn Wiltshire Regiment*
Service No.   24198   Age: 19
Place of Birth: Chippenham   Home Country: England
Date of Death: 10/04/1917   Cause of death: Died of wounds
Memorial: Chippenham & St. Andrew's Church Memorial
War cemetery: Warlincourt Halte British Cemetery Saulty
Theatre of war: France
Next of Kin: Thomas & Agnes Pearce
Address: 4 Mosley Row London Road, Chippenham

Nineteen year old Stanley enlisted with the 2nd Battalion Wiltshire Regiment. He was wounded most likely during fighting in the same action as Sylvester Thomas Cook near Arras on Easter Monday 1917. He was evacuated to a casualty clearing station at Warlincourt were he succumbed to his wounds on Tuesday 10 April 1917.

Private Albert Edward Allsop   *11th Labour Coy Lincolnshire Regiment*
Service No.   45607   Age: 30
Place of Birth: Lower Stanton, Wiltshire   Home Country: England
Date of Death: 10/04/1917   Cause of death: Died
Memorial: Not known
War cemetery: Bethune Town Cemetery
Theatre of war: France
Next of Kin: Jacob & Emma Allsop
Address: Lower Stanton, Stanton St. Quintin, Wiltshire

It is likely Albert, a groom, was conscripted into the army joining the Lincolnshire Regiment. He was a member of a labour company which were used for manual labour on duties such as repairing roads and preparing billets. He died most likely of illness or disease at one of the hospitals based at Bethune, France on Tuesday 10 April 1917.

Private Harold John Thomas Swain   *10th Loyal North Lancashire Regiment*
Service No.   33916   Age: 23
Place of Birth: Chippenham, Wiltshire   Home Country: England
Date of Death: 11/04/1917   Cause of death: Killed in action
Memorial: Not known
War cemetery: Arras Memorial
Theatre of war: France
Next of Kin: Hugh J & Emma M Swain
Address: 16 South Avenue, Oldfield Park, Bath, Somerset

Harold, a cycle repairer, originally joined the Army Cyclist Corps as an artificer but was transferred to the 10th Service Battalion Loyal North Lancashire Regiment. On Wednesday 11 April 1917 the Loyal North Lancashires were in action east of Arras and it is likely Harold was killed during heavy fighting at the capture of Monchy Le Preux. He is remembered on the Arras Memorial and has no known grave.

Corporal Percy Porter   *4th Bn Royal Fusilers*

Service No.	G/16566	Age:	26
Place of Birth:	Great Somerford, Wiltshire	Home Country:	England
Date of Death:	13/04/1917	Cause of death:	Killed in action
Memorial:	Great Somerford		
War cemetery:	Arras Memorial		
Theatre of war:	France		
Next of Kin:	Robert & Eliza Porter		
Address:	Great Somerford, Wiltshire		

Percy, a farm labourer, volunteered for service with the Kings Own Hussars in September 1914 and was later transferred to the 4th Battalion Royal Fusiliers arriving in France on 6 July 1915. Cannon Manley of Great Somerford had sent parcels to the men of the village who were serving at Christmas 1916 and Percy had acknowledged the gift especially thanking Cannon Manley for the small prayer book that was sent stating:

"The use of which he found most helpful."

Percy was killed on the night of Friday 13 April 1916 most likely south of Monchy Le Preux east of Arras. His commanding officer wrote to his parents stating that Percy had been recommended for gallant work in the past few days and again on the night he was killed. In May 1917 a well attended Memorial Service was held to the memory of Percy at the village church. Percy is today remembered on the Arras Memorial and has no known grave.

Private Herbert Henry Payne   *1st Bn Devonshire Regiment*

Service No.	23890	Age:	31
Place of Birth:	Frome, Somerset	Home Country:	England
Date of Death:	17/04/1917	Cause of death:	Died of wounds
Memorial:	Chippenham & St. Andrew's Church Memorial		
War cemetery:	Not known		
Theatre of war:	France		
Next of Kin:	George & Elizabeth Payne		
Address:	Frome, Somerset		

Herbert was a carter for the Great Western Railway and was a boarder at 18 St. Mary's Street, Chippenham. It is likely he was conscripted into the army joining the 1st Battalion Devonshire Regiment. On 14 April 1917 the 1st Devons were ordered to push patrols forward to ascertain the disposition of German forces east of Givenchy en Gohelle, a village south west of Lens, France. Each time a patrol went forward they were met by heavy machine gun and rifle fire and it is likely Herbert was wounded during one of these patrols and succumbed to his wounds on Tuesday 17 April 1917. At the time of writing this book Herbert is not listed by the Commonwealth War Grave Commission.

Able Seaman Cecil White   *Hawke Bn RN Div R.N.V.R.*

Service No.	Bristol Z/1395	Age:	19
Place of Birth:	Patney, Wiltshire	Home Country:	England
Date of Death:	18/04/1917	Cause of death:	Killed in action
Memorial:	Seagry & St Peter's Church Shipton Bellinger, Gloucestershire		
War cemetery:	Arras Memorial		
Theatre of war:	France		

Next of Kin: John Humphry & Mary White
Address: Minchinhampton, Gloucestershire

Prior to the Great War nineteen year old farm worker Cecil had lived with his parents at Upper Seagry. He volunteered for service with the Royal Naval Division on 17 November 1915 and after completing his training he arrived in France on 10 July 1916 joining Hawke Battalion on 25 November 1916. On 14 December 1916 Cecil was evacuated from the trenches suffering from trench foot, a condition caused by a persons feet being cold and wet for a long period, most likely from standing in waterlogged trenches. After his recovery he returned to Hawke Battalion on 7 April 1917. On Wednesday 18 April 1917 Hawke Battalion were in trenches near Gavrelle, North East of Arras France. The British front and support lines were subjected to a heavy German bombardment by guns of all calibres and a number of gas shells were sent over, catching some parties unawares. Cecil was one of six men killed on this day, most likely by German shelling. He is remembered on the Arras Memorial and has no known grave. John & Mary White were to lose two more sons; Leonard was to die of wounds in Belgium in July 1917 and Arthur was killed in France in April 1918.

Rifleman Walter George Mann		*1/8th TF Bn Hampshire Regiment*	
Service No.	331374	Age:	25
Place of Birth:	Castle Combe, Wiltshire	Home Country:	England
Date of Death:	19/04/1917	Cause of death:	Killed in action
Memorial:	Hullavington		
War cemetery:	Jerusalem Memorial		
Theatre of war:	Palestine		
Next of Kin:	Edwin Simeon & Elizabeth Mann		
Address:	New Town, Hullavington, Wiltshire		

Walter, known as George and a painter, volunteered for service initially with the 5th Battalion Wiltshire Regiment arriving in Gallipoli in July 1915. It is likely he was wounded or suffered from illness or disease and evacuated from the peninsular to Egypt. On his recovery he was transferred to the 1/8th Battalion Hampshire Regiment and sent to Palestine where in April preparations were taking place for the capture of Gaza from Turkish forces. Early on Thursday 19 April 1917 the British bombarded Turkish positions and two hours later the attack started with A and B companies of the 1/8th Hampshires supporting the 5th Norfolks and C and D companies following the 4th Norfolks toward the Gaza – Beersheba Road. Immediately the Tukish artillery started shelling the British they suffered heavy casualties and as they advanced over a low ridge they were caught by fire from a Turkish redoubt on their right. The redoubt was captured with the aid of a tank but the British were eventually forced to withdraw when ammunition became short. An attempt was made by about 100 Hampshires and a Lewis gun to stem the Turkish counter attacks at the low ridge. After dark many of those who had been lying in no man's land managed to get back to the British lines and the wounded that could be reached were brought in. Walter was posted as missing in action and later it was officially presumed that he had been killed on the day he was listed missing. He is remembered on the Jerusalem Memorial and has no known grave.

20 APRIL 1917 - BRITISH FORCES OCCUPY SAMMARAH, 60 MILES NORTH OF BAGHDAD

Private Herbert Richmond Coleman   *1st Bn Duke of Cornwalls Light Infantry*

Service No.	29168	Age:	21
Place of Birth:	Hanham, Bristol	Home Country:	England
Date of Death:	23/04/1917	Cause of death:	Killed in action
Memorial:	Kington Langley		
War cemetery:	La Chaudiere Military Cemetery Vimy		
Theatre of war:	France		
Next of Kin:	Henry & Edith Coleman		
Address:	New's Green, Kington Langley, Wiltshire		

Twenty one year old Herbert worked with his father as a carpenter and wheelwright and it is likely he was conscripted into the army joining the 1st Battalion Duke of Cornwall's Light Infantry. On Monday 23 April the 1st DCLI were preparing to attack German positions at Lacoulotte, east of Givenchy en Gohelle, a village south west of Lens, France. The British advanced and captured the railway embankment with little opposition and capturing the Germans described them as *"miserable specimens"*. However, as they reached the crest of the embankment they were met by heavy German rifle and machine gun fire. The advance continued and after a fierce bombing fight the position was consolidated. One of those killed was Herbert; his elder brother Henry was to die from heatstroke in Mesopotamia in July 1917.

Private George Weston   *7th Bn Wiltshire Regiment*

Service No.	12408	Age:	38
Place of Birth:	Chippenham, Wiltshire	Home Country:	England
Date of Death:	24/04/1917	Cause of death:	Died
Memorial:	Chippenham – St. Andrews Church, Chippenham & Derry Hill		
War cemetery:	Doiran Memorial		
Theatre of war:	Salonika		
Next of Kin:	Abraham & Sarah Weston		
Address:	Chippenham, Wiltshire		

George, a masons labourer, volunteered to serve with the 7th Service Battalion Wiltshire Regiment and arrived in France with them on 21 September 1915. In November 1915 the 7th Wiltshires were transferred to Salonika. In April 1917 the British forces in Salonika, Greece attacked Bulgarian lines near Lake Doiran. George was serving in A Company, 7th Battalion Wiltshire Regiment and during the night they attacked the Bulgarian trenches under cover of a British artillery barrage which had cut the first line of the enemy barbed wire. When they arrived at the second line of barbed wire they were held up due to the wire being almost intact, the Bulgarian trenches were heavily manned, and the enemy made great use of bombs, (hand grenades), causing many injuries and forcing A Company to retire. The War diary for the day states:

"The Bulgars supports were seen coming down the CT (communication trenches), on left and the front line was very strongly manned. Our advance was held up and the company was forced to lie down in shell holes in front of the wire. The main party never got through the wire. A few got into the enemy trenches but were not seen again."

George was listed as missing in the casualty return. Later he was officially reported killed in action on Tuesday 24 April 1917. He is remembered on the Dorian Memorial, Greece, and has no known grave.

Sergeant Henry Sidney Beaven

Service No.	8420	
Place of Birth:	Chippenham, Wiltshire	
Date of Death:	24/04/1917	
Memorial:	Melksham	
War cemetery:	Doiran Memorial	
Theatre of war:	Salonika	
Next of Kin:	Henry & Amelia Beaven	
Address:	Union Street, Melksham, Wiltshire	

7th Bn Wiltshire Regiment

Age:	33
Home Country:	England
Cause of death:	Killed in action

Regular soldier Henry originally joined the local volunteer corps in 1907 and later the regular army joining the 2nd Battalion Wiltshire Regiment, arriving on the continent with them on 7 October 1914. He was twice wounded and after several months treatment in a London hospital he was transferred to the 7th Battalion Wiltshire Regiment and sent to serve with them in Salonika, Greece in 1916. Henry was posted missing in action on Tuesday 24 April 1917 in the same action as George Weston. In August 1918 it was officially assumed that he had been killed in action on the same day he was listed as missing. He is remembered on the Dorian Memorial, Greece and has no known grave. His parents inserted the following memoriam in a local paper:

Farewell dear one we must leave you
On Salonika's battlefield
But as long as life and memory lasts
We will always remember you
We often sit and think of you
Your name we often recall
But there's nothing left to answer
But a photo on the wall
Ever remembered by his loving Father and mother, Sister and Brothers

Left: Henry Sidney Beaven killed at Salonika.

Below: Ramparts at Salonika, Greece.

Private Christopher James Cole

		7th Bn Wiltshire Regiment	
Service No.	26062	Age:	38
Place of Birth:	Kington Langley, Wiltshire	Home Country:	England
Date of Death:	24/04/1917	Cause of death:	Killed in action
Memorial:	Kington Langley		
War cemetery:	Doiran Memorial		
Theatre of war:	Salonika		
Next of Kin:	Edith Cole (wife) - Christopher and Lucy Cole (parents)		
Address:	Parkers Lane, Kington Langley – Kington Langley		

Builder's labourer Christopher was employed by Downing & Rudman's and toward the end of 1909 he married Edith Rogers. Christopher joined the army in June 1916 and after completing his training was sent to Salonika, Greece. He was posted missing in action on Tuesday 24 April 1917 in the same action as George Weston. Edith Cole made all possible enquiries with men from the Wiltshires and the Red Cross Society to gain information of her husband but with no success. A member of the 7th Wiltshires eventually wrote to Edith the following:

"Private Cole was wounded in the foot soon after leaving the lines for the attack and could not keep up, we lost sight of him afterwards. It was quite evident that Private Cole must not have gone on after being wounded, or he would have in all probability reached our lines again safely. No one appears to of heard of him since, so we can only fear that the worst has happened."

In August 1917 Edith was officially informed that her husband was presumed to have died on the day he was posted as missing. He is remembered on the Doiran Memorial and has no known grave. Edith inserted the following memoriam in a local paper:

We think of him in silence
No eye may see us weep
But deep within our heats
His memory dear we'll keep.
Mourned by his sorrowful wife

Private Edward Pegler

		A Coy 7th Bn Wiltshire Regiment	
Service No.	12292	Age:	24
Place of Birth:	Raybridge, Wiltshire	Home Country:	England
Date of Death:	24/04/1917	Cause of death:	Killed in action
Memorial:	Lacock - Lacock Church & Bowden Hill		
War cemetery:	Dorian Memorial		
Theatre of war:	Salonika		
Next of Kin:	William R. & Sarah J. Pegler		
Address:	The Wharf, Lacock, Wiltshire		

Edward, a trellis maker, was the second son of William and Sarah Pegler and volunteered for service joining the 7th Service Battalion Wiltshire Regiment and arrived in France on 21 September 1915. In November 1915 the 7th Wiltshires were transferred to Salonika, Greece. He was posted missing in action on Tuesday 24 April 1917 in the same action as George Weston. It was later assumed he had been killed in action during the attack. He is remembered on the Doiran Memorial, Greece, and has no known grave.

Private Maurice Jesse Sparrow   *5th Bn Wiltshire Regiment*
Service No.   18070   Age: 32
Place of Birth: Hankerton, Wiltshire   Home Country: England
Date of Death: 25/04/1917   Cause of death: Died of wounds
Memorial: Little Somerford
War cemetery: Basra War Cemetery
Theatre of war: Mesopotamia
Next of Kin: Alice Naomi Sparrow (wife) - Edmund & Harriet Sparrow (parents)
Address: Lea, Wiltshire – Hankerton

Maurice, known as Jesse and a carter, married Alice Naomi Comely in 1909. He volunteered for service with the 5th Battalion Wiltshire Regiment arriving at Gallipoli in August 1915. After the evacuation of the peninsular the 5th Wiltshires were initially sent to Egypt and then on to Mesopotamia, modern day Iraq. On 16 April 1917 Alice received a telegram informing her that Jesse had been seriously wounded and a little later she was informed he was dangerously ill. On 7 May 1916 a further telegram arrived, informing Alice that her husband had died from wounds received in action on Wednesday 25 April 1917. Jesse left a widow and three small children and in April 1918 Alice inserted the following memoriam in a local paper:

In Loving Memory of my dear husband
We loved him then we love him still
Forget him no we never will
God's will be done we'll meet again
And then we'll part no more
Inserted by his loving Wife and Children

Private Tom Sainsbury   *2nd Bn &Bucks Light Infantry*
Service No.   18797   Age: 19
Place of Birth: Chippenham   Home Country: England
Date of Death: 28/04/1917   Cause of death: Killed in action
Memorial: Chippenham & St. Pauls Church Memorial
War cemetery: Arras Memorial
Theatre of war: France
Next of Kin: Tom & Elizabeth Sainsbury
Address: 9 Park Field, Chippenham

Under age soldier Tom was the adopted son of Tom & Elizabeth Sainsbury and it is a likely he was a nephew of his foster mother, his true name being Talbot Tom Staples. He volunteered for service with the 2nd Battalion Ox & Bucks Light Infantry and arrived in France on 30 September 1915. He was killed in action on Saturday 28 April 1917 when the 2nd Ox & Bucks took part in the capture of the village of Oppy and Arleux north east of Arras, France. He is remembered on the Arras memorial and has no known grave. In May 1920 his foster parents inserted the following memoriam in a local paper:

In ever loving memory of our dear son Tom Sainsbury killed in action April 28th 1917.
Could I, his mother, have clasped the hand
Of the son I loved so well
And kissed the brow when death was nigh
And whispered, Tom, Farewell.
Sadly missed by his Mother, Dad and Sisters

Sapper William Henry Lumkin   *522nd Field Coy Royal Engineers*

Service No.	550958	Age:	40
Place of Birth:	Corsham, Wiltshire	Home Country:	England
Date of Death:	28/04/1917	Cause of death:	Died
Memorial:	Corsham		
War cemetery:	Longuenesse St.Omer Souvenir Cemetery		
Theatre of war:	France		
Next of Kin:	Charlotte Annie Mandy Lumkin (wife) - Henry & Fanny Lumkin		
Address:	Plough Lane, Kington Langley - Rose Cottage, Middlewick, Corsham		

William, a carpenter and joiner, married Charlotte Annie Mandy Trepte in Fulham in 1909 and it is likely he was conscripted into the Royal Engineers. It is likely he died of illness or disease at a stationary hospital at St. Omer France. He left a widow and three small children.

Lieutenant David Clutterbuck   *126th Bty 28th Bde Royal Field Artillery*

Service No.	N/a	Age:	26
Place of Birth:	Hardenhuish, Wiltshire	Home Country:	England
Date of Death:	06/05/1917	Cause of death:	Died of wounds
Memorial:	Hardenhuish Church		
War cemetery:	Aubigny Communal Cemetery Extension		
Theatre of war:	France		
Next of Kin:	Edmund & Madeline Clutterbuck		
Address:	Hardenhuish Park, Chippenham		

David was the second son of Edmund and Madeline Clutterbuck and was educated at Harris Hill and Winchester College where he held a scholarship before attending University College Oxford obtaining a B.A. After completing his studies he received an appointment with the Chinese Customs and at the outbreak of hostilities he was at Peking having just received a promotion. He returned to England in February 1915 and was given a commission with the Royal Field Artillery and proceeded to France in July 1915. He was wounded, most probably by German counter battery fire, and taken to a casualty clearing station at Aubigny, north west of Arras, where he succumbed to his wounds on Sunday 6 May 1917.

Memorial to David Clutterbuck at St. Nicholas Church Hardenhuish

Private Albert Henry Wellington Greenman   *1st Bn Devonshire Regiment*

Service No.	27688	Age:	32
Place of Birth:	Hullavington, Wiltshire	Home Country:	England
Date of Death:	09/05/1917	Cause of death:	Killed in action
Memorial:	Not known		
War cemetery:	Arras Memorial		
Theatre of war:	France		
Next of Kin:	Albert Andrew Wellington & Lucy Sarah Greenman		
Address:	Greens Farm, Hullavington, Wiltshire		

Albert worked on his father's farm and it is likely he was conscripted into the army joining the 1st Battalion Devonshire Regiment. Just after midnight on 9 May 1915 the 1st Devons were preparing to attack the German held Fresnoy Trench, north of the village of Fresnoy-en-Gohelle, which was south of Lens, France. Just before the attack two Canadian officers came to the 1st Devons trenches and begged them not to attack as they had only just received orders to support the 1st Devons attack and were unable to cooperate. There was no time to stop the attack and Captain Manton of the 1st Devons explained the situation to the men and they agreed to go on. At 2am the attack commenced and the 1st Devons passed through their own barrage which caused some casualties but they quickly captured the trench and consolidated the position. The 1st Devons were alone though and throughout the day with the aid of British Artillery they beat off German counterattacks. The 1st Devons numbers had been depleted and the situation remained the same as night fell. On Wednesday 9 May the remnants of the 1st Devon made their way back to their original positions. One of those killed during the attack was Albert. He is remembered on the Arras Memorial and has no known grave.

Private Walter Curtis   *4th Bn Wiltshire Regiment*

Service No.	202665	Age:	19
Place of Birth:	Sherston Parva, Wiltshire	Home Country:	England
Date of Death:	10/05/1917	Cause of death:	Died
Memorial:	Not known		

Left: Walter Curtis buried in St. Paul's Churchyard.

Below: The ruins of the Hotel de Ville, Arras.

War cemetery: Chippenham St. Paul's Churchyard
Theatre of war: Home
Next of Kin: Private Henry & Elizabeth Curtis
Address: Allington, Chippenham

Nineteen year old Walter was the third son of Henry and Elizabeth Curtis who had a family of fifteen children. His father was serving in France with the army and Walter joined the Wiltshire Regiment . While he was in training at Sutton Veny he developed pneumonia and died on Thursday 10 May 1917. His body was returned to his home and he was buried in St. Paul's Churchyard, Chippenham with military honours.

Private Frederick John Collier   *2/8th Bn Manchester Regiment*
Service No.   303471   Age: 21
Place of Birth: Kington St Michael   Home Country: England
Date of Death: 12/05/1917   Cause of death: Killed in action
Memorial: Kington St Michael
War cemetery: Sailly Labourse Communal Cemetery Extension
Theatre of war: France
Next of Kin: Charles & Sarah A Collier
Address: Kington St Michael, Wiltshire

It is likely farm labourer Frederick, known a Fred, was conscripted into the army initially joining the Suffolk Regiment before being transferred to the 2/8th Manchester Regiment, arriving in France in March 1917. It is likely he was killed when the 2/8th Manchesters were in so called 'training trenches' in what was considered to be a quiet part of the line south east of Bethune, France. Sarah collier received the following letter from his company commander:

"He was a good soldier, and it was as such he died. He was killed at his post by a shell bursting very close to him. His body was buried beside his comrades who have willingly given their lives for their King and country."

The Rev. A. Walters, a Wesleyan Chaplain, wrote:

"He was killed in action on the 12th May and we buried him in the British soldiers cemetery nearby. A cross will be erected to mark the place, may God help you to bear the loss. Your son gave his life in a great cause and it will not be in vain."

Private George John Little   *29th Bn British Columbia Regiment*
Service No.   423051   Age: 36
Place of Birth: Chippenham, Wiltshire   Home Country: Canada
Date of Death: 13/05/1917   Cause of death: Died of wounds
Memorial: Chippenham & St. Andrews Church Memorial
War cemetery: St Sever Cemetery Rouen
Theatre of war: France
Next of Kin: John & Anne Little - Louisa Little (sister)
Address: 9 Foghamshire, Chippenham

George was the youngest son of John and Anne Little and had been a carter in the employ of Chippenham Town Council. He emigrated to Canada prior to the Great War where he worked as a farmer. He volunteered for service with the Canadian army on 30 April 1915 being wounded during fighting at Vimy Ridge. He was evacuated to a stationary hospital at Rouen where he succumbed to his wounds on Sunday 13 May 1917.

Private Reginald Genvy Kaynes		*1st Middlesex Regiment*	
Service No.	TF/202992	Age:	21
Place of Birth:	Chippenham	Home Country:	England
Date of Death:	16/05/1917	Cause of death:	Died of wounds
Memorial:	Not known		
War cemetery:	Henin Communal Cemetery Extension		
Theatre of war:	France		
Next of Kin:	William & Florence Edith Kaynes (parents) - Mary Hemmings (stepmother)		
Address:	Chippenham - Box Cottage, Whitley, Wiltshire		

Reginald, known a Reggie and a trellis maker, was the nephew and adopted son of Mary Anne Hemmings who he and his brother Cecil had lived with since an early age. He attended the Wesleyan Sunday School and Shaw day school and was a keen footballer, playing for the Football Club in several matches. He volunteered for service with the Middlesex Regiment in May 1915 and was wounded in action between Monchy le preux and Fontaine Les Croissles on Wednesday 16 May 1917 but succumbed to his wounds soon after. His brother Cecil survived the war and in May 1919 his family inserted the following memoriam in a local paper:

In ever loving and proud remembrance of my darling Reggie
Died of wounds received in action near Monchy le preux
Think of me dear one while o'er life's waters I seek the land
Missing thy voice thy touch and true helping of thy pure hand
Till through the storm and tempest safely anchored on the other side
I find thy dear face looking through deaths shadows not changed but glorified
Ever fondly remembered by all

Gunner Herbert Teagle		*107th Bde Royal Field Artillery*	
Service No.	73564	Age:	33
Place of Birth:	Upper Seagry, Wiltshire	Home Country:	England
Date of Death:	05/06/1917	Cause of death:	Died
Memorial:	Seagry		
War cemetery:	Wimereux Communal Cemetery		
Theatre of war:	France		
Next of Kin:	Charles & Sarah Teagle		
Address:	Upper Seagry, Wiltshire		

Herbert was the second son of Charles & Sarah Teagle and enlisted with the army joining the Royal Field Artillery. He died of sickness or disease on Tuesday 5 June 1916 at a military hospital near Wimereux, France.

7 JUNE 1917 - THE BATTLE OF MESSINES, BELGIUM

2nd Lieutenant William Herbert Dickson		*2/4th Bn Loyal North Lancashire Regiment*	
Service No.	N/A	Age:	40
Place of Birth:	Preston, Lancashire	Home Country:	England

Right: Reginald Genvy Kaynes.

Far right: Orlando Edwards.

Date of Death: 07/06/1917   Cause of death: Killed in action
Memorial: Chippenham & St. Andrew's Church Chippenham
War cemetery: Motor Car Corner Cemetery
Theatre of war: Belgium
Next of Kin: George H & Mary E H Dickson
Address: Preston, Lancashire

William was educated at Cheltenham and was articled with Buck and Dickson Solicitors, a firm his father was a partner with. Prior to the war William was practicing as a solicitor in Chippenham and joined the London Scottish. He was attached to the officer training corps and received a commission with the 2/4th Territorial Battalion Loyal North Lancashire Regiment on 24 January 1917. He was sent to France in May 1917 and wounded after a few weeks service. After his recovery he rejoined his unit only to be killed in action on the first day of the battle of Messines near Ploegsteert, Belgium on Thursday 7 June 1917.

Private Orlando Edwards   *6th Bn Wiltshire Regiment*
Service No.   18589   Age: 31
Place of Birth: Chippenham   Home Country: England
Date of Death: 07/06/1917   Cause of death: Killed in action
Memorial: Chippenham & St. Andrews Church Memorial
War cemetery: Ypres Menin Gate
Theatre of war: Belgium
Next of Kin: Joseph & Salina Edwards
Address: 31 The Causeway, Chippenham

Orlando had trained as a blacksmith and in May 1912 he took employment with the Post Office, first as a temporary postman and then as an auxiliary postman responsible for Tytherton. He was described as a quiet and well conducted lad. He volunteered for service with the 6th Battalion Wiltshire Regiment on 25 January 1915 and arrived in France on 19 July 1915. On 7 June 1917 the 6th Wiltshires took part in the attack on the German held Messines – Wychaete Ridge in Belgium. At 3.10am three mines were exploded at the Hollandschschuur Farm forming the Hollande Salient near Vierstraat, Belgium. After capturing the Hollande Salient the Wiltshires went on to take the south east portion of the Grand Bois. At the end of June 1917 Joseph and Selina Edwards received the first intimation that their son had been killed in the following letter from Lieutenant Wing:

"He was as you doubtless know one of the special battalion bombers, so did not often parade with us, but we were always glad when he did so, for he was very smart, courageous, and painstaking and popular with every body. I hope it maybe some consolation in your bereavement to reflect that he died the death of an honourable and gallant man for his King and country."

Orlando's parents received the following letter from Signaller Macdonald of the Royal Dublin Fusiliers:

"In the last advance I found the body of your son, Orlando, with his pay book and letter lying beside him On seeing this I thought it best to write to you and let you know he died a hero's death, and accept my deepest sympathy with you. I may also add that he had an instantaneous death. I saw that his body was removed and he had a soldier's funeral, being buried with hundreds of the bravest of the brave."

Orlando's grave was lost in subsequent fighting and he is today remembered on the Ypres Menin Gate.

Lance Corporal Henry George Ash		*1st Bn Duke of Cornwall's Light Infantry*	
Service No.	3/6359	Age:	34
Place of Birth:	Chippenham	Home Country:	England
Date of Death:	29/06/1917	Cause of death:	Died of wounds
Memorial:	Bath		
War cemetery:	Mont Huon Military Cemetery Le Treport		
Theatre of war:	France		
Next of Kin:	Florence E. Ash		
Address:	47 Locksbrook Road, Lower Weston, Bath, Somerset		

Henry, an insurance agent, married Florence Ellen Floyd at the end of 1907 and it is likely he was conscripted into the army joining the 1st Battalion Duke of Cornwall's Light Infantry. He was wounded during fighting at the front and evacuated to a hospital at Le Treport, France where he succumbed to his wounds on Friday 29 June 1917. Henry left a widow and young daughter.

Bugler John Henry Hatherell		*6th Bn Wiltshire Regiment*	
Service No.	19452	Age:	19
Place of Birth:	Chippenham	Home Country:	England
Date of Death:	04/07/1917	Cause of death:	Died of wounds
Memorial:	Chippenham		
War cemetery:	Boulogne Eastern Cemetery		
Theatre of war:	France		
Next of Kin:	John William & Emily Hatherell		
Address:	9 Lowden Hill, Chippenham		

Nineteen year old John was employed as a signal worker with Saxby and Farmer Ltd prior to his enlistment with the 6th Battalion Wiltshire Regiment. He was sent to the continent where

Above: A captured German gun Emplacement.

Right: John Henry Hatherell.

on 4 June 1917 he was severely wounded during a German bombardment near Diependaalhoek, Belgium. He was evacuated to No 13 Base Hospital at Boulogne where he succumbed to his wounds. His parents received the following letter from Chaplain J. F. A. Branford:

"I am indeed most sorry to have to convey to you the sad news that your dear boy died this afternoon. Yesterday he seemed a little better, if anything, but he collapsed today. I saw him early this morning and we had a prayer together, but he quite suddenly, after dinner, got worse and expired in a few minutes. I know how much he longed to get back home and how much you longed to have him, so I can feel most sincere sympathy and I pray that our Heavenly Father may pour into your bleeding hearts His holy comfort and give you strength to bear bravely such a grievous blow."

In June 1918 John's parents inserted the following memoriam in a local paper:

In loving memory of our dear son
No one stood beside him to bid him a last farewell
Although his grave is far away he did his duty well
He's gone but not forgotten often we recall his name
But there is nothing left to answer but his photo in the frame
Sadly missed by his Mother, Father, Sisters and Brothers.

Private George Popham Garlike		*2/4th Bn Somerset Light Infantry*	
Service No.	201825	Age:	35
Place of Birth:	Sutton Benger, Wiltshire	Home Country:	England
Date of Death:	05/07/1917	Cause of death:	Died
Memorial:	Bath		
War cemetery:	Karachi 1914 - 1918 War Memorial		
Theatre of war:	India		
Next of Kin:	Dr James Percival & Sarah P Garlike		
Address:	30 Bathwick Street, Bath, Somerset		

George was the son of a former doctor of Sutton Benger and joined the Somerset territorials and was sent to India to serve on garrison duties and replace regular units which were needed in Europe. He died most likely of illness or disease on Thursday 5 July 1917 and was buried locally. He is today remembered on the Karachi 1914 - 1918 War Memorial in modern day Pakistan. The Commonwealth War Graves Commission do not tend most of the graves of fallen servicemen in what was formerly India.

Private Robert William Carter   *2/6th Bn Lancashire Fusiliers*

Service No.	38981	Age:	37
Place of Birth:	Chippenham, Wiltshire	Home Country:	England
Date of Death:	10/07/1917	Cause of death:	Killed in action
Memorial:	Chippenahm – St. Andrews Church Mem. & Devizes Odd Fellows Mem.		
War cemetery:	Coxyde Military Cemetery		
Theatre of war:	Belgium		
Next of Kin:	Matilda M. Wheeler (wife) - George & Jane Carter (parents)		
Address:	Chippeham - 51 London Road, Chippenham		

Robert was a machinist and a member of the Chippenham Odd Fellows Society. He married Matilda M.Wheeler in the summer of 1913 at Chippenham. It is likely he was conscripted into the army initially joining the Army Service Corps but because of a shortage of infantry recruits he was transferred to the 2/6th Battalion Lancashire Fusiliers, arriving in France in February 1917. Robert was killed on Tuesday 10 July 1917 during operations near Nieuport, Belgium to capture areas of the Belgium coast. Robert left a widow and two small children.

Lieutenant Sandford William Shippard   *1st Bn Loyal North Lancashire Regiment*

Service No.	N/A	Age:	21
Place of Birth:	Cape Colony	Home Country:	England
Date of Death:	10/07/1917	Cause of death:	Killed in action
Memorial:	Lacock – Lacock Church & Malthouse School Memorial		
War cemetery:	Nieuport Memorial		
Theatre of war:	Belgium		
Next of Kin:	Sir Sidney & Rosalind Shippard		
Address:	The Angel, Lacock, Wiltshire		

Sandford was the eldest son of Sir Sidney Shippard and his second wife Rosalind Shippard. He was educated the Old Malthouse School, Marlborough College and Sandhurst. On receiving his commission he was posted to the 1st Battalion Loyal North Lancashire Regiment. He was killed in action on Tuesday 10 August 1917 when his battalion were in preparation for Operation Hush along the Belgian coast. The operation was cancelled when the initial assaults of the Third Battle of Ypres failed to make their expected progress. He is remembered on the Nieuport Memorial and has no known grave.

Acting Bombardier Edward Willett   *C Bty 9st Bde Royal Field Artillery*

Service No.	130096	Age:	31
Place of Birth:	Banwell, Somerset	Home Country:	England
Date of Death:	13/07/1917	Cause of death:	Killed in action
Memorial:	Not known		
War cemetery:	Bard Cottage Cemetery		
Theatre of war:	Belgium		
Next of Kin:	James & Helen Willett		
Address:	Towerhiil Parcmain Street, Carmarthen, Carmarthenshire		

Edward was the only son of John and Helen Willett and worked as a shop assistant in Chippenham prior to the declaration of war. It is likely he was conscripted into the army joining the Royal Field Artillery. He was killed in action near Boezinge, Belgium on Friday 13 July 1917.

Gunner William Clifford   *324th Garrison Artillery RGA*

Service No.	46479	Age:	42
Place of Birth:	Chippenham, Wiltshire	Home Country:	England
Date of Death:	20/07/1917	Cause of death:	Died of wounds
Memorial:	Not known		
War cemetery:	Dozinghem Military Cemetery		
Theatre of war:	Belgium		
Next of Kin:	Ada Phylis Clifford (wife) - William & Sophia Clifford (parents)		
Address:	Euston Court Road, Epsom, Surrey		

William, an asylum assistant, married Ada Phylsis Beeching on 12 May 1907 at Epsom. He volunteered for service joining the Royal Garrison Artillery on 7 September 1914 arriving in France on 22 May 1915. In November 1915 William became ill and having spent a few days in hospital was granted extended leave, due to his medical condition, in order to return to England in December 1915. He rejoined his unit on 28 December 1915 but was admitted to hospital on 23 February 1916 and then evacuated to England on 3 March 1916. He then rejoined his unit on 1 May 1917. He was subsequently wounded with gunshot wounds on 20 July 1917 and evacuated to a casualty clearing station where he expired later that day. William's personal items were returned to his wife and included correspondence, two pipes, three pocket books, religious book, tobacco pouch, knife, whistle and strap, metal wrist watch (no glass). William left a widow and two children and in January 1918 Ada Clifford was granted a pension of 22 shillings and eleven pence a week.

Private Henry Arthur Coleman   *33rd Motor Amb. Convoy ASC*

Service No.	DM2/165578	Age:	26
Place of Birth:	Bristol, Gloucestershire	Home Country:	England
Date of Death:	22/07/1917	Cause of death:	Died
Memorial:	Kington Langley		
War cemetery:	Amara War Cemetery		
Theatre of war:	Mesopotamia		
Next of Kin:	Henry & Edith Coleman		
Address:	Kington Langley, Wiltshire		

Henry was the eldest son of Henry and Edith Coleman and worked with his father as a wheelwright and carpenter. It is likely he was conscripted into the army joining the Army Service Corps and was sent to Mesopotamia. He died of the effects of sun stroke at the General Hospital Amara on Sunday 22 July 1917. Henry's brother Herbert Richmond Coleman had been reported missing in April 1917 in France.

Lance Corporal Ernest Edwin Booy   *1st Bn Coldstream Guards*

Service No.	9283	Age:	27
Place of Birth:	Stanton St Quintin	Home Country:	England
Date of Death:	22/07/1917	Cause of death:	Killed in action
Memorial:	West Kington		
War cemetery:	Canada Farm Cemetery		

Theatre of war: Belgium
Next of Kin: Henry & Emma Booy
Address: Didmarton, Gloucestershire

Regular soldier Ernest was a farm labourer prior to his enlistment with the Coldstream Guards and arrived in France on 13 August 1914. He was killed in action on Sunday 22 July 1917 most likely by German shell fire near Bsoinge, north west of Ypres, Belgium, during preparations for the Third Battle of Ypres.

Private Gerald Harvey Barnfield   *1st Bn Wiltshire Regiment*
Service No.   32282   Age: 19
Place of Birth: Rangeworthy, Glos   Home Country: England
Date of Death: 23/07/1917   Cause of death: Killed in action
Memorial: Chippenham & St Andrews Church Memorial
War cemetery: Ypres Menin Gate
Theatre of war: Belgium
Next of Kin: William & Sarah Barnfield
Address: 46 Lowden, Chippenham

Nineteen year old Gerald was the eldest son of William and Sarah Barnfield and joined the 1st Battalion Wiltshire Regiment. On Monday 23 July 1917 the 1st Wiltshires were at Ypres, Belgium, and were called on to provide working parties in the forward area for burying dead animals. Throughout the night the Wiltshires were subjected to German shelling causing a number of casualties. One of these was Gerald. He is remembered on the Ypres Menin Gate and has no known grave. In August 1917 Gerald's parents inserted the following memoriam in a local paper:

Christ shall clasp the broken chain
Closer when we meet again

Private Philip Woodman   *2nd R M Bn R N Div RMLI*
Service No.   PLY/14116   Age: 27
Place of Birth: Liskeard, Cornwall   Home Country: England
Date of Death: 27/07/1917   Cause of death: Died of Wounds
Memorial: St. Pauls Church Chippenham
War cemetery: Naval Trench Cemetery Gavrelle
Theatre of war: France
Next of Kin: George & Eliza Woodman
Address: 78 Wallar Street, Ottawa, Ontario

Regular marine Philip enlisted with the Royal Marines on 5 September 1907 and served in the far east prior to the Great War. For the early part of the war he served mainly on board ships but on 9 May 1917 he joined the 2nd Royal Marine Battalion in France. He was wounded near Gavrelle north east of Arras, France and succumbed to his wounds shortly after on Friday 27 July 1917 and was buried in Naval Trench Cemetery, Gavrelle.

Private Gerald King   *3rd Bn Coldstream Guards*
Service No.   15458   Age: 26
Place of Birth: Athlone, West Meath   Home Country: Ireland

Date of Death: 29/07/1917   Cause of death: Killed in action
Memorial: Chippenham – St. Andrews Church & Wiltshire Police Memorial
War cemetery: Ypres Menin Gate
Theatre of war: Belgium
Next of Kin: George & Mary King
Address: 10 Myrtle Avenue, Warminster, Wiltshire

Gerald, a Wiltshire policeman lived at Lowden, Chippenham with his parents and volunteered for service with the Coldstream Guards arriving in France on 12 October 1915. On Sunday 29 July 1917 the 3rd Coldstream Guards were near Bosinge, north of Ypres, Belgium, preparing for the Third battle of Ypres. In mid August 1917 George and Mary received the following letter from Company Sergeant Major J. Gornall stating:

"Private King was my servant, or batman, as we say. We were digging quite close together when a shell burst very close to us. Your son was struck with a piece. I saw it myself. Death was instantaneous, there was no suffering, which is a mercy. He was very much liked by his officers and comrades, which shows that he always did his work well and pleasantly. He went to the sacrament on the Sunday before going to the trenches. That too says a lot, I think."

Captin Dorrian of the Coldstream Guards also wrote expressing his regrets and stating:

"Private King, poor fellow, was killed in action during the last battle of Ypres. All the men and myself will miss him. He was one of the finest soldiers we had and a great personal friend of mine. My sympathies are with you. The food parcel received from you has been given to his pals."

It is likely Gerald was buried and his grave lost during subsequent fighting. He is today remembered on the Ypres Menin Gate.

Gunner Leonard White   *D Bty 86th Bde Royal Field Artillery*
Service No.   59080   Age: 22
Place of Birth: Lea, Wiltshire   Home Country: England
Date of Death: 30/07/1917   Cause of death: Died of wounds
Memorial: Seagry
War cemetery: Hedge Row Trench Cemetery
Theatre of war: Belgium
Next of Kin: John Humphrey & Mary White
Address: West End, Minchinhampton, Gloucestershire

Leonard, a baker's assistant, was the second son of John and Mary White who had lived at Upper Seagry. He volunteered for service joining the Royal Field Artillery and arrived in France on 18 July 1915. He died of wounds on Monday 30 July 1917 on the eve of the Third Battle of Ypres just east of the town at Zillbeke, Belgium. It is likely his death was caused by German shelling. John & Mary White were to lose two more sons: Cecil had been killed in France in April 1917 and Arthur was to be killed in France in April 1918.

10
PASCHENDAELE

31 JULY 1917 - THE START OF THE THIRD BATTLE OF YPRES KNOWN AS PASCHENDAELE

Lance Cororal Arthur George Reed		*3rd Bn Grenadier Guards*	
Service No.	14577	Age:	22
Place of Birth:	Nettleton, Wiltshire	Home Country:	England
Date of Death:	31/07/1917	Cause of death:	Killed in action
Memorial:	Nettleton		
War cemetery:	Artillery Wood Cemetery		
Theatre of war:	Belgium		
Next of Kin:	Doris A. Reed (wife) - George & Sarah Reed (parents)		
Address:	Nettleton, Wiltshire.		

Arthur joined the Grenadier Guards in 1910 using the name George Reed and stated his age was nineteen years when in fact he was fifteen years of age. He left the army prior to the Great War and joined the police force in Abergavenny and at the outbreak of hostilities he was an attendant at the Brecon and Radnor Asylum. Being a member of the reserve he was called back to the colours rejoining the 3rd Battalion Grenadier Guards and arriving in France on 12 September 1914. He fought at the retreat from Mons, the Marne, the Aisne and the First Battle of Ypres. He was wounded at Le Bassee in the head by an explosive bullet and was sent to England to recover for six weeks and while convalescing he married nurse Doris A Pewtner. He returned to France taking part in the fighting at Loos, the Somme and the capture of Vimy Ridge. Arthur was killed instantly by a shell at about 10:30am on Tuesday 31 July 1917 while working in a trench near Bosinge, northwest of Ypres, Belgium. Sergeant W. Robertson, who was in the same company as Arthur, wrote:

"He was one of the bravest men I have ever seen, and was the most respected and best-liked non commissioned officer in his company."

At the time of his death Arthur had spent almost 3 years on the continent with the exception of six weeks in England. He left a widow and young son.

Private Herbert Pullin		*8th Bn Somerset Light Infantry*	
Service No.	27861	Age:	19
Place of Birth:	Nettleton, Wiltshire	Home Country:	England

Date of Death: 31/07/1917   Cause of death: Killed in action
Memorial: Leigh Dealamere
War cemetery: Ypres Menin Gate
Theatre of war: Belgium
Next of Kin: George & Ellen Pullin
Address: Green Barrow Farm, Summer Lane, Castle Combe, Wiltshire

Herbert volunteered for service with the Somerset Light Infantry in July 1915 at the age of seventeen and his character was described as bright and cheerful. At 7.50am on 31 July 1917 the 8th Somersets were in trenches East of Wijtschate, south of Ypres, Belgium, both in support and front line. As the British attacking troops advanced the German artillery shelled the British front line causing some casualties. Shortly after 8am the Somersets advanced to clear Beek Wood and establish a new line. Throughout the day the 8th Somersets were subjected to heavy German artillery and machine gun fire and enemy snipers were extremely active. Herbert was one of 58 members of the 8th Somersets to be killed on Tuesday 31 July 1917. He is remembered on the Ypres Menin gate and has no known grave.

Driver Walter Jacob Clark   *L Bty 15th Bde Royal Horse Artillery*
Service No.   63150   Age: 28
Place of Birth: Norton St Philip, Somerset   Home Country: England
Date of Death: 31/07/1917   Cause of death: Died
Memorial: Langley Burrell
War cemetery: Langley Burrell St Peter Churchyard
Theatre of war: Home
Next of Kin: Edith Evelyn Clark (wife) – Roland & Edith Clark (parents)
Address: 43 Peperhasow Road, Godalming, Surrey - Hill Corner, Langley Burrell

Regular soldier Walter joined the Royal Horse Artillery in 1910 and in the summer of 1914 he married Edith E. Berry at Guildford, Surrey. At the outbreak of the war he was sent to France arriving on 15 August 1914. He took part in the retreat from Mons and was then sent to Gallipoli and after the peninsular was evacuated he returned once again to France. In February 1917 he developed an illness and was invalided back to England, becoming a patient at Leicester Hospital. He was sent home on sick leave but his condition did not improve and he was sent to Bath Hospital where he died on Tuesday 31 July 1917. Because of the short notice for the funeral military honours were not paid and he was buried on the anniversary of the declaration of the war. At the close of the service at his graveside the Rector, the Rev. A. Pope said:

"This is the fourth anniversary of the war, and when we on this solemn occasion look back and review the past three years it is full of sorrow, but it is full of pride, pride for the devotion and loyalty of our people at home, pride in what our men have done, and what our women have done here co operating in the work. It is also a time of thankfulness, thankfulness to God for the help of our brethren over seas; thankfulness of the cooperation of our Allies, and our harmony with them; thankfulness for the success of our arms; and thankfulness that even now at the last moment the United States of America, the great Republic of the West, had joined the cause for which we entered this war. At this very moment a great battle is in progress which may decide the issue of this terrible war. Today when most of the parishes in England are keeping it as a day of prayer as well as of thankfulness it is in this meet that we should look up to the hills whence cometh our help. In what may follow we must rest assured that something will come out of this great spiritual upheaval which will help us to realise that God is on our side with the consequence of victory and peace. It is a coincidence we cannot pass that we have

Left: Walter Jacob Clark buried in Langley Burrell St Peter Churchyard.

Above: A knock out British Tank near Poelkapelle, Belgium.

laid to rest here this afternoon, on the anniversary of the war, one of those gallant fellows in the battery of the Royal Artillery, whose duty it was to face the onrush of the Great German Army which resulted in the fateful retreat from Mons: then the 29th Division, with which he was connected, went to Gallipoli, you know about that expedition; then France; then invalided home; then death. After his heroic service, it will be a comfort to his family to feel that he has given his life for his country, and that he has been laid to rest in this churchyard of the parish in which he lived nearly all his life. Lastly with bowed heads, we reverently salute the dead who have given their lives in this sacred cause, humbly thanking God for their courage and devotion, and solemnly resolving in His Name that we will not leave their work unfinished, nor suffer the great sacrifice to have been made in vain."

Private Frederick Angel Greenman   *1st Bn Wiltshire Regiment*

Service No.	24120	Age:	34
Place of Birth:	Hullavington	Home Country:	England
Date of Death:	01/08/1917	Cause of death:	Killed in action
Memorial:	Hullavington		
War cemetery:	Divisional Collecting Post Cemetery and Extension		
Theatre of war:	Belgium		
Next of Kin:	Thomas & Mirriam Greenman		
Address:	Jesamine Cottage, Hullavington, Wiltshire		

It is likely farm labourer Frederick was conscripted into the army joining the 1st Battalion Wiltshire Regiment. On Wednesday 1 August 1917 the 1st Wiltshires were at Half Way House Dugout east of Ypres, Belgium, and at noon were ordered to relieve the 1st Battalion Sherwood Foresters on the Westhoek Ridge. When they reached Bellewaerde Lake the Wiltshires were subjected to such heavy German shelling that no further movement could take place and they were forced to find what ever cover they could. At about 5pm the bombardment was less intense and the Wiltshires proceeded in small groups and relieved the Sherwood Foresters. Frederick was one of five men killed during the German bombardment at Bellewaerde Lake.

Corporal William John Bailey · *2nd Bn Wiltshire Regiment*

Service No.	32933
Place of Birth:	Malmesbury, Wiltshire
Date of Death:	03/08/1917
Memorial:	Little Somerford
War cemetery:	Ypres Menin Gate
Theatre of war:	Belgium
Next of Kin:	Mildred Jane Bailey (wife) - Edward & Georgina Bailey (parents)
Address:	Kingsmead, Mill Cottages, Little Somerford, Wiltshire

Age: 27
Home Country: England
Cause of death: Killed in action

Farm labourer William was the eldest son of Edward and Georgina Bailey and in the summer of 1911 he married Mildred Jane Minty. At the outbreak of war William joined the Wiltshire Yeomanry and in November 1916 he was transferred to the 2nd Battalion Wiltshire Regiment and sent to France. On Friday 3 August 1917 the Wiltshires were near Klien Zillebeke south east of Ypres, Belgium and while in the trenches they were subjected to German shelling. In late August 1917 Mildred Bailey received the following letter from William's platoon officer:

"It is with deep regret that I have to inform you of the death of your husband, Corporal W. Bailey. He was killed by a shell on the battlefield south east of Ypres, during the attack of July 31st He was a corporal in my platoon and both a capable and popular non commissioned officer, and his loss is keenly felt by all his comrades. He was killed after fighting bravely and doing invaluable service during an action, and he was buried where he fell. I trust you will find some consolation in the fact that he died the most noble death fighting for his country. Once again I express my deepest sympathy."

William's grave was lost during further fighting and he is today remembered on the Ypres Menin Gate, he left a widow and three young children.

Private Frank Henry Crewe · *8th Manitoba Regiment*

Service No.	100065
Place of Birth:	Great Somerford
Date of Death:	05/08/1917
Memorial:	Great Somerford
War cemetery:	Nouex Les Mines Communal Cemetery
Theatre of war:	France
Next of Kin:	Henry & Mary Anne Crewe
Address:	Great Somerford, Wiltshire

Age: 27
Home Country: Canada
Cause of death: Died of wounds

Frank, a farmer, emigrated to Canada prior to the Great War and volunteered for service on 29 June 1915. He died of wounds at a casualty clearing station at Noeux-les-Mines on Sunday 5 August 1917.

Private Walter George Cole · *7th Bn Suffolk Regiment*

Service No.	50580
Place of Birth:	Derry Hill, Wiltshire
Date of Death:	09/08/1917
Memorial:	Not known
War cemetery:	Arras Memorial
Theatre of war:	France
Next of Kin:	John Cole

Age: 25
Home Country: England
Cause of death: Killed in action

Address: Langley Burrell, Wiltshire

Walter, known as George, originally joined the Royal Army Service Corps and was later transferred to the 7th Service Battalion Suffolk Regiment. It is likely he joined under the Derby scheme or was conscripted. He was killed in action on Thursday 9 August 1917. George's Regiment was part of the 12th Eastern Division and between May and October 1917 held positions east of Monchy le Preux, near Arras, France. It is likely he was killed in a raid or a small attack in this area and has no known grave.

Rifleman Reginald Albert Butler   *5th London Regiment*
Service No   315215   Age: 25
Place of Birth: Chippenham   Home Country: England
Date of Death: 16/08/1917   Cause of death: Killed in action
Memorial: Chippenham - St Andrews Church & Devizes Odd Fellows Memorial
War cemetery: Ypres Menin Gate
Theatre of war: Belgium
Next of Kin: George & Maria Butler
Address: 27 Foghamshire, Chippenham

Reginald was a footman in service at Mayfair at the commencement of hostilities and it is likely that he was conscripted into the army joining the 5th Battalion London Regiment. He was killed in action on Thursday 16 August on the 1st day of the Battle of Langemarck North east of Ypres, Belgium. He is remembered on the Ypres Menin gate and has no known grave.

Sergeant Herbert Gladstone Brown   *20th Hussars*
Service No.   4478   Age: 38
Place of Birth: Purton, Wiltshire   Home Country: England
Date of Death: 17/08/1917   Cause of death: Died
Memorial: Not known
War cemetery: St Hilaire Cemetery Extension Frevent
Theatre of war: France
Next of Kin: Laura Louisa Brown (wife) - William & Pheobe Brown (parents)
Address: Biddestone, Wiltshire – Purton, Wiltshire

Herbert had been a regular soldier and had received a long service and good conduct medal. In the spring of 1914 he married Laura Louisa Long at Biddestone. At the outbreak of war he was called to the colours with the 20th Hussars and died of illness or disease on Friday 17 August at a military hospital at Frevent, west of Arras, France.

Second Officer Arthur Benjamin Panes   *SS Malda Mercantile Marine*
Service No.   N/A   Age: 26
Place of Birth: Axbridge, Somerset   Home Country: England
Date of Death: 20/08/1917   Cause of death: Died
Memorial: Not known
War cemetery: Hartland or Stokes St Nectan Churchyard
Theatre of war: At Sea
Next of Kin: Rev John Benjamin & Louisa C Panes
Address: The Rectory, Torver, Coniston, Lancashire

Arthur was the son of the Rev. John Benjamin Panes who had been a pastor for some time at St. Paul's, Chippenham. For many years Arthur had been with a Church Missionary Society in India and was described as:

"A clean living English gentlemen and seaman worthy of his race."

He was killed on Monday 20 August 1917 when the SS Malda en route from Boston to London was torpedoed and sunk by a German submarine U-70, 130 miles south west of Bishop's Rock, near the Scilly Isles, with the loss of 64 lives.

Rifleman James Smith   *24th Bn Rifle Brigade*

Service No.	206343	Age:	44
Place of Birth:	Lacock	Home Country:	England
Date of Death:	28/08/1917	Cause of death:	Died
Memorial:	Lacock		
War cemetery:	Karachi 1914 - 1918 War Memorial		
Theatre of war:	India		
Next of Kin:	Elizabeth Smith (wife) - Elias & Sarah Smith (parents)		
Address:	15 Tewksbury Road, Tottenham – Lacock		

James, a glazier and glass cutter, married in 1898 and lived with his wife in Croydon. At the outbreak of hostilities he initially joined the 2/4th Royal West Surrey Regiment and was transferred to the 24th Battalion Rifle Brigade and was posted to India on garrison duties. He died of illness or disease on Tuesday 28 August 1918 while serving in modern day Pakistan. The Commonwealth War Graves Commission do not tend the graves of service men who died in Pakistan and James is remembered on the Karachi 1914 - 1918 War Memorial. He left a widow and four children, his medals were sent to his wife but were returned to the army when she was not found at the address they had been given and it is likely they were eventually scrapped. James's brother Elias was to die in France in July 1918.

Sapper Henry George Panting   *227th Field Coy Royal Engineers*

Service No.	178172	Age:	23
Place of Birth:	Chippenham	Home Country:	England
Date of Death:	04/09/1917	Cause of death:	Died of wounds
Memorial:	Calne		
War cemetery:	Reninghelst New Military Cemetery		
Theatre of war:	Belgium		
Next of Kin:	Edith E Panting (wife) - Henry George & Rose Panting (parents)		
Address:	25 High Street, Wooton Bassett - 2 Oxford Villas, Pippin Road, Calne		

Henry, known as Harry, was a cabinet maker and the only son of Henry and Rose Panting . In the summer of 1915 he married Edith Ayers at Swindon. It is likely he joined the Royal Engineers by registering for the Derby Scheme or was conscripted. It is probable he was wounded somewhere around the Menin Road area of the front line. He died of wounds on Tuesday 4 September 1917 and was buried in Reninghelst New Military Cemetery which is where field ambulances were based at that time.

2nd Lieutenant Percival George Angood   *Royal Flying Corps*

Service No.	N/a	Age:	23
Place of Birth:	Chatteris, Cambridgeshire	Home Country:	England

Date of Death: 11/09/1917   Cause of death: Accident
Memorial: Chatteris & March Grammar School Old Boys
War cemetery: Meeks Cemetery Chatteris
Theatre of war: Home
Next of Kin: Grace Angood (wife) - George & Mary Ann Angood (parents)
Address: Kinley, Sussex & 48, New Road, Chatteris, Cambridgeshire

Percival was the only son of George and Mary Angood and was employed in his father's ironmongery. He enlisted in the Royal Flying Corps and in the summer of 1917 he married Grace A. Buck at Yarmouth, Norfolk. On Tuesday 11 September 1917 Percival was flying from Kinley, near Croyden where his wife resided, to Rendcomb near Cirencester. He had planned to use Swindon as a guide but missed the railway town and flew over Chippenham several times and as he could not ascertain where he was he decided to land. He came down landing near Showell farm which today lies to the north of the Lackham roundabout on the A350. Percival sent a message to the flying station at Yatesbury and several servicemen came to inspect the machine and it was found that it had run out of petrol. Percival then tried to restart the machine but had several futile attempts owing to the engine being choked and this was due to the throttle being worked too quickly and this was pointed out to the young officer. Eventually the engine started and Percival was warned about a tree in his take off path. As he took off he collided with the tree breaking the propeller and the aeroplane nose dived to the ground. Percival was found lying across the wires. Only his legs were in the seat and his neck was broken. A witness, Sergeant J. Kimberly, who was one of those sent from Yatesbury stated he had trained with Percival at Dover and that he was rather nervous, further he had been flying with other types of machines than the one in which he met his death.

Captain Geoffrey Stafford Wallington   *10th Bn Kings Royal Rifle Corps*
Service No.   N/A   Age: 20
Place of Birth: Bury, Lancashire   Home Country: England
Date of Death: 19/09/1917   Cause of death: Killed in action
Memorial: Eton School
War cemetery: Poelcapelle British Cemetery
Theatre of war: Belgium
Next of Kin: Colonel Charles D. & Edith Margaret Wallington
Address: 41 Portchester Road, Bournemouth, Dorset

Twenty year old Geoffrey, known as Geoff, was the elder son of Charles & Edith Wallington who had lived at The Priory, Chippenham and he was the grandson of Sir John Wallington of Keevil Manor. He was educated at Eton from 1910 to 1915 and was an exceptional athlete. He won the junior high jump in 1912 and in 1914 he won the school Field and Oppidian Wall colours, for the high jump and the hurldles. He played in the Eton XI gaining his colours for 12th man and in 1915 he was placed third for the Victor Ludorum Cup. Geoff was an active member of "pop" being secretary of the Musical Society and was Company Sergeant Major of the Officer Training Corps. He went to Sandhurst in August 1915 and joined the 60th Rifles in December 1915. He was sent to France in July 1916 and appointed adjutant and promoted to Lieutenant in early 1917. He was mentioned in dispatches on 25 May 1917 and promoted to Captain. On Wednesday 19 September 1917 the 10th Kings Royal Rifle Corps were near Langmarck north east of Ypres, Belgium. Geoff was killed together with his Colonel when a shell struck the dug out in which they were sheltering. His commanding officer wrote:

"We all loved Geoff and cannot yet realize that he has left us. One has had from time to time

to see other officers go, whom one could hardly bear to lose, but Geoff was quite apart. It was such a privilege to live with his wonderful personality, and the recollection of his cheerfulness, his ability, his own self, will always be a very great possession, a memory that will never, never fade. We cannot bear to think too much of what has happened, and it would be a presumption to tell you what you already know of his qualities as a man and as a leader of men, he was of course, ideal. That he and the Colonel should have been killed side by side is a great tragedy, but it was in battle, and some great comfort to us all."

Geoff's House master from his school wrote:

"We were all so proud of him and he was in life and death a worthy son of Eton."

Lance Corporal Charles Henry Ponting   *6th Bn Wiltshire Regiment*

Service No.   20880   Age: 21
Place of Birth: Kington St Michael   Home Country: England
Date of Death: 20/09/1917   Cause of death: Died of wounds
Memorial: Leigh Delamere
War cemetery: Locre Hospice Cemetery
Theatre of war: Belgium
Next of Kin: William G & Florence E Ponting
Address: Sevington, Wiltshire.

Charles, a farm labourer, was the eldest son of William and Florence Ponting and it is likely he was conscripted or joined the army under the Derby Scheme joining the 6th Battalion Wiltshire Regiment. He had only just returned from home leave in England when he was wounded. This most likely happened near Opaque Wood not far from Hill 60 near the Menin Road south east of Ypres and he was evacuated to a Field Ambulance at Loker, South west of Ypres, Belgium where he succumbed to his wounds on Thursday 20 September 1917. In September 1918 Charles's parents inserted the following memoriam in a local paper:

Sleep on dear one in an unknown grave
Your life for your country you nobly gave
No loved ones were with you to say goodbye
But safe in God's keeping now you lie
Never forgotten by his sorrowing Mother, Father, Sisters and Brothers

A concrete bunker at Hill 60, east of Ypres, Belgium.

Private Henry Stoneham   *6th Bn Wiltshire Regiment*

Service No.	18117	Age: 20
Place of Birth:	Hullavington	Home Country: England
Date of Death:	20/09/1917	Cause of death: Died of wounds
Memorial:	Hullavington	
War cemetery:	Bus House Cemetery	
Theatre of war:	Belgium	
Next of Kin:	William & Bertha Stoneham	
Address:	Hullavington, Wiltshire	

Henry was the second son of William and Bertha Stoneham and volunteered for service with the Wiltshire Regiment initially joining the 1st or 2nd Battalion and arriving in France on 27 April 1915. It is likely he was wounded and evacuated to England and on his recovery transferred to the 6th Battalion Wiltshire Regiment. He was wounded most likely near Battle Wood not far from Hill 60 and the Menin Road south east of Ypres on Thursday 20 September 1917 when the 6th Wiltshire formed part of an attack on German lines. Henry died later the same day.

Lieutenant William Thomas Granger   *6th Bn Wiltshire Regiment*

Service No.	N/A	Age: 24
Place of Birth:	Chippenham	Home Country: England
Date of Death:	21/09/1917	Cause of death: Died of wounds
Memorial:	Chippenham & St. Paul's Church Chippenham	
War cemetery:	Bus House Cemetery	
Theatre of war:	Belgium	
Next of Kin:	Thomas & Emily Granger	
Address:	40 Park Lane, Chippenham, Wiltshire	

William, known as Will, was educated at St. Pauls School in Park lane, Chippenham and was a member of the Boy Scout movement. He rose to the position of assistant scout master from which he resigned when he found employment with the Great Western Railway at Swindon. He lived with his Uncle and Aunt in Ferndale Road, Swindon taking an active role in the Scouting movement in the town. He initially worked as a porter before taking a role as clerk and at the outbreak of hostilities he was working in the Loco and Carriage Department. He volunteered for service in September 1916 with the Wiltshire Territorials and was sent to India on garrison duties. He was promoted to lance corporal and later recommended for a commission. He returned to England and in the qualifying examination he received the maximum marks and gained a first class military education certificate. He was gazetted to the rank of second Lieutenant on 16 November 1916 and was sent to France on 3 January 1917. He commenced service with the 6th Battalion Wiltshire Regiment on 16 January 1917 joining them at Sailly, in France. He was wounded in action near Battle Wood not far from Hill 60 and the Menin Road south east of Ypres on Thursday 20 September 1917 and died of his wounds the following day. In early October 1917 Will's parents received the following letter from the adjutant of the 6th Wiltshires:

"I am sorry to tell you that your son died from wounds received in battle on the 20th. He is a great loss to the regiment as he was both battalion musketry officer, and also a platoon commander. He was very keen in everything he did, and his men were ready to follow him at all times. On the 20th he led his men along a very difficult part of the advance, and it was due greatly to his leadership that we were able to gain the objective in the front allotted to his

company. He was always such a cheery fellow, and one could be certain that what ever job he was given to do would be done well. I truly sympathise with you in your great loss, which is felt by every officer and man in his battalion."

Will's cousin Bert Granger, who was also serving with the Wiltshires, made enquires to the fate of Will and ascertained that Will had volunteered to go forward and when he reached a fortified house he was shot through the kidneys. Will was brought to a dressing station and was just able to recognize the doctor, with who he was very friendly. He died shortly after and Bert was informed:

"I am glad to say he is decently buried in a recognized graveyard, and our pioneers have made a nice cross and painted it to put over the grave."

Sergeant Griffin of the Wiltshires wrote the following:

"I should like to mention that I was serving under Lieutenant Granger as a platoon sergeant last February, and I know that by his death the boys have lost a thorough good friend and leader."

Will's father received the following letter from W. R. Bird the District Commissioner North Wilts B.P. Scouts Association:

"I am very distressed to hear that Will has died of wounds received in the service of his country. I shall never forget what a true and faithful friend and loyal helper he was as my assistant officer in the Second Swindon Troop of Boy Scouts. His life here was very unselfish and happy one, spent in the service of others. From the beginning of the war he has not spared himself in the service of his country, and we have been proud of his advancement to the rank of lieutenant in the Wiltshire Regiment. Now he has made the greatest sacrifice, and the God in whom he trusted has called him to a higher service after a well spent life here. Officers and scouts of the Second Division troop present last night wish to join with me in tendering our very sincere sympathy with you and Mrs Granger and the rest of your family. I pray that our Heavenly Father may grant you all the comfort and consolation to bear the loss you have sustained with that faith and courage which we all need at this time."

In the London Gazette 23 November 1917 two months after his death, Will's promotion to Lieutenant was announced and along side it was written *"died of wounds"*.

Gunner Charles James Tompkin		*266th Siege Battery RGA*	
Service No.	99355	Age:	28
Place of Birth:	Bryanston, Dorset	Home Country:	England
Date of Death:	23/09/1917	Cause of death:	Killed in action
Memorial:	Chippenham & St Andrews Church Memorial Chippenham		
War cemetery:	Henin Communal Cemetry Extension		
Theatre of war:	France		
Next of Kin:	Mary Jane Tompkin (wife) - Charles & Hannah Tompkin (parents)		
Address:	14 Cornwill, St. Mary Street, Chippenham - 65 Salisbury Street, Blandford		

Charles, a coach and stable man, married Mary Jane Fry in the spring of 1915 in Chippenham and in May 1916 his employer Mr Daniels applied for an exemption from military service on the grounds that he was the only man left at the stables. Charles was granted an exemption until

1 July 1916. He was then conscripted into the army joining the Royal Garrison Artillery. He was killed in action most likely by German shell fire near Henin-sur-Cojeul south east of Arras France, on Sunday 23 September 1917.

Corporal Fred Hudd   *332nd Siege Bty RGA*

Service No.	125696	Age:	34
Place of Birth:	Hilperton, Wiltshire	Home Country:	England
Date of Death:	28/09/1917	Cause of death:	Died of wounds

Memorial: St. Andrews Church & Chippenham Secondary School
War cemetery: Dozinghem Military Cemetery
Theatre of war: Belgium
Next of Kin: Ada Hudd (wife) - Samuel & Emily Hudd (parents)
Address: 20 Athelstan Road, Clive Vale, Hastings – Chippenham

Fred, a solicitor's clerk, was the eldest son of Samuel and Emily Hudd of Foghamshire Nursery, Chippenham. In January 1896 at the opening of Chippenham Secondary School Fred was no.1 on the secondary school register and on leaving school was employed as a clerk with Wood and Audrey Solicitors. He was also a teacher at the Wesleyan Sunday School in the Causeway Chippenham. In 1901 he became a clerk with Gaby Stapleton and Smith of Bexhill and in 1906 he married Ada Ward in Bromley, Kent. He was badly wounded on 14 September 1917 and succumbed to his wounds at a hospital at Dozinghem, Belgium on Friday 28 September 1917. He left a widow and two small children.

Mr R.H. Gaby, Fred's employer, wrote to Samuel Hudd stating:

"I have always appreciated him and how much I have felt his absence. He was always doing something and always to be relied on. It is poor consolation to say that he was a son that you might well be proud of, but his steady, solid qualities commended him very much to me. A more loyal servant no man could have had."

Lance Corporal Frederick Bertram Pinfield   *13th Kings Royal Rifle Corps*

Service No.	R/38020	Age:	36
Place of Birth:	Goytre, Monmouthshire	Home Country:	England
Date of Death:	29/09/1917	Cause of death:	Killed in action

Memorial: Chippenham – St. Paul's Chuch & North Wilts Technical College
War cemetery: Tyne Cot Memorial
Theatre of war: Belgium
Next of Kin: Rosa Gertrude Pinfield (wife) - Henry G & Emily Pinfield (parents)
Address: 17 Audley Road, Chippenham - 44 Park Lane, Chippenham

Frederick, known as Bert, was the eldest son of Henry and Emily Pinfield and was first educated at St.Paul's School and then completed his education at the North Wilts Technical College at Swindon. At the age of 16 years he gained employment with Collen Brothers at Chippenham Flour Mills initially as a clerk before being promoted to outdoor representative and was employed with them for twenty years. Bert also had a great love of sport, he was Captain of Chippenham Football Club for several years before becoming a referee. He was a keen cricketer being a skillful batsman and played a good game of tennis. He helped form the Amateur Dramatic Society and was a member of St. Pauls Church choir and regularly took part in the services. In 1912 Bert married Rosa Gertrude Buckland at Doncaster and the couple set up home in Chippenham. At the outbreak of hostilities Bert joined the Wiltshire volunteers (home

Guard) and was in the cyclist section, he was described as a skilful marksman. Bert was called up joining the Army Service Corps but was transferred to the 13th Kings Royal Rifle Corps and was sent to France in February 1917 while also being promoted to lance corporal. He took part in the fighting at Arras and on Saturday 29 September 1917 the 13th KRRC were near Polygon Wood East of Ypres Belgium. In early October 1917 Rosa Pinfield received the following letter from a Captain, Bert's company commanding officer:

"I am very sorry to have to inform you of the death of your husband who was a non commissioned officer in the company in which I command. I only wish to say something to soften the shock of the sad news for you, but at such times words from anyone are very little good. I can only hope that in the course of time the fact that he made the supreme sacrifice in the fight for the freedom of the future generations may help you a little. Your husband was killed by a shell this morning at 6.45, during a heavy bombardment; he was only a few yards away from me at the time, in our trenches. I do not think he could have had time to realise he was even hit. You may feel glad, therefore, that he suffered no agony or physical pain. I had recommended your husband for a commission and he was expected very shortly to return to England for his course of training. I can only assure you of the sympathy felt by the whole of his company with you in your loss. Your husband was very popular with all his comrades."

Bert had written the following in a letter prior to his death:

"As you say, it is in the hands of God. I believe when I go over the great divide I am going to a better place, and I don't want any funeral music sung for me."

Bert's favourite hymn had been *"Hark, tis the watchman's cry"* and the words of the hymn seem to echo his message. He left a widow and small child and is today remembered on the Tyne Cot Memorial and has no known grave.

Leading Stoker George William James Hand   *HMS Brisk Royal Navy*

Service No.	309608		Age:	27
Place of Birth:	Biddestone, Wiltshire		Home Country:	England
Date of Death:	02/10/1917		Cause of death:	Died
Memorial:	Great Somerford			
War cemetery:	Plymouth Naval Memorial			
Theatre of war:	At Sea			
Next of Kin:	Annie Elizabeth Hand (wife) - Daniel & Elda Fanny Hand (parents)			
Address:	Holdfast Hall Cottage, Upton-on-Severn, Worcester - Great Somerford			

George enlisted in the Navy in 1906 at sixteen years of age and married Annie Elizabeth Kennedy in the summer of 1910 in Christchurch, Hampshire. While George was at sea Annie worked as a servant and lived at 40 Market Place, Chippenham. By 1917 George was a Petty Officer and leading stoker on H.M.S. Brisk a destroyer which was patrolling off Bull Point, County Antrim. On Tuesday 2 October the Brisk hit a mine which had been laid by the German submarine U 79. Of the Brisk's compliment of 141, thirty two were killed and one of these was George. The Brisk lost her bow in the explosion but the ship was saved and she was subsequently repaired. George is today remembered on the Plymouth Naval memorial, his brother Arthur Harvey was to die of wounds in France in October 1918.

Private George Chandler   *1st Bn Devonshire Regiment*
Service No.   44445   Age: 31
Place of Birth: Chippenham   Home Country: England
Date of Death: 04/10/1917   Cause of death: Killed in action
Memorial: Chippenham
War cemetery: Tyne Cot Memorial
Theatre of war: Belgium
Next of Kin: George & Anna Chandler
Address: Ashes Hamlet, Langley Burrell, Wiltshire

It is likely George, a carpenter and joiner, was conscripted into the army joining the 1st Battalion Devonshire Regiment. On the evening of 3 October 1917 the 1st Devons advanced to assembly positions just east of Veldhock, Belgium. The tracks were described as very slippery and they were shelled by the Germans continuously. At 6am the assault commenced; the 1st Devons objective was Polderhoek Chateau and they had to pick their way over a land of swamps, mud and German shells. The 1st Devons were met in no mans land by hard fighting as the Germans had at the same time been assembling for attack on the British. As they proceeded across no man's land, (which probably had a stream running through it at some point), it became a bog and continued to hamper the 1st Devons progress; however it was so soft and deep that it smothered shell bursts. The 1st Devons advance was finally brought to a halt west of Polerhoek Woods where they were forced to consolidate their position and repulse a number of German counter attacks. George was one of over a hundred men of the 1st Devons to be killed. He is remembered on the Tyne Cot Memorial and has no known grave. No one made an application for George's medals and in 1922 the Army Records Office applied to have the medals disposed of and, as with many others, it is likely they were melted down for scrap.

Private Ernerst David Hanks   *5th Bn Dorsetshire Regiment*
Service No.   19988   Age: 19
Place of Birth: Great Somerford, Wiltshire   Home Country: England
Date of Death: 04/10/1917   Cause of death: Killed in action
Memorial: Chippenham & St. Paul's Church Memorial
War cemetery: Poelcapelle British Cemetery
Theatre of war: Belgium
Next of Kin: Richard & Elizabeth Hanks
Address: 3 Old Road, Chippenham, Wiltshire

Nineteen year old Ernest, a farm labourer, joined the army enlisting with the 5th Battalion Dorsetshire Regiment. On Thursday 4 October 1917 the 5th Dorsets were supporting at attack at Poelkapelle, north east of Ypres, Belgium and in the early hours of the morning as they moved into position they sustained some casualties due to German shelling. Just after noon of the same day the 5th Dorsets were ordered forward to support attacking units, reaching the new forward positions at 3pm. Then it was realised that with all the force well forward the British were in a pronounced salient which would be hard to defend. The 5th Dorsets were ordered to return to theei original position. The 5th Dorsets suffered over 60 casualties and one of those killed was Ernest, he is buried Poelcapelle British Cemetery.

Private James Carey   *6th Bn Wiltshire Regiment*
Service No.   10283   Age: 41
Place of Birth: Seagry, Wiltshire   Home Country: England

Date of Death: 04/10/1917   Cause of death: Died of wounds
Memorial: Not known
War cemetery: Tyne Cot Memorial
Theatre of war: Belgium
Next of Kin: John & Sarah Carey
Address:,   Seagry, Wiltshire

James was employed by the Great Western Railway as a coach and wagon repairer and it is likely he was conscripted into the army joining the 6th Battalion Wiltshire Regiment. On Thursday 4 October 1917 the 6th Wiltshires were in trenches near Zillebeke south east of Ypres, Belgium. The front line consisted of a number of posts loosely connected and the Wiltshires spent the day improving these posts and improving the barbed wire. All through the day the Wiltshires were shelled by German artillery and it is likely James was wounded and died shortly after. He is remembered on the Tyne Cot Memorial and has no known grave.

2nd Lieutenant Harold Henry Reynolds   *1st Bn Bedfordshire Regiment*
Service No.   N/a   Age: 20
Place of Birth: Chippenham   Home Country: England
Date of Death: 04/10/1917   Cause of death: Killed in action
Memorial: Not known
War cemetery: Hooge Crater Cemetery
Theatre of war: Belgium
Next of Kin: Frank & Martha Reynolds
Address: 21 Ladyfield Road, Chippenham

Twenty year old Harold was educated and brought up in Winterslow. It is likely he volunteered for service with the Wiltshire territorials in India where he was promoted to lance sergeant. He was offered a commission and returned to England where he passed the army examinations with merit. He received his commission in March 1917 and was sent to France joining the 1st Battalion Bedfordshire Regiment. He was killed instantaneously by a shell near Polygon Wood, east of Ypres, Belgium, on Thursday 4 October 1917. He was described by his commanding officer as a young officer of exceptional promise.

Private William Henry Fry Vines   *3/4th Bn Royal West Surrey Regiment*
Service No.   205792   Age: 31
Place of Birth: Christian Malford   Home Country: England
Date of Death: 06/10/1917   Cause of death: Died of wounds
Memorial: Not known
War cemetery: Godewaersvelde British Cemetery
Theatre of war: France
Next of Kin: Joseph Daniel & Jane Vines
Address: Calstone, Wiltshire

William, a grocers assistant, was the youngest son of Joseph Daniel & Jane Vines. It is likely he joined the 3/4th Royal West Surrey Regiment by registering for the Derby Scheme or he may have been conscripted. He was wounded in the Battle of Broodseide on the ridge near the Menin Road, Belgium on 4 October 1917. He was then taken to one of the casualty clearing stations, based at Godewaersvelde, France where he died of his wound on Saturday 6 October 1917. He is buried in Godewaersvelde British Cemetery.

Private John Rowland Phillips   *162nd Coy Labour Corps*
Service No.   190257   Age: 41
Place of Birth: Chippenham, Wiltshire   Home Country: England
Date of Death: 07/10/1917   Cause of death: Died of wounds
Memorial: Chippenham & St.Andrews Church Memorial
War cemetery: Lijssenthoek Military Cemetery
Theatre of war: Belgium
Next of Kin: Emily Florence E Phillips (wife) - Matthew & Ann Phillips (parents)
Address: 27 River Street, Chippenham

John, known as Jack, was a milk seller and married Emily Florence E. Whyman in the summer of 1904. It is likely he was conscripted into the army initially joining the Wiltshire Regiment and then being transferred to the Labour Corps. He was wounded during fighting at the third battle of Ypres, most likely by German shell fire, and evacuated to a military hospital at Lijssenthoek west of Ypres, Belgium where he died of his wounds on Sunday 7 October 1917. He left a widow and three children. Soon after Emily Phillips received the news of the death of her husband, the family had another tragedy when her son, George, fell into a chaff cutting machine. George was taken to the Cottage Hospital in Chippenham but his arm was so badly mangled it had to be amputated.

Private Jesse Frank Tavenor Billett   *7th Bn Leicestershire Regiment*
Service No.   25255   Age: 23
Place of Birth: North Wraxall, Wiltshire Home Country: England
Date of Death: 08/10/1917   Cause of death: Died of wounds
Memorial: North Wraxall
War cemetery: Etaples Military Cemetery
Theatre of war: France
Next of Kin: Jesse & Dora Jane Billett
Address: 46 Hungerford Road, Lower Weston, Bath, Somerset

Jesse, a farm labourer, was the eldest son of Jesse & Dora Jane Billett and enlisted with the army joining the 7th Service Battalion Leicestershire Regiment. He was wounded most likely during fighting at Poygon Wood or Broodseide, Belgium in September 1917. He succumbed to his wounds on Monday 8 October 1917 at a military hospital at Etaples France.

Private Albert Fry   *4th Bn Wiltshire Regiment*
Service No.   1734   Age: 23
Place of Birth: Hullavington, Wiltshire Home Country: England
Date of Death: 09/10/1917   Cause of death: Died of wounds
Memorial: Hullavington
War cemetery: Hullavington St Mary Churchyard
Theatre of war: Home
Next of Kin: Edith E Fry (wife) - Richard & Sarah A. Fry (parents)
Address: Spa Road, Melksham - The Street, Hullavington, Wiltshire

Albert was a rubber worker and employed by Avon India Rubber Company at Melksham, he was also a member of the Wiltshire territorial which he joined on 1 October 1912. In the spring of 1913 he married Edith E Bodman at Melksham and at the outbreak of hostilities the 1/4th Territorial Battalion Wiltshire Regiment were sent to India to replace regular army units which were needed in Europe. Albert arrived in India in November 1914 and in January 1915 he realized that his sight was deteriorating. In March 1915 it was found that he was suffering from Retinitis Pigmentosa, an eye disease which leads to permanent blindness and on 30 December 1915 he returned to England. Albert was sent to Netley Hospital and on 13 June 1916 he was discharged from the army. On 13 July 1916 he attended a medical board where the army decided that the Retinitis Pigmentosa was caused when Albert had been employed as a rubber worker and the fumes of rubber manufacture had affected his vision. However, he was given a pension and returned to his home at Hullavington. In May 1917 he applied for an increase in pension because his health had deteriorated and on 30 August 1917 a further board found that Albert was suffering from pulmonary tuberculosis with only days to live. It was also stated that the onset of the pulmonary tuberculosis was caused by exposure on ordinary military service. Albert died on Tuesday 9 October 1917 at Hullavington and at this time he is not remembered by the Commonwealth War Graves Commission.

Private Arthur Thomas Benham		*9th Bn Devonshire Regiment*	
Service No.	291950	Age:	25
Place of Birth:	Alresford, Hampshireq	Home Country:	England
Date of Death:	10/10/1917	Cause of death:	Killed in action
Memorial:	Lacock - Lacock Church		
War cemetery:	Tyne Cot Memorial		
Theatre of war:	Belgium		
Next of Kin:	Mary Tryphena Benham (wife) - Thomas & Mary Benham (parents)		
Address:	High Street Lacock - Spring Garden's Tichborne, Hampshire		

Arthur married Mary Tryphena Farmer of Lacock at the end of 1914 at Tichborne, Hampshire. He initially joined the Cyclists Corps and was later transferred to the 9th Service Battalion Devonshire Regiment. In October 1917 the 9th Devons were at the Butte in Polygon Wood east of Ypres Belgium. The weather and the ground were awful and it had been raining insistently. At first they were in support but a message was sent to the 9th Devons from the front stating there was a gap in the British lines east of Judge Copse and they were to fill it. They moved in to position but because of the position of the ground it was impossible to dig adequate trenches. They were subjected to an intense German bombardment which was not only heavy but accurate and it is likely Arthur was killed by the German shelling. He is remembered on the Tyne Cot Memorial and has no known grave.

Tyne Cot Cemetery contains the graves of over 3500 servicemen and Tyne Cot Memorial, records the names of over 35,000 service men who have no known grave.

Private Frederick Edward Croker   *6th Bn Wiltshire Regiment*

Service No.	203261	Age:	20
Place of Birth:	Pewsham, Wiltshire	Home Country:	England
Date of Death:	11/10/1917	Cause of death:	Died of wounds
Memorial:	Lacock Church – Lacock & Bowden Hill Memorial		
War cemetery:	Tyne Cot Memorial		
Theatre of war:	Belgium		
Next of Kin:	Frederick & Julia Croker		
Address:	The Wharf, Lacock, Wiltshire		

Under age soldier Frederick was the eldest son of Frederick and Julia Croker and volunteered for service with the Wiltshire Yeomanry at the age of 17. He was transferred to the 6th Service Battalion Wiltshire Regiment and arrived in France on 4 December 1915. Frederick had spent 20 months on the continent before receiving his first leave, of ten days, in August 1917. On 10 October 1917 the 6th Wiltshire were at a position called the Spoil Bank near Zillebeke east of Ypres, Belgium. Frederick was wounded by a shell and died soon after on Thursday 11 October 1917 as the Wiltshires were being relieved and returning to a rest camp. It was the day after his twentieth birthday and he is today remembered on the Tyne Cot Memorial and has no known grave.

Acting Bombardier Arthur George Short   *93rd Cornwall Siege Bty RGA TF*

Service No.	322157	Age:	22
Place of Birth:	Chippenham, Wiltshire	Home Country:	England
Date of Death:	16/10/1917	Cause of death:	Killed in action
Memorial:	Chippenham & St. Andrews Church Memorial		
War cemetery:	Klein-Vierstraat British Cemetery		
Theatre of war:	Belgium		
Next of Kin:	Azor & Eliza Short		
Address:	11 Emery Lane, Chippenham, Wiltshire.		

Twenty two year old Arthur was the eldest son of Azor and Eliza Short, Azor Short was a postman in Chippenham and Arthur took employment with the post office firstly as a telegraph messenger boy, then an assistant postman and then being promoted postman and transferring to Truro in Cornwall. Soon after the outbreak of hostilities Arthur volunteered for service with the 93rd Siege Battery, Royal Garrison Artillery, part of the Cornish Territorial force, and was sent to France in May 1916. He was killed most likely by German counter battery fire near Kemmel, South east of Ypres Belgium on Tuesday 16 October 1917. His younger brother Maurice William Short was to be killed in France in May 1918.

Private George Henry Fennell   *9th Bn Devonshire Regiment*

Service No.	31371	Age:	26
Place of Birth:	Chippenham, Wiltshire	Home Country:	England
Date of Death:	26/10/1917	Cause of death:	Killed in action
Memorial:	Chippenham & St. Paul's Church Memorial		
War cemetery:	Tyne Cot Memorial		
Theatre of war:	Belgium		
Next of Kin:	Thomas & Mary Fennell		
Address:	17 Lowden, Chippenham		

George, a butcher, was the eldest son of Thomas and Mary Fennell and it is likely he was conscripted into the army joining the 9th Battalion Devonshire Regiment. On Friday 26 October 1917 the 8th & 9th Battalions were in position to attack Geluveld South east of Ypres on the Menin Road in Belgiun and were attacking over a sea of mud. This had not been helped by the constant rain prior to the attack and the only dry places were the German pill boxes. At 5.40am the 9th Devons advanced behind a creeping barrage which churned up the mud. The British attackers were immediately subjected to German machine gun fire from pillboxes. However the 9th Devons moved quickly forward and even though they were sustaining heavy casualties they managed to enter the village of Geluveld taking 15 German prisoners. The position was soon to become untenable and by 11am the advance was over and as the 9th Devons entered Geluveld they found that the majority of their rifles and Lewis guns were clogged with mud and were quickly overcome by German counterattacks. The 9th Devons casualties were 143 killed or missing and 151 wounded and there was only one officer who was not hit. One of those killed was George. He is remembered on the Tyne Cot Memorial and has no known grave.

Private Maurice Silver Pond		*9th Bn Devonshire Regiment*	
Service No.	31358	Age:	36
Place of Birth:	Chippenham, Wiltshire	Home Country:	England
Date of Death:	26/10/1917	Cause of death:	Killed in action
Memorial:	Chippenham & St.Pauls Church Memorial		
War cemetery:	Tyne Cot Memorial		
Theatre of war:	Belgium		
Next of Kin:	George William & Mary Ann Pond		
Address:	1 High Street, Chippenham		

Maurice was the youngest son of George and Mary Pond and worked for his father as a grocers assistant at their store at 1 High Street, Chippenahm. It is likely he was conscripted into the army joining the 9th Battalion Devonshire Regiment. He was killed in action on Friday 26 October in the same action as George Henry Fennell. He is remembered on the Tyne Cot Memorial and has no known grave.

Private Maurice Heath		*2nd Bn RN Div RM Light Infantry*	
Service No.	PO/17776	Age:	20
Place of Birth:	Chippenham, Wiltshire	Home Country:	England
Date of Death:	26/10/1917	Cause of death:	Killed in action
Memorial:	East Tytherton Morovian Church & St Andrews Church Memorial		
War cemetery:	Tyne Cot Cemetery		
Theatre of war:	Belgium		
Next of Kin:	Sidney & Kate Heath		
Address:	West Tytherton, Wiltshire		

At the age of seventeen years, seven months and twenty eight days Maurice, a farm labourer, volunteered for service with his brother Fred on 9 September 1914 at Bristol, arriving in France on 19 May 1917. On Friday 26 October 1917 Maurice was in the front line at Passchendaele and at 5.40am his battalion attacked a German position directly to the front, all the objectives were gained and consolidated. The 2nd Battalion Royal Marines suffered 308 casualties. Maurice was one of those listed as missing and as his parents prepared for Christmas 1917 they received the news that their 5th son had been killed in action at Passchendaele. He has no known grave and is remembered on the Tyne Cot Memorial. His brother Fred was to die in November 1918 when H.M.S. Britannia was torpedoed by a German Submarine.

Sergeant William George Russell   *14th Bn Royal Warwickshire Regiment*

Service No.	993	Age:	25
Place of Birth:	Chippenham, Wiltshire	Home Country:	England
Date of Death:	26/10/1917	Cause of death:	Killed in action
Memorial:	Bloxham, Oxfordshire		
War cemetery:	Tyne Cot Memorial		
Theatre of war:	Belgium		
Next of Kin:	James William & Annie Russell		
Address:	Near Little Green, Bloxham, Oxford		

William, a grocer's assistant, was the only son of James and Annie Russell and lived at Kenilworth prior to the Great War. He volunteered for service joining the 14th Service Battalion Royal Warwickshire Regiment and arrived in France on 21 November 1915. He was killed during fighting at Passchendaele on Friday 26 November 1917. William is remembered on the Tyne Cot Memorial and has no known grave.

Private Reginald Alfred Freegard   *2nd Bn Devonshire Regiment*

Service No.	30939	Age:	19
Place of Birth:	Sutton Benger, Wiltshire	Home Country:	England
Date of Death:	27/10/1917	Cause of death:	Killed in action
Memorial:	Bremhill - Foxham - East Tytherton Morovian Church		
War cemetery:	Lancashire Cottage Cemetery		
Theatre of war:	Belgium		
Next of Kin:	William & Sophia Freegard		
Address:	Foxham, Wiltshire		

Reginald was a rural postman and was well known in the Foxham area. It is likely he was conscripted into the army in late 1916 and sent to Exmouth, Devon for training. He was sent to France in July 1917 and was killed in action on Saturday 27 October 1917 near Ploegsteert, Belgium. The Chaplain, who buried Reginald beside two of his comrades who were killed at the same time by the same shell, wrote the following to Reginald's mother;

"The men were in a Lewis gun position and the shell burst in the middle of them, killing all three on the spot. One consolation is he did not suffer for an instant. Another consolation is that he died doing his duty, and doing it well, and has gone to join the noble army of men who have given their lives for the good of humanity."

The Corporal of the platoon wrote to Reginald's sister;

"Your brother was killed by the concussion of the shell as he had only a slight wound on his leg. He had been in my section of bombers all the time until last week, he was taken from me and put in the machine gun section, so as one of my old boys I knew him well. I always considered him one of the best in my section and for digging a bit of trench he was the master piece. You should be quite proud of Reg; he was a brave lad. He and four others were with me in a tight corner, but came through safe, so I knew his worth. He was quiet, reliable, and fond of you and home, also his girl."

Miss Hillier, Reginald's fiancée, received two letters, one from the Company Sergeant Major and the other from a private, one of Reginald's pals. The former stated:

"Reginald was well liked by the company and was admired by all the officers and N.C.O's. for his great coolness under fire. He would have done well if he had pulled through this terrible war."

His comrade also wrote to Miss Hillier:

"Bare your loss bravely and remember that he died fighting for you and he will be sadly missed by us all in the company, but much more so you and his dear mother."

In October 1918 the following memoriam was inserted in the local paper;

In loving memory of Reg
A few more struggles here
A few more partings o'er
A few more tolls a few more tears
And we shall weep no more

Corporal William Edwin Collett MM   *82nd Bde Royal Field Artillery*

Service No.	48324	Age:	21
Place of Birth:	Battersea, London	Home Country:	England
Date of Death:	27/10/1917	Cause of death:	Killed in action
Memorial:	Lacock – Lacock Church		
War cemetery:	Tyne Cot Memorial		
Theatre of war:	Belgium		
Next of Kin:	Maria Collett		
Address:	Nethcote Hill, Lacock, Wiltshire		

Twenty one year old William was the eldest son of Maria Collett and volunteered for service joining the Royal Field Artillery in October 1914. He arrived in France on 25 July 1915 serving continuously on the continent and being awarded the Military Medal in August 1917 for conspicuous work in the field. He was killed on Saturday 27 October 1917 east of Ypres, Belgium. In November 1917 Maria Collett received the following letter from and officer of her son's battery:

"I am writing on behalf of the officers and men of the battery to offer you the deepest sympathy in the loss of your son in action. Corporal W. Collett was one of the most valuable N.C.O.'s in the battery, especially in signaling, at which he had log training, but lately he was in charge of a gun detachment. We all miss him very much. He was wounded in the arm on the 27 October, and was on his way down to the dressing station when another shell burst near him and a piece struck him in the head, killing him instantly. He was buried on the battlefield, and his grave marked by a cross. I feel for you very deeply and trust that God will give you strength to bear your great sorrow."

William's grave was lost in subsequent fighting and he is today remembered on the Tyne Cot Memorial.

Sergeant Walter Mitchell MID   *5th Dorsetshire Regiment*

Service No.	9840	Age:	20
Place of Birth:	Cucklington, Somerset	Home Country:	England
Date of Death:	27/10/1917	Cause of death:	Died of wounds

Memorial:	Not known
War cemetery:	Bully Grenay Communal Cemetery British Extension
Theatre of war:	France
Next of Kin	Mary J. Sergeant (mother) – George & Elizabeth Mitchell (grandparents)
Address:	Notton, Lacock, Wiltshire – Cucklington, Somerset

Twenty year old Walter, a farm labourer, was the eldest son of Mary Sergeant and was brought up by his grandparents George and Elizabeth Mitchell. He volunteered for service with the 5th Service Battalion Dorsetshire Regiment and arrived at Gallipoli in August 1915. In December 1915 the 5th Dorsets were evacuated from the peninsular and sent to Egypt and then on to France arriving at Marseilles on 9 July 1916. He was promoted to regimental transport sergeant on 2 March 1916 and Mentioned in Dispatches for his actions on 7 October near Poelkapelle, north east of Ypres, Belgium. Walter was wounded while serving at the Loos Salient and died of his wounds on Saturday 27 October 1917 and is buried at Bully Grenay Communal Cemetery.

Private Ernest George Durbin   *20 Mt Base Workshops A.S.C.*

Service No.	M2-102898	Age:	33
Place of Birth:	Bath, Somerset	Home Country:	England
Date of Death:	29/10/1917	Cause of death:	Died
Memorial:	Chippenham & St. Paul's Church Memorial		
War cemetery:	Dae Es Salaam War Cemetery		
Theatre of war:	East Africa		
Next of Kin:	Caroline Durbin (mother)		
Address:	53 Park Lane, Chippenham, Wiltshire		

Ernest, a chauffeur, was the only son of Caroline Durbin and volunteered for service on 1 June 1915, arriving in France on 14 August 1915. He was attached to the Guards Division Field Artillery Workshops. In August 1916 he was admitted to No.2 General Hospital, Le Treport, France, with an inflamed stomach. He was then evacuated to England and sent to 2nd Canadian General Hospital and after his recovery he was sent, via South Africa, to East Africa where he arrived on 29 July 1917. Ernest was employed in the 20th Workshop at Nahungu, East Africa and on 21 October 1917 he became ill and was admitted to the Kilwa Indian Clearing Hospital. He died of dysentery on Monday 29 October 1917 and was buried in Dae Es Salaam War Cemetery in modern day Tanzania.

Private Thomas Francis Rose   *4th Bedfordshire Regiment*

Service No.	21274	Age:	35
Place of Birth:	Cirencester, Gloucestershire	Home Country:	England
Date of Death:	30/10/1917	Cause of death:	Killed in action
Memorial:	Sutton Benger		
War cemetery:	Tyne Cot Memorial		
Theatre of war:	Belgium		
Next of Kin:	Florence Mary Rose (wife) – Isaac & Emma Rose (parents)		
Address:	Sutton Benger, Wiltshire - 53 Castle Street, Cirencester		

Thomas, known as Frank, was the eldest son of Isaac and Emma Rose and married Florence Mary Weakley at the beginning of 1912 at Sutton Benger. The couple moved to Holt and it is likely Frank was conscripted into the army joining the Royal Horse Artillery, but because of a lack of infantry men Frank was transferred to the 4th Battalion Bedfordshire Regiment. At

5.50am on Tuesday 30 October 1917 the 4th Bedfords attacked Passchendaele, Belgium. As they advanced they were held up and eventually checked by the boggy ground that surrounded the Paddebeek a stream to the west of Passchendaele. An advance of between 150 and 200 yards was made and over ninety men of the 4th Bedfords were killed. One of those was Frank who is remembered on the Tyne Cot Memorial and has no known grave. He left a widow and two small children.

31 OCTOBER 1917 - BRITISH OCCUPY BEERSHEBA, PALESTINE

Private William John K Rumming   *12th Somerset Light Infantry*

Service No.	36196	Age:	37
Place of Birth:	Christian Malford, Wiltshire	Home Country:	England
Date of Death:	06/11/1917	Cause of death:	Killed in action
Memorial:	Not known		
War cemetery:	Beersheba War Cemetery		
Theatre of war:	Palestine		
Next of Kin:	Florence Hannah Rumming (wife) - George & Anna Rumming (parents)		
Address:	Bath Road, Hinton Charterhouse, Somerset - Christian Malford		

William, a bricklayer, was the only son of George & Anna Rumming and married Florence Hannah Swift in the spring of 1904. It is likely William was conscripted into the army and after a brief training period at Plymouth he was drafted to Egypt with the 12th Battalion Somerset Light Infantry in January 1917. At 5am on Tuesday 6 November 1917 the 12th Somersets attacked Turkish positions near Sheria Station on the Gaza Beersheba Railway. They had to advance over open ground a distance of 4000 yards while under fire of Turkish rifles, machine guns and field artillery. During the attack they suffered heavy casualties but by 7.15am the first objective at Cactus Garden Ridge was gained and the 12th Somerset captured 63 prisoners, 6 light field guns and 8 machine guns. Out of a compliment of 700 the Somerset suffered over 40 killed and nearly 200 wounded. On the day William's mother received the news of his death she also received a letter from him in which he stated he was in good health and sent affectionate messages to his six sisters. He also wrote:

"I hope that it would please the Almighty God to allow me to return home once more."

In January 1918 his family inserted the following memoriam in a local paper:

This day brings back our memory
Of one who is called to rest
And those who think of him today
Are those who loved him best

William is buried in Beersheba War Cemetery, he left a widow and four young children.

6 NOVENBER 1917 - PASENDAELE WAS CAPTURED BRINGING TO AN END THE THIRD BATTLE OF YPRES, BELGIUM

Private Percival John Hacker   *1st Bn Devonshire Regiment*

Service No.	205147	Age:	23
Place of Birth:	Hilmarton, Wiltshire	Home Country:	England
Date of Death:	06/11/1917	Cause of death:	Killed in action
Memorial:	Nettleton		
War cemetery:	Hooge Crater Cemetery		
Theatre of war:	Belgium		
Next of Kin:	Eli & Elizabeth Hacker		
Address:	Keeper's Cottage, West Kington, Wiltshire		

Percy was a cowman and carter employed at Fosse Farm. He was conscripted in late 1916 and originally joined the Dorset Regiment before being transferred to the Wiltshire Regiment and then on to the 1st Battalion Devonshire Regiment. He was killed in action on Tuesday 6 November when the 1st Devons captured a German position called the Mound near Polderhoek Chateau, Passchendaele Belgium; the same day the Canadians captured the Passchendaele village. Thirty one men of the 1st Battalion Devonshire Regiment were killed on the same day. Percy is buried in Hooge Crater Cemetery with nearly 6000 casualties of the Great War; his brother Ernest had been killed at the Somme in October 1916

7 NOVEMBER 1917 - BRITISH CAPTURE GAZA, PALESTINE

Private William Arthur Swanborough   *1/4th TF Bn Wiltshire Regiment*

Service No.	203662	Age:	24
Place of Birth:	Chippenham, Wiltshire	Home Country:	England
Date of Death:	07/11/1917	Cause of death:	Killed in action
Memorial:	Chippenham & St. Paul's Church Memorial		
War cemetery:	Gaza War Cemetery		
Theatre of war:	Egypt		
Next of Kin:	Hilda Swanborough (wife) - Joseph & Fanny Swanborough (parents)		
Address:	17 Sladesbrook, Bradford on Avon - 5 Lowden Avenue, Chippenham		

William, a grocer's assistant, was the eldest son of Joseph and Fanny Swanborough and initially joined the Wiltshire Yeomanry. He was transferred to the 1/4th Battalion Wiltshire Regiment and just before he left for Egypt he married Hilda Nellie Simms in the spring of 1917. On 6 November the 1/4th Wiltshires were near Sheik Abbas near Gaza, they had been involved in operations against the Turkish outposts of Outpost Hill and Maze Hill. Both had been evacuated by Turkish forces and the 1/4th Wiltshires spent the night consolidating the position. The following day the Turks shelled both Outpost and Maze Hills and the 1/4th Wiltshires were ordered to advance and capture a further Turkish post at Fryer Hill and as they advanced and took the position the Wiltshires were subjected to Turkish shell fire for the rest of the day. The Wiltshires suffered eight fatalities due to the shelling and one of these was William. In November 1918 William's wife inserted the following memoriam in a local paper:

Fondly I loved him he is dear to me still.
But in grief I must bend to God's holy will
My sorrow is great my loss hard to bear
But angels will guard my loved one with care.
When alone in my sorrow, and bitter tears flow
There Stealeth a dream of sweet long ago,

And unknown to the world, he stands by my side,
And whispers "My dear one, don't fret, death cannot divide
Fondly remembered by his sorrowing wife Nell.

Lieutenant Percival George Havelock Hunt   *92nd Trench Mortar Bty R.F.A.*

Service No.	N/a	Age:	26
Place of Birth:	Stroud, Gloucestershire	Home Country:	England
Date of Death:	08/11/1917	Cause of death:	Killed in action

Memorial: Chippenham & St.Andrew's Church Memorial
War cemetery: Roclincourt Military Cemetery
Theatre of war: France
Next of Kin: George & Matilda Emma Hunt
Address: 24 Langley Road, Chippenham

Percival, known as Tobe, was the only son of George and Matilda Hunt and was educated at Calne County Secondary School. On leaving he assisted his father in business as a boat dealer and prior to the war Tobe had been a member of the Territorials serving for four years with the Calne detachment of the Royal Army Medical Corps. In December 1914 he volunteered for service with the 1/4th Wiltshire Regiment but was transferred to the 8th Battalion Wiltshire Regiment and sent to Bovington Camp for training. He was promoted eventually reaching the rank of sergeant major and on 19 July 1916 he was given a commission and transferred to the Machine Gun Corps then attached to the Royal Field Artillery. On 5 March 1916 Tobe received a gunshot wound to his right arm and was sent to a military hospital at Boulogne. He wrote home stating that while at the hospital he went for a ride in a car and inscribed on the side was, *"Presented by Calne and District Red Cross Hospital Society".* In the summer of 1917 Percival became ill and was invalided back to England and on his recovery was sent back to France being promoted to full Lieutenant. On Thursday 8 November 1917 Tobe was in the line north east of Arras, France, and while directing the fire of his battery he was struck in the head by a piece of shell and killed instantly. In November 1918 Tobe's parents inserted the following memoriam in a local paper:

Memories affection precious thoughts
That shall not die such cannot be destroyed.

The private memorial to Percival George Havelock Hunt in St. Andrew's Church, Chippenham.

Private Frederick James Pullen   *16th Bn Welsh Regiment*

Service No.	54210	Age:	33
Place of Birth:	Noth Wraxall, Wiltshire	Home Country:	England
Date of Death:	12/11/1917	Cause of death:	Killed in action
Memorial:	Not known		
War cemetery:	Cite Bonjean Military Cemetery Armentieres		
Theatre of war:	France		
Next of Kin:	Albert & Emily Pullen (Uncle)		
Address:	Seagry, Wiltshire		

It is likely Frederick a gardener was conscripted into the army joining the 16th Service Battalion Welsh Regiment. He was killed in action Monday 12 November 1917 most likely during a raid on the German line in the Lys valley on the Armentieres front and buried in Cite Bonjean Military Cemetery, Armentieres.

Gunner Charles Large   *35th Bty 31st Bde R.F.A.*

Service No.	238354	Age	39
Place of Birth:	Upton Tetbury, Glos.	Home Country:	England
Date of Death:	12/11/1917	Cause of death:	Died of wounds
Memorial:	Not known		
War cemetery:	Wimereux Communal Cemetery		
Theatre of war:	France		
Next of Kin:	Elsie Elizabeth Large (wife) - Thomas & Hannah Large (parents)		
Address:	18 St Marys Street, Chippenham - Northfields, Tetbury		

Charles, a groom and gardener, married Elsie Elizabeth Harris at the end of 1900. It is likely he was conscripted into the army and because of his work with horses was sent to the Royal Field Artillery. He was wounded in fighting and evacuated to a military hospital at Wimereux, France where he succumbed to his wounds on Monday 12 November 1917. He left a widow and two children

Private Ernest William Rose   *1/4th TF Wiltshire Regiment*

Service No.	200990	Age:	24
Place of Birth:	Chippenham, Wiltshire	Home Country:	England
Date of Death:	13/11/1917	Cause of death:	Died of wounds
Memorial:	Chippenham - & St. Paul's Church & Causeway Methodist Church		
War cemetery:	Ramleh War Cemetery		
Theatre of war:	Egypt		
Next of Kin:	Alfred William & Harriet Rose		
Address:	42 Tugela Road, Chippenham		

Ernest was the eldest son of Alfred and Harriet Rose and employed at Saxby and Farmer Signal Works in Chippenham. He volunteered for service with the 1/4th Territorial Battalion Wiltshire Regiment in September 1914. The 1/4th Wiltshires were sent to India on garrison duties to replace regular regiments which were needed for the war, arriving in November 1914. In September 1917 the 1/4th Wiltshires were sent to Egypt and on Tuesday 13 November 1917 they were attacking Turkish forces which were defending Ramleh Junction. The 1/4th Wiltshires first objective was the village of El Kustineh which they found un occupied but as they passed through the village they were shelled by Turkish artillery At 11am the 1/4th Wiltshires were ordered to attack and capture El Mesmiyeh which involve a two mile advance under heavy shell fire. El Mesmiyeh was taken by the British and the 1/4th Wiltshires captured Two Turkish officers, about fifty other ranks and 2 machine guns. It is likely Ernest was wounded by Turkish shell fire while advancing to El Mesmiyeh and died soon after. Ernest' father received the following letter from Captain Talbot B. Pye Smith in January 1918:

"I very much regret that illness in hospital has prevented me from writing sooner to express my sincere sympathy in the loss of your son Ernest William. He was, as you no doubt have been officially informed, killed in action on the 13th November near the villages of Kustineh and El Mesmiyah, and he is buried near the former village. He is a great loss to our company, for he was popular, and during the last 18 months, the period I have been in command of B Company, and knew him, he developed wonderfully, and was a fine, strong, well set up and reliable soldier. Latterly he has been Mr Glendening's batman; I choose him at Kirkee, when Mr Glendening came to the regiment, for this work because I considered him a most trustworthy and loyal fellow. In this work I came into contact with him, as he helped with our little company officers mess and we always got on excellently. Mr Glendening was ill and did not come up to the trenches with us, so your son returned to ordinary company work, except that he acted as runner for his platoon commander, work which he performed creditably. I may add that I wanted to promote your son some months ago when we were still in India as I considered he was entitled to advancement, but he preferred to remain a private, much to my regret. We have indeed lost a splendid fellow, and I feel the deepest sympathy for you in losing him who had been absent from home for so long and whom you had not the opportunity of seeing since he had reached a full and exceptionally fine manhood."

It is likely Ernest's remains were relocated to Ramleh War Cemetery after the Armistice.

Private William Joseph John Comley   *1/4th Bn TF Wiltshire Regiment*
Service No.   200451   Age: 22
Place of Birth: Chippenham, Wiltshire   Home Country: England
Date of Death: 15/11/1917   Cause of death: Died of wounds
Memorial: Chippenham & St. Andrews Church Memorial
War cemetery: Dier El Belah War Cemetery
Theatre of war: Egypt
Next of Kin: John & Annie Comley
Address: 2 Cowleaze Terrace, Chippenham

Twenty two year old William was the eldest son of John and Annie Comley and also a territorial soldier who volunteered to serve in India with the 1/4th Territorial Battalion Wiltshire Regiment. The 1/4th Wiltshires arrived in India in November 1914, on garrison duties to replace regular regiments which were needed for the war. In September 1917 the 1/4 Wiltshires were sent to Egypt. It is likely William was wounded during fighting on Tuesday 13 November 1917 in the same action as Ernest William Rose and evacuated to a casualty clearing station at Dier El Belah where he succumbed to his wounds on Thursday 15 November 1917. In November 1919 his family inserted the following memoriam in a local paper:

With aching hearts we shook his hand
Tears glistened in our eyes
We wished him back, but never thought
It was his last good bye.

11

CAMBRAI

On 20 November 1917 the British mounted a surprise tank attack between the River Scarpe and St. Quentin, France. This was the first time a massed tank attack had taken place and 378 machines went into action at what was to be known as the Battle of Cambrai. Initially the advance was successful but the British failed to take advantage and the Germans mounted counter attacks retaking much of the ground that had been captured.

Private Henry George Couzens   *1/4th Bn TF Wiltshire Regiment*

Service No.	200151	Age:	34
Place of Birth:	Chippenham, Wiltshire	Home Country:	England
Date of Death:	22/11/1917	Cause of death:	Killed in action
Memorial:	Chippenham – St. Andrews Church & Liberal Club Memorials		
War cemetery:	Jerusalem War Cemetery		
Theatre of war:	Egypt		
Next of Kin:	Henry & Sarah Couzens		
Address:	1 Rowden Place, Chippenham		

Henry, known as George, was a stampsmith and the eldest son of Henry and Sarah Couzens. He was a territorial soldier and volunteered to serve in India with the 1/4th Territorial Battalion Wiltshire Regiment. The 1/4th Wiltshires arrived in India in November 1914, on garrison duties to replace regular regiments which were needed for the war. In September 1917 the 1/4th Wiltshires were sent to Egypt and on Thursday 22 November they were forming the advance guard of the British force and they had been tasked with capturing the villages of El Jib and Bir Nebal west of Jerusalem. After about a mile they came under fire from long range Turkish artillery from a ridge to the north. An attempt was made to advance on the ridge but owing to the broken stoney ground the attempt was abandoned and at night fall the British withdrew to Beit Izza. It is likely George was killed by Turkish shell fire during this advance.

Private George Alfred Knight   *1/4th Bn TF Wiltshire Regiment*

Service No.	201622	Age:	28
Place of Birth:	Kilburn, London	Home Country:	England
Date of Death:	22/11/1917	Cause of death:	Killed in action
Memorial:	Chippenham & Hardenhuish Church Memorial		
War cemetery:	Jerusalem War Cemetery		
Theatre of war:	Egypt		

Next of Kin: Alfred & Harriet Knight
Address: 12 Downing Street, Chippenham

George, a butcher, was the eldest son of Alfred and Harriet Knight and was a territorial soldier and volunteered to serve in India with the 1/4th Territorial Battalion Wiltshire Regiment. The 1/4th Wiltshires arrived in India in November 1914, on garrison duties to replace regular regiments which were needed for the war. In September 1917 the 1/4th Wiltshires were sent to Egypt and on Thursday 22 November they were forming the advance guard of the British force. George was killed by Turkish artillery fire as the Wiltshires advanced on a ridge in the same action as Henry Couzens. He is buried in Jerusalem War Cemetery.

Private Harold Alfred Hicks   *B Bn Tank Corps*
Service No.   95722   Age: 22
Place of Birth: Long Ashton, Somerset   Home Country: England
Date of Death: 23/11/1917   Cause of death: Killed in action
Memorial: Not known
War cemetery: Cambrai Memorial Louverval
Theatre of war: France
Next of Kin: Alfred & Jane Ann Hicks
Address: Woodlands Park Street, Chippenham

Twenty two year old Harold, a dairy man, volunteered for service with the Gloucester Regiment and arrived in France on 31 March 1915. He later transferred to the new Tank Corps and on 20 November 1917 the British successfully attacked the German lines at Cambrai, France with the first use of a massed tank attack. By Friday 23 November the German forces were beginning to recover from the initial shock of the tank attack but the British were still pushing forward. Thirteen tanks of B Battalion Tank Corps attacked the French village of Fontaine. The infantry was supposed to keep up with the Tanks but they had decided to keep back for fear of being hit by German artillery shells and were pinned down from German Machine gun fire from la Folie Chateau. The tanks of B Battalion entered the village alone and were subject to machine gun and hand grenade attacks from the upper stories of surrounding buildings. Only three tanks returned to base at the end of the day. It is likely Alfred was killed in one of the burning tanks left behind at Fontaine. He is remembered on the Cambrai Memorial Louverval and has no known grave

Gunner Cyril Richard Manners   *B Bty 47th Bde R.F.A.*
Service No.   184989   Age: 26
Place of Birth: Chippenham   Home Country: England
Date of Death: 26/11/1917   Cause of death: Killed in action
Memorial: Corsham
War cemetery: Tyne Cot Memorial
Theatre of war: Belgium
Next of Kin: Charles & Martha Manners
Address: Corshamside, Corsham, Wiltshire

Cyril, known as Richard, had been employed as a footman at Belton House, Grantham, Lincolnshire. He was the youngest son of Charles and Martha Manners who had previously run the Hare and Hounds at Corsham. It is likely Richard was conscripted into the army joining the Royal Field Artillery. He was killed in action on Monday 26 November 1917 most likely by German artillery fire during the Battle of Passchendaele, Belgium. He is remembered on the Tyne Cot Memorial and has no known grave.

Private Arthur Reginald Flower		*8th Bn Duke of Cornwall's Light Infantry*	
Service No.	34553	Age:	19
Place of Birth:	Chippenham	Home Country:	England
Date of Death:	29/11/1917	Cause of death:	Died
Memorial:	Chippenham - St Andres Church - Causeway Methodist & Liberal Club Mem.		
War cemetery:	Mikra British Cemetery		
Theatre of war:	Salonika		
Next of Kin:	Charles & Elizabeth Flower		
Address :	Sweet Briar Cottage, 42 Blind Lane, Chippenham		

Nineteen year old Arthur initially joined the Royal Wiltshire Yeomanry but was later transferred to the 8th Battalion Duke of Cornwall's Light Infantry and sent to Salonika Greece. At Salonika during the Great War for every man to be killed or die of wounds in battle four died of disease. Arthur was one of these men, he died of illness or disease on Thursday 28 November 1917 at 50th General Hospital. In February 1918 his parents inserted the following memoriam in a local paper.

"Now a mother's heart is aching for a son she loved so well
Who gave his life for his country and in honou's cause he fell
Had I but one last fond look into your loving face
Or had I the chance to kneel down in that far off place
And held your hand, dear son, whilst your young life ebbed away
My heart would not have felt so sore through tears I shed today
From his sorrowing Mother, Father, Sisters and Brother"

Right: Arthur Reginald Flower remebered on his mother's grave marker in Chippeham Cemetery.

Below: British Artillery in action at Salonika, Greece.

Private Edward Bath   *7th Somerset Light Infantry*

Service No.	36772	Age:	25
Place of Birth:	Lacock, Wiltshire	Home Country:	England
Date of Death:	30/11/1917	Cause of death:	Killed in action
Memorial:	Lacock & Lacock Church		
War cemetery:	Cambrai Memorial Louverval		
Theatre of war:	France		
Next of Kin:	Thomas & Emily Bath		
Address:	Raybridge, Lacock, Wiltshire		

Edward was the eldest son of Thomas and Emily Bath and prior to his enlistment was employed at the Avon Rubber works at Melksham. He was reported missing in action on Friday 30 November 1917 when the 7th Somersets were virtually wiped out near the canal at Masnieres during the German counter attack at Cambrai, France. In August 1918 Emily Bath was informed Edward had been killed in action as a result of the effects of mustard gas on the day he had been reported missing. He is remembered on the Cambrai Memorial at Louverval and has no known grave.

Guardsman George Henry Gleed   *1st Bn Grenadier Guards*

Service No.	17875	Age:	26
Place of Birth:	Chippenham, Wiltshire	Home Country:	England
Date of Death:	01/12/1917	Cause of death:	Killed in action
Memorial:	Not known		
War cemetery:	Cambrai Memorial Louverval		
Theatre of war:	France		
Next of Kin:	William Charles & Mary Ellen Gleed		
Address:	20 Mansfield Street, Bristol, Gloucestershire		

George was a porter employed by the Great Western Railway and volunteered for service arriving in France on 16 March 1915 He was killed on Saturday 1 December 1917 near Gouzeacourt, France, during the German counter attack at Cambrai. He is remembered on the Cambrai Memorial Louverval and has no known grave.

Rifleman Walter John Cook Brittain   *16th Bn Kings Royal Rifle Corps*

Service No.	C/1591	Age:	20
Place of Birth:	Foxham, Wiltshire	Home Country:	England
Date of Death:	02/12/1917	Cause of death:	Killed in action
Memorial:	Bremhill - Foxham - East Tytherton Morovian Church		
War cemetery:	Passchendaele New Cemetery		
Theatre of war:	Belgium		
Next of Kin:	William & Emma Brittain		
Address:	Lower Lodge, Pewsham		

Twenty year old Walter joined the 16th Battalion Kings Royal Rifle Corps by either registering under the Derby Scheme or was conscripted. He was the youngest son of William and Emma Brittain. William was wounded in the leg and foot at the Somme in August 1916 and after spending some time in the 3rd Western General Hospital at Cardiff once recovered he returned to the front. He was killed in action near Passchendaele village on Sunday 2 December 1917 and is buried in Passchendaele New Cemetery with over 500 casualties of the Great War.

Private John Marsh   *2nd Bn Hampshire Regiment*

Service No.   27813   Age: 34
Place of Birth: Chippenham   Home Country: England
Date of Death: 03/12/1917   Cause of death: Killed in action
Memorial: Chippenham & St.Pauls Church Memorial
War cemetery: Flesquieres Hill British Cemetery
Theatre of war: France
Next of Kin: Ebenezer & Eliza Marsh
Address: 13 Springfield Buildings, Chippenham

John, a fish and fruit salesman, was the eldest son of Ebenezer and Eliza Marsh and it is likely he was conscripted into the army joining the 2nd Battalion Hampshire Regiment. On Monday 3 December 1917 the 2nd Battalion Hampshire Regiment were facing German counter attacks east of Marcing at The Battle of Cambrai, France. At 11am after a heavy German bombardment, enemy infantry swarmed toward the Hampshires. The attack was most intense near the canal lock east of Marcing where the Hampshires were in hastily dug trenches with no barbed wire. The front line trenches were lost but the German attack was beaten off. John was one of seventeen men killed during the German attack. John's medals were never collected in the army and in February 1922 the army requested permission to dispose of his medals.

Private Henry John Baker   *2nd Bn Wiltshire Regiment*

Service No.   13608   Age: 29
Place of Birth: Biddestone, Wiltshire   Home Country: England
Date of Death: 04/12/1917   Cause of death: Killed in action
Memorial: Biddestone
War cemetery: Tyne Cot Memorial
Theatre of war: Belgium
Next of Kin: George & Hannah Baker
Address: Butts, Biddestone, Wiltshire

Henry, known as John, was a carter on a farm and volunteered for service with the 2nd Battalion Wiltshire Regiment arriving in France on 1 April 1915. On Tuesday 4 December 1917 the 2nd Wiltshire were in the trenches, south east of Zillbeke, near Ypres, Belgium. During the afternoon John was one of 5 men killed when Germans shelled the British with trench mortars. He is remembered on the Tyne Cot Memorial and has no known grave.

9 DECEMBER 1917 - JERUSALEM SURRENDERS TO BRITISH FORCES

Private George Henry Cole   *16th Bn Lancashire Fusiliers*

Service No.   47153   Age: 37
Place of Birth: Christian Malford Home Country: England
Date of Death: 11/12/1917   Cause of death: Killed in action
Memorial: Christian Malford
War cemetery: Tyne Cot Memorial
Theatre of war: Belgium
Next of Kin: John & Lucy Cole
Address: Christian Malford, Wiltshire

George had been a butler with the Schilizzi family at 3 Prince's Gate, London, for 14 years at the outbreak of hostilities. It is likely he joined under the Derby scheme enlisting with the Army service corps and arriving in France in January 1916 where he was employed in the Expeditionary Force canteen. In October 1917 he was transferred to the 16th Battalion Lancashire Fusiliers and after completing eight weeks training he was sent to the front. It is likely he was killed during his first tour in the front line as his sister had received a field post card dated 11 December which was the day he was killed. In January 1918 George's mother received the following letter from his commanding officer:

"I am very sorry to have to inform you of the death of Private G. H. Cole, which occurred on December 11th 1917. He suffered no pain as death was instantaneous. He had not been with the battalion long, but during the time he was in the Company he became very popular with his fellow men, and was a good soldier and a real man. It will be a great loss to you but please rest assured he died nobly doing his duty. Please accept all our heartfelt sympathy and convey the same to his people."

George is remembered on the Tyne Cot Memorial and has no known grave.

Private Richard Charles Silley   *17th Bn Manchester Regiment*
Service No.   51132   Age: 35
Place of Birth: Donyatt, Somerset   Home Country: England
Date of Death: 26/12/1917   Cause of death: Killed in action
Memorial: Chippenham & St. Andrews Church Memorial
War cemetery: Poelcapelle British Cemetery
Theatre of war: Belgium
Next of Kin: Charles & Flora Anne Silley
Address: Chiselborough, Stoke-under-Ham, Somerset

Richard, a grocer's assistant, was the second son of Charles and Flora Silley. It is likely he was conscripted into the army, initially joining the Army Service Corps and then being transferred to the 17th Battalion Manchester Regiment due to a shortage of infantry men. He was killed on Boxing day 1917 in trenches north east of Langemarck, Belgium and buried in Poelcapelle British Cemetery.

12
1918

Private Charles Hillman   *6th Bn Wiltshire Regiment*

Service No.   204240
Age: 19
Place of Birth: Chippenham, Wiltshire
Home Country: England
Date of Death: 11/01/1918
Cause of death: Died of wounds
Memorial: Chippenham
War cemetery: Rocquigny Equancourt Road British Cemetery Manancourt
Theatre of war: France
Next of Kin: John W. & Alice Hillman
Address: 45 Tegula Road, Chippenham

Nineteen year old Charles originally joined the 1/1st Wiltshire Yeomanry which was, on 20 September 1917, amalgamated with the 6th Battalion Wiltshire Regiment. It is likely Charles was wounded while in trenches near the Hiddenburg Line and taken to a casualty clearing station at Ytres, France where he succumbed to his wounds on Friday 11 January 1918.

Gunner Sidney Ernest Lock   *71st Heavy Bty Royal Garrison Artillery*

Service No.   163542
Age: 28
Place of Birth: Honiton, Devon
Home Country: England
Date of Death: 27/01/1918
Cause of death: Died of wounds
Memorial: Lacock & Lacock Church
War cemetery: Roisel Communal Cemetery Extension
Theatre of war: France
Next of Kin: Charles & Susan Lock
Address: Cheneys Farm, Honiton, Devon

Sidney was the third son of Charles & Susan Lock and worked on his father's farm, his brother Herbert John Lock was well known in Lacock. Sidney enlisted in the army and was sent to the Royal Garrison Artillery probably because of his ability to work with heavy horses. He was wounded most likely caused by German artillery fire north east of St. Quentin and died of his wounds shortly afterwards. It is likely he was buried near where his battery was stationed and his remains relocated after the Armistice.

Above: A British aircraft being inspected by the King in France.

Right: The grave of Levi James Berry at Christian Malford.

Sergeant Levi James Berry   *Royal Marine Artillery*

Service No.	3132	Age:	49
Place of Birth:	Higate, London	Home Country:	England
Date of Death:	04/02/1918	Cause of death:	Died
Memorial:	Christian Malford Church		
War cemetery:	Christian Malford		
Theatre of war:	Home		
Next of Kin:	Susan Kate Berry (wife) - Levi & Emma Berry (parents)		
Address:	Christian Malford, Wiltshire		

Levi enlisted with the Royal Marine Artillery on 12 November 1886 and served for thirteen years on board various ships. On 3 April 1899 he married Susan Kate Collins at Swindon and on 6 October 1907 he left the Marines being placed on reserve. He became a licensed victualler at Christian Malford where he and his wife Susan raised four children. In April 1915 he offered his service to the Marines and was given a clerical role at Portsmouth were he served until the 9 August 1916 when he became ill. He was invalided to the Naval Hospital at Haslar and later sent home. He died on Monday 4 February 1918 at his home in Christian Malford of morbris cordis, heart disease and dropsey an abnormal accumulation of fluid around the heart. He was buried in Christian Malford Churchyard and his funeral was attend by five of the sergeants mess members from Portsmouth and wreaths were sent from the President and members of the Royal Marine Artillery Sergeants Mess at Portsmouth. At the end of hostilities Levi was added to the War Memorial inside the church but was not added to the village war memorial. At this time Levi is not remembered by the Commonwealth War Grave Commission. He left a widow and four children. In February 1922 Susan received a gratuity from the Navy, the sum of £9.

Driver Edwin Minty   *20th Bde Royal Horse Artillery*

Service No.	206585	Age:	27
Place of Birth:	Lacock, Wiltshire	Home Country:	England
Date of Death:	05/02/1918	Cause of death:	Died
Memorial:	Bremhill - Foxham - East Tytherton Morovian Ch. - Chippeham Sec. Sch.		

War cemetery: Deir El Belah War Cemetery
Theatre of war: Egypt
Next of Kin: Myra Grace Minty (wife) - John Francis & Mary Jane Minty (parents)
Address: The Bakery, Bremhill, Wiltshire - Hare Street Farm, East Tytherton

It is likely Edwin, known as Ted and a farm worker, was conscripted into the Royal Horse Artillery. He married Myra Fry at Calne in 1917, just prior to leaving for Egypt. He died most likely due to illness or disease at the 69th General Hospital at the town of Deir el Belah on the Egypt Israel border, which was the site of a large British supply camp. He is buried in the cemetery that bears the same name as the town, with over 700 casualties of the Great War.

2nd Lt Tom Martindale Speechly   *Royal Flying Corps*
Service No.   N/a   Age: 20
Place of birth: Uttoxeter, Staffordshire Home country: England
Date of death: 08/02/1918   Cause of death: Accident
Memorial: Not known
War cemetery: London Road Cemetery, Salisbury
Theatre of war: Home
Next of kin: Tom Burge & Jessie Speechly (parents)
Address: Carter Street, Uttoxeter, Staffordshire

Tom was the eldest son of Tom and Jessie Speechly and was educated at Alleyne's School, Staffordshire. In May 1914 he emigrated to British Columbia, Canada to become a fruit Framer. On 8 December 1914, at just seventeen, Tom volunteered for service joining the 2nd Canadian Mounted Rifles arriving in England in January 1916. After completing further training in England the 2nd Canadian Mounted Rifles arrived in France on 23 September 1915. Tom was with the Canadians during the German attack at Sanctuary Wood, Belgium in June 1916 where he acted as a company runner. Clarence Bessette who volunteered on the same day as Tom gives us an idea of what life was like at the front:

"After leaving the trenches last time, we spent about six week, on working parties. We were billeted near a nice little town about seven miles back of the firing line; one of the few places along the front that has not been blown to bits by the Germans. We would walk about three miles everyday over the most wretched roads, sometimes in a downpour of rain. When it rains here it is generally accompanied by a cold penetrating wind. I think it was with pleasure we heard we were to have a few days in the trenches.

We moved on a Sunday night from our billets to a place about three miles closer to the front line into reserve. On Friday night we moved up to the front line. It was a tramp of some three miles and a half by the road, but unfortunately for us we found that the Germans were shelling the road, so we had to go by a longer way, over a wretched trail, over a steep hill. As I was carrying a very heavy pack, you may judge that it did not improve my temper any. Besides, I had just got over an attack of grippe. We arrived eventually at the front lines without any incident of importance. All was quiet along the lines, and we soon were shipshape. It was raining a little and misty.

That night I stood guard with another chap. We took spells of two hour shifts through the night, so you may judge we had not much sleep. In fact, you do not get much sleep in the trenches, one has to steal it between his various duties. When you consider that we do our own cooking, having to travel a considerable distance for water, and to rustle our own wood besides, you

Tom Martindale Speechly and his grave at Salisbury.

may judge we are busy. At night, of course, we take our spells on guard.

Our first day in the trenches was not very eventful, until about one o'clock in the afternoon, except that my troop sergeant, Sergt. McBane, was wounded in the foot by a stray bullet about ten minutes after arriving in the trenches. Pete Catt knows him I think. About eleven o'clock a.m. I had a cup of tea, and crawled into my dug-out to have some sleep. I was awakened about two hours later by a very inferno of noise. Word had been passed down the line in the morning that we were to lay low that afternoon as a big bombardment of the German lines was to take place. But it appears they started the show. Inside of a dugout is about the last place in the world to be in a bombardment, so you may be sure I wasted no time in vacating mine. We went through one of the severest bombardments that afternoon, which our line in that part had suffered for nearly three months. It is heartbreaking to suffer, because you must sit down and pretend to like it, hoping your artillery is giving them the same dose. Time and again, shells landed quite close to my bay, covering me in a shower of mud and rubbish, but fortunately we escaped serious damage on our part. Two six- inch shells struck the parapet right in front of me, but luckily they both failed to explode, otherwise you would not have heard from me except on the casualty lists. I have a small bit of shrapnel that struck the trench quite close to my head.

One shell, a six-inch one, went through the parapet and landed right between Speechly's feet, but it too failed to explode. All the boys were not so fortunate, however, as one shell landing on the parapet further up the line exploded, killing one and wounding six. Two of the Coldstream boys were in that lot, Malcolm and Malan K. They are both suffering from shock. The bombardment lasted about three hours, and in that time they put about 350 shells in our part. But I tell you, we have the satisfaction of knowing that the Germans got as much and more back.

The most serious losses from the bombardment were in the 3rd C. M. R. They lost over fifty wounded and killed that day, including a Major, a Captain and one Lieutenant. "B" squadron was not in the trenches, so they missed the fun. After the bombardment the remainder of the time in the front line was very quiet."

The 'Speechly' Clarence referred to was Tom he had been lucky. On 21 December 1916 Tom was given a commission in the British army and transferred to the 5th Reserve Regiment of Cavalry. In August 1917 Tom transferred to the Royal Flying Corps qualifying as a pilot on 2 February 1918. On Friday 8 February 1918 four aircraft took off from Old Sarum Airfield, on a planned flight via Warminster-Trowbridge-Chippenham-Swindon and then return to Old Sarum. The flyers were with an instructor who was teaching the young pilots to fly in formation. Tom Speechly's plane was on the left and he had been flying well until about midday when they reached Chippenham, where he had too much speed on and, instead of throttling back, he zig-zagged the machine to lessen the speed. The planes had been ordered to fly 100 feet apart, but it seemed Tom Speechly lost control and flew in front of one of the other aircraft and his machine was struck by its propeller, just behind the observer's seat. The aircraft had been flying at about 6,000ft and after the collision, Tom Speechly's plane went into a spin, disappearing through the clouds. Speechly had been flying with a passenger, Air Mechanic Walter Greenhalgh, and the machine crashed three miles from Chippenham at Poplar Farm, Sutton Lane. The pilot was killed in the impact and his air mechanic was found two fields away. Both men received what was described as frightful injuries, and death was instantaneous. Toms' commanding officer wrote to his parents stating:

"He is a very great loss to the squadron, in which he was extremely popular with both officers and men, and was killed in the execution of his duty. I had noted him as one of our most promising and capable pilots. He was very keen on his work and a splendid example to his brother officers."

Airman 2nd Class Walter Greenhalgh		*Recruits Depot Royal Flying Corps*	
Service No.	90699	Age:	26
Place of Birth:	Burnley, Lancashire	Home Country:	England
Date of Death:	08/02/1918	Cause of death:	Accident
Memorial:	Trinity Hall Memorial, Thomas Alleyne's School		
War cemetery:	Burnley Cemetery		
Theatre of war:	Home		
Next of Kin:	John & Priscilla Greenhalgh		
Address:	9 Hollingreave Road, Burnley, Lancashire		

Walter was the only son of John and Priscilla Greenhalgh and was educated at Burnley Wood Council School and was employed as an overlooker at R.P. Woodwards Cotton Mill at Burnley. It is likely he was conscripted into the Army joining the Royal Flying Corps on 1 August 1917. He was killed in the same accident as Tom Martindale Speechly on Friday 8 February 1918 at Poplar Farm in Sutton Lane. Walter was found two fields away from the aircraft and Tom Speechly. First Air Mechanic P. Waddington wrote to Walter's mother stating:

"He worked all the time under myself at Salisbury, and I know him to be a jolly good worker, and he had a very fine disposition and was very much liked by all his comrades."

Private Reginald Edward Sheppard		*1/4th Bn TF Northumberland Fusiliers*	
Service No.	235687	Age:	25
Place of Birth:	Chippenham, Wiltshire	Home Country:	England
Date of Death:	14/02/1918	Cause of death:	Died of wounds
Memorial:	Chippenham		
War cemetery:	Bucquoy Road Cemetery Ficheux		
Theatre of war:	France		

Next of Kin: Samuel & Emily Sheppard
Address: 1 Springfield Buildings, Chippenahm

It is likely Reginald, a labourer, was conscripted into the army initially being sent to the Nothumberland Yeomanry before being transferred to the territorial 1/4th Battalion Northumberland Fusiliers. He was wounded and taken to a casualty clearing station at Boisleux-au-Mont, south of Arras, France, where he succumbed to his wounds on Valentines Day 1918.

Corporal Algernon Aubrey Bakewell Warrilow   *816th MT Army Service Corps*
Service No.	M2-193786	Age:	29
Place of Birth:	Chippenham, Wiltshire	Home Country:	England
Date of Death:	26/02/1918	Cause of death:	Died
Memorial:	Chippenham		
War cemetery:	Mombasa British Memorial		
Theatre of war:	At Sea		
Next of Kin:	Agnes Warrilow (wife) – James B. & Clara Sophia Warrilow (parents)		
Address:	26 Princess Road, Evesham, Worcestershire - 12 New Road, Chippenham		

Algernon, a motor engineer, was the second son of James and Clara Warrilow, James Warrilow was a gun and cycle maker and dealer. In the summer of 1913 Algernon married Agnes Maud C. Taylor most likely at Ashton under Hill, Worcestershire. It is likely he was conscripted into the army and because he was a motor engineer he joined the Army Service Corps. He died after contracting enteric fever while travelling to east Africa on the ship Dunluce Castle on Tuesday 26 February 1918. He was buried at sea and today is remembered on the Mombasa British Memorial, in modern day Kenya. His brother Reginald was to be killed in an air accident in Hampshire in January 1919.

Memorial to Algernon Aubrey Bakewell Warrilow at St Barbara's Church. Ashton under Hill, Worcestershire.

Private Leonard Drewett   *152nd Lab. Coy. Labour Corps*
Service No.   90737   Age: 32
Place of Birth: Great Bedwyn, Wiltshire   Home Country: England
Date of Death: 12/03/1918   Cause of death: Died
Memorial: Kington Langley - Edington
War cemetery: Edington SS Mary and Katherine Allsaints Churchyard
Theatre of war: Home
Next of Kin: Stephen & Ellen Drewett (parents) – Jesse & Anne Coldrake (g/parents)
Address: Silver Street, Kington Langley – Tinhead, Westbury

Leonard worked as an attendant at Wiltshire County Asylum where he had worked for four and a half years prior to his enlistment in the army. He lived with his grandparents at Tin Head near Westbury where he had been the organ blower and a bell ringer. He was also a member of the Church of England Men's Society and it is likely he joined the army under the Derby Scheme on 12 December 1915 initially joining the Wiltshire Regiment on 29 February 1916 and a few days later was transferred to the 12th Devonshire Labour Battalion. He was sent to France arriving on 15 June 1916 and in 1917 was transferred to the 152nd Labour Battalion, Labour Corps. In August 1917 he was sent to the army school of cookery and the following month he was admitted to hospital after a blow on the head. In December 1917 Leonard started suffering from fits and after seemed to be in a dazed condition with head aches. He was evacuated to England and eventually sent to Colchester Military Hospital where after a Medical Board in January 1918 he was declared permanently unfit. Leonard died at 2.50pm on Tuesday 12 March 1918 of epilepsy at the Military Hospital at Colchester. His body was brought to Edington where he was buried on 19 March 1918, Leonard left £60 7s and 6d in his will.

Private Arthur Henry Holbrow   *Royal Marine Artillery*
Service No.   10200   Age: 33
Place of Birth: Kington St Michael   Home Country: England
Date of Death: 20/03/1918   Cause of death: Died
Memorial: Grittleton
War cemetery: Not known
Theatre of war: Home
Next of Kin: George & Ada Holbrow
Address: Foscote, Grittleton, Wiltshire

Arthur, a gardener, enlisted with the Royal Marine Artillery on 25 August 1902 and at the end of his time on 2 July 1914, he signed on again for further service. He continued to serve through the war at HMS Columbine, a shore base in Scotland, and on 1 July 1917 he was admitted to Royal Naval Hospital Haslar and was diagnosed with pulmonary tuberculosis He was discharged from the marines on 25 July 1917. He died most likely at his parent's house at Grittleton on 20 March 1918. The disease Arthur suffered from was attributable to his military service but at time of writing Arthur is not remembered by the Common wealth war grave commission. It is likely he is buried in Grittleton Churchyard.

13
KAISERSCHLACT

21 MARCH 1918 - THE GERMANS LAUNCH THEIR SPRING OFFENSIVE

Private Herbert William Osborne Burry   *1st Bn Wiltshire Regiment*

Service No.	18098	
Place of Birth:	Coate, Wiltshire	
Date of Death:	21/03/1918	
Memorial:	All Cannings	
War cemetery:	Achiet Le Grand Communal Cemetery Extension	
Theatre of war:	France	
Next of Kin:	Winifred Mary Burry (wife) - Sidney & Clara Burry (parents)	
Address:	25 Wood Lane, Chippenham - Home Farm, Allington, Devizes	

Age: 32
Home Country: England
Cause of death: Killed in action

Herbert, a farm labourer, was the only son of Sidney and Clara Burry and at the end of 1908 he married Winifred Mary Rich. He volunteered for service with the 1st Battalion Wiltshire Regiment and arrived in France on 17 February 1915. On Thursday 21 March 1918 the 1st Wiltshires were at a camp at Achiet Le Grand south of Arras. At 4.40am the German offensive began and the Germans starting shelling the French town with large calibre high velocity guns. One shell hit the Wiltshires camp and caused what was described as considerable casualties. The Bishop of Salisbury wrote to Herbert's parent's stating:

"I have heard with much regret of your great sorrow. May God help and comfort you. As your Bishop I desire to assure you of my sympathy, and to hope that you find consolation in the thought that your dear one has died for others, and is now in the loving care of One who died for him and for us all. I deeply grieve to hear that he is your only son. You have my most sincere sympathy."

Private William Richard Millin   *2/6th Bn Lancashire Fusiliers*

Service No.	242398
Place of Birth:	Christian Malford, Wiltshire
Date of Death:	21/03/1918
Memorial:	Swindon
War cemetery:	Roisel Communal Cemetery Extension

Age: 19
Home Country: England
Cause of death: Killed in action

Theatre of war: France
Next of Kin: Alfred George & Jane Millin
Address: The Lawn Stables, Swindon

Nineteen year old William was the second son of Alfred and Jane Millin. He joined the 2/6th Battalion Lancashire Fusiliers and in January 1918 because of a lack of replacements the 2/6th Lancashire were absorbed into the 1/6th Lancashire Fusiliers. He was killed on Thursday 21 March most likely by German shell fire, near Roisel east of Peronne, France. His brother Thomas was to be killed in Belgium in August 1918.

Corporal Maurice Cole	*2nd Bn Wiltshire Regiment*	
Service No. 18256	Age:	25
Place of Birth: Kington Langley, Wiltshire	Home Country:	England
Date of Death: 21/03/1918	Cause of death:	Killed in action
Memorial: Kington Langley		
War cemetery: Pozieres Memorial		
Theatre of war: France		
Next of Kin: Daniel & Mary Cole		
Address: Upper Common, Kington Langley, Wiltshire		

Maurice, a labourer, volunteered for service with the 2nd Battalion Wiltshire Regiment arriving in France on 4 May 1915. On Thursday 21 March 1918 the 2nd Wiltshires were south west of St.Quentin near the road to Ham. It was a misty morning and at 4.30am the Wiltshires were subjected to a German barrage consisting of high explosive and gas shells which continued throughout the day. At 10am the Germans attacked and owing to the dense mist broke through the British lines surrounding what was left of the Wiltshires. The last message heard from the Wiltshires was by carrier pigeon at 1.30pm and stated Lieutenant Colonel Martin was holding out in L'Epine Redoubt with about 50 men. Maurice was one of 93 men of the 2nd Wiltshire to be killed. He is remembered on the Pozieres Memorial and has no known grave.

Private Ernest Daniel Wilson	*4th Hussars*	
Service No. 261352	Age:	27
Place of Birth: Bristol, Glos.	Home Country:	England
Date of Death: 22/03/1918	Cause of death:	Killed in action
Memorial: Chippenham & St. Andrews Church Memorial		
War cemetery: Chauny Communal Cemetery British Cemetery Extension		
Theatre of war: France		
Next of Kin: Henry Charles & Kate Wilson		
Address: Sheldon Villa, Sheldon Road, Chippenham		

Ernest was the eldest son of Henry and Kate Wilson and served an apprenticeship as a tinsmith at Saxby and Farmer Signal Works. He later took employment at the aeroplane factory at Filton and at the commencement of hostilities he was employed in an engineering establishment in London. Ernest initially joined the Royal Army Medical Corps then was transferred to the London Yeomanry and then to the Hussars and was sent to Ireland. He was drafted to France in March 1917 joining the 4th Hussars and was killed in action neat Chauny, south of St. Quinton, France, on Friday 22 March 1918 during the German advance.

2nd Lieutenant Robert George Simmons   *11th Bn Royal Fusiliers*

Service No.	N/a	Age:	25
Place of Birth:	Rodbourne, Wiltshire	Home Country:	England
Date of Death:	22/03/1918	Cause of death:	Killed in action
Memorial:	Little Somerford		
War cemetery:	Pozieres Memorial		
Theatre of war:	France		
Next of Kin:	Theodore & Alice Florence Simmons		
Address:	Church Farm, Little Somerford, Wiltshire		

Robert, known as Bob, was the eldest son of Theodore and Alice Simons, and educated at Malmesbury Secondary School and then at Armstrong College at Newcastle. At the outbreak of the Great War Bob was still a student and in November 1914 he volunteered for service joining the 22nd Battalion Royal Fusiliers and arriving in France on 16 November 1915. On 20 November 1916 Bob was recommended for the Military Medal. While serving with a machine gun section, it became the target of German artillery and six out of the eight men present were severely wounded, Bob and a comrade administered first aid and carried the wounded men to safety and saved the machine gun. In January 1917 he returned to England and attended the officer training corps cadet school at Bushey and after passing his course he obtained a commission on 26 June 1917. In September 1917 he returned to France joining the 11th Battalion Royal Fusiliers. On one occasion he captured a German officer who was carrying valuable information. Bob was killed in action on Friday 22 March 1918 during the Battle of St. Quentin. He is remembered on the Pozieres Memorial and has no known grave.

Private Sidney William Crewe   *6th Bn Wiltshire Regiment*

Service No.	203260	Age:	21
Place of Birth:	Malmesbury, Wiltshire	Home Country:	England
Date of Death:	22/03/1918	Cause of death:	Died of wounds
Memorial:	Not Known		
War cemetery:	Queant Road Cemetery Buissy		
Theatre of war:	France		
Next of Kin:	Arthur Edward & Elizabeth Crewe		
Address:	Startley, Wiltshire		

Twenty one year old Sidney, a farm worker, was the youngest son of Arthur and Elizabeth Crewe and volunteered for service with the Royal Wiltshire Yeomanry and then the 6th Battalion Wiltshire Regiment. He arrived in France on 4 December 1915 and it is likely he was wounded when the 6th Wiltshires made a stand at Morchies, France, on the evening of Friday 22 March 1918 during the German advance. It is also likely his remains were relocated to Queant Road Cemetery, Buissy, at the end of the war.

Private Frederick Stevens   *2/7th Lancashire Fusiliers*

Service No.	282540	Age:	37
Place of Birth:	Lacock, Wiltshire	Home Country:	England
Date of Death:	22/03/1918	Cause of death:	Killed in action
Memorial:	Lacock & Lacock Church		
War cemetery:	Pozieres Memorial		
Theatre of war:	France		
Next of Kin:	Isaac & Eliza Stevens		
Address:	Notton, Lacock, Wiltshire		

Frederick, known as Fred and a carter, was the eldest son of Isaac and Eliza Stevens and it is likely he was conscripted into the army initially joining the Suffolk Regiment then being transferred to the 9th Service Battalion Lancashire Fusiliers. In February 1918 the 9th Lancashires were disbanded and Fred was transferred to the 2/7th Battalion Lancashire Fusiliers. He was reported missing on Friday 22 March 1918 near LeVerguier, northwest of St. Quentin, France, during the German offensive. At the end of April 1918 official news was received that Fred had been killed in action on the day he was posted missing. He is remembered on the Pozieres Memorial and has no known grave.

Private Harold Walter Jones		*6th Bn Wiltshire Regiment*	
Service No.	10973	Age:	25
Place of Birth:	Bradford on Avon, Wiltshire	Home Country:	England
Date of Death:	23/03/1918	Cause of death:	Killed in action
Memorial:	Chippenham & St. Andrews Church Memorial		
War cemetery:	Arras Memorial		
Theatre of war:	France		
Next of Kin:	Henry & Annie Jones		
Address:	8 Nelsons Place, Chippenham		

Harold was the youngest son of Henry and Annie Jones and had been a member of the Wiltshire Yeomanry. He volunteered for service with the 5th Battalion Wiltshire Regiment and arrived at Gallipoli in November 1915. He was wounded in fighting in December 1915 and evacuated to England. On his recovery he was transferred to the 6th Battalion Wiltshire Regiment and sent to France. He was wounded at the Somme in the summer of 1916 and after recovery was again returned to the front. On Saturday 23 March 1918 the 6th Wiltshires were at Morchies, France, facing continued German attacks. During the morning the 6th Wiltshires were subjected to heavy German shell fire. During the afternoon they were ordered to retire but because of the rising ground to the rear and the continuing German attacks it was decided it was safer to stay where they were until night fall. However at 5pm the 6th Wiltshires were forced to withdraw under a heavy German barrage and German machine gun fire. When the 6th Wiltshires reformed at 6pm 6 officers and 32 men were present. Harold was on one of over 50 men killed. He is remembered on the Arras Memorial and has no known grave.

Private Jack Smith		*7th Bn Somerset Light Infantry*	
Service No.	29473	Age:	18
Place of Birth:	Chippenham, Wiltshire	Home Country:	England
Date of Death:	23/03/1918	Cause of death:	Killed in action
Memorial:	Chippenham & Hardenhuish Church Memorial		
War cemetery:	Pozieres Memorial		
Theatre of war:	France		
Next of Kin:	Charles & Anne Smith		
Address:	12 Park Street, Woodlands, Chippenham		

Eighteen year old Jack was the youngest son of Charles and Anne Smith He initially joined the Hussars before being transferred to the 7th Bn Somerset Light Infantry. On Saturday 23 March 1918 the Somersets were at Jussy south west of St.Quentin, France. They had taken up a defensive position on the west bank of the canal. During the morning the charges beneath the bridge at Jussy failed to explode and the Germans poured across. The Somersets headquarters company moved forward to form a defensive line but it was quickly overcome and the majority of the Somersets were surrounded. Jack was one of 16 men killed and he is remembered on the Pozieres Memorial and has no known grave.

Private Benjamin John Miles	*5th Bn Ox and Bucks Light Infantry*
Service No.　30068	Age:　19
Place of Birth:　Hullavington, Wiltshire	Home Country:　England
Date of Death:　23/03/1918	Cause of death:　Killed in action
Memorial:　Hullavington	
War cemetery:　Pozieres Memorial	
Theatre of war:　France	
Next of Kin:　John & Lucy Miles	
Address:　Vine Tree Row, Hullavington, Wiltshire	

Nineteen year old Benjamin was the second son of John and Lucy Miles. He joined the army enlisting with the 5th Service Battalion Oxfordshire and Buckinghamshire Light Infantry. He was killed in action during the German advance south west of St. Quentin on Saturday 23 March 1918. He is remembered on the Pozieres Memorial and has no known grave.

Private Walter Feltham	*3rd Bn Coldstream Guards*
Service No.　17201	Age:　33
Place of Birth:　Bratton, Wiltshire	Home Country:　England
Date of Death:　23/03/1918	Cause of death:　Killed in action
Memorial:　Lacock – Lacock Church – Bowden Hill &Bratton	
War cemetery:　Arras Memorial	
Theatre of war:　France	
Next of Kin:　Agnes Annie Feltham (wife) - Charles & Betsy Feltham (parents)	
Address:　Bowden Hill, Lacock – Thornicombe, Bratton	

Walter, a carter for a brewery, married Agnes Annie Nash at the end of 1908 and it is likely he was conscripted into the army joining the 3rd Battalion Coldstream Guards. He was killed in action on Saturday 23 March 1918 during the German offensive. Walter is remembered on the Arras Memorial and has no known grave.

Private Charles Frederick Mooney	*2nd Bn Ox & Bucks Light Infantry*
Service No.　25450	Age:　28
Place of Birth:　Trowbridge, Wiltshire	Home Country:　England
Date of Death:　24/03/1918	Cause of death:　Died of wounds
Memorial:　Trowbridge	
War cemetery:　Arras Memorial	
Theatre of war:　France	
Next of Kin:　Eliza Mooney	
Address:　St.Thomas's Passage, Trowbridge	

Charles, known as Charlie, worked in a butchers shop in Chippenham and it is likely he was conscripted into the army joining the Worcestor Regiment before being transferred to the 2nd Battalion Oxfordshire and Buckinghamshire Light Infantry. He was reported wounded and missing in France on Sunday 24 March 1918 and was last seen walking towards Bapaume, France, one hour before the town was captured by German forces. In February 1919, Eliza Mooney inserted an advert in a local paper asking for information concerning her son. It was

Above: British Dead awaiting burial.

Left: Charles Frederick Mooney last seen walking towards Bapaume.

assumed later that Charlie had died of wounds on the day he was reported missing. He is remembered on the Arras Memorial and has no known grave.

Private George Millard		*2nd Bn Wiltshire Regiment*	
Service No.	10350	Age:	29
Place of Birth:	Chippenham, Wiltshire	Home Country:	England
Date of Death:	24/03/1918	Cause of death:	Died of wounds
Memorial:	Chippenham		
War cemetery:	Guise La Desolation French National Cemetery, Flavi		
Theatre of war:	France		
Next of Kin:	Eliza Rebecca Jones		
Address:	31 Timber Street, Chippenham		

George was a shop assistant in a book shop and it is likely he was a member of the special reserve. He volunteered for service with 2nd Battalion Wiltshire Regiment arriving in France on 11 December 1914. It is probable that he was wounded and captured by the Germans on 21 March 1918, in the same action in which Maurice Cole was killed on 21 March 1918, and died as a prisoner of war on Sunday 24 March 1918 near Guise, east of St. Quentin.

Private William Arthur King		*11th Bn Cheshire Regiment*	
Service No.	50803	Age:	22
Place of Birth:	Pimlico, London	Home Country:	England
Date of Death:	24/03/1918	Cause of death:	Died of wounds
Memorial:	Castle Combe		
War cemetery:	St Sever Cemetery Extension Rouen		
Theatre of war:	France		
Next of Kin:	Emma Alice Totham (mother) – Mary Anne King (grandmother)		
Address:	2A, Tasman Rd, Stockwell, London - Castle Combe, Wiltshire		

William, known as Arthur and a games keeper, was the son of Emma Alice King and after he was born he was taken to Castle Combe where he was brought up by his grandmother and two years after Arthur's birth Emma king married Arthur Totham. Arthur had grown up in Castle Combe and was a member of the local Boy Scouts. He joined the army initially being sent to the Army Service Corps, was then transferred to the training reserve before joining the 11th Cheshire Regiment. He was wounded in fighting during the German advance and died of his wounds on Sunday 24 March 1918 on a hospital train while being evacuated to a base hospital at Rouen.

Major Charles Selwyn Awdry DSO   *6th Bn Wiltshire Regiment*

Service No	N/a.	Age:	41
Place of Birth:	Bloomsbury, London	Home Country:	England
Date of Death:	24/03/1918	Cause of death:	Killed in action
Memorial:	Lacock Church & MCC Memorial		
War cemetery:	Pozieres Memorial		
Theatre of war:	France		
Next of Kin:	Constance Lilias Awdry (wife) - Charles & Margaret H. Awdry (parents)		
Address:	Hitchambury, Taplow, Buckinghamshire		

Charles was the son of Charles & Margaret Awdry who resided at Notton near Lacock. He was educated at Waynflete School then Winchester College before attending New College, Oxford. He was a keen sportsman and played in Winchester's XI in 1896 and played cricket for the Army, Wiltshire and the M.C.C which he became a member of in 1897. He served in the South African War with the Imperial Yeomanry and was mentioned in dispatches. On 27 October 1903 he married Constance Lilias Bateson and the following year became a partner in the stationers W.H. Smith & Son. He was appointed to the Royal Wiltshire Yeomanry on it's formation in 1908 and remained with them until the Wilts Yeomanry were amalgamated with the 6th Battalion Wiltshire Regiment in Belgium on 30 September 1917. On 23 March 1918 the 6th Wiltshires were near Beugy east of Bapaume, France facing the German Offensive. At the risk of being surrounded the 6th Wiltshires were forced to withdraw whilst being subjected to German artillery fire and suffering heavy casualties. Charles was posted as missing most probably during the early hours of Sunday 24 March east of Bapaume. In June his wife Constance inserted articles in local papers asking for information about her husband from any relatives of prisoners who had been taken during the German advance and in August 1918 news was received that her husband was a prisoner of war in Germany. No further news was heard of Charles and it was later assumed that he had been killed in action on the day he was reported missing. In December 1918 he was posthumously awarded the Distinguished Service Order for taking command and leading the 6th Wiltshires in March 1918, the citation reads:

"Maj. Charles Selwyn Awdry, R. Wilts. Yeo., attd. 6th Bn., Wilts. R.
For conspicuous gallantry and devotion to duty. He showed the greatest coolness and contempt of danger in conducting the retirement of the remnants of his battalion, and though greatly exhausted organised a new line of defence during the night. Next day, by his fine example he did much to steady the men of many scattered units."

Charles is remembered on the Pozieres Memorial and has no known grave.

Private Charles Henry Field   *2nd Bn Devonshire Regiment*

Service No.	30938	Age:	19
Place of Birth:	Coleford, Somerset	Home Country:	England

Above: Stretcher bearers struggle to an aid post.

Left: Charles Henry Field

Date of Death:	25/03/1918	Cause of death:	Killed in action
Memorial:	Trowbridge		
War cemetery:	Roye New British Cemetery		
Theatre of war:	France		
Next of Kin:	Charles & Mary Field		
Address:	129 Rock Road, Trowbridge		

Nineteen year old Charles was a farm labourer and it is likely he was conscripted into the army joining 2nd Battalion Devonshire Regiment. He was killed in action on Monday 25 March 1918 most likely as the Devons withdrew eastwards between Misery and Villers Cabonnel south of Peronne, France. He is today burried in Roye New British Cemetery.

Lieutenant Thomas Holt Fogg   *288th Army Troops Coy Royal Engineers*

Service No.	N/a	Age:	35
Place of Birth:	Ludworth, Derbyshire	Home Country:	England
Date of Death:	25/03/1918	Cause of death:	Killed in action
Memorial:	Chippenham		
War cemetery:	Heath Cemetery Harbonnieres		
Theatre of war:	France		
Next of Kin:	Charles T. & Agnes Fogg		
Address:	Heath Bank Babbcombe, Torquay, Devon		

Thomas came to Chippenham in 1909 and was an architect and surveyor for the Building and Land Agency with offices in the market place, acting for Mrs Lysley of Pewsham. He lived at 4 Tugela Road and was a prominent member of the Chippenham Swimming Club where he taught boys to swim and dive. He had been the honorary secretary of the Sports Club, was a keen tennis and cricket player and had served as an official at many competitions. He was a member of the musical Society, and amateur dramatic and operatic society of which he was a founder member. Thomas had been the choirmaster of St. Mary's Roman Catholic Church for seven years and was well known for the improvements he made. He volunteered for service with the Royal Engineers in 1915 and was given a commission arriving in France on 14 December 1916. He was promoted to lieutenant on 26 October 1917 and the following month his hand was badly injured while he was operating a gun. He returned to England in December 1917 to attend the funeral of his father and while on leave he received special treatment to his hand. He returned to France on New Years Day 1918. He was killed on Monday 25 March 1918 by a shrapnel shell bursting over the trench he was sheltering in near Vauvillers, between Amiens and St Quentin, France, during the German advance. He was taken unconscious to the rear where he expired on a stretcher within a quarter of an hour after receiving his fatal wound. Thomas was originally buried at Copse Corner Cemetery at Vauvillers and his remains were later relocated to Heath Cemetery Harbonnieres.

Guardsman David Brinkworth Croker   *4th Bn Grenadier Guards*
Service No.   28800   Age: 21
Place of Birth: Langley Burrell, Wiltshire   Home Country: England
Date of Death: 25/03/1918   Cause of death: Killed in action
Memorial: Bradford on Avon & Bradford on Avon Christ Church Memorial
War cemetery: Arras Memorial
Theatre of war: France
Next of Kin: Walter James & Happy Emily Croker
Address: Field Barn Farm, Ford, Wiltshire

David, known as Davie, was the second son of Walter and Happy Croker and he worked with his father as a market gardener. He enlisted with the army joining the 4th Battalion Grenadier Guards and was last seen wounded near Aytte between Arras and Bapaume, France, on Monday 25 March 1918. In March 1919 David's mother inserted a notice in a local paper asking if any soldier returning from the war could give any information about her missing son. It was later assumed that Davie had died on the day he was posted as missing. He is today remembered on the Arras Memorial and has no known grave.

Private Thomas Henry Carpenter   *2nd Bn Leinster Regiment*
Service No.   5388   Age: 37
Place of Birth: Chippenham, Wiltshire   Home Country: England
Date of Death: 27/03/1918   Cause of death: Killed in action
Memorial: Chippenham & St. Andrews Memorial Chippenham
War cemetery: Pozieres Memorial
Theatre of war: France
Next of Kin: Lydia Jane Carpenter (wife) - Annie Maria Carpenter (mother)
Address: 10 London Road, Chippenham

Thomas, a cask washer, married Lydia Jane Strugnell in 1905 and it is likely he was conscripted into the army initially joining the Dorsetshire Regiment then being transferred to the 2nd Battalion Leinster Regiment. He was killed in action on Wednesday 27 March 1918 south of Albert, France, during the German advance. Thomas left a widow and four young children. He is remembered on the Pozieres Memorial and has no known grave.

Bugler Frederick Charles Nutt   *2nd Bn Rifle Brigade*
Service No.   6270   Age: 20
Place of Birth: Bath, Somerset   Home Country: England
Date of Death: 31/03/1918   Cause of death: Killed in action
Memorial: Lacock Church & Lacock Memorial

War cemetery: Pozieres Memorial
Theatre of war: France
Next of Kin: Mary Anne Howell
Address: Cumberwell, Bardford on Avon.

Frederick was the auxiliary postman at Lacock and was the only son of Mary Anne Howell. He volunteered for service on 22 April 1915 initially joining the Royal Field Artillery before being transferred to the 2nd Battalion Rifle Brigade. He arrived in France on 29 September 1915 and had been wounded twice previously during his two years four months active service on the continent. In May 1918 it was reported that Frederick was wounded and a prisoner of the Germans but no confirmation of this news was heard and it was later assumed he had been killed in action on Sunday 31 March 1918 along with 61 men of the 2nd Rifle Brigade. He is remembered on the Pozieres Memorial and has no known grave.

Private Gabriel Wicks   *6th Bn Shropshire Light Infantry*
Service No.   27311   Age: 19
Place of Birth: Sherston, Wiltshire   Home Country: England
Date of Death: 31/03/1918   Cause of death: Killed in action
Memorial: Hullavington & Sherston
War cemetery: Pozieres Memorial
Theatre of war: France
Next of Kin: James & Annie Elizabeth Wicks
Address: Newtown, Hullavington, Wiltshire

Nineteen year old Gabriel was the eldest son of James and Annie Wicks and initially joined the army being sent to the Training Reserve before being transferred to the Worcestershire Regiment and then onto the 6th Battalion King's Shropshire Light Infantry. He was killed in action during a German attack on Sunday 31 March 1918 south east of Dormat-sur-la-Luce near Amiens, France. He is remembered on the Pozieres Memorial and has no known grave.

Lance Coporal Charles Pinnell   *3rd Hussars*
Service No   .   26390   Age: 23
Place of Birth: Lea, Wiltshire   Home Country: England
Date of Death: 01/04/1918   Cause of death: Killed in action
Memorial: Little Somerford
War cemetery: Moreuil Communal Cemetery Allied Extension
Theatre of war: France
Next of Kin: William & Annie Pinnell
Address: Park Farm Cottages, Little Somerford, Wiltshire

Charles, known as Charlie and a farm labourer, was the second son of William and Annie Pinnell. He volunteered for service with the 3rd Hussars arriving in France on 18 October 1915. He was killed in action on Monday 1 April 1918 near Moreuil Wood, south east of Amiens, France, during the German advance.

Private Thomas Edward Cole   *1st Bn Wiltshire Regiment*
Service No.   22220   Age: 23
Place of Birth: Chippenham   Home Country: England
Date of Death: 01/04/1918   Cause of death: Died of wounds

Memorial: Not known
War cemetery: Ontario Cemetery Sains Les Marquion
Theatre of war: France
Next of Kin: John & Rose Amelia Cole
Address: 1 Baydons Lane, Chippenham

Thomas, a general labourer, had been a student at the Western Counties Asylum Learning Institution for the Feeble Minded at Starcross, Devon. It may have been he was deaf or dumb as the Asylum specialized in training young people with learning difficulties for work. He volunteered for service with the Wiltshire Regiment on 22 August 1914 at the age of 18 years and 135 days. Thomas had been given a medical by an army doctor the previous day and had been declared fit for service. However just twenty five days later he was discharged from the army his record stating *"not likely to become an efficient soldier."* It is likely that Thomas was later conscripted into the army when the situation had become desperate and the army could not pick and choose. He again joined the Wiltshire Regiment being sent to the 1st Battalion. It is likely Thomas was wounded and captured during the German advance succumbing to his wounds on Monday 1 April 1918. He was later buried in Ontario Cemetery Sains Les Marquion

Private Charles King   *2nd Wiltshire Regiment*
Service No.   23746   Age :   29
Place of Birth: Lacock, Wiltshire   Home Country: England
Date of Death: 01/04/1918   Cause of death: Died of wounds
Memorial: Not known
War cemetery: St Souplet British Cemetery
Theatre of war: France
Next of Kin: Jessie & Harriet King
Address: Higher Coombe, Shaftesbury, Dorset.

Charles a cabinet maker was the only son of Jessie and Harriet King and it is likely he was conscripted into the army and sent to the 2nd Battalion Wiltshire Regiment. It is probable that Charles was wounded captured during the German offensive when the 2nd Wiltshires were surrounded on 21 March 1918 in the same action as Maurice Cole. He succumbed to his would while a prisoner of war on Monday 1 April 1918 and was originally buried in St. Quentin German Cemetery and his grave was later lost. He is now remembered on a memorial at St. Souplet British Cemetery.

Rifleman Stanley Beconsfield Collett   *1st/3rd Bn New Zealand Rifle Brigade*
Service No.   25/1689   Age: 36
Place of Birth: Langley Burrell, Wiltshire   Home Country: New Zealand
Date of Death: 05/04/1918   Cause of death: Died of wounds
Memorial: Hardenhuish Church Memorial
War cemetery: Doullens Communal Cemetery Extension No 1
Theatre of war: France
Next of Kin: Henry & Rosa Collett
Address: The Folly, Chippenham, Wiltshire

Stanley, a solicitor's clerk, was the youngest son of Henry of Langley Burrell Brewery and Rosa Collett. Prior to emigrating to New Zealand he was employed by Wood and Awdry Solicitors in Chippenham. He joined the New Zealand Army embarking from Wellington on

1 April 1916. Stanley was wounded during the German advance and succumbed to his wounds at a casualty clearing station at Doullens, France on Friday 5 April 1918 and was buried in Doullens Communal Cemetery Extension No 1.

Private Walter Charles Selman		*4th Wiltshire Regiment*	
Service	No.35151	Age:	18
Place of Birth:	Lacock, Wiltshire	Home Country:	England
Date of Death:	07/04/1918	Cause of death:	Died
Memorial:	Not known		
War cemetery:	Burrington Holy Trinity Churchyard		
Theatre of war:	Home		
Next of Kin:	Walter George & Annie Selman		
Address:	West Hay Road, Wrington, Somerset		

Eighteen year old Walter born at Nethercote Hill was the youngest and only son of Walter and Annie Selman and joined the Wiltshire Regiment. He died of illness or disease on Sunday 7 April 1918 while at a training camp near Amesbury and his body was sent home for burial in Burrington Holy Trinity Churchyard.

9 APRIL 1918 - 'GEORGETTE' THE SECOND GERMAN SPRING OFFENSIVE IS LAUNCHED

CSM William Penney		*1st Bn Wiltshire Regiment*	
Service No.	5361	Age:	34
Place of Birth:	Valetta, Malta	Home Country:	England
Date of Death:	10/04/1918	Cause of death:	Killed in action
Memorial:	Devizes - Lacock Church & Bowden Hill		
War cemetery:	Strand Military Cemetery		
Theatre of war:	Belgium		
Next of Kin:	Lilian Penney (wife) – John & Amelia Penney (parents)		
Address:	Glen Helen Wick Devizes - Bowden Hill		

Regular soldier William a musician the third son of John and Amelia Penney and was serving with the 1st Battalion Wiltshire Regiment at the outbreak of hostilities He arrived in France on the 14 August 1914 and was gassed in April 1916 and evacuated to England. In the summer of 1916 he married Lilian S Ridgley. He was killed in action on Wednesday 4 April 1918 near Rijselseweg north of the River Lys. The Wiltshires were subjected to a very heavy German bombardment and then attacked and German forces penetrating both flanks. William was a member of D Company who were subjected to an attack for an hour before being forced to retire from Zambuk Post. It is likely he was killed in action during this attack and is today buried in Strand Military Cemetery near Ploegsteert Wood, Belgium.

Private Wilfred James Frederick Griffin		*25th Coy Machine Gun Corps*	
Service No	23062	Age:	20
Place of Birth:	Chippenham, Wiltshire	Home Country:	England
Date of Death:	11/04/1918	Cause of death:	Killed in action

Above: British prisoners of war captured during the German offensive.

Right: Wilfred James Frederick Griffin.

Memorial:	Trowbridge & Hilperton
War cemetery:	Ploegsteert Memorial
Theatre of war:	Belgium
Next of Kin:	Frederick & Clara J. Griffin
Address:	39 Wyke Road, Trowbridge

At the outbreak of hostilities Wilfred was employed at the Trowbridge Club and being a member of the special reserve was called up. He arrived in France with the Wiltshire Regiment on 6 July 1915 at 17 years of age and an underage soldier. He served nearly three years in France before being transferred to the Machine Gun Corps. Wilfred was killed in action, being shot through the neck during heavy fighting in Belgium, on Thursday 11 April 1918. He is remembered on the Ploegsteert Memorial and has no known grave. His brother Gilbert William Frank Griffin was to be killed on 21 May 1918.

Private Reginald John Lane   *6th Bn Wiltshire Regiment*

Service No.	203306	Age:	23
Place of Birth:	Kington St. Michael	Home Country:	England
Date of Death:	13/04/1918	Cause of death:	Died of wounds
Memorial:	Purton		
War cemetery:	HAC Cemetery Ecoust-st Mein		
Theatre of war:	France		
Next of Kin:	Frederick William & Sarah Rebecca Lane		
Address:	Bagbury Lane, Purton, Wiltshire		

Reginald, known as John, was the second son of Frederick and Sarah Lane and he was employed on his father's farm. He volunteered for service initially joining the Wiltshire Yeomanry and then transferring to the 6th Battalion Wiltshire Regiment arriving in France on 4 December 1915. He was wounded and captured during the German advance and succumbed to his wounds on Saturday 13 April 1918 while a prisoner of war. John is today buried in the HAC Cemetery Ecoust-st Mein, France.

Private Arthur Sidney Rawlings   *2/6th Bn South Staffordshire Regiment*

Service No.	46621	Age:	19
Place of Birth:	Chippenham, Wiltshire	Home Country:	England
Date of Death:	15/04/1918	Cause of death:	Killed in action

Memorial: Chippenham & St. Andrew's Church Memorial
War cemetery: Ploegsteert Memorial
Theatre of war: Belgium
Next of Kin: Frederick & Jane Rawlings
Address: 59 Parliament Street, Chippenham

Nineteen year old Arthur was the second son of Frederick and Jane Rawlings and Arthur and his father were both members of the Chippenham Salvation Army. It is likely he was conscripted into the army initially joining the Army Service Corps before being transferred to the 2/6th Battalion South Staffordshire Regiment. On 14 April 1918 the 2/6th South Staffordshires were moved to reinforce the line near Loker, south of Ypres, Belgium and were subjected to a German attack and suffered heavy casualties. The British line broke and the defending units fell back in disarray. Arthur was posted as missing on Monday 15 April 1918 near Bailleul, France. In January 1919 Arthur's parents received an official intimation that their son was presumed dead. He is remembered on the Ploegsteert Memorial and has no known grave.

Private John Thomas Richards   *1/4th Bn West Riding Regiment*

Service No.	26616	Age:	19
Place of Birth:	Hullavington, Wiltshire	Home Country:	England
Date of Death:	15/04/1918	Cause of death:	Died of wounds

Memorial: Not known
War cemetery: Mendinghem Military Cemetery
Theatre of war: Belgium
Next of Kin: William & Sarah Ann Richards
Address: 5 Trafford Street, Scunthorpe, Yorkshire

John was the second son of William & Sarah Richards and enlisted in the army joining the 1/4th Battalion West Riding Regiment. He was wounded in fighting on the Belgium front during the German advance and was evacuated to a casualty clearing station at Mendinghem, near Poperinge, Belgium, where he succumbed to his wounds on Monday 15 April 1918. The Commonwealth War Graves Commission web site states John died on 15 April 1919 while information on his medal card states he died on 15 April 1918.

Gunner Henry William Bull   *12th Siege Bty RGA*

Service No.	110760	Age:	34
Place of Birth:	Yatton Keynell, Wiltshire	Home Country:	England
Date of Death:	17/04/1918	Cause of death:	Died of wounds

Memorial: Trowbridge & Corsham
War cemetery: Etaples Military Cemetery
Theatre of war: France
Next of Kin: Annie Bull (wife) - John & Isabella Bull (parents)
Address: 60 Mortimer Street, Trowbridge – Broadstone, Corsham

Henry was a bricklayer and a popular sportsman. He was the captain of Corsham Football Club for three years and led the team to three victories in the League Cup. He was also well known

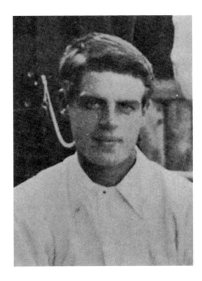

Gunner Henry William Bull

for his bowling skills for Corsham Cricket Club. He attested under the Derby Scheme on 12 February 1916 and married Mary Ann Brewer at St. Thomas' Church, Trowbridge on 5 June 1916. He was called up in August 1916 and after training he was sent on a signals course. He arrived in France in May 1917 and was wounded in the abdomen on 9 April 1918 while going to the aid of a wounded comrade. He succumbed to his wounds on Wednesday 17 April 1918 at the Canadian Hospital Etaples, France. Henry's parents received the following letter from Lieutenant A. C. Hampson:

"Probably by this time you will have received news of your son. I feel it is useless for one to say what our feelings are when compared with what yours must be, but I must say that he was a man beloved, and better still, respected by all of us. It may come as some consolation to you to know that you have every reason to be proud of him. He received his wound when carrying in a wounded comrade under observation and fire of the enemy. Such acts have a far more reaching effect than the actual saving of life which he undoubtedly effected. These are the sacrifices which build up the morale of our Army. No one of whatever constitution, can fail to live up to such an example.
May I, on behalf of his officers and comrades offer you our sincere sympathy. I know how empty words are. I wish I could force into them some of our feelings of "one who has also known adversity," and may we in the light of these glorious achievements of our friends play the game as they have played it for the honour of our country and our Battery."

Sergeant Ernest Lane   *8th Bn Gloucestershire Regiment*
Service No.   5617   Age: 36
Place of Birth: Overbury, Worcestershire   Home Country: England
Date of Death: 17/04/1918   Cause of death: Died of wounds
Memorial: Chippenham - St Andrews Church Memorial - Overbury & Conderton
War cemetery: Haringhe (Bandaghem) Military Cemetery
Theatre of war: Belgium
Next of Kin: Emily Lane (wife) – William & Fanny Lane (parents
Address: Frogwell, Chippenham - Conderton, Tewkesbury

Ernest, a postman, married Emily Walkley in the spring of 1909 and volunteered for service most likely with the 2nd Battalion Gloucestershire Regiment and arrived in France on 23 February 1915. In late November 1915 the 2nd Gloucesters were sent to Salonika where for every soldier to be killed or die from wounds in battle, four were to die from disease. Ernest developed malaria and was evacuated to England. On his recovery he was transferred to the 8th Battalion Gloucestershire Regiment and sent to France in March 1917. He was wounded during the German offensive at Messines, Belgium in April 1918 and sent to a casualty clearing station at Bandaghem near Haringe, west of Ypres Belgium. Here he succumbed to his wounds on Wednesday 17 April 1918, leaving a widow and two young children.

Private Reginald John Wood		*1st Bn Somerset Light Infantry*	
Service No.	40691	Age:	18
Place of Birth:	Chippenham	Home Country:	England
Date of Death:	22/04/1918	Cause of death:	Killed in action
Memorial:	Chippenham & St.Andrews Church Memorial		
War cemetery:	Loos Memorial		
Theatre of war:	France		
Next of Kin:	William & Frances Annie Wood		
Address:	Jamaica Villa, Ethelwulf Road, Worthing, Sussex		

Eighteen year old Reginald, known as Reggie, was the youngest son of William and Frances Wood and who had previously run a fruit and fish shop at Station Hill, Chippenham. Reggie joined the 1st Battalion Somerset Light Infantry and it is likely he was sent to France in response to the German offensive of 1918. He was one of nine members of the Somersets to be killed by German shell fire near Bethune on Monday 22 April 1918. He is remembered on the Loos Memorial and has no known grave.

2nd Lt. Herbert Charles Vallentine Sharps		*1st Bn Rifle Brigade*	
Service No.	N/a	Age:	25
Place of Birth:	Lyneham, Wiltshire	Home Country:	England
Date of Death:	22/04/1918	Cause of death:	Killed in action
Memorial:	Seagry		
War cemetery:	Le Vertannoy British Cemetery, Hinges		
Theatre of war:	France		
Next of Kin:	Robert J. & Louisa Sharps		
Address:	Manor Farm, Seagry, Wiltshire		

Herbert, known as Valentine or Val, was the second son of Robert and Louisa Sharps, a member of the parish choir and well known in Seagry. He joined the King's Own Hussars as a trooper with his brother Sidney in September 1914. They were both transferred to the 7th Service Battalion Gloucestershire Regiment and arrived at Gallipoli in August 1915. Val was evacuated from the peninsular in December 1915 suffering with severe frost bite and invalided to England. He was recommended for a commission and promoted to 2nd Lieutenant on 28 August 1917. He was then transferred to the 1st Battalion Rifle Brigade and sent to France in October 1917. In May 1918 Val's parents received the following letter from the Colonel commanding the 1st Rifle Brigade:

"It is with the very deepest regret that I have to inform you of the death of your gallant son. He was killed on the 22nd by a shell during the most terrific bombardment that we were subjected to. I can't tell you what a loss he is to the battalion. I had formed a very high opinion of him as an officer, and he was quite one of the best subalterns, a keen, enthusiastic officer

and most popular with everyone. I offer you my very deepest sympathy in the great loss that you have sustained, and it is a loss that the whole battalion feels also. He was buried last night in a cemetery about 1000 yards S.W. of a place called Hinges; two other officers, including your son's company commander, were buried there also."

Private Wilfred Thomas Newman   *1st Bn Hampshire Regiment*
Service No.   28627   Age: 18
Place of Birth: Christian Malford   Home Country: England
Date of Death: 22/04/1918   Cause of death: Killed in action
Memorial: Not known
War cemetery: Loos Memorial
Theatre of war: France
Next of Kin: John & Kate Newman
Address: Railway Cottages, Acton Turville, Gloucestershire

Eighteen year old Wilfred, a porter at Badminton Station, was the second son of John & Kate Newman. He joined the army in April 1917 and arrived in France in March 1918, being sent to the 1st Battalion Hampshire Regiment. Wilfred had only been in France three weeks when he was killed by heavy German shell fire near Pacaut Wood , Bethune, France, on Monday 22 April 1918. He is remembered on the Loos Memorial and has no known grave.

Corporal Arthur John White   *38th Bn Machine Gun Corps*
Service No.   105325   Age: 24
Place of Birth: Lea, Wiltshire   Home Country: England
Date of Death: 22/04/1918   Cause of death: Killed in action
Memorial: Seagry
War cemetery: Bouzincourt Communal Cemetery Extension
Theatre of war: France
Next of Kin: John Humphrey & Mary Jane White
Address: West End, Minchinhampton, Gloucestershire

Arthur, a gardener, was the eldest son of John & Mary White and initially joined the Royal Warwickshire Regiment and then transferred to the Machine Gun Corps. He was killed by a bomb (hand grenade) on Monday 22 April north west of Albert, France. John & Mary White had already lost two sons, Cecil was killed in France in April 1917 and Leonard died of wounds in Belgium in July 1917.

Corporal Richard Henry Reginald Neate   *4th Bn Royal Marine Light Infantry*
Service No.   CH/18066   Age: 22
Place of Birth: Castle Combe   Home Country: England
Date of Death: 23/04/1918   Cause of death: Killed in action
Memorial: Chippenham & Castle Combe
War cemetery: Castle Combe St Andrew's Church Yard
Theatre of war: Home
Next of Kin: Richard & Annie Taylor Neate
Address: 100 Wood Lane, Chippenham, Wiltshire

Richard, known as Richie, was a member of the church choir educated at Castle Combe School and later on the Training Ship Warspite at Dartford Kent. He was then apprenticed to a tyre

Left: Richard Henry Reginald Neate and above his grave marker at St Andrew's Church Yard Castle Combe.

manufacturing company in Birmingham and while there enlisted with the Royal Marines on 30 April 1913 at the age of 17 years 3 months and 8 days. However because he was under age his recognized service did not start until 27 January 1914. He served on ships in the North Sea and was stationed in the Orkney Isles. He was promoted to Corporal on 3 April 1918. On 23 April 1918 a raid was to take place at Zeebrugge, Belgium, the aim was to block the channel which led to the canal leading to the docks at Brugge, which the Germans were using as a U Boat base. To enable the block ships to be sunk in the channel a naval raiding party and Royal Marines were to be landed on Mole (concrete pier which protected the Channel) and were to attack the German shore batteries. Unfortunately H.M.S. Vindictive which was carrying many of the marines came alongside the mole at the wrong position and even before the marines disembarked they were subject to German shell fire and suffered heavy casualties. When the Marines left the ships it was found that there were not enough left to take the planned objectives and in one platoon of 45 men only 12 landed. At About 1am H.M.S. Vindictive left the mole and sailed for England. It is likely Richie was killed while waiting to leave the ship or close by on the Mole as his body was brought back to England and he was buried at Castle Combe with full military honours. In June 1918 a memorial stone subscribed by the parishioners of Castle Combe was erected over Richies' grave.

Private John Thomas Gough   *8th Bn Ox & Bucks Light Infantry*

Service No.	28118	Age:	22
Place of Birth:	Hullavington, Wiltshire	Home Country:	England
Date of Death:	23/04/1918	Cause of death:	Died
Memorial:	Hullavington		
War cemetery:	Mikra British Cemetery		
Theatre of war:	Salonika		
Next of Kin:	William & Miriam Gough		
Address:	Watts Lane, Hullavington, Wiltshire		

Farm worker John was the eldest son of William and Miriam Gough. He initially joined the Wiltshire Regiment but was transferred to the 8th Oxfordshire and Buckinghamshire Light Infantry. He was sent to Salonika, Greece where for every man to be killed or die of wounds form battle, four were to die from illness or disease. John died of illness or disease at one of the military hospitals based at Mikra, Greece on Tuesday 23 April 1918.

Private Herbert Compton   *19th Bn Middlesex Regiment*
Service No.   G/21328   Age: 28
Place of Birth: Avon, Wiltshire   Home Country: England
Date of Death: 25/04/1918   Cause of death: Died of wounds
Memorial: Seagry
War cemetery: Haringhe (Bandaghem) Military Cemetery
Theatre of war: Belgium
Next of Kin: Robert & Emily Compton
Address: Lower Seagry, Wiltshire

Herbert was the second son of Robert and Emily Compton and had been a member of the choir in Seagry. Prior to the war he had been employed as a footman at Welton Place near Daventry, Northamptonshire. He volunteered for service joining the 19th Middlesex Service Battalion 2nd Public Works Pioneers and it is likely he arrived in France in May 1916 before serving in Italy. It is likely he was wounded during actions around the River Lys in Belgium in April 1918 and died of his wounds at a Casualty Clearing Station near Haringhe Belgium on Thursday 25 April 1918

Private Lewin James Billett   *1st Bn Royal Warwickshire Regiment*
Service No.   306675   Age: 42
Place of Birth: Kington St Michael   Home Country: England
Date of Death: 26/04/1918   Cause of death: Died of wounds
Memorial: Kington St Michael
War cemetery: Etaples Military Cemetery
Theatre of war: France
Next of Kin: Ephraim & Jane Billett
Address: Kington St Michael, Wiltshire

Labourer Lewin joined the army under the Derby Scheme and registered on 16 November 1916. He was called up on 20 March 1916 and after completing his training was posted to the 8th Battalion Warwickshire Regiment arriving in France on 5 June 1917. He was wounded in action on the 27 August 1916 with a gun shot wound to the chest and taken to No. 11 Casualty Clearing Station and then on to the 26th General Hospital at Etaples, France. After his recovery he rejoined his unit in November 1916 but he was admitted to the No. 53 Field Ambulance on 29 December 1916 with inflammation to the connecting tissue of the left leg and was eventually evacuated to England in January 1917 and was found to be suffering from tuberculosis. He returned to France on 17 May 1917 and in June was posted to the 1st Battalion Royal Warwickshire Regiment. He was wounded in the right shoulder on 15 April 1918 and admitted to the 56th General Hospital and was found to be suffering from tetanus and septicaemia and died of his wounds on Friday 26 April 1918. His personal possessions were sent to his brother and consisted of disc, cap badge, pipe, 2 pairs of scissors, 2 German buttons, 2 Cards and coins (farthing). Lewin is buried in Etaples Military Cemetery

Gunner Reginald James Victor Clifford   *85th Siege Bty RGA*

Service No.	171002	Age: 27
Place of Birth:	Cherhill, Wiltshire	Home Country: England
Date of Death:	27/04/1918	Cause of death: Killed in action
Memorial:	Calne – Lacock Church & Keevil	
War cemetery:	Ploegsteert Memorial	
Theatre of war:	Belgium	
Next of Kin:	Emily Jane Clifford (wife); George Hyde & Anne Jane Clifford (parents)	
Address:	Lacock; 1 Freeth, Compton Bassett, Wiltshire	

Reginald, known as Victor, was a farm labourer and in 1915 married Emily Jane Walker. It is likely that he was conscripted into the army and then sent to the Royal Garrison Artillery, probably because he was used to working with horses. In May 1918 Emily received a notice informing her that Victor had been missing since 23 April, when he was last seen transporting munitions to the firing line. It was later found that he had been killed in action on Saturday 27 April 1918. He is remembered on the Ploegsteert Memorial with over 11,000 casualties of the Great War. He has no known grave.

Rifleman Maurice William Short   *8th Bn London Regiment*

Service No.	374823	Age: 20
Place of Birth:	Chippenham, Wiltshire	Home Country: England
Date of Death:	02/05/1918	Cause of death: Killed in action
Memorial:	Chippenham & St. Andrews Church Memorial	
War cemetery:	Pozieres Memorial	
Theatre of war:	France	
Next of Kin:	Azor & Eliza Short	
Address:	7 River Street, Chippenham	

It is likely twenty year old Maurice was a postman like his father and brother. He initially joined the 17th Battalion London Regiment then transferred to the 8th Battalion London Regiment known as the Post Office Rifles. He was killed in action on Thursday 5 May 1918 east of Amiens, France. He is remembered on the Pozieres Memorial and has no known grave. His brother Arthur George Short was killed in Belgium in 1917.

Private William Henry Freegard   *2nd Battalion Wiltshire Regiment*

Service No.	202515	Age: 32
Place of Birth:	Christian Malford	Home Country: England
Date of Death:	08/05/1918	Cause of death: Died of wounds
Memorial:	Christian Malford	
War cemetery:	Tyne Cot Memorial	
Theatre of war:	Belgium	
Next of Kin:	Edward & Julia Freegard	
Address:	82 Thornend, Christian Malford, Wiltshire	

William, a farm labourer and cowman, volunteered for service with the Wiltshire Regiment arriving in France on 20 July 1915. On Wednesday 8 May 1918 the 2nd Battalion Wiltshire Regiment supplied a working party to the 2nd Battalion Bedforshire Regiment at Watou, west of Poperinge, Belgium. When the working party returned the following day it was found that they had sustained a number of casualties, 7 killed, 20 wounded and 37 missing. One of those posted as missing was William, official information was late received that William had died of wounds while on the working party, which were probably inflicted by German artillery. He is remembered on the Tyne Cot Memorial and has no known grave.

Sergeant Walter Baston		*Tank Corps*	
Service No.	206259	Age:	27
Place of Birth:	Kencott, Oxfordshire	Home Country:	England
Date of Death:	09/05/1918	Cause of death:	Died
Memorial:	Biddestone		
War cemetery:	Biddestone Churchyard Extension		
Theatre of war:	Home		
Next of Kin:	John George and Elizabeth Ellen Baston		
Address:	The Butts, Biddestone, Wiltshire		

Regular soldier Walter enlisted with the Wiltshire Regiment on 3 August 1909 and in 1913 he passed an army course to be a blacksmith. At the outbreak of war the 2nd Battalion Wiltshire Regiment were serving in Gibraltar and after their return to England were sent to the continent landing at Zeebrugge, Belgium on the 7 October 1914. After serving with the Wiltshires for the first two years of the war and being promoted to corporal, Walter transferred to the Machine Gun Corps on 5 February 1916 and while serving at the Somme with 21 Coy he was promoted to Sergeant on 23 September. At some stage Walter transferred to the Heavy Branch of the Machine Gun Corps who in July 1917 became the Tank Corps. Walter and his platoon were caught in a gas attack most likely in Belgium in June 1917 and he was wounded with gas poisoning while trying to save his men. He was evacuated to England and on 13 August 1917 Walter was discharged from the Army being deemed no longer fit for military service. Walter died at his home in Biddestone on Thursday 9 May 1918. As a measure of respect practically the whole village attended his funeral and he was buried with full military honours.

Lieutenant John Basil Robert Langley		*Royal Air Force*	
Service No.	N/a	Age:	29
Place of Birth:	Heytesbury, Wiltshire	Home Country:	England

Right: Walter Baston buried at Biddestone Churchyard Extension

Below: A Sopwith aircraft similar to the one flown by John Basil Robert Langley.

Date of Death:	15/05/1918
Memorial:	North Wraxall
War cemetery:	Gosport Annes Hill Cemetery
Theatre of war:	Home
Next of Kin:	Lorna Leslie Langley (wife) - Rev. John & Bertha V. Langley
Address:	Sky, Amesbury, Wiltshire - The Rectory, North Wraxall

Cause of death: Accident

John, known as Robert, was the eldest son of Rev. John and Bertha Langley and emigrated to Canada where he was employed as a builder. He volunteered for service with the Canadian army on 23 September 1914 joining the 19th Alberta Dragoons and was with the first Canadian contingent to arrive in England and served in France. He transferred to the Royal Flying Corps, obtained a commission and was employed as an artillery observer in France. In June 1916 he qualified as a pilot being presented with his "wings" and almost at once became an instructor in Special Flying. On Saturday 28 July 1917 Robert married Lorna Leslie Lodge, the daughter of Sir Oliver Lodge, at St. George's, Edgbaston. The following month Robert was graded as a flight commander while serving at The Special Flying School at Fort Grange, Gosport. The Special Flying School was used to teach new pilots air combat skills in an attempt to prepare them for enemy action. Robert always maintained it was possible to roll a Sopwith Camel to the left, because of the torque of the rotary engine the Camel turned left rather slowly, which resulted in leaving the nose of the aircraft up. The engine torque also resulted in the ability to turn to the right in half the time of other aircraft and many pilots preferred to turn to the right and do almost a full circle rather than turn left. Robert had, on two previous occasions, completed a left role in the Camel and on Wednesday 15 May 1918 he took off in Camel B.847 from Fort Grange, Gosport. While practicing aerial combat he rolled the Camel to the left and his machine entered a vicious spin and plunged to the ground. It is likely his aircraft stalled during the left roll, Robert was killed instantly by the impact, suffering a broken neck. He was buried in Gosport Anne's Hill Cemetery on 19 May 1918 and left a widow and son of only 15 days old. Robert's brother Francis would be killed in action in France in August 1918.

Lieutenant Terence McHugh   *13th Vet Hospital Army* Veterinary*Corps*

Service No.	N/a		Age:	39
Place of Birth:	Bradford, Yorkshire		Home Country:	England
Date of Death:	20/05/1918		Cause of death:	Died of wounds
Memorial:	Not known			
War cemetery:	Etaples Military Cemetery			
Theatre of war:	France			
Next of Kin:	Mrs P. W. McHugh (wife) - Terence & Mary McHugh (parents)			
Address:	25 Pembridge Gardens, Notting Hill Gate, London			

Regular soldier Terence had served in the South African campaign and was a holder of the Long Service and Good Conduct Medal. He originally joined the 5th Lancers and rose to the rank of Sergeant Major and for three years he was Regimental Sergeant Major of the Royal Wiltshire Yeomanry at Chippenham. His son Terry McHugh was a chorister at Westminster Cathedral and during the war entertained audiences in Bath. Terence arrived in France on 3 December 1915 and was promoted Quarter Master with the honoury rank of Lieutenant with the Royal Veterinary Corps on 12 July 1916. He was wounded most likely by German shell fire and evacuated to a military hospital at Etaples, France where he died on Monday 20 May 1918. He was burried at Etaples Military Cemetery

27 MAY 1918 - 'BLUCHER' THE THIRD GERMAN SPRING OFFENSIVE

Private Walter Charles Cole   *1st Bn Wiltshire Regiment*

Service No.	10378	Age:	21
Place of Birth:	Lacock, Wiltshire	Home Country:	England
Date of Death:	27/05/1918	Cause of death:	Killed in action
Memorial:	Lacock - Lacock Church & Bowden Hill Memorial		
War cemetery:	Soissons Memorial		
Theatre of war:	France		
Next of Kin:	Walter & Lydia Cole		
Address:	Bewley Common, Lacock, Wiltshire		

Twenty one year old Walter known as Charles was the eldest son of Walter & Lydia Cole. He volunteered for service with the 1st Battalion Wiltshire Regiment and arrived in France on 4 December 1915. On Monday 27 May 1918 the 1st Wiltshires were at Guyencourt, east of Soissons France, and at 1am they were subjected to a heavy German gas bombardment at 5pm the bombardment ceased and the German attack commenced. Soon after the 1st Wiltshires were ordered forward at by 10.15am they were in the line at Bouffignereux. The Germans constantly shelled and machine gunned the 1st Wiltshires position and at 5.30pm the Germans attacked with an overwhelming force. The 1st Wiltshires were compelled to retire splitting into small groups and fighting rear guard actions. Charles was killed during the attack he is remembered on the Soissons Memorial and has no known grave.

Corporal Harry George Hunt   *B Coy1st Bn Wiltshire Regiment*

Service No.	8185	Age:	27
Place of Birth:	Chippenham	Home Country:	England
Date of Death:	27/05/1918	Cause of death:	Killed in action
Memorial:	Not known		
War cemetery:	Soissons Memorial		
Theatre of war:	France		
Next of Kin:	Frances Emily Hunt (wife) - William Henry & Maria Hunt (parents)		
Address:	Oak Tree Cottage, , Brockenhurst – 33 Malmesbury Road, Chippenham		

Harry worked in his fathers bakers and grocers shop and volunteered for service with the 1st Battalion Wiltshire Regiment arriving in France on 17 February 1915. In the summer of 1917 he married Francis Emily Harrison at Brockenhurst, Hampshire, returning to France shortly after. On monday 27 May 1918 the 1st Wiltshires were at Guyencourt, east of Soissons, France.. Arthur was one of over 37 men killed during the German attack in the same action as Walter Cole. He is remembered on the Soissons Memorial and has no known grave.

Private Albert Edward Chivers   *11th Bn Essex Regiment*

Service No.	38417	Age:	19
Place of Birth:	Chippenham	Home Country:	England
Date of Death:	28/05/1918	Cause of death:	Killed in action
Memorial:	Chippenham & St. Andrews Church Memorial		
War cemetery:	Tyne Cot Memorial		
Theatre of war:	Belgium		
Next of Kin:	George H & Rosanna Chivers		
Address:	1 St Mary Place, Chippenham		

Nineteen year old Albert was the youngest son of George and Rosanna Chivers and prior to his enlistment had been employed as a shop assistant by the Royal Wilts Bacon Company.

Albert was sent to the 11th Battalion Essex Regiment and in July 1918 George and Rosanna Chivers were informed he had been killed in action on Tuesday 28 May 1918. They had already lost two sons to the war, Sidney was killed in Belgiun in October 1914 and Edwin had died of wounds in Mesopotamia in April 1916. Albert is remembered on the Tyne Cot Memorial and has no known grave.

Private Thomas Brinkworth		*14th Bn Australian Infantry AIF*	
Service No.	2152	Age:	27
Place of Birth:	Chippenham	Home Country:	Australia
Date of Death:	31/05/1918	Cause of death:	Killed in action
Memorial:	St. Andrews Church Memorial		
War cemetery:	Allonville Communal Cemetery		
Theatre of war:	France		
Next of Kin:	George & Sarah Montague Brinkworth		
Address:	Frogwell, Chippenham		

At seventeen Thomas, known as Tom, had been employed as a nurseryman and in 1908 decided to emigrate to Australia. At the outbreak of war he was working as a manager at a cattle ranch for the Queensland National Pastoral Company Limited. He volunteered for service with the Queensland Light Horse at Brisbane on 9 December 1915. He was first sent to Egypt arriving in May 1916 and then sent on to France arriving on 24 June 1916 before being granted 10 days leave which he spent at home. In September 1916 he was transferred to the 14th Battalion and was twice wounded in October 1917 and December 1917. He was killed on Friday 31 May 1918 while in a rest camp at Allonville, north east of Amiens, France. In June 1918 Tom's father received the following letter from one of his son's comrades:

"It is with some hesitation that I, a stranger, come intruding on your sorrow, but you will, I trust permit my regard for Tom to be sufficient reason for taking it on myself, to let you know how the end came. I can at least tell you that your boy did not suffer; it was all over in a flash. The Battalion was resting in billets at Allonville, and about two o'clock in the morning of the 31st two long range shells landed and burst amongst the sleepers. Tom was one very close to it, and received the full concussion. When the debris of the broken bard was cleared away, he was found lying just as in sleep. Could you have seen some of the painful wounds that some got you would, I am sure, find some measure of relief in the knowledge that Tom was spared all suffering. He lies with a number of his comrade in the cemetery at Allonville, where one looks across the country to Amiens. I had learned to appreciate Tom's worth when up at Zonnebeke last November; he had just joined the Battalion, and his behaviour through a trying period in the line there won my respect, so that on my getting a change from company duty he was one of the few I still kept in touch with. As evidence of his worth in the lines I may state that he was specially mentioned after our Zonnebeke tour of duty for meritorious work. Unfortunately many of such recommendations go no further than the unit, so Tom's name did not figure in the honour's list. But he was one of those men who could be depended on in an emergency, and both as a soldier and a friend his loss is distinct. One does not grow callous over here and I think you will understand that my brief note is written with anything but the intention of intruding on your grief and sorrow."

Tom's brother Claude had spent some time with him the day before he was killed. Tom was buried in Allonville Communal Cemetery

Private Herbert Thomas James Fortune
Service No. 290779
Place of Birth: Calne, Wiltshire
Date of Death: 31/05/1918
Memorial: Chippenham – St. Andrews Church, Chippenham - Derry Hill
War cemetery: Soissons Memorial
Theatre of war: France
Next of Kin: Thomas & Mary Jane Fortune
Address: Fair View, Sheldon Road, Chippenham, Wiltshire

2nd Bn Devonshire Regiment
Age: 20
Home Country: England
Cause of death: Killed in action

Herbert worked for his father who was a market gardener and it is likely he was conscripted into the army joining the 2nd Battalion Devonshire Regiment. He was reported missing during the German advance toward the river Marne when the Devons stopped the enemy advance at Bligny Hill east of Soisons, France, on Friday 31 May 1918. Later he was listed as killed in action on that day. He is remembered on the Soissons Memorial and has no known grave.

Private Gilbert Arthur Kennaugh Higgins
Service No. 44043
Place of Birth: Chippenham, Wiltshire
Date of Death: 31/05/1918
Memorial: Chippenham & St. Andrews Church Memorial
War cemetery: Wimereux Communal Cemetery
Theatre of war: France
Next of Kin: Fitzroy & Laura Higgins
Address: 91 London Road, Chippenham

9th Yorkshire Light Infantry
Age: 21
Home Country: England
Cause of death: Died

Twenty year old Gilbert, known as Bert, was the only son of Fitzroy and Laura Higgins and initially joined the Training Reserve before being posted to the 9th Battalion Yorkshire Regiment and was then sent to France. He died of illness or disease at a military hospital Wimereux, France, on Friday 31 May 1918.

Gunner Albert Edward Wilkins
Service No. 861002
Place of Birth: Chippenham, Wiltshire
Date of Death: 01/06/1918
Memorial: Leigh & Upper Waterhay
War cemetery: Madras 1914-1918 War Memorial Chennai
Theatre of war: India
Next of Kin: Elizabeth Burrows
Address: Malmesbury Road, Leigh, Wiltshire

104th Bty216th Bde Royal Field Artillery
Age: 31
Home Country: England
Cause of death: Died

Albert, known as Edward and a carpenter, was the only son of Elizabeth Burrows and it is likely he joined the Royal Artillery Territorial Force and was sent to India on garrison duties. He died of illness or disease on Saturday 1 June 1918 and was buried at Agra Cantonment Cemetery. The Commonwealth War Graves Commission do not tend many of the graves of soldiers who are buried in India and Edward is remembered on the Madras 1914-1918 War Memorial Chennai.

Private Francis Herbert Harding   *12th Bn Suffolk Regiment*
Service No.   42577   Age: 19
Place of Birth: Chippenham, Wiltshire   Home Country: England
Date of Death: 03/06/1918   Cause of death: Died of wounds
Memorial: Chippenham & St. Andrews Church Memorial
War cemetery: Cologne Southern Cemetery
Theatre of war: Germany
Next of Kin: George & Annie Maria Harding
Address: 58 Forest View Englands, Chippenham

Francis, known as Herbert, was the second son of George and Annie Harding and initially joined the Training Reserve before being posted to the 12th Battalion Suffolk Regiment. He was wounded and captured during the German advance in March and April 1918 and transported to Germany. He died a prisoner of war on Monday 3 June 1918 and was buried in Germany. In June 1919 Herbert's parents inserted the following memoriam in a local paper:

Out in a foreign country there is a silent grave
Of one we loved so dearly but yet we could not save
His king and country called him, he bravely did his best
Till God saw fit to take him for his eternal rest
Sadly missed and ever fondly remembered by his sorrowing Mother, Father, Sisters and Brothers

Corporal Herbert John Kington   *1st Bn Royal Dublin Fusiliers*
Service No.   15035   Age: 21
Place of Birth: Grittleton, Wiltshire   Home Country: England
Date of Death: 03/06/1918   Cause of death: Killed in action
Memorial: Grittleton
War cemetery: Ploegsteert Memorial
Theatre of war: Belgium
Next of Kin: Thomas & Clara Kington
Address: Clapcote Cottage, Grittleton, Wiltshire

Herbert, a farm labourer, originally volunteered for service in 1914 with the Wiltshire Regiment but because there were too many volunteers for the Wiltshires he was transferred to the Royal Dublin Fusiliers. He served nearly two years in France and was killed in action on Monday 3 June 1918. He is remembered on the Ploegsteert Memorial and has no known grave.

Private Walter George Parsons   *2/4th TF Bn Wiltshire Regiment*
Service No.   202576   Age: 39
Place of Birth: Chippenham, Wiltshire   Home Country: England
Date of Death: 05/06/1918   Cause of death: Died
Memorial: Chippenham & St. Andrews Church - Trowbridge St James Church Mem.
War cemetery: Madras 1914 1918 War Memorial Chennai
Theatre of war: India
Next of Kin: Thomas & Elizabeth Parsons
Address: 51 Lowden, Chippenham

Walter was a Wiltshire Territorial was sent to India for garrison duties. He died of illness or disease at Allahabad, India and was buried in Allahabad New Cantonment Cemetery. The

Commonwealth War Graves Commission do not tend the graves of British soldiers in many cemeteries in India and he is remembered on the Madras 1914-1918 War Memorial Chennai.

Private William Thomas Hibberd MM		*2nd Bn Wiltshire Regiment*	
Service No.	22329	Age:	32
Place of Birth:	Battersea, London	Home Country:	England
Date of Death:	16/06/1918	Cause of death:	Died of wounds
Memorial:	Not known		
War cemetery:	Marfaux British Cemetery		
Theatre of war:	France		
Next of Kin:	Elizabeth Hibberd (wife) - William & Helen Hibberd (parents)		
Address:	South Wraxhall – Lacock, Wiltshire.		

William was the second son of William and Helen Hibberd as was employed at Melksham Flour Mills. He volunteered for service with the 2nd Battalion Wiltshire Regiment as a stretcher bearer in November 1915. Before he left for the front he married Elizabeth Hollister at the beginning of 1916 at Bradford on Avon. In September 1917 William received the Military Medal for gallantry in the field near Kemmel, Belgium. William was reported wounded and missing on the 1 June 1918 near Chambrecy, West of Rheims, France when the 2nd Wiltshires were forced to withdraw. It was later discovered he had been taken to 59th Field Ambulance at Chambrecy, where he succumbed to his wounds on Sunday 16 June 1918. In October 1918 Elizabeth Hibberd inserted the following memoriam in a local paper:

A soldier does not ask or choose the place to serve
And from the path that that duty points no soldiers steps may swerve
So when from that red field of strife, Death's bugle called him far
He turned his face toward the steep where Heaven's outposts are

Below Left: The Military Medal - Below Right: William Thomas Hibberd MM

Private Cyril Chivers   *11th Bn Hampshire Regiment*

Service No.	30034	Age:	19
Place of Birth:	Lacock, Wiltshire	Home Country:	England
Date of Death:	17/06/1918	Cause of death:	Died of wounds
Memorial:	Lacock – Lacock Church & Bowden Hill		
War cemetery:	Pernes British Cemetery		
Theatre of war:	France		
Next of Kin:	Alfred & Charlotte Chivers		
Address:	Naish Hill, Lacock, Wiltshire		

Nineteen year old Cyril was the youngest son of Alfred and Charlotte Chivers he enlisted in the army joining the 11th Battalion Hampshire Regiment. He was wounded most likely by German artillery or trench mortar fire at Pacaut Wood, near Riez du Vinage north of Bethune, France. He died of his wounds on Monday 17 June 1918 and was buried at Pernes British Cemetery. In June 1919 Cyril's parents inserted the following memoriam in a local paper:

It's only a mother who knows the sorrow
It's only a mother who feels the pain
Of losing a son she loved most dearly
And to know she will never meet him again

When last we saw his smiling face
He looked so strong and brave
We little though how soon he'd be
Laid in a soldiers grave

Sleep on dear one in a far off land
In a grave we may never see
As long as life and memory last
We shall always remember thee

Private Harry Burridge   *7th Bn Duke of Cornwalls Light Infantry*

Service No.	27825	Age:	21
Place of Birth:	Chippenham, Wiltshire	Home Country:	England
Date of Death:	19/06/1918	Cause of death:	Died
Memorial:	Not Known		
War cemetery:	Sarralbe Military Cemetery		
Theatre of war:	France		
Next of Kin:	Thomas & Mary Jane Burridge		
Address:	Knighton, Sherborne, Dorset		

Harry was the eldest son of Thomas and Mary Burridge and was employed on his father's farm. He enlisted in the army initially joining the Somerset light Infantry before being transferred to the 7th Battalion Duke of Cornwall's Light Infantry. He was captured during the German offensive in March and April 1918 and taken to a prisoner of war camp near Sarralbe east of Metz, France, where he died of illness or disease on Wednesday 19 June 1918.

Private Gilbert Tom Rudman   *3rd Dorset Regiment*

Service No.	Not known	Age:	27
Place of Birth:	Kington St Micheal	Home Country:	England

Date of Death: 26/06/1918   Cause of death: Died
Memorial: Kington St Michael
War cemetery: Not known
Theatre of war: Home
Next of Kin: Florence E. Rudman (wife) - George & Emily Rudman (parents)
Address: Kington St Micheal, Wiltshire

Gilbert a stone mason's labourer and was the second son of George and Emily Rudman and late in 1916 he married Florence E. Hazell. It is likely he was conscripted into the army joining the 3rd Battalion Dorset Regiment. While serving Gilbert was taken ill and sent home where he died of cancer of the rectum on Wednesday 26 June 1918. He left a widow and a young child. At this time Gilbert is not commemorated by the Commonwealth War Graves Commission.

Private Harry Button   *Base Depot Army Service Corps*
Service No.   M-285588   Age: 36
Place of Birth: Chippenham, Wiltshire   Home Country: England
Date of Death: 29/06/1918   Cause of death: Died
Memorial: Chippenham & St. Andrews Church Memorial
War cemetery: Mikra British Cemetery
Theatre of war: Salonika
Next of Kin: Gwen Button (wife) - George & Emily Button (parents)
Address: 25 Market Place, Chippenham - 13 New Road, Chippenham

At the outbreak of hostilities Harry was employed by John Coles (Alderman of Chippenham) who ran a chemist and grocers shop in the Market Place, Chippenham. Harry was a prominent member of the Wednesday Cricket and Football Club. He was a keen swimmer and could often be found at the bathing place of the river at 6.30am in the morning. He was also a member of the operatic society and took part in all their performances. On 6 December 1915 Harry attested for service in the army under the Derby Scheme where men registered and were not called up until the army needed them. John Coles died in April 1916 and in his will he bequeathed Harry a small legacy and for his faithful service for 22 years he was given the option of purchasing the business. Harry purchased the business becoming the proprietor and because he managed a chemist shop he was at that time exempted from military service. On 26 January 1917 Harry was called up and was sent to Army Service Corps Motor Transport Depot at Grove Park. On 6 March 1917 he married Gwendolyn Llewellyn, the daughter of Captain Llewellyn, at Chippenham and in June 1917 he was sent to Salonika, Greece. Shortly after his arrival in Salonika in August 1817 Harry contracted malaria and he had not long recovered when he was stricken with black water fever. While he was convalescing the military authorities ordered his return to England but while he was waiting for a ship he was suddenly take ill with diarrhoea and admitted to 49th General Hospital on 10 June 1918. He was diagnosed with dysentery and malaria and his condition became gradually worse and because of his previous illnesses he was in a weakened state. He died at 4.20am on Saturday 29 June 1918 at 49th General Hospital and he was later buried in Mikra British Cemetery

Private Ernest Leonard Stevens   *1st Bn Wiltshire Regiment*
Service No.   33556   Age: 19
Place of Birth: Lacock, Wiltshire   Home Country: England
Date of Death: 02/07/1918   Cause of death: Died of wounds
Memorial: Lacock & Lacock Church

War cemetery: Niederzwehren Cemetery
Theatre of war: Germany
Next of Kin: James & Bessie Stevens
Address: Rose Cottage, Wick Lane, Lacock, Wiltshire

Nineteen year old Ernest was the youngest son of James and Bessie Stevens and at the age of 15 years he volunteered to serve with the Wiltshire Regiment on 20 April 1915 stating his age as 19 years and two months. However on 30 July 1915 he was discharged due to having made a false statement at the time of enlistment and being under the age of 17 years. Then on 15 September 1915 he volunteered to serve with the Wiltshire Yeomanry and again he was discharged from the army on 25 February 1916 for exactly the same reason. When Ernest was old enough he volunteered for a third time joining the 1st Battalion Wiltshire Regiment. He was wounded and captured during the German offensive of March and April 1918 and taken to Germany where he died of his wounds on Tuesday 7 July 1918 at Giessen east of Bonn. After the Armistice Ernest's remains were relocated to Niederzwehren Cemetery, in July 1919 his parent's inserted the following memoriam in a local paper:

Somewhere afar in a soldiers grave
Lies our dear brother amongst the brave
We little thought his time so short
In this world to remain
Or that when from his home he went
He would never return again
He was one of the best and one of the many to answer the call
For those who loved he gave his all
Safe in the arms of Jesus
Ever remembered by his sorrowing Mother, Father, Sisters and Brothers

Corporal Elias Smith   *344th Road Construction Coy RE*
Service No.   WR/10665   Age: 50
Place of Birth: Lacock, Wiltshire   Home Country: England
Date of Death: 03/07/1918   Cause of death: Died
Memorial: Lacock Church
War cemetery: Les Baraques Military Cemetery Sangatte
Theatre of war: France
Next of Kin: Elias & Sarah Smith
Address: Lacock, Wiltshire

Elias a railway labourer initially enlisted with the Rifle Brigade then was transferred to the West Riding Regiment before being transferred to the Royal Engineers. He died on Wednesday 3 July 1918 of illness or disease at a military hospital at near Callais, France. His brother James had died in August 1917.

Private Alfred William Porter   *16th Royal Warwickshire Regiment*
Service No.   242606   Age: 25
Place of Birth: Great Somerford   Home Country: England
Date of Death: 04/07/1918   Cause of death: Died of wounds
Memorial: Not known
War cemetery: Aire Communal Cemetery
Theatre of war: France

Next of Kin: George & Annie Porter
Address: Startley Street, Somerford, Wiltshire

Alfred, known as William and a mason's labourer, was the youngest son of George & Anne Porter and enlisted in the army joining the 16th Battalion Warwickshire Regiment. He was wounded near Bethune, France and evacuated to a Military Hospital at Aire where he succumbed to his wounds on Thursday 4 July 1918. Willaim is buried at Aire Communal Cemetery

Private Edwin George Hayward   *17th Bn Lancashire Fusiliers*
Service No.   46799   Age: 25
Place of Birth: Sandy Lane, Wiltshire   Home Country: England
Date of Death: 07/07/1918   Cause of death: Killed in action
Memorial: Chippenham – St. Paul's Church Memorial & Melksham
War cemetery: Lindenhoek Chalet Military Cemetery
Theatre of war: Belgium
Next of Kin: Edwin George & Elizabeth Hayward
Address: Manor Farm, Castle Combe, Wiltshire

Edwin was the youngest son of Edwin and Elizabeth Hayward and worked on his father's farm. He enlisted in the army initially joining the Army Veterinary Corps and was later transferred to the 17th Battalion Lancashire Fusiliers. He was killed south west of Ypres, Belgium, most likely by German artillery on Sunday 7 July 1918. Edwin is buried in Lindenhoek Chalet Military Cemetery

Captain Douglas Ridley Clunes Gabell   *Royal Air Force*
Service No.   N/a   Age: 20
Place of Birth: Charlton Kings, Glos   Home Country: England
Date of Death: 12/07/1918   Cause of death: Accident
Memorial: Swindon Village Glos.
War cemetery: Swindon St.Lawrence Churchyard
Theatre of war: Home
Next of Kin: Rev. Arthur Charles & Emma Gabell
Address: Battledown Gates, Cheltenham, Gloucestershire

Douglas was the youngest son of the Rev. Arthur & Emma Gabell and was educated at Cheltenham College before attending Sandhurst. He obtained a commission with the Gloucester Regiment and in August 1916 was transferred to the Royal Flying Corps, soon after being promoted to flying officer. He was described as an experienced flying Officer, having served over the Western Front, and in July 1918 he was an instructor at R.A.F. Yatesbury near Calne. On the afternoon of Friday 12 July 1918, Sir Audley Dallas Neeld and Lady Edith Neeld were entertaining a company of wounded soldiers at Grittleton House. The gathering was about to be brought to a close when an aeroplane attracted the attention of the party. The aircraft was seen to make several extensive circles when suddenly the machine was seen to turn over and crash to the earth, where it caught fire. The lifeless bodies of the occupants were removed as quickly as possible from the Debris. Douglas had been flying with George Frederick Delmar-Wilson and the bodies were removed to the mortuary at Yatesbury. An inquest was held the following day, the verdict being accidental death. There was a rumour that the flight had been a part of the entertainment for the wounded soldiers but this was denied by Sir Audley Dallas Neeld and it was assumed that Douglas was attracted to the spot by the gathering. When

*Far left:
Douglas Ridley
Clunes Gabell*

*Left: George
Frederick
Delmar-
Williamson*

an article appeared in the local paper the editor stated:

*"We are not permitted to disclose the localities where flying accidents take place and the
following communication from one of our representatives, alluding to the double fatality can
only be published with the names blank."*

Douglas's remains were taken to Swindon Village, Gloucestershire and he was buried in
St.Lawrence Churchyard.

Lt. George Frederick Delmar-Williamson		*Royal Air Force*	
Service No.	N/a	Age:	19
Place of Birth:	Kensington, London	Home Country:	England
Date of Death:	12/07/1918	Cause of death:	Accident
Memorial:	Cheltenham – Leckhampton Christ Church		
War cemetery:	Leckhampton St Peter Churchyard		
Theatre of war:	Home		
Next of Kin:	Frederick & Emily Delmar-Williamson		
Address:	Firs Lodge, Leckhampton, Gloucestershire		

George was the only son of Frederick, a famous singer, and Emily Delmar-Williamson and
was educated at Glyngarth School, Cheltenham then at Cheltenham College before attending
Sandhurst. He was commissioned as a 2nd Lieutenant in the Black Watch on 23 September
1916 and attached to the Royal Flying Corps in October 1916. He was promoted to flying
officer and obtained his wings in February 1917 then serving in France and Belgium from
March 1917. He was highly commended for photographic and reconnaissance duty and in
August 1917 he was invalided back to England suffering concussion. After his recovery he
served with the Home Squadron on air raid duty and was appointed instructor at Yatesbury in
March 1918. He was killed near Grittleton House on Friday 12 July 1918 in the same incident

as Douglas Ridley Clunes Gabell. His remains were taken to Leckhampton and buried in Leckhampton St Peter Churchyard. His commanding Officer wrote the following:

"He was a first class pilot, with the most promising career in front of him."

Private James Victor Wakeling   *1st Bn Royal Berkshire Regiment*

Service No.	39190	Age:	19
Place of Birth:	Redcombe, Glos	Home Country:	England
Date of Death:	25/07/1918	Cause of death:	Died of wounds
Memorial:	Little Somerford		
War cemetery:	St Hilaire Cemetery Extension Frevent		
Theatre of war:	France		
Next of Kin:	Leslie James & Sarah Wakeling		
Address:	5 Western Street, Swindon, Wiltshire.		

Nineteen year old James initially enlisted with the Somerset Light Infantry and was then transferred to the 1st Battalion Royal Berkshire Regiment. On 23 July 1918 the 1st Royal Berks carried out a trench raid on German positions south west of Arras, France. The raid was deemed a success, 5 prisoners were taken and 50 Germans were killed. The Royal Berks casualties consisted of 1 officer killed and 1 officer and 37 other ranks wounded. It is likely James was one of those wounded and he succumbed to his wounds on Thursday 25 July at a casualty clearing station at Frevent, West of Arras. James is buried in St Hilaire Cemetery Extension, Frevent.

Private Arthur Hull   *2/4th TF Bn Somerset Light Infantry*

Service No.	201805	Age:	32
Place of Birth:	Chippenham, Wiltshire	Home Country:	England
Date of Death:	31/07/1918	Cause of death:	Killed in action
Memorial:	Chippenham		
War cemetery:	Soissons Memorial		
Theatre of war:	France		
Next of Kin:	Albert H. J. & Phoebe Hull		
Address:	11 Park Fields, Chippenham		

Arthur a coach painter was the eldest son of Albert and Phoebe Hull and he enlisted with the 2/4th Battalion Somerset Light Infantry, a territorial battalion. The Somerset were sent to India in 1914 for garrison duties, then in September 1917 they were transferred to Egypt and then brought back to France landing at Marseilles on 1 June 1918. The Somersets became part of a Corps that was to be attached to the French army between the Ourcq and the Aisne on the western side of the salient from Rheims to west of Soissons. On Wednesday 31 July 1918 the Somersets were holding part of the Paris Line near Beugneux, south east of Soissons, France and were subject to heavy German shell fire which included using a large quantity of gas shells. Arthur was one of nine men killed. He is remembered on the Soissons memorial and has no known grave.

2nd Lieutenant Wilfred Henry Brinkworth   *215th Sqdn Royal Air Force*

Service No.	N/A	Age:	29
Place of Birth:	Corsham, Wiltshire	Home Country:	England
Date of Death:	04/08/1918	Cause of death:	Killed in action

Memorial:	Corsham & Chippenham Secondary School
War cemetery:	Arras Flying Services Memorial
Theatre of war:	France
Next of Kin:	Lily Mary Brinkworth
Address:	13 Churchill Road, Exeter, Devon

Regular soldier Wilfred was a clerk and enlisted with the Army Service Corps on 29 October 1908 and was promoted to corporal on 5 August 1914, the day war was declared. He arrived in France on 16 August 1914 and on August 1915 he married Lily Mary Hunt at Exeter. On 15 June 1916 he was mentioned in dispatches and in September 1916 Wilfred was accepted for officer training. After receiving a commission he joined the 3rd Battalion Royal Fusiliers and later transferred to the Royal Air Force in 1918. It is likely Wilfred was posted as missing on 4 August 1918 while flying east of Arras, France. He is remembered on the Arras Flying Services Memorial and has no known grave.

Private Frederick John Holder		*11th Bn Cheshire Regiment*	
Service No.	53399	Age:	29
Place of Birth:	North Wraxall, Wiltshire	Home Country:	England
Date of Death:	07/08/1918	Cause of death:	Died
Memorial:	North Wraxall		
War cemetery:	Terlincthun British Cemetery Wimille		
Theatre of war:	France		
Next of Kin:	Elizabeth Holder (wife) - Isaac Holder (parent)		
Address:	60 Dyfodwg Street, Treorchy, Glamorgan - North Wraxall		

Frederick, known as Fred, was a collier and married Elizabeth Davies on 13 November 1909 in South Wales. He volunteered for service with the 15th Service Battalion Welsh Regiment on 13 October 1914 and was sent to France arriving on 2 December 1915. On 31 March 1918 Fred was transferred to the 11th Battalion Cheshire Regiment and while serving with them he was posted as missing in action on 10 April 1918 during the German offensive known as the Battle of Lys. No further information was heard of Fred until his wife Elizabeth was given information from returning prisoners of war in December 1918. A friend wrote the following letter to the commanding officer of the Cheshire Regiment Depot at Chester:

"Sir
On information received of at least two returned prisoners of war who have been released from Germany both of who state that Pte. F.J. Holder has died whilst a prisoner in German hands. I beg to make an application for a verification of the above mentioned statement so as to get the official notification. I also venture to apply for any gratuities and medals for active service or monies due to the above (deceased) mentioned soldier. Hoping to get a reply to the statement of death shortly as the suspense for the wife is unnerving."

After much correspondence with the military it was officially established that Fred had died of dysentery while a prisoner of war on 7 August 1918 in a hospital at Friedrichsfeld, Mannheim, Germany and was buried locally. His remains were later exhumed and re-interred in Terlincthun British Cemetery, Wimille. He left a widow and four children.

14
A BLACK DAY FOR THE GERMAN ARMY

Private Arthur Herbert George Tavinor

Service No.   G/29390
Place of Birth: Chippenham, Wiltshire
Date of Death: 08/08/1918
Memorial: Chippenham – St Paul's Church – Congregational Church Memorial
War cemetery: Vis En Artois Memorial
Theatre of war: France
Next of Kin: George & Emily Tavinor
Address: 62 Marsh Field Road, Chippenham

7th Bn Royal West Kent Regiment

Age: 19
Home Country: England
Cause of death: Killed in action

Below left: Arthur Herbert George Tavinor remembered on his fathers fallen grave stone in St Paul's Churchyard Chippenham. - Below right: German prisoners of war.

Nineteen year old Arthur, known as Bertie, was the only son of George and Emily Tavinor and initially enlisted with the Devonshire Regiment and then being transferred to the 7th Battalion Royal West Kent Regiment. He was killed east of Arras France on Thursday 8 August 1918. He is remembered on the Vis En Artois Memorial and has no known grave.

Private Harry Parsons   *2nd Bn Wiltshire Regiment*
Service No.   9649   Age: 24
Place of Birth: Calne, Wiltshire   Home Country: England
Date of Death: 08/08/1918   Cause of death: Killed in action
Memorial: Sutton Benger
War cemetery: Loos Memorial
Theatre of war: France
Next of Kin: Henry & Sarah Parsons
Address: Sutton Benger, Wiltshire

Farm labourer Harry volunteered for service with the 2nd Battalion Wiltshire Regiment and arrived in France on 19 July 1915. On Thursday 8 August 1918 the Wiltshires were in shell hole posts north east of Hinges at a position called Vertbois Farm and sending out patrols probing German positions. They were subjected to heavy German shelling and Harry was one of seven men killed. He is remembered on the Loos memorial and has no known grave.

Sergeant Frederick William Sinclair   *1/6th Bn Gloucestershire Regiment*
Service No.   33618   Age: 28
Place of Birth: Sydney, Australia   Home Country: Australia
Date of Death: 09/08/1918   Cause of death: Killed in action
Memorial: Biddestone
War cemetery: Barenthal Military Cemetery
Theatre of war: Italy
Next of Kin: Daisy Maud Sinclair (wife) - George Sinclair (father)
Address:,   Biddestone, Wiltshire - North Sydney, Australia

Frederick, known as Cyril, married Daisy Maud Bushell from Biddestone at the end of 1915 in Portsmouth, Hampshire. He enlisted with the 1/6th Battalion Gloucestershire Regiment who in November 1917 were sent to Italy. Cyril was killed in the early hours of Friday 9 August 1918 when the Gloucesters raided the Austrian held Norfolk Trench south of Gaiga on the Asiago plateau. He was one of three men killed during the action and left a widow and small child. Cyril was buried in Barenthal Military Cemetery and in August 1920 Daisy Sinclair inserted the following memoriam in a local paper:

Only those who have loved and lost
Know how hard it is to bear
Only God knows how I miss him
Only God knows how I care

Private Thomas Geoffrey Millin   *15th Bn Hampshire Regiment*
Service No.   28758   Age: 18
Place of Birth: Christian Malford   Home Country: England
Date of Death: 09/08/1918   Cause of death: Killed in action
Memorial: Swindon Christ Church

War cemetery: Tyne Cot Memorial
Theatre of war: Belgium
Next of Kin: Alfred G & Jane Millin
Address: The Lawn Stables, Swindon, Wiltshire

Eighteen year old Thomas was the youngest son of Alfred and Jane Millin and he enlisted in the army and was sent to join the 15th Bn Hampshire Rregiment. On Friday 9 August the 15th Hampshires were at the Kemmel sector of the front attacking a salient at La Clytte (Klijte). They quickly moved forward capturing their objectives in the centre and on the right, but on the left the Germans resisted stubbornly. The position was bristling with machine guns and the Hampshires sustained heavy casualties before the opposition was overcome and the ground consolidated. Thomas was one of 39 men posted as killed or missing. He is remembered on the Tyne Cot Memorial and has no known grave. Thomas's brother William Richard Millin had been killed in France in March 1918.

Able Seaman Samuel Stutt   *Hood Bn Royal Naval Division RNVR*
Service No.   R/581   Age: 35
Place of Birth: Bristol, Glos   Home Country: England
Date of Death: 11/08/1918   Cause of death: Died
Memorial: Chippenham & St Andrews Church Memorial
War cemetery: Niederzwehren Cemetery
Theatre of war: Germany
Next of Kin: Annie Maria Stutt - Edward & Elizabeth Stutt
Address: 13 Wood Lane, Chippenham – Crosses Gardens, St Paul's, Bristol

Samuel was a stoker at Chippenham Gas Works and attested for service under the Derby Scheme on 12 December 1915, being called up on 3 January 1917 joining the Royal Naval Volunteer Reserve. After completing his training he was sent to France on 15 April 1917 and was posted to Hood Battalion on 5 June 1917. At the beginning of 1918 Samuel was granted home leave and married Annie Maria Weston at Chippenham returning afterwards to France. On 24 March 1918 he was posted as missing during the German advance and information was later obtained that Samuel had been wounded and captured and was a prisoner of war in Germany. He died after developing septicaemia from his wounds at Langensalza Hospital, Saxony on Sunday 11 August 1918. He was initially buried in Langensalza Prisoner of War Cemetery and after the Armistice his remains were relocated to Niederzwehren Cemetery.

Lieutenant Basil William Ramsbottom   *12th Bn Norfolk Regiment*
Service No.   N/a   Age: 22
Place of Birth: Colesberg, Cape Colony   Home Country: England
Date of Death: 19/08/1918   Cause of death: Killed in action
Memorial: Lacock & Lacock Church
War cemetery: Le Grand Hasard Military Cemetery Morebecque
Theatre of war: France
Next of Kin: Rev. William Henry & Annie Ramsbottom
Address: Lacock Vicarage, Lacock, Wiltshire

Basil was the youngest son of Rev. William and Annie Ramsbotton of Lacock. He initially joined the 2/1st Wiltshire Yeomary and then was transferred to the Norfolk Yeomanry then to the 12th Battalion Norfolk Regiment. He was killed after a few days after returning from home leave in England on Monday 19 August 1918 at Vieux Berquin, South of Hazebrouck.

Private Arthur Alexander Gameson   *2nd South Wales Borderers*

Service No.	20845	Age:	31
Place of Birth:	Tredegar, Monmouthshire	Home Country:	England
Date of Death:	20/08/1918	Cause of death:	Killed in action
Memorial:	Not known		

War cemetery: Outterstreene Communal Cemetery Extention Bailleul
Theatre of war: France
Next of Kin: Ellen G. Gameson (wife) - William J. & Elizabeth Gameson (parents)
Address: 24 London Road, Chippenham - 74 High Street, Tredegar, Tredegar

Arthur, a coal miner, was the eldest son of William and Elizabeth Gameson and volunteered for service with the 2nd Battalion South Wales Borderers. It is likely that while he was in training he met Ellen Gertrude Davis from Chippenham and they married at Winchester just prior to him leaving for France where he arrived on 3 December 1915. He was killed in action on Tuesday 20 August 1918 during fighting around the village of Outtersteene, France. In August 1919 Ellen Gameson inserted the following Memoriam in a local paper:

He stood at his post like a soldier brave
He answered his country's call
He sleeps faraway in a hero's grave
For a country's call he did fall
Ever remembered by his loving wife

21 AUGUST 1918 - THE SECOND BATTLE OF ALBERT

2nd Lieutenant Francis Charlton Lanaway   *7th Bn Royal Fusiliers*

Service No.	N/A	Age:	36
Place of Birth:	Dartford, Kent	Home Country:	England
Date of Death:	21/08/1918	Cause of death:	Killed in action
Memorial:	Not Known		

War cemetery: Achiet Le Grand Communal Cemetery Extension
Theatre of war: France
Next of Kin: Frances Grace Lanaway (wife) - Hugh and Elizabeth Lanaway (parents
Address: Bouveret, Borstal Road, Rochester, Kent

Francis was the only son of Hugh and Elizabeth Lanaway and in the spring of 1914 he married Frances Grace Huxham. He was employed by the Westminster Bank at Cambridge and it is likely he was conscripted into the army and sent to the Royal Berkshire Regiment. He was then offered a commission in January 1918 and after completing his cadet training he was posted to the Royal Sussex Regiment and then attached to the 7th Battalion Royal Fusiliers. He was reported missing on the 24 August 1918 South of Arras and Francis's sister Elizabeth Stewart-Craig of Lacock inserted an advert in the paper asking for information concerning her brother. It was later found that Francis had been killed in action on Wednesday 21 August 1918 and was buried in Achiet Le Grand Communal Cemetery Extension.

Private John Reginald Hayes   *15th Bn Royal Warwickshire Regiment*

Service No.	26642	Age:	19
Place of Birth:	Chippenham, Wiltshire	Home Country:	England
Date of Death:	24/08/1918	Cause of death:	Killed in action

Memorial:	Chippenham - St. Paul's Church & Secondary Schhol Memorial
War cemetery:	Adanac Military Cemetery Miraumont
Theatre of war:	France
Next of Kin:	Albert & Sarah Hayes
Address:	Audlee, Lowden Avenue, Chippenham

Nineteen year old John, known as Reginald, was the eldest son of Albert & Sarah Hayes. He entered Chippenham Secondary School with a foundation scholarship, and afterward obtained a junior scholarship. On leaving school he found employment as a clerk in the goods department of the Great Western Railway. He enlisted in the army at the age of eighteen years joining the 15th Battalion Royal Warwickshire Regiment. Reginald was chosen to be a signaler with the Warwickshires and was awarded a first class certificate while training in Northumberland and was given another award in France. Reginald was shot through the temple on Saturday 24 August 1918 during fighting around the villages of Miraumont and Pys north East of Albert, France. He had been involved in all the fighting since the German offensive in March 1917. Reginald is buried in Adanac Military Cemetery, Miraumont.

Private Ernest Jasper Notton *34th Coy Machine Gun Corps*

Service No.	114858	Age:	21
Place of Birth:	Great Somerford	Home Country:	England
Date of Death:	25/08/1918	Cause of death:	Died of wounds
Memorial:	Pewsey		
War cemetery:	Croix Rouge Military Cemetery Quaedypre		
Theatre of war:	France		
Next of Kin:	Alfred George & Mary Notton		
Address:	Sunnyhill Farm, Pewsey, Wiltshire		

Ernest was the eldest son of Alfred and Mary Notton. He joined the army initially enlisting with the Army Service Corps and then being transferred to the Machine Gun Corps. He was wounded and evacuated to the 44th casualty clearing station at Quaedypre, south east of Dunkerque France, where he died on Sunday 25 August 1918. Ernest is buried in Croix Rouge Military Cemetery, Quaedypre

2nd Lieutenant Francis Jasper Langley *2nd Bn Grenadier Guards*

Service No.	N/A	Age:	28
Place of Birth:	Heytesbury, Wiltshire	Home Country:	England
Date of Death:	27/08/1918	Cause of death:	Killed in action
Memorial:	North Wraxall		
War cemetery:	Mory Abbey Military Cemetery Mory		
Theatre of war:	France		
Next of Kin:	Rev. John & Bertha V. Langley		
Address:	The Rectory, North Wraxall, Wiltshire		

Francis was the second son of Rev. John and Bertha Langley and originally joined the Navy on 15 July 1907 and was employed as a clerk. In 1910 the Rev. John Langley applied for his son to be released from the Navy on account of a problem with his eyesight, he was prescribed spectacles for mild myopia and his release was approved. Francis had planned to join his brother in Canada but in June 1911 he applied to rejoin the Navy and was promoted to Paymaster in 1912. In 1913 Francis resigned again with plans to go to South Africa and become a farmer, but he decided to remain with the Navy and his resignation was cancelled. On 21 May 1916

Francis made a further application to resign from the Navy in order to enlist with the army. His resignation was accepted and he obtained a commission with the 2nd Battalion Grenadier Guards. Francis was killed in action near Bapaume, France, on Tuesday 27 August 1918 during the British advance. He is today buried in Mory Abbey Military Cemetery. His brother John Basil Robert Langley was killed in an air accident in May 1918.

Private Albert Edward Thomas Rose (Rusher)   *1st Bn Dorsetshire Regiment*
Service No.   20923   Age: 18
Place of Birth: Chippenham   Home Country: England
Date of Death: 27/08/1918   Cause of death: Killed in action
Memorial: Chippenham & St. Andrews Church Memorial
War cemetery: Vis En Artois Memorial
Theatre of war: France
Next of Kin: James & Edith Rusher
Address: 96 Wood Lane, Chippenham

Eighteen year old Albert was the eldest son of James and Edith Rusher and was born before his parents were married. He was brought up as Albert Rusher but when he went to enlist with the army it is likely that he had to take his birth Certificate and he served as Albert Rose. He initially joined the Wiltshire Regiment but later was transferred to the 1st Battalion Dorsetshire Regiment. On Tuesday 27 August 1918 the 1st Dorsets were ordered to clear Starry Wood and advance to the village of Soyecourt south of Roye, France. As they advanced the 1st Dorsets were held up for the best part of a day by the German rear guard and then German artillery heavily shelled the approaches to the wood. It is likely Albert was killed during this action, he is remembered on the Vis En Artois Memorial and has no known grave.

Rifleman George Joseph Spooner   *5th Bn London Regiment*
Service No.   315468   Age: 35
Place of Birth: Southwark, London   Home Country: England
Date of Death: 29/08/1918   Cause of death: Killed in action
Memorial: Not known
War cemetery: H A C Cemetery Ecoust St Mein
Theatre of war: France
Next of Kin: Mary Elizabeth Spooner (wife) - Robert & Hannah Eliza Spooner (parents)
Address: 28 Palmer Street, Chippenham - 141 Plough Road, Battersea, London

George, a builder, was the eldest son of Robert and Hannah Spooner and married Mary Elizabeth Wythe on 19 August 1911 at Fulham, London. It is likely he was conscripted into the army initially joining the 6th London Regiment before being transferred to the 5th Battalion London Regiment. He was killed in action East of Arras during the British Advance on Thursday 29 August 1918. George is buried in H. A. C. Cemetery Ecoust St Mein.

Private Frank Gregory   *1st Bn Devonshire Regiment*
Service No.   30744   Age: 29
Place of Birth: Lacock, Wiltshire   Home Country: England
Date of Death: 30/08/1918   Cause of death: Killed in action
Memorial: Lacock Church
War cemetery: Vis En Artois Memorial
Theatre of war: France

Next of Kin: Ellen Gregory (wife) - Charles & Sarah A. Gregory (parents)
Address: The Mead, Lacock, Wiltshire - Lackham Lodge

Frank, a milkman, was the eldest son of Charles and Sarah Gregory and in the summer of 1915 he married Ellen Hunt. Frank originally joined the Wiltshire Regiment but was transferred to the 1st Battalion Devonshire Regiment. On Friday 30 August 1918 the 1st Devons were part of a British attack at Beugny East of Bapaume, France. Their objective was a knoll known as Hill 140 and the 1st Devons were met by exceptionally thick German barbed wire and the four tanks that had been assigned to them were knocked out. However, before 7.30am Hill 140 was captured and a German counter attack was beaten off. The 1st Devons sustained heavy casualties and one of those killed was Frank. He is remembered on the Vis En Artois Memorial and has no known grave.

Private Percy George Brookman   *12th Bn Gloucestershire Regiment*

Service No.	40130	Age:	22
Place of Birth:	Acton Turville, Glos	Home Country:	England
Date of Death:	31/08/1918	Cause of death:	Killed in action
Memorial:	Nettleton		
War cemetery:	Vis En Artois Memorial		
Theatre of war:	France		
Next of Kin:	Hugh & Lydia Brookman		
Address:	Burton, Wiltshire		

It is likely Percy was conscripted into the army initially joining the Welsh Regiment before being transferred to the 12th Battalion Gloucestershire Regiment. He was killed in action near Bapaume, France on Saturday 31 August 1918. He is remembered on the Vis En Artois Memorial and has no known grave.

Private Noah Davis   *10th Bn West Riding Regiment*

Service No.	25938	Age:	31
Place of Birth:	Chippenham, Wiltshire	Home Country:	England
Date of Death:	01/09/1918	Cause of death:	Died
Memorial:	Chippenham - St. Andrews Church – Liberal Club Memorial.		
War cemetery:	Dueville Communal Cemetery Extension		
Theatre of war:	Italy		
Next of Kin:	May Helena Davis (wife) - Noah & Mary Davis (parents)		
Address:	17 The Causeway, Chippenham - 18 Timber Street, Chippenham		

Noah, a fish and fruit salesman, was the second son on Noah and Mary Davis. He married May Helena Sage on 20 February 1912 and was conscripted into the army joining the Royal ArmyVeternary Cory on 6 June 1916, being sent to France on 20 Septemer 1916. He was granted home leave in June 1917 and just after his return he was compulsorily transferred to the 10th Battalion West Riding Regiment and in November 1917 the 10th West Riding Regiment were sent to Italy. He was admitted to the 9th Casualty Clearing Station with jaundice on 21 August 1918 and re admitted on 28 August with pneumonia. He died of jaundice on Sunday 1 September 1918 and his personal possessions were return to his wife consisting of disc, photos, cards, wallet, bladesin case, pencil case, silver ring (broken), cap badge, belt and note book. Noah left a widow and a young son. In September 1919 Noah's parent's inserted the following memoriam in a local paper:

When we last saw his smiling face
He looked so strong and brave.
We little thought how soon he'd be
Laid in a soldier's grave.
We pictured his home returning,
We longed to clasp his hand,
But God has postponed the meeting
Till we meet in a better place

Private Herbert Holloway		*2/8th Bn Worcestershire Regiment*	
Service No.	42367	Age:	18
Place of Birth:	Chippenham, Wiltshire	Home Country:	England
Date of Death:	03/09/1918	Cause of death:	Killed in action
Memorial:	Chippenham & Hardenhuish		
War cemetery:	Pont Du Hem Military Cemetery La Gorgue		
Theatre of war:	France		
Next of Kin:	Charles & Anne Holloway		
Address:	15 Downing Street, Woodlands, Chippenham		

He was christened Albert Frank Holloway but known as Herbert and was the youngest son of Charles and Anne Holloway. He originally enlisted with the Wiltshire Yeomanry and was then transferred to the 2/8th Battalionn Worcestershire Regiment. Herbert was killed in action when the 2/8th Worcesters forced a crossing of the River Lys at Estaires, France capturing the only two bridges that remained over the river while under fire from the German rear guard. One of the bridges was in need of repair before it could be crossed and the 2/8th Worcesters gathered material repairing the bridge under the cover of darkness. It is likely Herbert was buried at Estaires and relocated to Pont Du Hem Military Cemetery, La Gorgue, after the Armistice.

Private Charles Opie		*8th Bn Royal Berkshire Regiment*	
Service No.	45945	Age:	18
Place of Birth:	Castleton, Lancashire	Home Country:	England
Date of Death:	06/09/1918	Cause of death:	Died of wounds
Memorial:	Chippenham – St. Paul's Church & Secondary School Memorial		
War cemetery:	Dernancourt Communal Cemetery Extension		
Theatre of war:	France		
Next of Kin:	Charles H & Mary Anne Opie		
Address:	Pew Hill Cottages, Chippenham		

Charles, known a Charley, was the only son of Charles & Anne Holloway was educated at St. Paul's School and then Chippenham Secondary School and was a member of St. Pauls Church Choir. On leaving school he found employment with Saxby and Farmer Signal Works, where his father had a department. He enlisted with the army in March 1918 initially joining the Devonshire Regiment and was then transferred to 8th Battalion Royal Berkshire Regiment and sent to France on 26 August 1918. He was promoted to lance corporal and then transferred to the Lewis gun section. On 4 September the 8th Royal Berkshires were near Combles at the Somme and were sending out patrols to keep in touch with the retreating German forces. The British patrols had been probing enemy positions on the east bank of the river Tortille and as they were withdrawn to Bivouacs on the Fricourt Road in the early hours of 5 September they were subjected to a German gas bombardment. It is likely Charley was wounded at this time and evacuated to a dressing station at Dernancourt where he succumbed to his wounds on Friday

6 September 1918. Charley is buried in Dernancourt Communal Cemetery Extension.

Shoeing Smith Frederick George Edgar Bull   *C Bty 112th Bde Royal Field Artillery*
Service No.   86568   Age: 30
Place of Birth: East tytherton Wiltshire   Home Country: England
Date of Death: 07/09/1918   Cause of death: Killed in action
Memorial: Chippenham – St. Andrews Memorial & Langley Burrell Memorial
War cemetery: Peronne Communal Cemetery Extension
Theatre of war: France
Next of Kin: Elsie Bull (wife) - George & Ellen Bull (parents)
Address: 19 Crickets Lane, Chippenham - Langley Burrell

Frederick was a brewer's labourer and at the end of 1912 he married Elsie E. Poole at Chippenham. He volunteered for service with the Royal Artillery and arrived in France on 27 September 1915. He was originally a driver but was promoted to Shoeing Smith after the completion of a course and would have been responsible for ensuring horses of his battery were correctly shod. He was killed in action on Saturday 7 September 1918 during the British advance. He is buried at Peronne Communal Cemetery Extension with over 1400 casualties of the Great War.

Private David Barnes   *8th Bn Somerset Light Infantry*
Service No.   31029   Age: 18
Place of Birth: Little Somerford   Home Country: England
Date of Death: 08/09/1918   Cause of death: Died of wounds
Memorial: Little Somerford
War cemetery: Varennes Military Cemetery
Theatre of war: France
Next of Kin: Frank & Caroline Barnes
Address: Little Somerford, Wiltshire

Eighteen year old David initially enlisten with the Wiltshire Regiment but was transferred to the 8th Battalion Somerset Light Infantry. In early September the Somersets were advancing near Havrincourt east of Bapaume, France. It is likely David was wounded when the Somersets were clearing German forces at Havrincourt Wood. He was evacuated to a casualty clearing station at Varennes where he succumbed to his wounds on Sunday 8 September 1918. David is buried in Varennes Military Cemetery.

2nd Lieutenant Edwin John Brinkworth   *15th Bn Durham Light Infantry*
Service No.   N/a   Age: 27
Place of Birth: Chippenham   Home Country: England
Date of Death: 09/09/1918   Cause of death: Died of wounds
Memorial: Chippenham - St. Andrews-Congregational - Seconday School Memorial
War cemetery: Rocquigny Equancourt Road British Cemetery Mananco
Theatre of war: France
Next of Kin: Major William H. & Charlotte A Brinkworth
Address: 6 The Causeway, Chippenham

Edwin, known as Jack, was the elder of twin sons of William and Charlotte Brinkworth and was educated at Chippenham Secondary School. In 1907, on leaving school, Jack gained employment with the savings bank department of the London Post Office and in 1909 he joined Capital and Counties Bank at Bristol and was subsequently employed at Swansea, Tewkesbury and Swindon Branches. After passing examinations coming top in economics he was transferred to the Banks headquarters in London where he worked in the chief inspectors office. Jack volunteered for service with the 26th Battalion Royal Fusiliers, known as the Banker Battalion, and was sent to France in 1916 going through all of the Somme campaign and spending two winters in the trenches. On 25 September 1917 Jack received a commission and was posted to the 15th Battalion Durham Light Infantry. In July 1918 Jack was given home leave and while at rest he stated that in all the tight corners he had been, he was fortunate in not having received any serious wounds, and thought he possessed a charmed life. On 11 September Jack's parents received two letters dated 4 and 5 September stating he was at rest and about to proceed to the front once more. Jack was wounded most likely near Havrincourt Wood and evacuated to a casualty clearing station at Ytrs east of Baupaume France where he died on Monday 9 September 1918. Jack is buried in Rocquigny Equancourt Road British Cemetery, Mananco.

Rifleman George Dixon   *1/5th Bn London Regiment*

Service No.	45406	Age:	23
Place of Birth:	Durham	Home Country:	England
Date of Death:	09/09/1918	Cause of death:	Killed in action
Memorial:	Chippenham		
War cemetery:	Windmill British Cemetery Monchy Le Preux		
Theatre of war:	France		
Next of Kin:	William & Rhoda Dixon		
Address:	2 Park Street, Woodlands, Chippenham		

George was employed as a labourer with Saxby and Farmer Signal Works, Chippenham and enlisted with the army initially joining the Durham Light Infantry and then being transferred to the 1/5th Battalion London Regiment. He was killed in action on Monday 9 September 1918 during the British advance toward the Hindenburg line south east of Arras, France. In September 1919 George's parents inserted the following memoriam in a local paper:

Can ever a mother forget
The son she loved so dear
Oh, no, the voice that is now still
Keeps ringing in my ear
In the quiet hours of the night
When sleep forsakes my eyes
My thoughts are ever far away
Where my dear son George lies
Somewhere in France he lies at rest
For his King and Country he did his best
With other comrades he played his part
And did his duty with a loyal heart
From his loving Mother, Father, Brothers and Sisters

Private Charles Herbert Archibald Tasker   *16th Bn Devonshire Regiment*

Service No.	345163	Age:	25
Place of Birth:	Chippenham, Wiltshire	Home Country:	England
Date of Death:	10/09/1918	Cause of death:	Killed in action
Memorial:	Not known		

War cemetery: Ste Emilie Valley Cemetery Villiers Faucon
Theatre of war: France
Next of Kin: Sidney Herbert & Sarah Jane Tasker
Address: Rowde, Wiltshire

Charles, known as Archie, was the eldest son of Herbert and Sarah Tasker, a member of the Rowde Church choir and was employed as a baker with the Cooperative Stores in Devizes, later working in Yeovil. He volunteered for service in September 1914 with the 1st Devon Yeomanry and arrived in Gallipoli in October 1915. After the evacuation of the peninsular he was sent to Egypt where for some time he served as a scout for the Australian Light Horse and had been to Jerusalem and Jericho before being transferred to the Western Front in May 1918 joining the 16th Battalion Devonshire Regiment. After three years continuous service Archie was given home leave in July 1918 and after two weeks he returned to the front. On Tuesday 10 September 1918 the 16th Devons were attacking Horshoe Trench system in front of Ronssoy, France, where they succeeded in getting into the enemies trenches and gained a foothold on the ridge beyond. The Devons faced strong opposition in the initial attack and were then subject to German counter attacks which led to the Devons withdrawing and returning to the British line from where they had commenced the attack. One of those killed was Archie. Herbert Tasker received the two letters from Archies company officers Captain F.R. Archer and Lieutenant Thomas. Captain Archer stated:

"You can feel proud as all of us that he died a gallant soldier."

Lieutenant Thomas wrote:

"His company had twice made a most gallant attack on a German trench at night, and he was lying in the trench by his company commander when a shell fell in the trench, killing him and four others instantaneously."

Lt. Robert Edward Leslie Scott MC&Bar   *129th Bty Royal Garrison Artillery*
Service No.   N/A   Age: 21
Place of Birth: Pembury, Kent   Home Country: England
Date of Death: 14/09/1918   Cause of death: Killed in action
Memorial: Langley Burrell – Memorial Window Langley Burrell & Matfield, Kent.
War cemetery: Lebucquiere Communal Cemetery Extension
Theatre of war: France
Next of Kin: Edward Lucas Montgomery Scott & Emily Letitia Scott
Address: Cryals Matfield, Paddock Wood, Kent

Robert was the eldest son of Edward and Emily Scott and the grandson of Robert Martyn Ashe of Langley House. He was educated at Tonbridge School and then the Royal Military Acadamy Woolwich. He was given a commission in the Royal Garrison Artillery on 26 May 1916 and arrived in France on 4 July 1916 being promoted to Lieutenant in November 1917. He was killed in action on Saturday 14 September 1918 at Havrincourt Wood east of Bapaume, France. Robert's Major wrote:

"Liked by all for his many personal attractions, and very much respected for his fine abilities, most courageous under all circumstances, he was one of a type very seldom met with. It would be a vain endeavour to replace him, and his going has left a gap that cannot be filled. His name will never be forgotten and his deeds bear glorious testimony to his fine character."

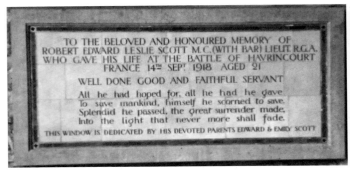

The memorial plaque and window remembering Robert Edward Leslie Scott at
St. Peter's Church Langley Burrell

The Adjutant wrote:

"He did not seem to know the meaning of fear. His commanding officer told me he considered
he was one of the best artillery officers in France. I never saw anyone keener at his job. He
was an extraordinary efficient section officer. He inspired his men with the same devotion of
duty and disregard of danger that he showed himself. No one could help being struck by his
personality: he was a first rate officer, and a gallant gentleman."

Robert was awarded the Military Cross and Bar for gallantry and devotion to duty in the field.
He was originally buried at Bertincourt but after the Armistice his remains were relocated to
Lebucquiere Communal Cemetery Extension. In Langley Burrell Church there is a window
dedicated to Robert by his parents.

Corporal Stephen Rose		*12/13th Bn Northumberland Fusiliers*	
Service No.	56249	Age:	27
Place of Birth:	Chippenham	Home Country:	England
Date of Death:	17/09/1918	Cause of death:	Died of wounds
Memorial:	Chippenham & St. Andrews Church Memorial		
War cemetery:	St Sever Cemetery Rouen		
Theatre of war:	France		
Next of Kin:	Agnes E. Rose (wife) – James & Emily Rose (parents)		
Address:	Moor End Lane, Eaton Bray, Dunstable, Bedfordshire		

Stephen, a groom, volunteered for service with the Army Service Corps and was later transferred
to the 12/13th Battalion Northumberland Fusiliers. He was wounded in action during actions
against the Germans at the Hindenburg Line, east of Bapaume, France. He died of his wounds
at a military hospital at Rouen on Tuesday 17 September 1918 and is buried in St. Sever
Cemetery, Rouen.

Private Francis John Griffin		*1/4th Bn TF Wiltshire Regiment*	
Service No.	201006	Age:	28
Place of Birth:	Ford, Wiltshire	Home Country:	England
Date of Death:	19/09/1918	Cause of death:	Died
Memorial:	Chippenham & St. Andrews Church Memorial		

War cemetery:	Gaza War Cemetery
Theatre of war:	Palestine
Next of Kin:	John Sherman & Eliza Griffin
Address:	22 Parliament Street, Chippenham

Francis, known as Frank, was a milk factory worker and enlisted with the army joining the 1/4th Territorial Battalion Wiltshire Regiment. He died of dysentery at No.36 Stationary Hospital, Gaza on Thursday 19 September 1918. Frank is buried in Gaza War Cemetery. His Brother John Edward Griffin had been killed in Salonika in December 1915.

Private Thomas Michael Alexander Puttock *1/4th Bn TF Wiltshire Regiment*

Service No.	21300	Age:	37
Place of Birth:	Bath, Somerset	Home Country:	England
Date of Death:	19/09/1918	Cause of death:	Killed in action
Memorial:	Chippenham & St. Andrews Church Memorial		
War cemetery:	Ramleh War Cemetery		
Theatre of war:	Palestine		
Next of Kin:	Thomas & Annie Puttock (parents) – Edward & Mary Dempsey (uncle)		
Address:	Not known - 18 St. Mary Street, Chippenham		

Thomas, a blacksmith's striker, was brought up by his uncle and aunt and enlisted with the army joining the 1/4th Territorial Battalion Wiltshire Regiment. He was one of sixteen fatalities during action in the early hours of the morning of Thursday 19 September 1918 when the Wiltshires advanced and captured Turkish positions near Ramleh, in modern day Israel. Thomas is buried in Ramleh War Cemetery.

Rifleman Fred Powney *12th Bn London Regiment*

Service No.	50140	Age:	19
Place of Birth:	Chippenham, Wiltshire	Home Country:	England
Date of Death:	21/09/1918	Cause of death:	Killed in action
Memorial:	Chippenham & St. Andrews Church Memorial		
War cemetery:	Pigeon Ravine Cemetery Epehy		
Theatre of war:	France		
Next of Kin:	Mary Hancock		
Address:	9 River Street, Chippenham		

Nineteen year old Fred was the only son of Mary Hancock and enlisted with the army initially being sent to the Training Reserve, then onto King's Royal Rifle Corps and then posted to the 12th Battalion London Regiment. He was killed in action during the British advance to the Hindenburg line near Epehy on Saturday 21 September 1918. Fred is buried in Pigeon Ravine Cemetery Epehy.

Private William Francis Emery *14th Bn Royal Warwickshire Regiment*

Service No.	50626	Age:	18
Place of Birth:	Malmesbury	Home Country:	England
Date of Death:	27/09/1918	Cause of death:	Killed in action
Memorial:	Chippenham		
War cemetery:	Gouzeaucourt New British Cemetery		
Theatre of war:	France		

Next of Kin: Harry & Rhoda Emery
Address: Horse Fair, Malmesbury, Wiltshire

Eighteen year old William was the second son of Harry & Rhoda Emery and enlisted in the army joining the 14th Battalion Royal Warwickshire Regiment. He was killed in action during the British adance to the Hindenburg line south west of Cambria, France on Friday 27 September 1918. William is buried in Gouzeaucourt New British Cemetery.

Private William Rose   *1st Bn Wiltshire Regiment*

Service No.	24569	Age:	20
Place of Birth:	Chippenham	Home Country:	England
Date of Death:	27/09/1918	Cause of death:	Died
Memorial:	Chippenham		
War cemetery:	Cologne Southern Cemetery		
Theatre of war:	Germany		
Next of Kin:	Nelson & Annie Rose		
Address:	4 Shrubbery Lane, Wyke Regis, Weymouth, Dorset		

William, known as Willie, was the youngest son of Nelson and Annie Rose and lived at Park Street, Chippeham. It is likely he was captured during the German offensive in Mach and April 1918 and taken prisoner. He died of illness or disease as a prisoner of war in Germany. Willie is today buried in Cologne Southern Cemetery

Sapper George Enos Farmer   *275th Railway Coy Royal Engineers*

Service No.	WR/258385	Age:	40
Place of Birth:	Lacock, Wiltshire	Home Country:	England
Date of Death:	28/09/1918	Cause of death:	Accident
Memorial:	Not known		
War cemetery:	Varennes Military Cemetery		
Theatre of war:	France		
Next of Kin:	Jennie Farmer (wife) - John & Elizabeth Farmer (parents)		
Address:	2 Lawley Court, Shrewsbury, Shropshire – Lacock		

George had spent twelve years serving with the Wiltshire Regiment prior to the war and was working as a bricklayer's labourer for the Great Western Railway at Shrewsbury. He married Jennie Stevens at Chippenham on 4 November 1907 and attested for service under the Derby Scheme on the 11 December 1915. He was called up for service on 7 July 1916 and joined the Royal Engineers and arrived in France on 21 August 1916. On Saturday 28 September 1918 George was mortally wounded after accidentally kicking a Stokes mortar bomb which was hidden by long grass. He died a few minutes later, at a court of enquiry held after the accident Corporal J. Bufton was called and stated:

"I arrived at Buire-Sur-L'Ancre by train on Saturday 28 September 1918 at about 7.40am. Five minutes later I was going, in accordance with orders, from the train towards the well situated near the R.T.O's Office, in order to get a wash. I was accompanied by Sapper G. Farmer for a short distance but soon he inclined away to my left about four yards away. I walked on, and after going a few paces, I heard an explosion. I turned around and heard Farmer call to me "Come Here Corporal". He was lying flat on the ground and saw him trying to raise himself into a sitting posture. I went to him and laid him down and I found he was badly injured in the right thigh as well as in other places. I cut away his clothes and found that

*something had gone right through his thigh from front to back at about three inches below the
groin, and that the bone was broken and sticking out behind. He was bleeding badly and I tried,
with the assistance with a Corporal in the 5th Gloucesters (from a waiting train) and Sapper
Smith of the 275th Coy. R.E, to apply a tourniquet, but the wound was too high up to admit
this. He was also wounded in the left thigh, the abdomen, and in the head. He died in about
eight minutes after the explosion. The Military Police came up and took charge of the body
which was removed in an ambulance. I saw a Stokes bomb lying a few yards away from where
Sapper Farmer was lying and several more about."*

George's body was taken to No. 75 Field Ambulance and later buried in Varennes Military
Cemetery. He left a widow and two children.

Stoker 1st Class Henry John Cleaver   *HMS Seagull Royal Navy*

Service No.	O/2163	Age:	30
Place of Birth:	Langley Burrell, Wiltshire	Home Country:	England
Date of Death:	30/09/1918	Cause of death:	Died
Memorial:	Langley Burrell		
War cemetery:	Plymouth Naval Memorial		
Theatre of war:	At sea		
Next of Kin:	Isaac & Hannah Cleaver		
Address:	Barrow Cottage, Langley Burrell, Wiltshire		

Henry, known as John, was the second son of Isaac and Hannah Cleaver had joined the Navy
Prior to the outbreak of hostilities. He died when the Torpedo Gunboat H.M.S. Seagull collided
with a merchant ship in the Firth of Clyde on Monday 30 September 1918. He is remembered
on the Plymouth Naval Memorial, his brother Gilbert Cleaver would be killed just over a week
later in October 1918.

Sergeant Elisha Frank Jones MM   *B Bty 232 Bde Royal Field Artillery*

Service No.	10738	Age:	22
Place of Birth:	Chippenham, Wiltshire	Home Country:	England
Date of Death:	03/10/1918	Cause of death:	Killed in action
Memorial:	Chippenham – St Andrews Church & Causewat Methodist Church		
War cemetery:	Bellicourt British Cemetery		
Theatre of war:	France		
Next of Kin:	Samuel John & Mary Jane Jones (parents) – Fanny Perrott (Sister)		
Address:	1 Timber Street, Chippenham		

Elisha volunteered for service with the Royal Field Artillery and arrived in France on 17 July
1915 and during his service he won the Military Medal. He was killed most likely due to German
artillery fire at the Battle of the St. Quentin Canal near Bellicourt, France on Thursday 3 October
1918. In October 1919 Elisha's brothers and sisters inserted the following memoriam in a local
paper:

*He heard the call, he held not back
But went straight forth to fight
When for our homes it looked most black
He fell with victory in sight
Ever remembered by his loving Sisters and Brothers*

Corporal William Henry Walker *1st Bn Worcestershire Regiment*

Service No.	1171	Age:	27
Place of Birth:	Lacock, Wiltshire	Home Country:	England
Date of Death:	03/10/1918	Cause of death:	Died
Memorial:	Melksham		
War cemetery:	Melksham Church Cemetery		
Theatre of war:	Home		
Next of Kin:	Amelia Frances Walker (wife) – Jane Farmer		
Address:	King Street, Melksham – Lacock		

William had served nine years in the army prior to the outbreak of the war and was in Egypt at the commencement of hostilities. The Worcesters were recalled to England and then sent to France arriving on 6 November 1914. After serving some time in France he was evacuated to England after suffering shock and an injury to his back caused by a bursting shell. After his initial recovery he was deemed unfit for service and transferred to the Royal Defence Corps in which he remained until being discharged on the 31 July 1918. For a short time he took employment as a van man with the Cooperative Society but after a few weeks he was forced to resign when his health deteriorated and he died on Thursday 3 October 1918 at Melksham and was buried in the cemetery. He left a widow and a young child.

Private 2nd Class George Alfred Bothwell *Wireless School (Winchester) RAF*

Service No.	294023	Age:	20
Place of Birth:	Kirkee, Clare	Home Country:	England
Date of Death:	04/10/1918	Cause of death:	Died
Memorial:	Not known		
War cemetery:	Winchester West Hill Old Cemetery		
Theatre of war:	Home		
Next of Kin:	James & Margaret Bothwell		
Address:	48 New Road, Chippenham, Wiltshire		

George was the eldest son of James and Margaret Bothwell, James was a master photographer having a studio in New Road, Chippenham. George enlisted with Royal Air Force and was sent to the Wireless School at Winchester where he died of illness or disease on Friday 4 October 1918.

Private Arthur Frederick George Skuse *7th Bn Wiltshire Regiment*

Service No.	33669	Age:	41
Place of Birth:	Chippenham, Wiltshire	Home Country:	England
Date of Death:	07/10/1918	Cause of death:	Killed in action
Memorial:	Biddestone		
War cemetery:	Templux Le Guerard British Cemetery		
Theatre of war:	France		
Next of Kin:	Frederick & Eliza Skuse		
Address:	Cuttle Lane, Biddestone, Wiltshire		

Arthur was the only son of Frederick and Eliza Skuse and it is likely he was conscripted into the army joining the 7th Battalion Wiltshire Regiment. He was killed on Monday 7 October 1918 when the Wiltshires attacked the German forces north of Guisencourt Farm east of Templux Le Guerard and were held up by barbed wire and machine gun fire. Arthur is buried in Templux Le Guerard British Cemetery.

Private Edward Aaron Wicks   *7th Bn Wiltshire Regiment*
Service No.   18624   Age: 40
Place of Birth: Hullavington, Wiltshire   Home Country: England
Date of Death: 07/10/1918   Cause of death: Killed in action
Memorial: Hullavington
War cemetery: Templeux Le Guerard British Cemetery
Theatre of war: France
Next of Kin: Giles & Sarah A Wicks
Address: Hullavington, Wiltshire

Edward, a hurdle maker, was the eldest son of Giles and Sarah Wicks and volunteered for service with the 7th Battalion Wiltshire Regiment arriving in France on 21 September 1915. In November 1915 the 7th Wiltshires were sent to Salonika and returned to France in July 1918. He was one of 42 men killed in action on Monday 7 October 1918 when the Wiltshires attacked the German forces north of Guisencourt Farm east of Templux Le Guerard when they were held up by barbed wire and machine gun fire.

Corporal Walter Gilbert Cleaver   *54th Ammo. Sect RAOC*
Service No.   O/2163   Age: 20
Place of Birth: Hill Corner, Wiltshire   Home Country: England
Date of Death: 07/10/1918   Cause of death: Died of wounds
Memorial: Langley Burrell
War cemetery: Delsaux Farm Cemetery Beugny
Theatre of war: France
Next of Kin: Isaac & Hannah Cleaver
Address: Barrow Cottage, Langley Burrell, Wiltshire

Walter, known as Gilbert, was the youngest son of Isaac and Hannah Cleaver. He volunteered for service joining the Royal Army Ordinance Corps arriving in France on 21 December 1915. He was wounded during the British advance east of Bapaume, France most likely by German artillery fire and succumbed to his wounds on Monday 7 October 1918 at a casualty clearing station at Beugny, France. His brother Henry John Cleaver died at sea just eight days earlier.

Captain Wallace Mortimer Rooke   *2nd Bn Wiltshire Regiment*
Service No   N/A   Age: 28
Place of Birth: Hanover Square, London   Home Country: England
Date of Death: 08/10/1918   Cause of death: Died
Memorial: Chippenham
War cemetery: Chippenham London Road Cemetery
Theatre of war: Home
Next of Kin: Mortimer & Fredericka Charlotte Louisa Rooke
Address: The Ivy, Chippenham

Wallace was the youngest son of Mortimer and Fredericka Rooke and at the outbreak of hostilities he joined the Royal Wiltshire Yeomanry being promoted to Captain in June 1916. He was later attached to the 2nd Battalion Wiltshire Regiment arriving in France on 9 December 1916 and in the two years he spent with the Wiltshires he took part in all the engagements they were involved with. He was made transport office for the 2nd Wiltshires and during the retreat form St. Quentin he was mentioned in dispatches. He contacted influenza while in France and

Left: The grave of Wallace Mortimer Rooke in Chippenham Cemetery and above the memorial plaque in St. Andrews Church Chippenham.

was invalided home for leave on 30 September 1918 his condition grew worse and developed into pneumonia which proved fatal and he died at home on Tuesday 8 October 1918. Wallace was buried at Chippenham Cemetery and his grave was lined with trails of Ivy. He was given full military honours. Mortimer and Fredericka Rooke were to have more grief and sadness at their home. On 14 October their youngest daughter, eighteen year old Doris died of pneumonia following Spanish influenza and two days later another daughter Ellen Marjory aged twenty, died from meningitis, following Spanish influenza. Both of the daughters had served as Voluntary Aid Detachment nurses at the Red Cross hospital at Chippenham's Neeld Hall.

Sergeant W. Snelgrove wrote to Wallace' father stating:

"I was very sorry and much surprised to hear of the death of your son, Captain Rooke, also of your daughters. I was very much attached to Captain Rooke, as transport officer, and I was his sergeant. I have been in the service for 15 years, and your son was one of the finest officers I have had anything to do with. I had been with him for about eighteen months on the transport, and doing our tour of duty together we have had some very lively and exciting times. He was one of the coolest officers I ever saw under fire, he never had any fear. No doubt you have heard him mention the duck boards, a small track about three feet wide; we used to get our pack animals along there for about three miles, and if you got off you were up to your waist in mud. It was on this track last November that we experienced one of the worst evenings we ever had. We had twenty two pack animals, and "Jerry" started his games, putting a couple in front of our animals, wounding two, and then put his shells at the rear of our animals. Captain Rooke always took the lead, and I at the rear. That evening "Jerry" just gave us what he thought he would. Our casualties were one man killed and four wounded, and six animals killed. We made double trips until we got the rations up to battalion headquarters, which were in the line. One of his great pals was Dr Blickley of Warminster who was with the 2nd Wilts, as M.O. He left us about the 16th of last March very lucky fellow, or he might have been with the Regiment. Captain Rooke was only about 100 yards from me when I met with my accident, and he helped

me to walk about a mile."

The incident on the duckboard track that Sergeant Snelgrove referred to was well known by the officers and men of the 2nd Wiltshires and bears testament to the bravery of Wallace:

Wallace was in command of the transport column taking food to the frant line. He was stopped at one place by an officer who said: *"You cannot go on; there is a barrage in front of us."*

Wallace*: "I am not blind; I can see the barrage; but I must go on."*

Officer: *"You cannot; I have orders to stop all forward traffic."*

Wallace*: "Then you must now take orders from me, and I order you to let us pass, for this food must get to the fighting line."*

On they went, right through the barrage and safely delivered the goods, only losing two mules and having two men wounded. The General who told this story to a Major added:

"Rooke is the best transport officer in the whole of France."

Private Richard Wheeler Porter		*1st Bn Monmouthshire Regiment*	
Service No.	227879	Age:	30
Place of Birth:	Great Somerford	Home Country:	England
Date of Death:	08/10/1918	Cause of death:	Killed in action
Memorial:	Great Somerford		
War cemetery:	Sequehart British Cemetery No 1		
Theatre of war:	France		
Next of Kin:	George & Sarah Annie Porter		
Address:	44 The Barton, Great Somerford, Wiltshire		

Richard was the eldest son of George & Sarah Porter and prior to the war worked as a navvie. He enlisted in the army joining the 1st Battalion Monmouthshire Regiment and was killed in action Tuesday 8 October 1918 north east of St.Quentin, France, during the Bristish advance on the Hindenburg Line. Richard is buried in Sequehart British Cemetery No 1.

Private Percival Victor Elms		*1st RM Bn RN Div RMLI*	
Service No.	PLY/2379(S)	Age:	25
Place of Birth:	Yatton Keynell, Wiltshire	Home Country:	England
Date of Death:	08/10/1918	Cause of death:	Killed in action
Memorial:	Langley Burrell		
War cemetery:	Vis En Artois Memorial		
Theatre of war:	France		
Next of Kin:	Rosa Georgina Elms (wife) - Charles & Phoebe Elms (parents)		
Address:	Hardenhuish - Barrow Cottage, Langley Burrell, Wiltshire		

Percival, known as Victor, was a loader for the Great Western Railway and married Rosa Georgina Lewis at the end of 1915. He enlisted on 11 August 1917 and joined the Royal Marines on 5 October 1917 being sent to France on 29 December 1917. He was first posted to the 2nd Battalion Royal Marines on 15 January 1918 and then posted to the 1st Battalion Royal Marines on the 28 April 1918. He was killed in action during the Battle of Cambrai on the 8 October 1918 during the British assault on the Hindenburg Line. He is remembered on the Vis En Artois Memorial and has no known grave. He left a widow and baby son.

Private Herbert Neal		*22nd Vet Hosp. Army Veterinary Corps*	
Service No.	SE/24832	Age:	42
Place of Birth:	North Wraxall, Wiltshire	Home Country:	England
Date of Death:	11/10/1918	Cause of death:	Died
Memorial:	North Wraxall		
War cemetery:	St Germain Au Mont D'or Communal Cemetery Extension		
Theatre of war:	France		
Next of Kin:	Mary Adeline Neal (wife) - Edwin & Sarah Anne Neal (parents)		
Address:	20 Bradley Street, Roath, Cardiff - North Wraxall, Wiltshire		

Herbert, a draper's delivery cart driver, married Mary Adeline Williams in the spring of 1907. It is likely he was conscripted into the army joining the Army Veterinary Corps. He died of illness or disease at a British military hospital St Germain-au-Mont-d'Or north of Lyon, France, on Friday 11 October 1918. Herbert left a widow and four children.

Private Percy William Little		*Wiltshire Yeomanry*	
Service No.	320295	Age:	25
Place of Birth:	Chippenham	Home Country:	England
Date of Death:	12/10/1918	Cause of death:	Died
Memorial:	Chippenham - St. Pauls Church Memorial		
War cemetery:	Not Known		
Theatre of war:	Home		
Next of Kin:	Henry & Mary Anne Little		
Address:	36 Tugela Road, Chippenham		

Percy was the third son of Henry and Mary Anne Little and was a machinist at Saxby and Farmer Signal Works. He volunteered for service with the Wiltshire Yeomanry on 4 September 1914. He was discharged due to sickness on 19 July 1917 and died at home on Saturday 12 October 1918 of tuberculosis of the spine and Pulmonary tuberculosis. It is probable that he is buried in St. Paul's Churchyard. At this time Percy is not commemorated by the Commonwealth War Grave Commission.

Private Arthur Harvey Hand		*1st Bn Worcestershire Regiment*	
Service No.	238136	Age:	26
Place of Birth:	Seagry, Wiltshire	Home Country:	England
Date of Death:	14/10/1918	Cause of death:	Died of wounds
Memorial:	Great Somerford		
War cemetery:	Orchard Dump Cemetery Arleux en Gohelle		
Theatre of war:	France		
Next of Kin:	Daniel & Elda Hand		
Address:	Detenie, Great Somerford, Wiltshire		

Arthur, an agricultural labourer, joined the Gloucester Hussars at the end of 1915 and was then transferred to the 1st Battalion Worcestershire Regiment. The last time he was seen by his parents was during a short leave in December 1917. He was wounded on Monday 14 October

1918 during the occupation of Douai at German positions on the outskirts of Flers-en-Escrebieux. He died later the same day most likely at 26th Field Ambulance at Fresnes-les-Montauban and was buried locally. His remains were relocated after the armistice. His brother George William James Hand had died at sea in October 1917.

Private George Arthur Hurst *880th MT Coy Army Service Corps*

Service No.	M2/264754
Place of Birth:	Strutham, Bedfordshire
Date of Death:	17/10/1918
Memorial:	Little Somerford
War cemetery:	Skopje British Cemetery
Theatre of war:	Balkans
Next of Kin:	Evelyn Hurst (wife) – Philip Ernest & Mary Anne Hurst (parents)
Address:	School Cottage, Little Somerford, Wiltshire

Age: 35
Home Country: England
Cause of death: Died

George, a motor driver and commercial grocer married Evelyn Hurst in the summer of 1908 at Little Somerford. It is likely he was conscripted into the army joining the Army Service Corps and sent to Salonika, Greece. He died of pneumonia on Thursday 17 October 1918 and was buried locally. His remains were relocated to Skopje British Cemetery which is in the former Yugoslav Republic of Macedonia.

Private Frederick Thomas Butler *2nd Bn Wiltshire Regiment*

Service No.	46974
Place of Birth:	Hardenhuish, Wiltshire
Date of Death:	19/10/1918
Memorial:	Broad Hinton
War cemetery:	St Aubert British Cemetery
Theatre of war:	France
Next of Kin:	Thomas & Fanny Butler
Address:	152, Broad Hinton, Wiltshire

Age: 20
Home Country: England
Cause of death: Killed in action

Frederick was the eldest son of Thomas and Fanny Butler and enlisted in the army joining the 2nd Battalion Wiltshire Regiment. At 3pm on Saturday 19 October 1918 the 2nd Wiltshires were near the River Selle at St. Aubert east of Cambrai, France and a patrol was sent out to ascertain whether German forces were occupying the railway embankment. They managed to cross the River Selle and were fired on with only the non commissioned officer returning. It is likely Frederick was one of six members of the patrol killed in this action with German forces. He is buried in St. Aubert British Cemetery.

Private Charles Edward Coles *1st Res. Bn British Columbia Regiment*

Service No.	140532
Place of Birth:	West Kington, Wiltshire
Date of Death:	21/10/1918
Memorial:	North Wraxall
War cemetery:	North Wraxall St James Churchyard
Theatre of war:	Home
Next of Kin:	Job & Julia Coles
Address:	Lanhill Cottages, Yatton Keynell, Wiltshire

Age: 42
Home Country: England
Cause of death: Died

Charles Edward Coles buried at St James Churchyard North Wraxall.

Charles was the eldest son of Job and Julia Coles and emigrated to the United States prior to the war. He lived at Duart Los Angeles, California and was a teamster on a fruit farm. He volunteered for service with the Canadian army on 18 July 1918 at Victoria British Columbia joining the 1st Reserve Battalion. It is likely he died of illness or disease soon after his arrival in Great Britain and his body was taken to North Wraxall and buried in the Churchyard.

Private Wilfred Baker   *1st Bn Wiltshire Regiment*

Service No.	11887	Age:	24
Place of Birth:	Biddestone, Wiltshire	Home Country:	England
Date of Death:	23/10/1918	Cause of death:	Died
Memorial:	Biddestone		
War cemetery:	Cologne Southern Cemetery		
Theatre of war:	Germany		
Next of Kin:	Arthur & Mary Jane Baker		
Address:	Biddestone, Wiltshire		

Wilfred a labourer was the eldest son of Arthur and Mary Baker and after the death of Arthur Baker, his mother Mary married George Woodman. Wilfred volunteered for service with the Wiltshire Regiment and arrived in France on 21 April 1915. He was captured by the Germans in subsequent fighting and died of illness or disease while a prisoner of war in Germany on Wednesday 23 October 1918. Wilfred is today buried in Cologne Southern Cemetery.

Corporal Herbert John Ford MM   *2nd Bn Royal Dublin Fusiliers*

Service No.	15841	Age:	26
Place of Birth:	Ilfracombe, Devon	Home Country:	England
Date of Death:	26/10/1918	Cause of death:	Died of wounds
Memorial:	Chippenham - Calne - St Paul's Church Chippenham		
War cemetery:	Abbeville Communal Cemetery Extension		

Theatre of war: France
Next of Kin: Frederick John & Fanny Ellen Ford
Address: Chippenham, Wiltshire.

Herbert, known as Bert, had been adopted by his uncle and aunt, Benjamin & Angeline Jones of 3 York Place, Calne. He had been employed at C & T Harris Bacon Factory for a number of years and afterwards worked in the stores department at Saxby and Farmers Ltd of Chippenham. He volunteered for service in September 1914 joining the 5th Wiltshire Regiment but was later transferred to the Royal Dublin Fusiliers and went to the Dardanelles with them arriving on 9 August 1915. He saw active service in Salonika, Palestine and France. He was seriously wounded in Salonika in September 1916 and was sent to Malta for treatment. On his return to duty he was sent to France and had been home on leave from there in July 1918. Bert died of wounds on Saturday 26 October 1918 most likely received at the battle of the Selle during the final advance through Picardy. In June 1919 it was announced he would posthumously receive the Military Medal for action during this battle. His fiancee Kate Bailey was heart broken using the following words in a local paper to express her grief:

In loving memory of my dear Bert
Who died from wounds received in France,
If only round the bedside
I could but just have stayed
Or seen that lonely spot
Where my dear boy is laid
But the hardest part is yet to come
When the heroes all come home
I shall miss among those cheering lads
The face of my darling boy

Lieutenant Henry Hope Hunt   *1st Sqdn Royal Air Force*
Service No.   N/A   Age: 24
Place of Birth: Chippenham   Home Country: England
Date of Death: 26/10/1918   Cause of death: Accident
Memorial: Chippenham & St. Paul's Church Memorial
War cemetery: Tincourt New British Cemetery
Theatre of war: France
Next of Kin: Henry Hope & Sarah Ann Hunt
Address: 62 Park Lane, Chippenham

Henry known as Tom, was the eldest son of Henry and Sarah Hunt and his father was an assistant master at St. Paul's School, Chippenham. Tom was educated at St. Pauls School and the Secondary School where he passed the Oxford Local Examination. He wished to become a teacher like his father and served twelve months as a student teacher under Mr Hinton of Ivy Lane School. At the end of the year he went to St. John's Training College at Battersea. Soon after war was declared Tom volunteered to serve with the 10th Battalion Middlesex Regiment, known as Queen Victoria's Rifles. In a competitive examination he came first being promoted to the position of chief non commissioned officer of the Intelligence Staff at Brigade Headquarters. After several months he was sent to France and was wounded at the Battle of Arras, shortly afterwards he was offered a commission. Tom returned to England and joined the Officers' Cadet Battalion at Pirbright and finished his training course at Reading. Having obtained his commission he was attached to the 10th London Regiment and at his request was transferred to the Royal Air force and qualified as a pilot at Upavon. On 25 October 1918 Tom's father received a letter from his son stating:

"I am quite safe. You probably read on a casualty list that I was missing since the 23rd. After spending one day and a part of another miles from anywhere with my machine, I returned to the aerodrome on the 25th."

Tom went on duty the next morning but the next information about him stated he was posted as missing on 26 October 1918. Henry Hunt senior received the following letter from a Major of his son's squadron:

"I very much regret that it is my sad duty to inform you of very bad news. I regret to say your son, Lieutenant H. H. Hunt, of this squadron, has been killed in an aeroplane accident. The squadron moved from one aerodrome to another on the 26th of this month, and your son failed to arrive at the new aerodrome. The formation with which he was flying ran into a bank of fog, and was forced to fly very close to the ground. The leader of the formation missed your son about this time and nothing more was heard of him until today. We made exhaustive enquiries, and searched the ground where he was last seen, but could find no trace of him, and, of course, we all hoped that he had lost himself and had landed a long way away, and had been unable to get through on the telephone. We finally heard this morning that the machine had crashed shortly after it was last seen by the leader of the formation, and the only consolation I can offer you is that your son must have been killed outright, and was consequently spared any pain or suffering. We are making arrangements for the funeral, which will take place this afternoon, and I need hardly say that any officers who are not on duty will be attending. I was the last man to speak to your son before his death, as I gave him some instructions to be carried out after arrival at the new aerodrome. We all miss your son very much, and although he had been with us for such a short time he seemed very promising, and I am sure would have done well had he been spared. On behalf of the whole squadron I wish to offer you our deepest sympathies in your irreparable loss. It seems particularly hard that your son should have been taken after the long period he had served in France previously."

2nd Lieutenant Edgar Taviner		*Royal Air Force*	
Service No.	N/A	Age:	26
Place of Birth:	Giddea Hall, Wiltshire	Home Country:	England
Date of Death:	28/10/1918	Cause of death:	Accident
Memorial:	Chippenham & Secondary School Memorial		
War cemetery:	Hollybrook Memorial Southampton		
Theatre of war:	Home		
Next of Kin:	William John & Sarah Agnes Taviner		
Address:	Cold Harbour, Kington Langley, Wiltshire		

Edgar, known as Bertie, was the eldest son of Alderman John and Sarah Taviner and prior to the war he travelled to United States of America and was employed as a hotel and transportation clerk at the Keystone Hotel in San Francisco, California, now the Mosser Hotel on 544th Street. He volunteered for service with the Canadian army at Victoria British Columbia on 17 July 1917 joining Forestery Depot of the Canadian Expeditionary force. He came to England with the Canadians and in January 1918 transferred to the Royal Flying Corps as a Temporary 2nd Lieutenant, his rank being confirmed on 24 September 1918. He was killed over the sea in an aeroplane accident on Monday 28 October 1918 at Marske-by-Sea, near Redcar, Yorkshire. His body was never recovered and he is today remembered on the Hollybrook Memorial.

Sapper Albert Skinner   *Railway Operating Div. R. E.*

Service No.	WR/260841	Age:	28
Place of Birth:	Kington Langley	Home Country:	England
Date of Death:	28/10/1918	Cause of death:	Died
Memorial:	Not known		
War cemetery:	Blargies Communal Cemetery Extention		
Theatre of war:	France		
Next of Kin:	Charles & Sarah Anne Skinner		
Address:	20 Buyshey Road, Upton Park, London		

Albert, a crane driver, was the eldest son of Charles and Sarah Skinner and attested for service on 12 December 1915 joining the army under the Derby Scheme. He was called up on 8 February 1916 being sent to the 6th Battalion Royal Fusiliers and was drafted to France arriving on 9 August 1916. On 29 September 1916 Albert was transferred to the Royal Engineer Railway Operating Division and was granted his first home leave on 26 January 1917. Shortly after returning to the front he was admitted to hospital at Blargies, France on 25 October 1918 with influenza which developed into pneumonia causing his death on Monday 28 October 1918. Albert is buried in Blargies Communal Cemetery Extention.

Private Harold Roy Bowden   *15th Bn London Regiment*

Service No.	535255	Age:	20
Place of Birth:	Codford St Mary, Wiltshire	Home Country:	England
Date of Death:	29/10/1918	Cause of death:	Died
Memorial:	Hardenhuish		
War cemetery:	Hautmont Communal Cememtery		
Theatre of war:	France		
Next of Kin:	Frederick & Ada E. Bowden		
Address:	The Folly, Park Side, Chippenham		

Harold, a clerk, was the eldest and only son of Frederick and Ada Bowden and attested for service on 8 June 1916 at the age of eighteen years and two months. He was called for service joining on 26 February 1917 and after completing his training was posted to the London Regiment arriving in France on 23 May 1917. He joined 15th Battalion on 18 June 1917 and was posted as missing on 23 March 1918 during the German offensive. It was later found out that he was a prisoner of war and had been taken to Hautmont, France by the Germans. He died of dysentery on Tuesday 29 October 1918 while in captivity. In May 1919 Harold's parents inserted the following memoriam in a local paper:

We pictured him safe returning
We longed to clasp his hand
But God has postponed the meeting
It will be in a better land
His loving ways his smiling face
A pleasure to recall
Though there is nothing left to answer
but his picture on the wall
A good life is often too short but a good name will live forever
Still sadly missed and remembered by his sorrowing Mother, Father and Sister

Harold is buried in Hautmont Communal Cememtery.

Private William Alfred Knight　　　　　*1st Bn Middlesex Regiment*

Service No.	G/53399	Age:	19
Place of Birth:	Colyton, Devon	Home Country:	England
Date of Death:	29/10/1918	Cause of death:	Died of wounds
Memorial:	Lacock – Lacock Church & Bowden Hill		
War cemetery:	Awoingt British Cemetery		
Theatre of war:	France		
Next of Kin:	Alfred Charles & Emily Ann Knight		
Address:	29 Alderville Road, Fulham, London		

William was the eldest and only son of Alfred and Emily Knight who had lived at Bowden Park Lodge. He enlisted with the army initially with the East Kent Regiment before being transferred to the 1st Battalion Middlesex Regiment. William was wounded most likely near Englefontaine, East of Cambrai, France, during the Battle of the Selle. He was evacuated to Awoingt east of Cambrai and admitted to a casualty clearing station with a gun shot wound to the thigh. He died on Tuesday 29 October 1918 at the casualty clearing station after the amputation of his leg. He was buried in Awoingt British Cemetery.

Lance Corporal Oliver Reuben H Oatley　　　*2nd Bn Wiltshire Regiment*

Service No.	203322	Age:	32
Place of Birth:	Box, Wiltshire	Home Country:	England
Date of Death:	04/11/1918	Cause of death:	Killed in action
Memorial:	Box		
War cemetery:	Cross Roads Cemetery Fontaine Au Bois		
Theatre of war:	France		
Next of Kin:	Leah Priscilla Smith (mother)		
Address:	Parliament Street, Chippenham, Wiltshire		

Oliver, a gardener, initially joined the Royal Wiltshire Yeomanry and was transferred to the 2nd Battalion Wiltshire Regiment. At 1 am on Monday 4 November 1918 the 2nd Wiltshires were at Jenlain, north east of St. Quentin, they advanced clearing the village with little opposition and by 10.15am they had reached all their objectives. At 12 noon patrols were were pushed out toward the village of Eth and were met by heavy German artillery and machine gun fire and it was decided to put a barrage down and advance at 4.30pm. Eth was captured but Oliver was one of those killed during the advance. He was originally buried at Eth British Cemetery and his remains were relocated after the armistice. Oliver left over £150 in his will.

Driver Charles Henry Neath　　　　　*210th Bde Royal Field Artillery*

Service No.	249572	Age:	Not known
Place of Birth:	Not known	Home Country:	England
Date of Death:	04/11/1918	Cause of death:	Killed in action
Memorial:	Langley Burrell		
War cemetery:	Capelle Beaudignies Road Cemetery		
Theatre of war:	France		
Next of Kin:	Not known		
Address:	Not known		

It is likely Charles was conscripted into the army joining Royal Field Artillery. He was killed in action near Capelle, France, south east of Mons, Belgium on Monday 4 November 1918. He is buried in Capelle Beaudignies Road Cemetery.

Private William James Hatherell   *11th Bn Somerset Light Infantry*

Service No.	265919	Age:	40
Place of Birth:	Chippenham	Home Country:	England
Date of Death:	06/11/1918	Cause of death:	Killed in action

Memorial: Chippenham & St. Andrews Church Memorial
War cemetery: Pecq Communal Cemetery
Theatre of war: Belgium
Next of Kin: Annie Hatherell (wife) - John Hatherell (parent)
Address: 1 Cowleaze Terrace, Sheldon Road, Chippenham - Lowden, Chippenham

William a painter married his wife Annie Noad in 1903 and it is likely he was conscripted into the army initially joining the Wiltshire Regiment before being transferred to the 11th Battalion Somerset Light Infantry. On 5 November 1916 the 11th Somersets were at Esquelmes, Belgium and across the River Cabaret was the village of Lietard, held by the Germans. A British patrol was sent out, establishing that the Germans had left and A Company of the 11th Somersets was ordered to occupy the village. As they approached Lietard in the early hours of Wednesday 6 November they were subjected to heavy German machine Gun fire. William was killed during this action and left a widow and four young daughters. In November 1919 Annie Hatherell inserted the following memoriam into a local paper:

In the field of battle he bravely took his place
And fought and died for England and the honour of his race;
He sleeps not in his native, but 'neath a foreign sky,
Far from those who loved him best, in a hero's grave he lies.
Fondly remembered by his sorrowing Wife, Children, Brothers and Sisters.

Private John William Kingsland   *1/4th Bn TF Seaforth Highlanders*

Service No.	S/43485	Age:	19
Place of Birth:	Pundle, Northamptonshire	Home Country:	England
Date of Death:	06/11/1918	Cause of death:	Died of wounds

Memorial: Devizes & Chippenham & United Reform Church Chippenham
War cemetery: Cambrai East Military Cemetery
Theatre of war: France
Next of Kin: Rev. John Paddon & Helen Priscilla Kingsland
Address: Victoria Street Congregational Church, St Helier, Jersey.

John was the only son of John Kingsland a Congregational Minister at Devizes and Helen Kingsland an author living at The Haven, The Breach, Devizes. John junior was an employee of Lloyds Bank in Chippenham. He enlisted with the army and was initially sent to the Royal Warwickshire Regiment and was then transferred to the Royal Inniskilling Fusiliers and finally to the Seaforth Highlanders. He was wounded during the final advance most likely during the The Battle of the Selle near Cambrai, France, and was taken to No. 30 Casualty Clearing Station where he succumbed to his wounds on Wednesday 6 November 1918. He was aged nineteen and two months. John seniors' Ministery in Devizes came to an end as a consequence of so many men being away at the war and the Congregation Chapel could not afford a paid minister and he eventually found a new minister role in the Channel Islands. In November 1918 Johns's parents inserted the following memoriam in a local paper:

Is it well with the lad? It is well

In 2006 Chippenham refurbished the town War Memorial. John William Kingsland was the only soldier from the Great War added, his position being confirmed as a result of a plaque bearing his name in the United Reform Church, Chippenham.

Gunner William Merritt   *Royal Garrison Artillery*

Service No.	136681	Age:	22
Place of Birth:	Chippenham	Home Country:	England
Date of Death:	06/11/1918	Cause of death:	Died
Memorial:	Not known		
War cemetery:	Milborne Port Cemetery		
Theatre of war:	Home		
Next of Kin:	John & Elizabeth Merritt		
Address:	High Street, Milbourne Port, Somerset		

William, a shoeing smith, was the only son of John and Elizabeth Merrit and volunteered for service with the Dorset Yeomanry on 17 November 1914 and was appointed as a shoeing smith on 20 December 1914. On 1 March 1916 he was transferred to the Dorset Royal Garrison Artillery and served throughout the war in England. He was admitted to the 1st Birmingham War Hospital at Rednal with influenza which had developed into pneumonia on Tuesday 5 November 1918 and he died at 4am the following day. His body was returned to Milbourne Port and he as buried in Milborne Port Cemetery.

Private Samuel Wiltshire Frankcom   *Depot Tank Corps*

Service No.	304706	Age:	19
Place of Birth:	North Wraxall, Wiltshire	Home Country:	England
Date of Death:	08/11/1918	Cause of death:	Died
Memorial:	North Wraxall		
War cemetery:	North Wraxall St James Churchyard		
Theatre of war:	Home		
Next of Kin:	Maurice & Ann Frankcom		
Address:	North Wraxall, Wiltshire		

Nineteen year old Samuel was the eldest son of Maurice and Ann Frankcom and enlisted in the army joining initially the Training Reserve before being transferred to the Tank Corps. He died of illness or disease on Friday 8 November 1918 and was buried in St. James Churchyard, North Wraxall .

Private Fred Heath   *H.M.S. Brittania RMLI*

Service No.	PO/17762	Age:	25
Place of Birth:	West Tytherton, Wiltshire	Home Country:	England
Date of Death:	09/11/1918	Cause of death:	Died
Memorial:	East Tytherton Morovian Church & St. Andrews Church Memorial		
War cemetery:	Portsmouth Naval Memorial		
Theatre of war:	At Sea		
Next of Kin:	Sidney & Kate Heath		
Address:	West Tytherton, Wiltshire		

Fred, a farm labourer, volunteered for service with his brother on 9 September 1914 and joined the Royal Marine Light Infantry. After he completed his training he was posted to H.M.S.

Britannia, a pre-dreadnought battleship which had been launched in 1904. He was killed on 9 November 1918. The Britannia was on her way to Gibraltar when she was torpedoed by the German submarine UB 50. After the first explosion caused by the torpedo the Britannia listed to port and there were two further explosions, the last being in her cordite magazine. Fred was killed by one of these explosions. The ship sank after two and a half hours with the loss of 50 of her crew. Fred is remembered on the Portsmouth Naval Memorial, his brother Maurice was killed in action in October 1917 at the Battle of Passchendaele.

Gunner Lancelot Coulter Witts *1st North Midland Heavy Bty RGA*

Service No.	95863	Age:	35
Place of Birth:	Chippenham, Wiltshire	Home Country:	England
Date of Death:	10/11/1918	Cause of death:	Died
Memorial:	Hullavington		
War cemetery:	St Sever Cemetery Extension Rouen		
Theatre of war:	France		
Next of Kin:	Fanny Ellen Witts (wife) – Francis James & Ann Witts (parents)		
Address:	New Town, Hullavington - 12 St Mary's Place, Chippenham		

Lancelot, known as Masher and an insurance agent, was the youngest son of Francis and Ann Witts who ran a shoeing forge in Chippenham. He married Fanny Ellen Walters on 4 March 1912 at Bristol and it is likely he attested for service under the Derby Scheme on 29 November 1915. He was called up on 10 June 1916 and was sent to the Royal Garrison Artillery and arrived in France on 19 February 1917. In July 1918 he was promoted to Shoeing Smith. Masher was admitted to No. 3 Stationary Hospital, Rouen, on 9 November 1918 with Broncho Pneumonia and died the following day. His personal possessions were retuned to his wife and consisted of brush, safety razor, 3 pipes, lighter, badge, watch, postcards, photo and a paper wallet. He left a widow and a young son and Fanny Witts received a pension of 20 shillings and 5 pence per week. Masher is buried in St. Sever Cemetery Extension Rouen

15

ARMISTICE DAY - MONDAY 11 NOVEMBER 1918

The War is Over but the Deaths Continue:

Private Reginald Deane Pinnell　　　　*2nd Bn Wiltshire Regiment*

Service No.	28272	Age:	17
Place of Birth:	Chippenham	Home Country:	England
Date of Death:	13/11/1918	Cause of death:	Died
Memorial:	Not known		
War cemetery:	Mont Huon Military Cemetery Le Treport		
Theatre of war:	France		
Next of Kin:	John Dudley & Maria Pinnell		
Address:	Sunnyside, The Marsh, Calne		

Seventeen year old Reginald was the youngest son of John and Maria Pinnell and it is likely he lied about his age because he should have been eighteen and a half to serve on the continent at this time. He originally joined the Royal Wiltshire Yeomanry but was transferred to the 2nd Battalion Wiltshire Regiment. He died of pneumonia at one of the hospitals based at Le Treport on Wednesday 13 November 1918, two days after the armistice. He is buried in Mont Huon Military Cemetery, Le Treport, with over 2000 casualties of the Great War.

Private Ernest Brimble　　　　*55th Bn Machine Gun Corps*

Service No.	12684	Age:	19
Place of Birth:	Somerford, Wiltshire	Home Country:	England
Date of Death:	13/11/1918	Cause of death:	Died
Memorial:	Holt		
War cemetery:	Don Communal Cemetery Annoeullin		
Theatre of war:	France		
Next of Kin:	James W & Mary Anne Brimble		
Address:	Star Cottage, Holt, Wiltshire		

Nineteen year old Ernest originally enlisted with the Wiltshire Regiment and later transferred to the Machine Gun Corps. He died most likely of illness or disease at No. 15 Casualty Clearing Station at Don South west of Lille France on Wednesday 13 November 1918.

Private Arthur George Reynolds   *2nd Bn Wiltshire Regiment*

Service No.	8786
Place of Birth:	Chippenham
Date of Death:	15/11/1918
Memorial:	Not known
War cemetery:	Winterslow All Saints Churchyard Extension
Theatre of war:	Home
Next of Kin:	Dorothy Rose Reynolds (wife) - Frank & Martha Reynolds (Parents)
Address:	51 Wine Street, Bradford on Avon - Groveley Middle, Winterslow

Age:	27
Home Country:	England
Cause of death:	Died

Regular soldier Arthur was the eldest son of Frank and Martha Reynolds and had been a territorial soldier and enlisted with the 2nd Battalion Wiltshire Regiment on 16 December 1912. At the outbreak of hostilities the 2nd Wiltshires were serving at Gibraltar and after returning to England they landed at Zeebrugge, Belgium on 7 October 1914. In late October 1914 the 2nd Wiltshires were facing the German onslaught at Beselare, Belgium and during a German bombardment Arthur was buried alive in a trench. When he was rescued Arthur had lost his memory and his mind was a perfect blank with regard to his past. He was evacuated to England arriving on 1 November 1914 and had no knowledge of his parents, home, reading, writing, or that he had been a skilled musician. Arthur was hypnotized and under it's influence he remembered his previous life but as soon as he was wakened from the trance his memories were lost again. He was discharged from the army on 26 June 1915 and never really recognized his father or mother. He found employment as a skilled weaver and at the start of 1918 he married Dorothy Rose Pratten at Bradford on Avon. In November 1918 Arthur contracted influenza which became pneumonia and he died on Friday 15 November at the Military Hospital in Salisbury. He was buried with full military honours at Winterslow All Saints Churchyard. Because Arthur had married after his discharge Dorothy Reynolds did not receive a widow's pension from the army.

Private William Webb   *9th Northamptonshire Regiment*

Service No.	226074
Place of Birth:	Melksham, Wiltshire
Date of Death:	23/11/1918
Memorial:	Chippenham & St. Andrew's Church Memorial
War cemetery:	Thetford Cemetery
Theatre of war:	Home
Next of Kin:	Beatrice Alice Webb (wife) - Frederick and Hanna Webb (parents)
Address:	6 Ladd's Lane, Chippeanham

Age:	47
Home Country:	England
Cause of death:	Died

William, a boot repairer, married Beatrice Alice Fisher in the spring of 1902. It is likely he was conscripted into the army joining the 9th Battalion Northamptonshire Regiment, a home service battalion based in Norfolk. He died most likely of illness or disease on Saturday 23 November 1918 and left a widow and six children.

Private Edwin Ernest Herbert Lough   *Royal Army Medical Corps*

Service No.	155330
Place of Birth:	Whitby, Yorkshire
Date of Death:	29/11/1918
Memorial:	Chippenham
War cemetery:	Chippenham London Road Cemetery
Theatre of war:	Home

Age:	30
Home Country:	England
Cause of death:	Died

Next of Kin: Majorie Lough (wife) - Arthur Dudley & Mary Jane Lough (parents)
Address: Church House, Sheldon Road, Chippenham – Aust, Glocestershire

Edwin was the youngest son of Reverend Arthur & Mary Lough and had studied theology. On 14 September 1915 Edwin married Marjorie MacCormack at Northwick, Bristol. He had been the curate of Bitton, Swindon and Chiseldon Camp and since 1915 he had held the post at St. Andrews Church, Chippenham. He joined the Royal Army Medical Corps on 5 July 1918 and had been stationed at Blackpool and Marsham Camp, Rippon, Yorkshire. Edwin was admitted to Colsterdale Military Hospital on 20 November 1918 with influenza which developed into pneumonia and he died at 2am on Friday 29 November 1918. His body was returned to Chippenham and he was buried in the Town Cemetery with full military honours. He left a widow and two small Children.

Private Jack Richmond Pugh   *6th Bn Wiltshire Regiment*
Service No.   203345   Age: 26
Place of Birth: Presteigne, Radnorshire   Home Country: England
Date of Death: 05/12/1918   Cause of death: Died
Memorial: Kington Langley
War cemetery: Cologne Southern Cemetery
Theatre of war: Germany
Next of Kin: William & Mary Ann Pugh
Address: 10 Wem Road Cline, Shrewsbury, Shropshire

John known as Jack had originally joined the Royal Wiltshire Yeomanry and on the 20 September 1917 they were amalgamated with the 6th Battalion Wiltshire Regiment. He was reported missing during the German offensive on 23 March 1918 and in August 1918 his sweetheart, Edith Fortune of Foghamshire, Chippenham, inserted an advert in the paper requesting information about his whereabouts. Jack had been taken prisoner and was in Germany, he died of illness or disease after his release on Thursday 5 Deceber 1918. He is today buried in Cologne Southern Cemetery.

1919

Private Charles Ernest Hawkins   *M.T. Army Service Corps*
Service No.   DM2/189781   Age: 22
Place of Birth: Kington St Michael   Home Country: England
Date of Death: 03/01/1919   Cause of death: Died
Memorial: Kington St Michael
War cemetery: Montecchio Precalcino Communal Cemetery Extension
Theatre of war: Italy
Next of Kin: Frederick & Bertha Hawkins
Address: Kington St Micheal, Wiltshire

Charles was the second son of Frederick and Bertha Hawkins and enlisted in the army joining the Army Service Corps. He was sent to Italy and attached to the 240th Siege Battery Royal Garrison Artillery. He died of illness or disease on Friday 3 January 1919.

Right: the grave of Rifleman Alfred George Self at Lacock Cemetery.

Far right: Edwin Ernest Herbert Lough buried in Chippeham Cemetery.

Rifleman Alfred George Self   *2/10th London Regiment*

Service No.	50049	Age:	25
Place of Birth:	Seend, Wiltshire	Home Country:	England
Date of Death:	10/01/1919	Cause of death:	Died of wounds
Memorial:	Lacock – Lacock Church & Devizes Odd Fellows Society		
War cemetery:	Lacock Cemetery		
Theatre of war:	Home		
Next of Kin:	William & Rebecca Annie Self		
Address:	White Hall Farm, Lacock, Wiltshire		

Alfred was the second son of William and Rebecca Self and was employed on his father's farm. He initially joined the Royal Flying Corps but was transferred to the 2/10th London Regiment. He was wounded most likely near Epehy, south of Cambrai, France on 22nd September 1918 and evacuated to England and sent to the 4th London General Hospital, Denmark Hill, where he died on Friday 10 January 1919. His body was transported to Lacock and a service was held at the Congregational Chapel .The service was conducted by the Rev. W.J.Farr of Melksham and the Hymns *"Rock of Ages"* and *"Nearer My God to Thee."* Alfred was buried in Lacock Cemetery with military honours.

2nd Lt. Reginald Arthur Bakewell Warrilow   *29th Training Depot Sqdn RAF*

Service No.	N/A	Age:	24
Place of Birth:	Chippenham	Home Country:	England
Date of Death:	13/01/1919	Cause of death:	Accident
Memorial:	Chippenham & St Paul's Church Memorial		
War cemetery:	Chippenham St.Paul's Churchyard		
Theatre of war:	Home		
Next of Kin:	James Bakewell Warrilow & Clara Sophia Warrilow		
Address:	Amesbury House, Chippenham, Wiltshire		

Reginald joined the Royal Air Force and was killed in an flying accident on Monday 13 January 1919 at RAF Beaulieu, later East Boldre, he body was returned to Chippenham and he was buried at St. Paul's Churchyard with full Military honours. His brother Algernon Aubrey Bakewell Warrilow had died in February 1918.

Lance Corporal Francis Edward Baker   *46th Anti-Aircraft Search-light Sect RE*
Service No.   466975   Age: 34
Place of Birth: Chippenahm, Wiltshire   Home Country: England
Date of Death: 16/01/1919   Cause of death: Died
Memorial: Chippenham - St Andrews Church & Liberal Club Memorial
War cemetery: Dunkirk Town Cemetery
Theatre of war: France
Next of Kin: Harriet Baker (wife) - Frederick and Eliza Baker (parents)
Address: 39 Factory Lane, Chippenahm

Francis, an iron moulder was the youngest son of Frederick and Eliza Baker and married Harriet Whale in the summer of 1907. He initially joined the Territorial Force of the Royal Engineers and transferred to a regular unit and was employed in a search light section. He died of pneumonia on Thursday 16 January 1919 and was buried in Dunkirk Town Cemetery. Francis left a widow and four young children.

Corporal John Wicks   *8th Coy Royal Army Medical Corps*
Service No.   71288   Age: 27
Place of Birth: Grittleton, Wiltshire   Home Country: England
Date of Death: 17/01/1919   Cause of death: Died
Memorial: Grittleton
War cemetery: Grittleton St Mary Churchyard
Theatre of war: Home

Far left: The grave of John Wicks in Grittleton St Mary Churchyard.

Left: Reginald Arthur Bakewell Warrilow.

Next of Kin: Joseph & Mary Jane Wicks
Address: Gas House, Grittleton, Wiltshire

John a labourer was the youngest son of Joseph and Mary Wicks and lived at Pontypridd, Glamorgan. He volunteered for service with the Royal Army Medical Corps on 15 March 1915 and arrived in France on 9 October 1915. He served throughout the war and was promoted to Corporal. On 12 October 1918 he was admitted to the Wharncliffe War Hospital with what was described as feeble mindedness. He was then transferred to the Northumberland War Hospital at Gosforth, Newcastle-on-Tyne with acute mania and congestion of lungs where he died of the same ailment at 8.30am on Friday 17 January 1919. His body was brought to Grittleton and he was buried in Grittleton St. Mary Churchyard.

Driver Frank Moss   *61st Div. Ammunition Col RFA*
Service No.   846381   Age: 23
Place of Birth: Cirencester, Glos.   Home Country: England
Date of Death: 31/01/1919   Cause of death: Died
Memorial: Chippenham & St. Paul's Church Memorial
War cemetery: Gosforth St. Nicholas Churchyard
Theatre of war: Home
Next of Kin: Henry George & Annie Margaret Moss
Address: 32 Tugela Road, Chippenham

Frank a steam wagon steersman was the youngest son of Harry & Annie Moss and attested for service under the Derby Scheme on 11 December 1915 and was called up and sent to the Royal Field Artilley on 1 March 1916 arriving in France on 27 May 1916. He served for the next thirty months in France and on 21 November 1918 he was admitted to No. 22 Casualty Clearing Station at Cambrai, France with Influenza. He was evacuated to England and sent to the Northumberland War Hospital at Gosforth, Newcastle-on-Tyne arriving on the 4 December 1918 where his condition deteriorated In January 1919 his mother was informed that he was seriously ill and travelled to his bedside. Frank died at 8.10pm on Friday 31 January 1919 of influenza and abscess of the liver and it was his mother's wish that he was buried with full military honours at South Gosforth Cemetery.

Private George Henry Wakefield   *New Zealand Div MT NZASC*
Service No.   M2/081823   Age: 24
Place of Birth: Not known   Home Country: England
Date of Death: 15/02/1919   Cause of death: Died
Memorial: Biddestone
War cemetery: Cologne Southern Cemetery
Theatre of war: Germany
Next of Kin: Hilda May Wakefield
Address: Rose Cottage, Biddestone, Wiltshire

George volunteered for service with the Army Service Corps and arrived in France on 9 July 1915 he served throughout the war and was attached to the New Zealand Army. He married Hilda M. Davis at the end of 1918 and returned to Germanay where he was serving when he developed influenza and died at 44th Casualty Clearing Station, Cologne on Saturday 15 February 1919.

Private Leonard Humphries
Service No.   97604
Place of Birth: Sutton Benger, Wiltshire
Date of Death: 01/03/1919
Memorial: Sutton Benger
War cemetery: Terlincthun British Cemetery Wimille
Theatre of war: France
Next of Kin: Tom & Bessie Humphries
Address: Mount Pleasant Farm, Sutton Benger, Wiltshire

12th Labour Corps
Age: 27
Home Country: England
Cause of death: Died

Leonard a farmer, was the second son of Tom and Bessie Humphries and attested most likely under the Derby Scheme, to serve in the army on 8 November 1915 and was called up on 21 February 1916 and sent to Weymouth to serve with the Wiltshire Regiment. He was admitted to Weymouth Hospital on 28 February 1916 with Influenza and broncho pneumonia and spent 6 weeks in care. In July 1916 he was transferred to the 12th Labour Battalion Royal Berkshire Regiment arriving in France on 19 August 1916. He was then transferred to the Labour Corps in May 1917 and on 10 February 1919 Leonard was admitted to the 3rd Canadian General Hospital at Boulogne with pyrexia of unknown origin (unknown disease with a high temperature) where he died of broncho pneumonia on Saturday 1 March 1919. His personal possessions were returned to his parent's consiting of disc, letters, photos, cardboard folder, belt, safety razor, snuff box, metal ring, scissors, badge, 2 souvenir notes and 3 souvenir coins. He is buried in Terlincthun British Cemetery, Wimille.

Private Henry James Collar
Service No.   189210
Place of Birth: Yatton Keynell, Wiltshire
Date of Death: 03/03/1919
Memorial: Hardenhuish Church Memorial
War cemetery: Chippenham London Road Cemetery

445th Agricultural Coy Labour Corps
Age: 41
Home Country: England
Cause of death: Died

Far left: Henry James Collar buried in Chippenham Cemetery.

Left: Iron harvest shells are still found today.

Theatre of war: Home
Next of Kin: Martha Collar (wife) - Joseph & Honor Collar (parents)
Address: 97 London Road, Chippenham - Yatton Keynell

Henry a mason's labourer, was the eldest son of Joseph and Honor and married Martha Cuss early in 1906. It is likely he was conscripted into the army joining the labour corps. He died of illness or disease at Chippeham on Monday 3 March 1919. He left a widow and a young son.

Private Edward Chivers   *651st Agricultural Coy Labour Corps*

Service No.   1106
Place of Birth: Naish Hill, Wiltshire
Date of Death: 04/03/1919
Memorial: Not Known
War cemetery: Bowden Hill St.Anne Churchyard
Theatre of war: Home
Next of Kin: Alfred & Charlotte Chivers
Address: Naish Hill, Lacock, Wiltshire

Age: 29
Home Country: England
Cause of death: Died

Edward a farm labourer was the third son of Alfred & Charlotte Chivers. He enlisted with the army joining the Royal Wiltshire Yeomanry. He died of illness or disease on Tuesday 4 March 1919 and was buried at Bowden Hill St. Anne Churchyard. His brothers were to die soon after Edgar Reginald Chivers on 6 March 1919 and George Chivers, not a serviceman, on 11 March 1919. All three are buried at St. Anne's Churchyard, Bowden Hill.

Private Edgar Reginald Chivers   *651st Agricultural Coy Labour Corps*

Service No.   506987
Place of Birth: Naish Hill, Wiltshire
Date of Death: 06/03/1919
Memorial: Not Known

Age: 25
Home Country: England
Cause of death: Died

The grave markers of Edward, Edgar and George Chivers at St. Anne Churchyard, Bowden Hill.

Far left: Edward Bull buried in Chippenham Cemetery.

Left: George Rafferty buried in St. Paul's churchyard.

War cemetery: Bowden Hill St.Anne Churchyard
Theatre of war: Home
Next of Kin: Alfred & Charlotte Chivers
Address: Naish Hill, Lacock, Wiltshire

Edgar known as Reginald and a farm labourer was the sixth son of Alfred & Charlotte Chivers. He initially joined the Royal Wiltshire Yeomanry and was then transferred to the Training Reserve before being sent to the Gloucestershire Regiment and then the Labour Corps. He died of illness or disease on Thursday 6 March 1919. His brothers were to die with in days Edward Chivers on the 4 March 1919 and George, not a serviceman, on 11 March 1919. All three are buried at St. Anne's Churchyard, Bowden Hill.

Private Edward Bull		*2nd Bn Wiltshire Regiment*	
Service No.	11105	Age:	29
Place of Birth:	Chippenham, Wiltshire	Home Country:	England
Date of Death:	25/03/1920	Cause of death:	Died
Memorial:	Chippenham & St. Andrews Church Memorial		
War cemetery:	Chippenham London Road Cemetery		
Theatre of war:	Home		
Next of Kin:	George & Eliza Bull		
Address:	26 The Causeway, Chippenham		

Edward volunteered for service with the Wiltshire Regiment on 5 September 1914 and arrived in France on the 24 March 1915. He was wounded on Tuesday 18 May 1915 when the Wiltshires were in trenches at Rue De L'Epinette near Festubert, France and were subjected to heavy German shelling which was composed of high explosive and shrapnel shells which fell every eight or nine seconds. He was evacuated to England and after a long spell in hospital was discharged from the army on 12 February 1916 and died at Brentford, Middlesex on Thursday 25 March 1920. His body was returned to Chippenham and he was buried in the Cemetery.

Private George Rafferty   *Depot Royal Fusilers*

Service No.   142777   Age: 35
Place of Birth:,   Birmingham   Home Country: England
Date of Death: 22/05/1920   Cause of death: Accident
Memorial: Not known
War cemetery: Chippenham St. Paul's Churchyard
Next of Kin: Annie Elizabeth Rafferty
Address: 310 Beckwith Street, Birkenhead, Cheshire

George, a painter, married Annie Owens at Liverpool on 21 October 1910. He had served twelve years in the army with the Shropshire Light Infantry and volunteered for service with the Lancashire Fusilers on 19 March 1915. In October 1915 he was posted to Gallipoli landing at Suvla Bay and after the evacuation of the peninsular he was sent to Alexandria and from there invalided home to England in May 1915. George was discharged from the army having valvular disease of the heart and being medically unfit on 10 July 1916. On 17 November 1916 George enlisted with the Shropshire Light Infantry but was discharged on 17 January 1917. Some time later George enlisted with the Royal Fusilers and served at Ypres where he was wounded and sent to Netley Hospital. On Saturday 22 May 1920 a report was made that a man had fallen from the night train from London to Bristol in the early hours of the morning. Later on Great Western Railway driver George Gregory was told of the incident and informed that no body had been found and as he was driving a light engine from Corsham to Swindon he was asked to keep a look out. At 4.10am when he was at the home up signal at Dauntsey he saw the body of a man lying between the up and down rails. He pulled up at Dauntsey and informed the signalman. He then returned to the body and found that he was quite dead. P.C. Read from Sutton Benger was called to Dauntsey station and he proceeded along the line about half a mile in the direction of Chippenham and found the body of a soldier. He was lying face down and both legs were severed, one leg was about thee yards away the other 66 yards away in the direction of Chippenham. It was apparent that the body had been dragged about 36 yards. At the coroners inquest John Davidson a travelling ticket examiner stated that he had been on the train and between Reading and Swindon he had came across two soldiers lying down in a third class compartment. One man Robert Ray produced his warrant (rail ticket) and and also took one from the pocket of the other man. Both men appeared to be under the influence of drink. When the train reached Bath at 12.33am John Davidson noticed that one of the men was missing and the door of the compartment on the off side was open. Robert Ray stated that he and George had served in the same regiment in France, but he did not become acquainted with George until they were both at Netley Hospital where they had been on the same ward for three weeks. George intended spending his leave with Robert Ray in Bristol. They had journeyed from Southampton to London and visited the pay office at Hounslow and drew £3 each and then went back to London where they did some shopping. About 7pm in the evening they arrived at Paddington and then went for a drink. They visited two public houses and had some beer, Robert Ray stated he did not remember giving up his ticket, the first thing he remembered was being asked for his name by an official at Bath. A verdict of accidental death was returned and George Rafferty was buried at St. Paul's Churchyard.

Private Water Frank Haines   *Hawke Bn Royal Naval Division*

Service No.   Z/1337   Age: 24
Place of Birth: Chippenham, Wiltshire Home Country: England
Date of Death: 02/06/1921   Cause of death: Died
Memorial: St Andrews Church Chippenham
War cemetery: Chippenham London Road Cemetery

Theatre of war: Home
Next of Kin: William & Mary Maria Haines
Address: 13 Nelson's Place, Chippeham

Walter was the youngest son of William and Mary Haines and had been employed by Royal Wells Bacon Factory. He volunteered for service on 15 November 1915 and arrived in France on 10 July 1916. He was posted wounded and missing at Beaucourt, France and no news was heard until Walter's parents received a post card in April 1917 stating that he was a prisoner of war at Lazarett III, Kriegsgefangenenlager, Eppindorf, Hamburg, where he remained until the end of the war. He was repatriated on Boxing Day 1919 and discharged on 25 March 1919. Walter had suffered many deprivations while a prisoner of war and he died of tuberculosis on Thursday 2 June 1921 and was buried with full military honours in Chippenham Cemetery. At this time Walter is not remembered by the Commonwealth War Graves Commission.

16
REMEMBRANCE

A competition was set to design a War Memorial for Chippenham and the winner being a plan by Mr G. Parker-Pearson of Grittleton, using as a base the fountain in the Market Place which had been erected in the 1870's to mark the opening of the new waterworks. The fountain had fallen into a bad state of repair. Part of the scheme was to re-use as much of the valuable granite as possible. The structure was originally supposed to have a light on each of the side pillars. One half of the drinking trough for cattle was to be retained facing the Waverley Restaurant. The unveiling took place on Sunday 4 September 1921. At 3pm the ceremony commenced with the crowd singing the hymn O God, our help in ages past. There followed a reading of the 90th Psalm by Archdeacon Talbot of Swindon. Prayers were said by Rev WH Gorham. Then the memorial was unveiled. The memorial was covered by a large Union Jack, which was removed by George Wood MM, son of Mr Joseph Wood, a late Company Sgt Major of the Wiltshire Regiment, and Reginald Neate. The Mayor said that they had unveiled the Cenotaph to the memory of their Country men who went forth, endured hardship, faced danger and finally passed out of sight of men in the path of sacrifice, through the gate of death. The care of the memorial devolved upon the corporation of that borough for all time and on whose behalf he accepted that responsibility and trust.

Left: On Sunday 17 July 1921 a Rood Screen was unveiled at St. Andrews Church by Sir Audley Neeld and dedicated by the Bishop of Bristol. The Memorial was a thanks-offering to the men who had lost their lives in the Great War. The Screen is flanked by two panels containing the names of 132 men of the parish. It was designed by F.E. Mombray of Oxford and build at a cost of £1,150. Sir Audley Neeld remarked that he was disappointed the tablets could not be finished because of the ongoing coal strike.

Above: Two wooden panels containing the names of the fallen flank a small wooden alter in the centre of which is a wooden cross which came from a chapel of a Great War Military Hospital at Rouen France.

Above left: Hardenhuish Memorial unveiled on Sunday 5 June 1921 by Colonel Hankey and the dedication was performed by Canon Wrangham.

Above right: Chippenham Liberal Club Memorial unveiled by the Mayor on the evening of Saturday 12 November 1921. It was originally sited behind the bar but some time later it was moved to the snooker room.

Above left: Allington Memorial can now be found in St. Paul's Church Chippenham. It was originally sited in Allington Church which was a converted ox house in the yard at Manor Farm but was closed in the 1960's.

Above right: Chippenham Secondary School Memorial was unveiled in the presence of the Mayor and Mayoress on Thursday 20 October 1920 and was performed by Teacher Miss Morgan who had taught two thirds of the boys who had died and she had known all but four. The memorial was originally sited in the Gymnasium but was at some time relocated to a corridor in the main building.

Bowden Hill Memorial　　　　　*Castle Combe village memorial*

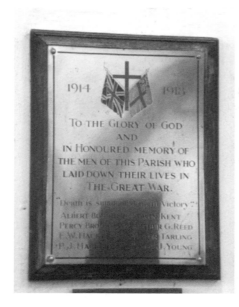

Burton and Nettleton Memorial　　　　　*Castle Combe Church Memorial*

Top left: Christian Malford Village Memorial.

Top right: Christian Malford Church Memorial.

Bottom left: Great Somerford Church Memorial.

Bottom right: Great Somerford Village Memorial.

Top left: Grittleton Memorial.

Top right: Hullavington Memorial.

Bottom left: Kington Langley Memorial.

Bottom right: Kington St. Michael Memorial.

Top left: Lacock Cemetery Memorial

Top right: Lacock Village Memorial.

Middle right: Lacock Church Memorial.

Bottom right: Leigh Delamere Memorial.

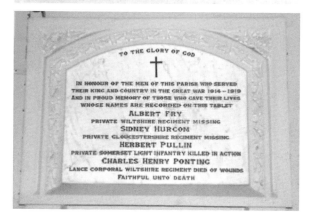

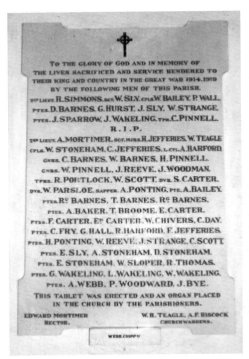

Little Somerford Memorial.

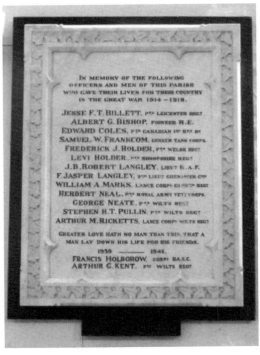

North Wraxall Memorial.

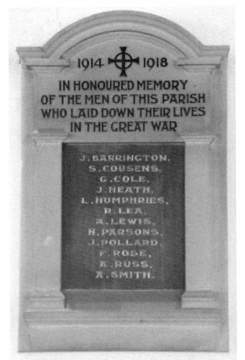

Sutton Benger Church Memorial.

Sutton Benger Churchyard Memorial.

Top left: Langley Burrell Memorial.

Top right: Yatton Keynell Memorial.

Middle right: West Kington Memorial.

Bottom right: Seagry Memorial.

MAPS

The Western Front

Gallipoli 1915 to 1916

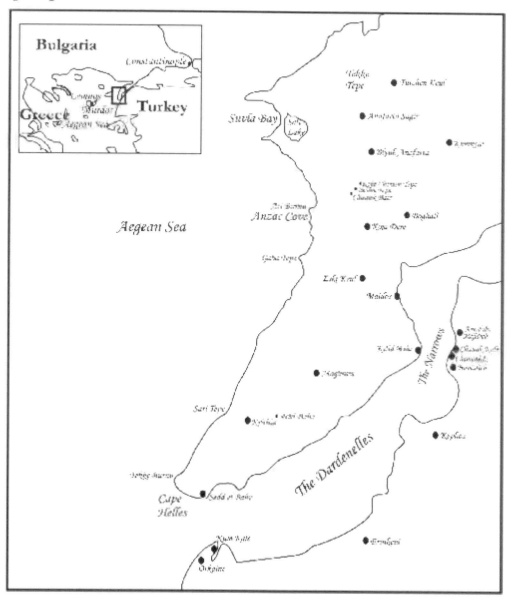

Mesopotamia 1914 to 1918

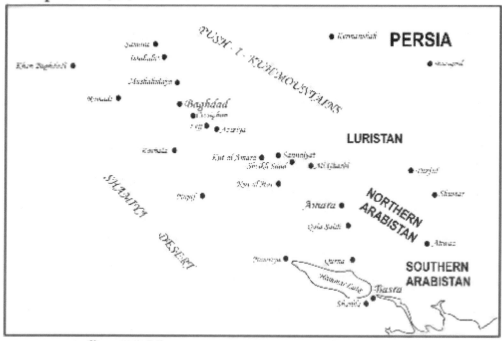

Balkans 1914 to 1918

A-Z OF MEMORIALS

7th Field Ambulance Cem.
George William Fields
AIF Burial Ground Flers
Frederick John Pollard
Abbeville Communal
Cemetery & Extension
Henry Crook
Herbert John Ford
Achiet Le Grand
Communal Cemetery Ext.
Herbert W O Burry
Francis Charlton Lanaway
Adanac Military Cemetery
John Reginald Hayes
Aire Communal Cemetery
Alfred William Porter
Alexandria Chatby Cem.
John Randolph Lea
Alexandria Hadra War
Memorial Cemetery
Albert George Daniels
Allonville Comunal Cem.
Thomas Brinkworth
Amara War Cemetery
George Bodman
Edwin George Chivers
William James Lemm
Henry Godfrey V Chapman
Henry Arthur Coleman
Harold Augustus Lewis
Herbert Raymond Wilson
Arras Flying Services Mem.
Wilfred Henry Brinkworth
Arras Memorial
Charles Frederick Mooney
Harold Walter Jones
William Bert Mills
Tom Sainsbury
Harold John Thomas Swain
Frederick Willis
Cecil White
David Brinkworth Croker
Albert Henry W Greenman
Walter Feltham
Percy Porter
Walter George Cole
Artillery Wood Cemetery
Arthur George Reed

Aubigny Communal
Cemetery Extension
David Clutterbuck
Awoingt British Cemetery
William Alfred Knight
Baghdad North Gate War
Cemetery
William Albert Baker
Edwin Frank Scammell
Robert Wilton Tuck
Bailleul Communal
Cemetery Ext. Nord
Albert George Bishop
Arthur Noel Edwards
Bard Cottage Cemetery
Edward Willett
Barenthal Military Cem.
Frederick William Sinclair
Basra Memorial
George Edwin Duck
Ladas Harcourt Hancock
Arthur George Hiscox
Arthur John Payne
Ernest Townsend
Hugh Guy Daniel Clutterbuck
William Augustus Marks
Ernest William Maslen
Frederick Orlando Goulding
Reginald P Daly
Frank Monk
William Francis Vines
Frederick James Drewett
Arthur Tanner
Wilfred Hunt
James Egbert Wilkins
Glenville Richard Cattarns
William Sutton
Alfred Tom Drew
Basra War Cemetery
Maurice Jesse Sparrow
Arthur Tom Humphries
Beaurains Road Cemetery
Alfred Henry Herbert Brain
Bedford House Cemetery
Walter Hancock
Archibald Herbert Wheeler
Beersheba War Cemetery
William John K Rumming

Bellicourt British Cemetery
Elisha Frank Jones
Berlin South Western Cem.
Frank Phillips
Bernafay Wood British Cem.
Frederick Mark Wilkins
Francis John Pullen
Herbert Jesse Wiltshire
Bethune Town Cemetery
Herbert Knighton
Albert Edward Allsop
Harry Vincent Calkin
Biddestone Churchyard Ext.
Walter Baston
Blargies Communal
Cemetery Extention
Albert Skinner
Bordon Military Cem.
Albert John Payne
Boulogne Eastern Cemetery
John Henry Hatherell
Alfred Edward Bray
John Griffiths
Bouzincourt Communal
Cemetery Extension
Arthur John White
Bowden Hill St.Anne Church
Edgar Reginald Chivers
Edward Chivers
Bronfay Farm Military
Cemetery Bray Sur Somme
Robert Barclay
Bucquoy Road Cem. Ficheux
Joseph Hawkins
Reginald Edward Sheppard
Bulford Church Cemetery
James Edward Bindon
Bully Grenay Communal
Cemetery British Extention
Walter Mitchell
Burnley Cemetery
Walter Greenhalgh
Burrington Holy Trinity
Churchyard
Walter Charles Selman
Bus House Cemetery
William Thomas Granger
Henry Stoneham

Cambrai East Military Cem.
John William Kingsland
Cambrai Mem. Louverval
Edward Bath
Harold Alfred Hicks
George Henry Gleed
Cambrin Churchyard Ext.
Arthur James Blackford
Canada Farm Cemetery
Ernest Edwin Booy
Capelle Beaudignies Road Cemetery
Charles Henry Neath
Castle Combe St Andrew Church Yard
Richard Henry Reginald Neate
Roland Alpheus Pullin
Chauny Communal Cemetery British Cemetery Extension
Ernest Daniel Wilson
Chippenham London Road Cemetery
Henry James Collar
Robert Blanchard
Edward Bull
Edwin Ernest Herbert Lough
Wallace Mortimer Rooke
Arthur Harry J. Swanborough
George Ralph Thomas
Raymond Stubbert
Water Frank Haines
Chippenham St. Paul's Churchyard
Walter Curtis
Reginald Arthur B. Warrilow`
George Rafferty
Chocques Military Cemetery
Charles William Scriven
John Taylor
Christian Malford
Levi James Berry
Cite Bonjean Military Cemetery Armentieres
Frederick James Pullen
Cologne Southern Cemetery
Wilfred Baker
Francis Herbert Harding
William Rose
George Henry Wakefield
Thomas Baker
Jack Richmond Pugh

Combles Communal Cemetery Extension
Percy Tucker
Corsham St Bartholemew Burial Ground
Ernest Egbert O Slade
Coxyde Military Cemetery
Robert William Carter
Croix Rouge Military Cememtery Quaedypre
Ernest Jasper Notton
Cross Roads Cemetery Fontaine Au Bois
Oliver Reuben H Oatley
Dantzig Alley British Cemetery Mametz
Albert Kearton
Thomas Percy Snell
Harold Melsom
Dar es Salaam War Cem.
Ernest George Durbin
Deir El Belah War Cem.
Edwin Minty
William Joseph John Comley
Delsaux Farm Cemetery
Gilbert Cleaver
Dernancourt Communal Cemetery Extension
Charles Opie
Dickebusch New Military Cemetery
Joseph Stanley Victor Fox
Dive Copse British Cemetery Sailly Le Sec
Reginald Staney James
Divisional Collecting Post Cemetery and Extension
Frederick Angel Greenman
Doiran Memorial
John Edward Griffin
George Weston
Henry Sidney Beaven
Christopher James Cole
Edward Pegler
Don Communal Cemetery Annoeullin
Ernest Brimble
Doullens Communal Cemetery Extension No 1
Stanley Beconsfield Collett

Dozinghem Military Cem.
Fred Hudd
William Clifford
Dueville Communal
Cemetery Extension
Noah Davis
Dunkirk Town Cemetery
Francis Edward Baker
Ecoivres Military Cemetery
Mont St Eloi
Percy James Perkins
Edington SS Mary and
Katherine Allsaints Church
Leonard Drewett
Elzenwalle Brasserie Cem.
Henry John Whale
Embarkation Pier Cem.
James Sly
Etaples Military Cemetery
Henry William Bull
Lewin James Billett
Ernest Albert Young
Terence McHugh
Jesse Frank Tavenor Billett
Flatrion Copse Cemetery Mametz
Walter George Brain
Flesquieres Hill British Cemetery
John Marsh
Fricourt British Cemetery
Ronald Henry Greig
Frome Vallis Road Cem.
Everett Ferriday
Gaza War Cemetery
Francis John Griffin
William A. Swanborough
Godewaersvelde British Cemetery
William Henry Fry Vines
Gommecourt British
Cemetery No2 Hebuterne
Reginald W. Davies
Gordon Dump Cemetery Ovillers La Boisselle
Edgar Thomas Pearce
Anthony George Greenway
Arthur Frederick Clark
Gosforth St Nicholas Churchyard
Frank Moss

Gosport Annes Hill Cemetery
John Basil Robert Langley
Gouzeaucourt New British Cermetery
William Francis Emery
Great Somerford (SS.Peter and Paul) Churchyard
William Hadrill
Green Hill Cemetery
James William Milford
Grittleton St Mary Church
John Wicks
Guards Cemetery Lesboeufs
Victor Clare Tarling
Josiah Whitmore
Guise La Desolation French National Cemetery
George Millard
H A C Cemetery Ecoust St Mein
George Joseph Spooner
John Reginald Lane
Haringhe (Bandaghem) Military Cemetery
Herbert Compton
Ernest Lane
Hartland or Stokes St Nectan (St Nectan)Churchyard
Arthur Benjamin Panes
Hautmont Communal Cem.
Harold Roy Bowden
Heath Cemetery Harbonnieres
Thomas Holt Fogg
Hedge Row Trench Cemetery
Leonard White
Helles Memorial
Frederick Gideon Beasley
Oscar James Kidd
Albert George Newman
Albert Russ
Frederick John Walker
Harold Mortimer
Edward James Greenman
Frank Goulding
Allen Richard Wicks
Joseph Harry Dew
Charlie Clifford
Percy Harold A. Knighton
Ernest Walter Scott

Henin Communal Cemetry Extension
Reginald Genvy Kaynes
Charles James Tompkin
Hollybrook Memorial Southampton
Edgar Taviner
Hooge Crater Cemetery
Percival John Hacker
Harold Henry Reynolds
Hullavington St Mary Churchyard
Joseph John Hulance
Albert Fry
James Idle
Hyde Park Corner Royal Berks Cemetery
Reginald Tucker
Jerusalem War Cemetery
Henry George Couzens
George Alfred Knight
Walter George Mann
Karachi 1914 - 1918 War Memorial
James Smith
George Popham Garlike
Kemmel Chateau Military Cemetery
Sidney Iver Morse
Klein-Vierstraat British Cemetery
Arthur George Short
Kut War Cemetery
Albert Walter Cullimore
La Chaudiere Military Cemetery Vimy
Herbert Richmond Coleman
La Ferte Sous Jouarre Memorial
James Webb
Lacock Cemetery
Alfred George Self
Lancashire Cottage Cem.
Reginald Alfred Freegard
Lancashire Landing Cem.
Stephen Bull
Langley Burrell St Peter Churchyard
Walter Jacob Clark

Laventie Military Cemetery
La Gorgue
Frederick Arthur Howard
Le Grand Hasard Military Cemetery Morebecque
Basil William Ramsbottom
Le Touret Memorial
Albert Fry
Frank Stapleford
Frederick Eli George Ashe
Frederick Escott
Sidney Allen Penny
John Waddie Wishart
Harvey William Cole
Maurice Dancey
Herbert Gainey
Thomas Henry W Powell
George Blackman
Stephen Henry T Pullen
William Herbert Spencer
Isaac Charles Watts
John Smith
Harry Oswald Smith
Thomas Self
William Pearce
Clifford Alfred J Wiltshire
Le Vertannoy British Cemetery Hinges
Herbert Charles V Sharps
Lebucquiere Communal Cemetery Extension
Robert Edward Leslie Scott
Leckhampton St Peter Churchyard
George Delmar-Williamson
Les Baraques Military Cemetery Sangatte
Elias Smith
Lijssenthoek Military Cemetery
Jack Rowland Phillips
Roland Baish
Lindenhoek Chalet Military Cemetery
Edwin George Hayward
Locre Hospice Cemetery
Charles Henry Ponting
Longfleet St Mary Church
Reginald Percy Bennett

Longuenesse St.Omer Souvenir Cemetery
William Henry Lumkin
James Richard Few
Jesse Heath
Loos Memorial
Edward Hinchliffe Carvey
Alfred George Hunt
Mervyn Percy Powell
Evelyn Seppings Wilson
Geoffrey Mervyn U Wilson
Reginald John Wood
Richard Edward John Wilkins
William Arthur Sealy
Arthur Henry Selby
Tom Canter
Harry Parsons
Edward Scott
Wilfred Thomas Newman
Reginald Frank Bailey
Madras 1914 1918 War Memorial Chennai
Walter George Parsons
Albert Edward Wilkins
Marfaux British Cemetery
William Thomas Hibberd
Meeks Cemetery Chatteris
Percival George Angood
Melksham Church Cemetery
William Henry Walker
Mendinghem Military Cemetery
John Thomas Richards
Merville Communal Cem.
William James Taylor
John Newman
Eustace A De St Barbe Sladen Watkins
Mikra British Cemetery
Harry Button
Arthur Reginald Flower
John Thomas Gough
Milborne Port Cemetery
William Merritt
Millencourt Communal Cemetery Extension
Harry Lucas
Mombasa British Memorial
Algernon A Bakewell Warrilow

Mont Huon Military Cemetery Le Treport
Bertie Basil Blackman
Reginald Deane Pinnell
Henry George Ash
Montecchio Precalcino Communal Cemetery Extension
Charles Ernest Hawkins
Moreuil Communal Cemetery Allied Extention
Charles Pinnell
Mory Abbey Military Cemetery Mory
Francis Jasper Langley
Motor Car Corner Cem.
William Herbert Dickson
Narbone East Cemetery
Frederick Bishop
Naval Trench Cemetery Gavrelle
Philip Woodman
Netley Military Cemetery
Arthur Francis Baggs
Nettleton St Mary Church
Edwin Kent
Neuville-Vitasse Road Cemetery
Sylvester Thomas Cook
Niederzwehren Cemetery
Samuel Stutt
Ernest Leonard Stevens
Nieuport Memorial
Sandford William Shippard
No 2 Outpost Cemetery
Montague Douglas Snell
North Wraxall St James Churchyard
Samuel Wiltshire Frankcom
Charles Edward Coles
Nouex Les Mines Communal Cemetery
Clement Harold Taylor
Frank Henry Crewe
Ontario Cemetery Sains Les Marquion
Thomas Edward Cole
Orchard Dump Cemetery Arleux en Gohelle
Arthur Harvey Hand

Outterstreene Communal Cemetery Extention Bailleul
Arthur Alexander Gameson
Passchendaele New Cem.
Walter John Cook Brittain
Pecq Communal Cemetery
William James Hatherell
Pernes British Cemetery
Cyril Chivers
Peronne Communal Cemetery Extension
Frederick George Edgar Bull
Peronne Road Cemetery Maricourt
Edgar George Vines
Perth Cemetery China Wall
Sidney James Chivers
Pigeon Ravine Cemetery pehy
Fred Powney
Ploegsteert Memorial
Wilfred James F Griffin
Reginald James V Clifford
Arthur Sidney Rawlings
Felix C H Hanbury-Tracy
Herbert John Kington
Herbert Kington
Herbert James Fishlock
Ploegsteert Wood Military Cemetery
Gilbert John Mahoney
Plymouth Naval Memorial
Henry George Morse
Frederick Pepler
George William James Hand
Henry John Cleaver
Francis John Eddolls
Plymouth Weston Mill Cemetery
Richard Harold Marsden
Poelcapelle British Cem.
Ernerst David Hanks
Richard Charles Silley
Geoffrey Stafford Wallington
Pont Du Hem Military Cemetery La Gorgue
Herbert Holloway

Pont Du Hem Military Cemetery La Gorgue
William John Hoye
Poperinghe Old Military Cem
Oscar Bush
Portsmouth Naval Memorial
Fred Heath
George Stevens
Frank Beaven
Pozieres Memorial
Thomas Henry Carpenter
Maurice William Short
Jack Smith
Robert George Simmons
Frederick Charles Nutt
Benjamin John Miles
Gabriel Wicks
Maurice Cole
Charles Selwyn Awdry
Frederick Stevens
Puchevillers British Cemetery
Reginald Hancock
Frank Porter
Henry Charles Bowsher
Frederick James Young
Queant Road Cemetery Buissy
Sidney William Crewe
Railway Dugouts Burial Ground
Edmund John Clark
Ramleh War Cemetery
Thomas Micheal A Puttock
Ernest William Rose
Regina Trench Cemetery Grandcourt
Ivan Cecil Francis Joy
Walter John Martin
Reninghelst New Military Cemetery
Henry George Panting
Ridge Wood Military Cem.
Simeon Rowe
Roclincourt Military Cem.
Percival George H Hunt
Rocquigny Equancourt Road British Cemetery Mananco
Edwin John Brinkworth
Charles Hillman

Roisel Communal Cemetery Extension
William Richard Millin
Sidney Ernest Lock
John William Purnell
Roye New British Cemetery
Charles Henry Field
Sailly Labourse Communal Cemetery Extension
Frederick John Collier
Salisbury London Road Cemetery
Tom Martindale Speechly
Sarralbe Military Cemetery
Harry Burridge
Seagry St Mary Churchyard
Edgar William Godwin
Sequehart British Cemetery No 1
Richard Wheeler Porter
Skopje British Cemetery
George Arthur Hurst
Soissons Memorial
Herbert Thomas J Fortune
Arthur Hull
Walter Charles Cole
Harry George Hunt
Soupir Communal Cemetery
Richard William M Lockwood
St Aubert British Cemetery
Frederick Thomas Butler
St Germain Au Mont D'or Communal Cemetery Ext.
Herbert Neal
St Hilaire Cemetery Extension Frevent
James Victor Wakeling
Herbert Gladstone Brown
St Pierre Cemetery Amiens
Allen Llewellyn Palmer
St Sever Cemetery Extension Rouen
Herbert William Carter
Lancelot Coulter Witts
William Arthur King
St Sever Cemetery Rouen
George John Little
Stephen Rose
Herbert Arthur Tanner
Walter Victor Bridgeman

St Souplet British Cem.
Charles King
St Vaast Post Military Cemetery Richebourg Lavoue
Joseph Alfred Wood
St Venant Communal Cem
Walter George Greenman
Ste Emilie Valley Cemetery Villiers Faucon
Charles Herbert A Tasker
Strand Military Cemetery
William Penney
Swindon St.Lawrence Churchyard
Douglas Ridley C Gabell
Templeux Le Guerard British Cemetery
Edward Aaron Wicks
Arthur Frederick G Skuse
Terlincthun British Cemetery Wimille
Leonard Humphries
Frederick John Holder
Thetford Cemetery
William Webb
Thiepval Memorial
Frederick Edward Avery
George Frederick Bright
George Hulbert
Leopold John Jordan
Albert Edward Millard
Willis Spear Robbins
Frederick Walter Whale
Henry John Wicks
William Bryan Wood
George William Tanner
William James Barrow
George Neate
Francis Edward Porter
Eric Robert Donner
George Goodwin Cook
William Sly
Thomas Strange
Henry John G Herrington
Arthur Lewis
William Ernest Rose
John Monk
Fred Purbrick
Frank Mason

Thiepval Memorial
Walter Stiles
Frederick James Tanner
Richard Elmes
George John Collins
Ernest William Hacker
Edward James Barrington
Frederick Henry Keyte
Gilbert Arthur Robbins
Alfred John Smith
Gerald Herbert Wooster
Arthur Thomas
Tincourt New British Cem.
Henry Hope Hunt
Trois Arbres Cemetery
Steenwerck
Harry Arthur William Penton
Trowbridge Cemetery
George Victor Jim Elmes
Twelve Tree Copse Cemetery
Philip Simons Picot
Tyne Cot Cemetery
Maurice Heath
Tyne Cot Memorial
George Chandler
Albert Edward Chivers
George Henry Fennell
Frederick Bertram Pinfield
Maurice Silver Pond
Henry John Baker
Cyril Richard Manners
Frederick Edward Croker
Thomas Geoffrey Millin
William George Russell
Arthur Thomas Benham
William Edwin Collett
George Henry Cole
William Henry Freegard
Francis Thomas Rose
James Carey

Uffington Lincolnshire
William Preston Ainley
Vailly British Cemetery
John Cole
Varennes Military Cemetery
David Barnes
George Enos Farmer
Verberie French National Cemetery
Charles Ernest Yates
Vielle-Chappelle New Military Cem. Lacouture
Percy Saunders Pearce
Vimy Memorial
Frank Moritmer Webb
Vis En Artois Memorial
Arthur Herbert G Tavinor
Frank Gregory
Albert Edward Thomas Rose
Percy George Brookman
Percival Victor Elms
Voormezeele Enclosure No 3
Christopher Herbert Dawson
Warlencourt British Cem.
Francis Tom Tanner
Arthur Bridgeman
Arthur Martin Ricketts
Warlincourt Halte British Cemetery Saulty
Stanley William James Pearce
Weymouth Cemetery
Harry John Wheeler
William Isaac Henry T Hobbs
Wimereux Communal Cem.
Gilbert Arthur K Higgins
William Ernest Jones
Charles Large
Herbert Teagle

Winchester West Hill Old Cemetery
George Alfred Bothwell
Windmill British Cemetery Monchy Le Preux
George Dixon
Winterslow All Saints Churchyard Extension
Arthur George Reynolds
Wytschaete Military Cem.
Frederick Evans
Ypres Menim Gate
Montague R Bridgeman
Ernest Alfred Tuck
John William Blanchard
William Arthur Brewer
Reginald Albert Butler
Orlando Edwards
Frederick Philip Cole
Edgar Wallace Couzens
Herbert Pullin
Arthur Joseph Ricketts
Gerald Harvey Barnfield
Alfred Joseph Hand
Gerald King
Harold George Pearce
Roland John Rose
Arthur Stinchcombe
William James Wilkins
Herbert Ernest Crew
William John Bailey
Sutcliffe Cousins
Ernest Philip Morris Panes
Guy Clark
Arthur Hillier
George Bishop
Sidney Hurcom

The Missing

Men remembered on local memorials who I have yet to find military details.

Name	Memorial
Horace Blackman	Chippenham & St. Paul's Church
Ernest Victor Hayward	Chippenham & St. Paul's Church
W Hancock	Chippenham
J Hill	Chippenham
L G Morton	Chippenham & St. Andrews Church
James Thomas	Chippenham & St. Andrews Church
William Robinson	Chippenham & St. Andrews Church
A H Swayne	Chippenham
Arthur William Wilkins	St Andrews Church Memorial
Edward Hopkins	St Andrews Church Memorial
George Davis	Chippeham Secondary School Memorial
Edmund Hibberd	Secondary School Memorial
Ronald White	Chippenham Secondary school Memorial
William Joseph Reeves	Hullavington
W C Hawkins	Kington St. Michael
Harry Hunt	Christian Malford
P Wall	Little Somerford
W Strange	Little Somerford
Albert Boucher	Nettleton & Burton

Also

Available

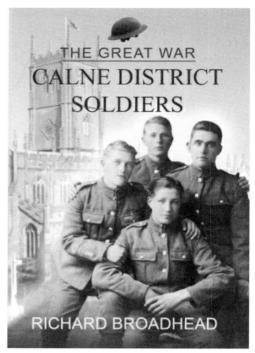

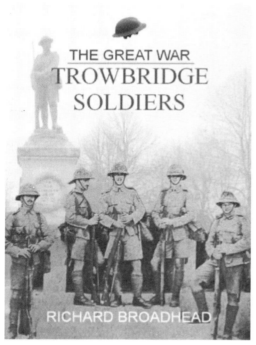

For more information
www.hrrec.co.uk